AFRICAN ETHNOGRAPHIC STUDIES
OF THE 20TH CENTURY

Volume 30

IDEAS AND PROCEDURES IN
AFRICAN CUSTOMARY LAW

IDEAS AND PROCEDURES IN AFRICAN CUSTOMARY LAW

Studies Presented and Discussed at the Eighth International African Seminar at the Haile Sellassie I University, Addis Ababa, January 1966

Edited by
MAX GLUCKMAN

LONDON AND NEW YORK

First published in 1969 for the International African Institute by Oxford University Press

This edition first published in 2018
by Routledge
2 Park Square, Milton Park, Abingdon, Oxon OX14 4RN

and by Routledge
711 Third Avenue, New York, NY 10017

Routledge is an imprint of the Taylor & Francis Group, an informa business

© 1969 International African Institute

All rights reserved. No part of this book may be reprinted or reproduced or utilised in any form or by any electronic, mechanical, or other means, now known or hereafter invented, including photocopying and recording, or in any information storage or retrieval system, without permission in writing from the publishers.

Trademark notice: Product or corporate names may be trademarks or registered trademarks, and are used only for identification and explanation without intent to infringe.

British Library Cataloguing in Publication Data
A catalogue record for this book is available from the British Library

ISBN: 978-0-8153-8713-8 (Set)
ISBN: 978-0-429-48813-9 (Set) (ebk)
ISBN: 978-1-138-59656-6 (Volume 30) (hbk)
ISBN: 978-0-429-48757-6 (Volume 30) (ebk)

Publisher's Note
The publisher has gone to great lengths to ensure the quality of this reprint but points out that some imperfections in the original copies may be apparent.

Disclaimer
The publisher has made every effort to trace copyright holders and would welcome correspondence from those they have been unable to trace.

IDEAS AND PROCEDURES
IN AFRICAN CUSTOMARY LAW

*Studies presented and discussed at the Eighth
International African Seminar at the
Haile Sellassie I University, Addis Ababa, January 1966*

Edited by MAX GLUCKMAN
with an Introduction by A. N. Allott, A. L. Epstein,
and M. Gluckman

Published for the
INTERNATIONAL AFRICAN INSTITUTE
by the
OXFORD UNIVERSITY PRESS
1969

Oxford University Press, Ely House, London W.1

GLASGOW NEW YORK TORONTO MELBOURNE WELLINGTON
CAPE TOWN SALISBURY IBADAN NAIROBI LUSAKA ADDIS ABABA
BOMBAY CALCUTTA MADRAS KARACHI LAHORE DACCA
KUALA LUMPUR SINGAPORE HONG KONG TOKYO

© International African Institute 1969

*Printed in Great Britain by Richard Clay (The Chaucer Press), Ltd.,
Bungay, Suffolk*

To
DARYLL FORDE
in tribute to his work as Director of the International
African Institute, and in organizing these Seminars,
this Seminar being held during his twenty-first year
in that office

Contents

Editorial Preface ... xi

INTRODUCTION
By A. N. Allott, A. L. Epstein, and M. Gluckman

PART I. PROBLEMS OF RESEARCH
I. The Seminar ... 1
II. Research Problems and Methods ... 4
III. The Time Factor and the Definitional Problem: What is Customary Law? ... 9
IV. The Problem of Description ... 15

PART II. PROCEDURES
V. Proceedings and Evidence in African Customary Law ... 22
VI. The New Personnel of Local Courts ... 25
VII. Codification and Recording of Customary Law ... 31
VIII. Reason and the Occult in Customary Law ... 34

PART III. CONCEPTIONS IN THE SUBSTANTIVE LAW
IX. The Conception of Legal Personality ... 38
X. Succession and Inheritance ... 48
XI. Rights in Land ... 55
XII. Marriage and Affiliation ... 59
XIII. Injuries: Liability and Responsibility ... 66
XIV. Agreements and Transactions: Contracts? ... 71
Bibliography ... 79
Résumé français ... 82

SPECIAL STUDIES

I. J. POIRIER. *Directeur, Département des Sciences humaines, Université de Madagascar*
L'Analyse des Espèces juridiques et l'Étude des Droits coutumiers africains ... 97

Contents

II. N. A. OLLENNU. *Judge of the Court of Appeal, Ghana*
The Structure of African Judicial Authority and Problems of Evidence and Proof in Traditional Courts   110

III. S. S. RICHARDSON. *Formerly Director, Institute of Administration and Pro-Vice-Chancellor, Ahmadu Bello University, Zaria*
Whither Lay Justice in Africa?   123

IV. J. VAN VELSEN. *Reader in Sociology, University of Zambia*
Procedural Informality, Reconciliation, and False Comparisons   137

V. WILLIAM A. SHACK. *Associate Professor of Anthropology in the University of Illinois at Chicago; formerly Assistant Professor of Anthropology, Haile Sellassie I University*
Guilt and Innocence: Problem and Method in the Gurage Judicial System   153

VI. H. DESCHAMPS. *Professeur d'Histoire de l'Afrique moderne et contemporaine à la Sorbonne, Paris*
La première Codification africaine: Madagascar 1828–81   169

VII. A. N. ALLOTT. *Professor of African Law in the University of London (School of Oriental and African Studies)*
Legal Personality in African Law   179

VIII. A. M. R. RAMOLEFE. *Lecturer in Law, University of Lesotho, Botswana, and Swaziland; formerly Customary Law Commissioner, Lesotho*
Sesotho Marriage, Guardianship, and the Customary-Law Heir   196

IX. M. G. SMITH. *Professor of Anthropology in the University of California, Los Angeles*
Idda and Secondary Marriage among the Northern Kadara   210

X. J. M. PAUWELS. *Professor at the University of Louvain; Visiting Professor at the Lovanium University (Kinshasa)*
Legitimation of Children in Customary Law in Kinshasa   223

Contents

XI. J. VANDERLINDEN. *Lecturer in African Law and Legal Anthropology in the University of Brussels; Director, Centre for African Legal Development, Haile Sellassie I University, Addis Ababa*

Réflexions sur l'Existence du Concept de Propriété immobilière individuelle dans les Droits africains traditionnels ... 236

XII. M. GLUCKMAN. *Professor of Social Anthropology in the University of Manchester*
Property Rights and Status in African Traditional Law ... 252

XIII. C. M. MCDOWELL. *Lecturer in Law in the University of Birmingham; formerly Lecturer in Law in the Ahmadu Bello University, Zaria*
The Breakdown of Traditional Land Tenure in Northern Nigeria ... 266

XIV. P. J. NKAMBO MUGERWA. *Solicitor-General, Uganda*
Status, Responsibility and Liability: A Comparative Study of two Types of Society in Uganda ... 279

XV. A. L. EPSTEIN. *Professorial Fellow in the Australian National University; formerly Senior Lecturer in Social Anthropology in the University of Manchester*
Injury and Liability in African Customary Law in Zambia ... 292

XVI. J. O. IBIK. *Formerly Customary Law Commissioner, Malawi*
The Customary Law of Wrongs and Injuries in Malawi ... 305

XVII. I. SCHAPERA. *Professor of Anthropology at the London School of Economics and Political Science*
Contract in Tswana Law ... 318

XVIII. Y. P. GHAI. *Professor of Law and Dean of the Faculty of Law in the University College of Dar es Salaam, Tanzania*
Customary Contracts and Transactions in Kenya ... 333

INDEX ... 347

Editorial Preface

At a meeting held in Ibadan, Nigeria, in April 1964, I was asked by the Executive Council of the International African Institute to be chairman of the eighth of its series of Seminars in Africa on conceptions and procedures in African customary law. An initial drafting of a programme and selection of personnel was done at Ibadan by a panel of the Executive Council, consisting of M. le Gouverneur Professeur H. Deschamps, Professor M. Fortes, Professor G. Malengreau, and myself, and discussed with the Director, Professor Daryll Forde. Subsequently Professor Forde and I consulted on the planning of the Seminar in London. Most of the planning of the Seminar was carried out by Professor Forde with the assistance of Mrs. Olga Wolfe and Miss Moyna Young of the Institute. We are most grateful to them.

The policy of the International African Institute is to hold its seminars in various centres of learning in Africa in turn and at Ibadan we had discussed with Professor R. Pankhurst the possibility of holding the Seminar at the Haile Sellassie I University. This proposal was welcomed and supported by Professor Pankhurst, as Director of the Institute of Ethiopian Studies, and by Dr. James Paul, as Dean of the Law School. We are most grateful to them for their close co-operation throughout and also to the authorities and staff of the University for making arrangements for the Seminar. For their welcome help and hospitality we are especially indebted to Lij Kassa Wolde Mariam, President of the Haile Sellassie I University, Ato Wubishet Dilnessahu, Business Vice-President of the Haile Sellassie I University, and Ato Terrefe Woldetsadik, Director of Public Relations, and Dr. Jacques Vanderlinden of the Faculty of Law, also of Haile Sellassie I University.

It has been customary for the Director of the Institute to write the preface to reports of its seminars and to express the thanks of the Institute and of participants to the many people on whom, obviously, the success of such an international gathering must depend. I am doing so for this volume, as Chairman of the Seminar, because we wished to state how much the

xii *Editorial Preface*

success of our own Seminar was due to the Director, Professor Forde. I had previously appreciated his work when I participated in the first seminar in the series, held at Kampala, Uganda, in 1959 (*Social Change in Modern Africa*, edited by A. W. Southall, 1961); but only when I was organizing a seminar did I become fully aware how much depended on the general direction, as well as attention to details, that he gave. I should add that at the Seminar itself, even while he was contributing to our discussions, he was still engaged in arranging for the comfort of its members and in planning visits which would enable them to see as much as possible, in a short time, of their fascinating host country. Chairmen of previous seminars would endorse my tribute; and it seems appropriate to dedicate this volume to Professor Forde, since our Seminar was held during the twenty-first year of his tenure of the Directorship of the Institute.

The International African Institute has aimed in its series of seminars not only to produce symposia on a specific series of problems, but also to bring together a number of scholars at various centres of learning in Africa in order to assist in developing those centres. Most of the scholars have been drawn from African universities and research institutes, with a few from America or Europe. Since the Seminar was limited in numbers, both because funds were limited and because discussion proceeds best within a relatively small group, we had perforce to leave out scholars we should have liked to invite. Some we invited could not attend (I note particularly Professor P. J. Bohannan and a number of African lawyers); and at the last minute Ibik, Richardson, Schapera, and Smith, who had contributed papers, were unable to come. Mr. John Howard came to represent the University of Yaounde and Mr. C. M. McDowell in place of Richardson from Zaria. We were joined at the Seminar by members of the Law Faculty and the Institute of Ethiopian Studies at the Haile Sellassie I University. Professor K. Bentsi-Enchill had planned to attend the Seminar as an observer but could not; he did however send to it a long paper on 'The Comparative Analysis of Property Rights'. This is not reproduced here, but we are able to refer to it in the *Introduction* because some of the central ideas are given in his *Ghana Land Law: An Exposition, Analysis and Critique* (1964).

Editorial Preface

Since the Seminar consisted of lawyers and social anthropologists, French-speaking and English-speaking scholars, many of whom had never met before, I had expected there to be difficulties in intercommunication. It is with great pleasure that I can record that we soon settled down into a cheerful and harmonious, if argumentative, group; and we all felt that the Seminar was a memorable occasion in which we had gained friendships as well as understanding. The Seminar recorded with acclamation its thanks to the Ford Foundation whose generosity to the International African Institute had made its meeting possible. Personally, I have to add my thanks to the Center for Advanced Study in the Behavioral Sciences, at Stanford, California, as a Fellow of which I have completed my editorial work. The administrative and technical staff of the Center were most generous in their help: my special thanks are due to Mrs. Dorothy Brothers and Mr. Charles Short. It is worthy of record, in thanking the Ford Foundation for financing the Seminar itself, that it was also the initial generosity of the Foundation which established the Center.

MAX GLUCKMAN

University of Manchester
January 1968

Introduction

by A. N. ALLOTT, A. L. EPSTEIN, and M. GLUCKMAN

PART I PROBLEMS OF RESEARCH

I THE SEMINAR

The major objectives of the Seminar might be briefly described as the isolation and characterization of the fundamental ideas and procedures to be found in African traditional systems of law, and an assessment of their adaptation to new conditions. Given the limited number of scholars it was possible to invite, nevertheless four traditions of law were represented: there were lawyers trained in the European Continental civil codes with their Roman law background, Anglo-Saxon common law, and Roman–Dutch law, as well as Africans thus trained who had experience of living under customary law. The anthropologists were all sociological in their orientation; and five of them had training also in law, covering the civil code, common-law, and Roman–Dutch traditions. Some of the lawyers had been or were administrators applying introduced and customary law in Africa, both Francophone and Anglophone, or had been or were involved in its official compilation; and they had severally worked under colonial direct and indirect rule and under independent African governments. Hence we feel able to say that the several varied methods that have been deployed in the study of African customary law were adequately represented and that we can hope that our statements of agreement and clarification of differences apply more generally than among our own small group.

In the nature of a seminar based on a limited number of essays, each restricted in length, we started from specific topics often illustrated for a single society or cultural region. Inevitably much of the discussion, despite general introductions on selected problems by various participants, involved citation of other examples, representing different forms of organization, each with its varied rules. But in the end there was a consistent attempt to see whether it was possible to arrive at generalizations which would cover ranges of systems of African customary law, to classify together some systems, and to see whether some wide general principles for all African law might be adduced. Of the last step, hardly anyone remained sceptical, though a few queried specific modes of comparison (see van Velsen below). On the whole, we concluded that some general principles did emerge, despite the variety of specific rules found in Africa. Divergences of opinion on particular problems are recorded below. Strikingly, on this point there was no division between lawyers and anthropologists, though they proceeded from similar facts to different kinds of analyses.

The main aim of the theoretical lawyer (as against the practitioner of law) is to isolate and state in a clear and comprehensive way the general principles which underlie a particular branch of the law. In this task his primary responsibility is to the practitioners and judges who administer the law and who require such a statement for advising clients and disposing of cases. The legal analyst may also have broader aims, e.g. to relate the given branch of the law to the legal system, to incorporate the work in some wider jurisprudential or comparative analysis, or to promote the harmonization or unification of legal rules nationally or internationally. Here he may become the servant of those concerned with directing the affairs of the nation, who may demand a greater certainty and simplicity in the law, or the development of new legal institutions, or the reform of old ones. In Africa he is particularly responsible for the development of the customary laws: he may have to put forward legislative proposals for the unification of customary law or its harmonization with other laws. In comparative analysis he tries to establish and define legal principles which recur in different systems and to show which legal institutions are unique in their application; while if he belongs to the historical or sociological schools of jurisprudence he may be interested in relating these occurrences to the course of historical development or to the pattern of social and economic conditions.

The social anthropologist shares much of this ground with the theoretical jurist. Even though he may lack some skill in refining and analysing the problems set out above, he does make statements of rules, in so far as he gets them from jurists or can set them out for himself. These are a starting-point for an analysis in a comparative framework of the relation of rules to other elements in socio-cultural systems. He is interested in the setting of specific disputes within social relationships where varied methods of control operate; and he analyses how these relationships are structured in relation to technical purposes, to economic variables, to political co-operation and competition, and so forth. He studies the manner in which processes of settling disputes work. He is also concerned to relate legal to other types of actions and beliefs, and to examine how their variations can be referred to different socio-economic conditions. On the practical side, he may indicate where changes in law run into unexpected difficulties (see Pauwels and Smith, below). Thus lawyer and anthropologist complementarily serve each other from the peripheries of their respective fields, though there are, of course, scholars who are able to practise both types of analysis.

In writing this 'Introduction', we have inevitably seen the problems from the background of English law. Lack of space, as well as lack of expertise, have prevented our attempting to add a corresponding approach from the other major system of law introduced into Africa—the French civil code. In addition, since we had to make notes of the discussions in English, we worked largely from Dr. Pauwels's English summaries of French contributions; and we are happy to record the thanks of the Seminar to Pauwels for taking on this onerous burden which both imposed a strain on him and affected his participation in debate. The result was that our records of the contributions in French were briefer than our records of those in English. If we have clarified the problems for English-speaking scholars, we can hope that what we have written may be of use to a civil-law jurist, or an anthropologist from the same background, in essaying a task parallel with ours.

We ourselves have necessarily, with some disagreement, provided the frame of analysis in this 'Introduction'; but we did not wish to impose our own several ideas on it. As far as space allowed, we have tried to bring out the dialogue that went on between professions and persons.

II RESEARCH PROBLEMS AND METHODS

The ideas and procedures of African customary law can only be discovered through a series of investigations of that law at work in particular societies. A similar study of modern European law might concentrate on legal texts (legislation, case reports, and jurists' commentaries) to arrive at fundamental ideas, rather than on the day-to-day behaviour of courts and persons involved in the legal process. Textual study appears to treat law as a set of formal and explicitly stated norms and procedures, laid down and enforced by appropriate authorities, apparently largely detached from the total social situation in which they operate and which they seek to modify. Practising lawyers are fully aware that social and cultural facts, and their development, influence the law; but they believe that sensitivity to these processes comes from experience in chambers and in court. Hence academic preparation for practice and research in Europe (possibly rightly) largely concentrates on learning the rules of law themselves, and on acquiring skill in analysing and disposing of legal problems. But Europe has produced sociologically minded jurists; and these have been far more numerous in the United States. Many jurists there have for a long time emphasized the extent to which changing social currents and presumptions influence, e.g., the judicial process. Eventually the so-called realist schools of rule-sceptical and fact-sceptical lawyers questioned the established modes of studying law, and focused attention increasingly on the role of law in society, and on the influence of society on law. These developments were reciprocally encouraged by the burgeoning of the social and behavioural sciences from the last quarter of the nineteenth century to their high development from the 1930s onwards.

Jurists could concentrate on records when they studied legal systems with a long tradition of writing which allowed an accumulation of reports and commentaries on which there could be a high degree of refined, self-conscious reflection. Writing also provided fuller historical backgrounds for the different stages of legal development, and the wider dissemination of information on current and changing situations, abroad as well as at home. In Africa there were no indigenous written codes or records save where Islam prevailed.[1] Our first written studies come from early travellers, missionaries, and administrators, and in the early years of colonial rule these were supplemented by more systematic reports of commissions and other special inquiries. Judgments by higher-grade courts, largely staffed by personnel from the colonizing country, sometimes assisted by indigenous assessors or taking evidence on customary law, were recorded, and the introduction of Roman script also enabled indigenous authorities to compile codes and briefly record decisions.[2] In time, Western-type courts and Western-educated officials, both European and African, concerned with administering and supervising customary courts, and with trying cases on appeal from those courts, clarified, crystallized, and formalized customary law as operated from the centre; and, most importantly, they attempted to translate its terms into a language intelligible to European lawyers. At the same time there appeared a number of professional studies by lawyers and anthropologists, including Africans. But for deeply informed research into comparative African law there was lacking the body of documentary material, historical and current, about the social systems and cultures from which law springs.

In addition, with the economic and social differentiation of society in Europe and North America, 'the law' is considerably differentiated out from other institutions so that it can be more or less separately studied. The 'external' connections of 'law' with society can be left to other specialists, though many jurists have given notable leads in studying these connections. On the other hand, in the absence of marked social differentiation in African societies, the principles and rules of its customary laws were not detached from their social environment. In this situation they were mostly not enunciated in authoritative texts or edicts, but were rather felt to be embedded in the

[1] Islamic law was excluded from this Seminar, since the International African Institute had already organized a seminar dealing with *Islam in Tropical Africa* (edited by I. M. Lewis, 1966), and to bring it in would have widened the field too much. But see Smith's essay on the effects of an Islamic rule on a community's domestic life and corporate groups.
[2] See essays by Deschamps, Ramolefe, and Schapera below.

usages and customs of the people. The criterion by which it could be decided whether a given norm was legal or non-legal was difficult to determine. The social background had to be investigated, and this background too was not described in writing. An investigation of law as social fact might, therefore, seem to be the only way to discover the principles of such systems, even though there were some written codes, and some societies did recognize the capability of certain authorities or experts to enunciate the law—*jus dicere*.

In this situation, it is not surprising that when research lawyers and anthropologists wished to study the 'living' customary law, rather than the law crystallized in decisions of higher courts, they focused on trials in the courts of customary law, both by study of the recorded decisions and by observation of trials in progress. The lawyers brought with them to interpret these facts the background of the total legal system of the territory; the anthropologists brought the detail of their long-term observations in social life itself. These different approaches stemmed from their analytic divergences outlined above.

It is easier to state these divergences abstractly than to observe them in practice. To understand 'legal personality' in African law, Allott has in his essay to examine how the members of African groups work their land and organize their interdependent relationships. Moreover, in practice when a well-informed lawyer deals with an acute social problem, he has to investigate and try to use the social groups for which he is legislating. This is well shown in Mugerwa's essay which analyses how the Uganda Government legislated to prevent cattle raids by the Karamojong on their neighbours, as well as to control their internal blood-feuds, by thrusting responsibility and liability on those elders whose positions in the tribal structure would both induce them, and give them power, to control the raiding and feuding warriors. On the other hand, Pauwels shows how the introduction from Belgian law into Leopoldville (now Kinshasa) of ideas about the status of illegitimate, and especially adulterine, children, produced a situation in which parts of the law controlling family relations within the city are being influenced by reaction to certain administrative regulations dealing with allowances for children and schooling rather than by a coherent familial policy. Customary law as developed in urban courts now distinguishes rights of guardianship from rights of paternity: while a man may be made guardian of his natural children, he can only be recognized as *pater* (social father) if he pays the traditional bridewealth (marriage-payment) to the kin of the mother, who in turn if she has been married must have been properly divorced. Thus the legitimation of adulterine children is ruled out. Pauwels feels that the law is developing here by what may be called 'uncontrollable drift' of decisions by inadequately trained judges, rather than by knowledge illumined by combined legal and anthropological research. In this analysis of historical developments Pauwels relies on knowledge of legal rules from several systems operating together in a new social context.

The essay by Smith, an anthropologist, examines how a legislative change to customary law can have consequences that were not even considered worthy of contemplation by the initiators. The introduction of the Islamic rule forbidding a woman to remarry before she has menstruated three times (*idda*) has affected the law of a Nigerian people practising 'secondary marriage' of a woman to a new spouse even while her extant marriage to her 'primary husband' remains in being. These secondary marriages were made in previously set links between lineages. Some enforcement of the *idda* rule has altered the relative powers and liabilities of women, their several husbands, the women's fathers, and the kin of the spouses, so as to affect the stability of the lineages which controlled much of social life. Thus new problems have been created which in turn require further legislative action.

Clearly, then, lawyers and anthropologists may co-operate fruitfully in studying the complex reality of social action. It seemed also fruitful for them to do so when they essayed theoretical comparative analyses. But there was fairly heated debate about the appropriateness of particular comparisons. Throughout the discussions, some sought to illuminate the principles of African law by comparing its doctrines with those of modern Western law: others argued that there are many dangers in polarizing contrasts between 'a pan-African customary law' and something called 'Western modern law'. The case was put most strongly by van Velsen, recurrently; but in his essay he argues that if procedures in African customary courts are compared with procedures in European 'magistrates' courts' and some American 'small claims courts' and with specialized conciliation tribunals, rather than with courts at higher levels of jurisdiction, there is found a similar informality marking a similar striving after 'common-sense justice'.[1] This example illustrates that comparisons of aspects of African customary law and modern Western law can be made in various ways, depending on the problems set.

There was general agreement that any comparison may illuminate understanding: it is no use arguing about theoretical research methods and theoretical objectives in the abstract; one must first define the problem that one is investigating. The problem obviously influences what data have to be collected to solve it; and the problem further determines how useful it is or may be to make any particular comparison or series of comparisons.

All emphasized, as Poirier does in his essay, that any statement of rules should be supported by reports of cases tried in customary courts, together with a search for specific incidents of different types of contract, marriage, etc., for divergences between the theory of rules and actual practice, for the history of individuals in litigation, and so forth. But the use of cases raised two problems. First, how far can a clear rule of law, in its full context, be derived from a single judicial decision? Where one has only a short statement of a decision, without full presentation of the arguments and judicial reasoning, it is difficult to see how the decision was arrived at to fit the particular set of circumstances before it. Since any body of law is likely to consist of a whole series of principles and rules, some very general and others more specific, it may be illegitimate to deduce any principle from a solitary case on a particular issue, since the same principle may be applied differently, or not at all, in circumstances which seem similar but which in the eyes of the court vary in other significant respects from those of the case under trial. Secondly, since only a few, or even no, cases in certain areas of dispute may occur in any period of time, information has to be collected by discussions both with customary judges and with ordinary citizens, on remembered

[1] This example is further explored below, pp. 23–25, where Ollennu's views are cited.

disputes and on cases stated, varied as much as possible, as well as on statements of what customary rules were and are. These have to be presented with as much care as possible by setting them in the context through such direct observation as the researcher has been able to make, on other issues in court and in social life at large. There was only one of us who doubted whether this would produce a relatively accurate and comprehensive statement of the law of a particular community.

III THE TIME FACTOR AND THE DEFINITIONAL PROBLEM: WHAT IS CUSTOMARY LAW?

If we are to investigate the customary law of an African people, when and where do we find it? Is it the traditional or ancient law, or the modern (traditionalists might say 'perverted') law, infected as it is by non-African ideas, administered by non-customary courts, studied by jurists, challenged by the younger generation of those allegedly subject to it, and recorded in a form which may fundamentally alter its whole character and style (whether the form be the technical language of the lawyer or the technical language of the anthropologist)?

The importance of the time factor in this cannot be overemphasized. The view that customary law was ancient and immutable, retaining its principles through long periods of time, its origins lost in the mists of antiquity, has been discarded. Not only are customary laws changing today but also they were subject to constant change in the pre-colonial past. Furthermore, even where the formulation of laws remains fixed, we have to take into account that there may be substantial respecifications in the application of persisting legal formulae both to recurrent and to new situations. Thus (as in Europe and America) even where legal rules in Africa retain their form, their content may be highly flexible.

Have these developments, manifesting the adaptability of customary law to new conditions, gone so far that its rules have become too unstable and unpredictable in their application for us to be able to speak legitimately of law, with its implication of some order and regularity and certainty?

The answer to these very worrying problems has to be made at various levels and in various forms. It has been established that African customary law, like any system of law, consists of a variety of different types of principles, norms, and rules. Some of them state wide and general principles of morality and public policy to constitute an apparently enduring ideological framework for justice. Such principles of wide connotation, stated in multivocal terms covering many referents or wide ranges of action, are flexible and can be adapted to changing conditions and standards. This applies to a lesser extent to medium-level principles which inform the application of the highest principles, and it continues to apply to the form of much more specific rules. These qualities enable law to exhibit a continuity and certainty in many areas where attempts are being made to control substantially changed circumstances. Meanwhile, some principles or rules may be declared forgotten, or even declared obsolete under what is a principle of obsolescence stated quite explicitly, while on the other hand new principles and rules are introduced. These changes can occur at any of the various levels outlined above. It is the skill of the judges in selecting from this variety of principles and rules those which in a particular case will give the 'just decision' that marks a living, adaptable, functional system of law, as against a hidebound, unadaptable system in any field of social life. Hence a first task in research on any system is to determine how adaptable it is to new conditions and demands in the various areas of legal relationships, and to what extent adaptation as it occurs is framed in terms of old or newly devised principles, as well as what principles block adaptation. Studies of African customary courts show that adaptation is easier in some fields than in others (see discussion of contract law below). The problem of these courts is not different from the problems which have faced, and face, courts elsewhere in the world: in Europe and America judges have been guided by changing principles of justice, public policy, and morality, as socio-economic conditions have altered, to amend the definition and application of legal rules where they could do so. Hence the study of European and American law is largely a study of decisions applying, with fresh specification, enduring linguistic formulae. No one would consider trying to expound the law outside of specific decisions, exhibiting the extent to which new forms of relationships with altering standards permeate the application of legal principles and rules. Further problems arise in examining how courts' decisions in these circumstances are related to the varying distribution of new developments through the population, since these developments may be associated, though not perfectly, with the indigenous and new status of persons, and their sex, age, education, religious affiliation, and so forth. It is important to assess which judges are in touch with what currents of opinion in the community at large.

We see thus that certain general principles are able to continue operating to cope with new legal problems. These most general statements acquire significance as they are applied through a series of subsidiary rules, involving less widely ranging principles and procedures. In all this, legal development does not keep exactly in step with socio-economic development; and that more general development itself is not precisely phased in all its parts. A system of law may be kept in some accord with developments by judge-made law; but normally where change is rapid it depends also on legislation to declare some rules obsolete and to enact new rules. In the absence of such clarifying action, it may be difficult to state exactly when judicial or popular disregard of a traditional rule means that the rule is abrogated and loses the force of law. In recent times individual Kipsigis in Kenya began to enclose and appropriate community grazing lands: at what point in time does what was originally a flagrant disregard of established and legally protected rights become an approved method of acquiring property? Breach of the old rule would appear as 'the law' if the investigator adopts the policy that he reports what he sees happening, whether in the customary courts or outside among the people; and this will provide us with an excellent legal behavioural study. But will it give us a fair picture of the law? Will it enable us to criticize a court decision as revealing ignorance of the law? Or to comment on the people's conduct in acting in a manner so contrary to law? Does it define obsolescence of old rules and institutionalization of new rules? On the other hand, if the investigator insists on the validity of stated rules, he may be contributing to the perpetuation in theory of a law which is disregarded in practice. To support this, one can argue the paramount public necessity that law, when it changes, should do so in an unmistakable manner, either by legislation (which seems necessary in this Kipsigis example) or by long-maintained, general non-observance. It is common elsewhere, as in Africa, for there to be a time-lag between social and legal evolution: and people find it acceptable where they expect their law to be well-established, even if this implies that it is sometimes somewhat old-fashioned.

The same difficulties are met in studying any extant system of law. Even for the practitioner in a well-developed written system it is often impossible to predict the decision of a court on seemingly straightforward issues, though he can turn to many decisions and texts. In recording an African system, we have to consult informants, and we have to select those who seem most appropriate. The local judges in practice decide cases; and each decision is the law in that case, subject to appeal. Hence it seems sensible in the first place to get theoretical decisions from local judges on cases stated, on the assumption that the law is whatever the judges will probably say it is. Where the judges are traditional jurists, we may be getting the law of an age that is passing, and which is being rejected by many of those who are amenable to their jurisdiction, but that raises other problems involving the study of changing public opinion. If the judges are no longer those traditionally indicated, but new types of persons selected by recently independent governments (see below, pp. 25–28), they may speak without knowledge of what the law of the community has been, or is, while a situation may be arising in which some people take their disputes for most satisfactory settlement, according to the law they support and the decisions they desire, to unofficial arbitrators. There would then be two sets of customary laws, as Deschamps, McDowell, Poirier, and Shack describe, applied in two sets of 'courts' which the unscrupulous could play against each other.

We believe again that the answer to these difficulties will depend on the task set himself by the investigator. For theoretical academic study it may be possible to describe the total situation, in all its complexity, with divergence of the practices of some people from what certain specified others state to be 'the law'. Lawyer or anthropologist may here delight in the difficulties and complexities we have discussed, and out of these build the most fascinating parts of his analysis, without feeling the need to solve them as the practical lawyer or politician must do. He may similarly avoid the difficulties inherent in another problem these practical men must solve: What is law, as it is to be enforced, and how does it differ from moral rules, conventions, etiquette, mere customary practices, and the like?

The lawyer must solve these problems when he is called upon to apply his expert knowledge of customary law to a task such as recording[1] or restating[2] customary law for a government. The Government's objective is limited and practical: write down a comprehensive list of operational instructions for our courts and legal practitioners to use, and our legislators to act on. What is included in the list is law; what is omitted is not. How is this list to be compiled? Clearly it is impossible to prescribe, in advance, specific rules for observation, or for collection of data, or for interpretation. A pragmatic, comprehensive approach seems sensible. To record any particular system of modern or traditional African law requires the development of experience and scholarly judgment, as in all research. Ramolefe's paper herein on Sesotho family law neatly illustrates the possible sources available for the elucidation of customary law: he draws on (i) *The Laws of Lerotholi*, an official but non-technical compilation of various rules of Sesotho customary law made under the authority of the then Paramount Chief at the beginning of the century; (ii) reports of a British Government Commission in 1873, and the writings of missionaries, lawyers, and anthropologists; (iii) cases decided in the High Court; (iv) the opinions of a contemporary Panel for the Restatement of Sesotho Law and Custom; and (v) his own personal experience as Registrar of Sesotho customary courts and Customary Law Commissioner, adding (vi) his own personal opinions on what traditional law was and what the law should be on certain points in present-day circumstances.

That is Ramolefe, as all restators must, turns to written sources, to judgments known, and to 'customary law' as embodied in the rules of behaviour observed by the members of a given community.

These problems have always arisen for judges in superior

[1] I.e. producing a handbook or code of legal rules to be used in courts.

[2] *A restatement of the law* is a systematic, analytical, and comprehensive account of a branch of the law which is unwritten or to be found in a variety of sources, or which has diverged in application by different courts; it is generally unofficial, as were the American Restatements prepared by the American Law Institute.

courts in cases involving customary relationships. Under colonial régimes which recognized customary law in so far as it was not repugnant to principles of their morality and their conceptions of natural justice, superior court judges, whether African or European, in both British and French territories, often sat with African assessors who informed them what was the customary law in question. The statements of such assessors were subject to some of the hazards we have described. Alternatively, the litigants would call experts on the customary law, or cite authorities, and judges had to consider this evidence and come to a decision on it as best they could. Ollennu stated that under these processes, African customary law was in a sense a foreign law which had to be proved in its own land, a law external to the main body of law enforced in the superior courts. He went on to say that this colonial distinction between introduced and customary law is now felt to be undesirable in an independent country in Africa, and there is a movement for 'integration'[1] of all types of law, which are regarded as equal in status, and so connected as to form a systematic whole. In Ghana part of the law may be special personal law applicable to one tribe, and part of the law may have been introduced: but all are one law of the land, emanating from different sources, and applied in disputes as required. Though conflicts may arise between different systems of customary law (in succession, marriage, tort), all these systems of law enjoy parity of esteem. They are administered by all courts of the land: there is conflict of laws, but it is between bodies of law on the basis of equality. Ghana now has one system of courts from the highest court to the local courts; and all these courts are deemed to know the indigenous customary law. Litigants do not have to lead evidence to prove this law. In practice, the change means that a court can use its personal knowledge, take cognizance of what has been written on a topic, or itself institute an inquiry into what is customary law. Other African territories have adopted different solutions (these will be discussed below, pp. 25–33): we cite the Ghanaian solution here to indicate that the problems which confront the researcher and law officer confront the judge as he settles cases.

[1] This is different from 'unification' and 'codification' of the law discussed below at pp. 28–30, 31–33.

We reiterate that these same problems confront judges, and researchers and practitioners, in all legal systems. Everywhere there is uncertainty over which rules may be applied to a dispute, and everywhere not all the standards, customs, conventions, and even rules, that are enforced by judges, are recorded in statements of law and statutes. Conceptions of public policy, morality, and justice, which guide judges and permeate their judgments within the framework of established rules, all contribute to the formation of what is called judicial law: and hence the critical importance, in Africa as in Europe and America, of the mode of selecting judges for determining the style and orientation of the legal system in action.

The problem of the time-factor may be solved in various ways by the theoretical research worker, depending on what problems he has posed. For example, if he is interested in the relation between the customary law and the socio-economic conditions which prevailed when African societies were more self-subsistent, before the large-scale development of mining, farming, and industry, then obviously he may be compelled to reconstruct, as best he can, traditional law at that period. Here he must combine the use of written records and oral traditions, with all the scholarly safeguards he can employ, as Ramolefe has done. Such a study would be research in historical jurisprudence and anthropology. It may well have practical implications: e.g. in helping to determine the effectiveness of legislation to change customary law, and indicating the sorts of unintended consequences which may flow from proposed changes, however beneficial these be; in showing what is the capacity and incapacity of customary law to deal with new problems; and in illuminating a variety of other problems discussed below.

IV THE PROBLEM OF DESCRIPTION

When he has solved the above difficulties, the investigator has to report his findings in a set of interconnected terms which will most accurately, appropriately, and intelligibly convey to other scholars as well as practical men the exact range and effect of the rules of customary law.

Obviously any particular system of African law can be reported in its own language; but this would raise two difficulties.

First, the range of most African languages is relatively small, and even within a single African state there are several mutually unintelligible languages: communication might therefore be very restricted. Secondly, many of the key terms of any legal system are imprecise, ambiguous, multivocal; this causes difficulties even in legal systems where scholars, aided by writing, have long worked on refining legal concepts and delineating their contexts of use. Each African language still has to develop its own scholarship of refinement; and meanwhile this use of the native language would restrict communication even among Africans.

In the past, four courses have been followed, though inevitably they have been combined:

(i) professional lawyers have attempted to assimilate the features and institutions of the given customary law to an existing technical legal vocabulary belonging to one or more of the major legal systems of the world (e.g. the civil law, the common law, the Roman–Dutch law, or Roman law), with retention of some untranslatable African concepts (as in the Natal Native Code, 1896);

(ii) some lawyers have (like the Dutch students of Indonesian law) reacted against this ethnocentricity, as have anthropologists. They have tried to work out a vocabulary of neutral or indifferent words from the language of analysis, and to strip these of their technicalities or overt reference to the legal system of that language, by using qualificatives of various kinds;

(iii) a few comparative jurists have tried to develop a new universal legal language, corresponding to universals believed to subsist in all legal systems; this has been done for very restricted sections of comparative law and so far remains at best a hope; and

(iv) a few anthropologists have maintained that it is essential, after expounding the implications of African terms in the language of the study, to retain them in constant use, if their meaning is not to be destroyed.

Each of these courses has weaknesses and difficulties, as well as strengths and advantages. For the reasons given, we assume that for the time being most scholars will find the last course most difficult and unsatisfactory for analysis. While some recording of law has been done in some African languages and they will be used in time for analysis, it is probable that work will be in a major language of European origin, or in Arabic, or some other Asian language. The use of a non-African extraneous language, or the wider application of an African language outside or even inside its own region, immediately creates problems which have to be overcome: its terms, even when apparently not technical, are already loaded with special meaning, both more narrowly linguistic and more broadly social. The specialization of a technical language from an everyday vocabulary, and the use of another language for translation, always raises these problems. They are further complicated because languages are conventional human constructs, in which words have only the meanings attributed to them by user and audience, and they do not in themselves stand for things.

This being so, the language of analysis also must be established by convention, and it should be possible to stipulate what referents apply to each term used. Whether the language be borrowed or novel, it clearly should be consistent, economical, as unambiguous as possible, and in correspondence with the system or systems described.

There was little difficulty in getting agreement on these rules, or on the importance of developing terms which would allow comparison. Forde put the view of the anthropologists, and the lawyers agreed with the implications of what he said. He affirmed that social anthropology operates extra-culturally and super-societally, and that therefore the idea that a researcher has exhausted his task when he has expounded the terminology of one society is quite inadequate. It is essential to go on to relate one society's concepts to a category of analytical concepts. As social anthropologists, and presumably also as comparative jurists, we are trying to find concepts to denote particular types of phenomena. The difficulty is that in human societies the phenomena being studied, including legal phenomena, have been named by those who use and reflect about them—a difficulty not encountered in natural sciences. But if we stick to the nomenclature of one society, comparative analysis is stultified. We have to ask what categories are found significantly recurrently, or significantly uniquely, over varied ranges of societies.

Again, agreement on these points was general: the debate arose, and it still persists, about which are the most suitable terms to use for a specific type of phenomena, and whether certain terms in, say, English, are confusing if applied to other systems. Thus some considered that the use of words like 'property' and 'ownership' and 'contract' in some English treatises on African law is objectionable on this ground. Others felt that analysis is facilitated, and no confusion is created, if certain very important, and perhaps therefore inherently multivocal, terms in the field of law—words like law itself, justice, right, duty, property, crime, debt, contract, tort, court, proof, evidence, and the like[1]—are used in translation of African terms which seem equivalent. They considered that these English words were so general in meaning that the use of an adjective to locate their provenance or type would distinguish them sufficiently, where the context did not make clear what the immediate connotation of the word was. It was suggested that if the same terms were to be used in analysis, this might be indicated by printing them in heavy black type or by some other device. It was argued further that this is possible if terms for analysis are used within a hierarchy or series embracing more specialized words with narrower and narrower specifications of meaning. Thus when goods are transferred to obtain a bride from her kin, it is possible to speak of claims on these as one set among many of property rights; of the transfer itself as marriage-payment[2] to cover this institution in many African and other systems, including early Germanic law, even though the transfers may have different further implications

---

[1] For discussions of the multivocality of similar African terms, see Biebuyck, 1963, 'Introduction', pp. 15–16; Gluckman, 1955, Chapter IV; Schapera, 1938, pp. 37–38. For proposals for the use of more neutral English terms, see Moore, 1969b.

[2] There has been considerable discussion among anthropologists in English about the most suitable term: Radcliffe-Brown used 'marriage-payment' in his 'Introduction' to *African Systems of Kinship and Marriage* (1950). Some have continued to use 'bride-price' which came early into use, while 'bride-wealth', which avoids the implication of purchasing the bride, is in common use. One has suggested 'child-wealth' since in some systems the payment is largely to gain the affiliation of children born to the bride. We consider that 'dowry' and the French '*dot*' are inappropriate.

in various systems. These can be handled by speaking of payments for uxorial or genetricial services (see below). Where the payment consists of several items, variously named, these may be referred to by literal translations, or by vernacular terms.

This set of participants argued that it was possible to restrict the connotation of terms high in the hierarchy by adjectives; so that if we use 'contract' widely to refer to enforceable agreements, we can distinguish between 'status contracts' (e.g. marriage, adoption) and 'commercial contracts', and between 'medieval English commercial contracts' or 'modern English commercial contracts' or 'traditional African commercial contracts', and the like, with more narrower specifications possible. They considered that the elaboration of an interdependent vocabulary appeared to be the most suitable path for success in comparative analysis.

A few argued that only by the use of a single term, in one language or another, was it possible to bring together phenomena in several systems in order to scrutinize them for differences as well as for similarities. Thus Gluckman cited his use of the phrase 'the reasonable man' to analyse the process of Barotse trials:[1] some critics had said this immediately raised connotations attaching to the phrase in English law. But Gluckman contended that if we speak of 'the reasonable man' in English law, '*vir pius gravissimusque*' in Roman law, '*bon père de famille*' in French law, '*mutu yangana*' in Barotse law, '*umuntu ohlakaniphileyo*' in Zulu law, and so forth, we are left dealing with systems in perpetual isolation from one another. For a scholar writing in English, use of the phrase 'the reasonable man' enables attention to be drawn to the common element of measurement of degree of fulfilment of duty required at law, whether it be a reasonable degree of care in maintaining a wife or administering lineage property in Africa, or care in driving an automobile or manufacturing pure food in Britain. Emphasis can then be shifted to the hypothesis that, say, in Barotse law 'reasonableness' focuses on the extent to which persons concretely fulfil the expectations inherent in their roles as occupants of specific positions of status, while in the texts of English law and in English superior courts 'the reasonable man' is

---

[1] 1955, Chapter III, and new edition (1967), pp. 387 f., where various criticisms are cited and discussed.

much more of a judicial fiction within the differentiated realms of the law to assess fulfilment of duty within restricted dyadic relationships. This was why (to enable comparison of difference as well as similarity to be worked out) he had not, as he once planned to do, used instead the phrase 'the sensible man'. Allott agreed with this in principle, but said he preferred the use of verbs and adverbs to handle these situations: 'requirement to act reasonably' would be clearer of itself.

On the whole, members of the Seminar agreed with Gluckman's point, provided that the terms so employed were carefully chosen. They considered one term preferable, despite the difficulties and even dangers of translation and transposition, to the course of remaining in the terms of each separate legal system. No one was prepared to defend this point of view.[1]

In short, the problems of comparison were seen to lie in creating an analytic system for comparative analysis, where such an analytic system might consist partly of terms in current use in the jurisprudence of the language of analysis, and partly of especially devised terms. The solution was seen to lie in careful and clear specification of the terms used; and we trust this will appear in later sections, particularly those on succession and ownership of land, which raised the most heated debates (see below, pp. 45–48, 49–59).

Given that there were differing, and even opposed, views on the possibility of achieving anything like a universal legal language, or of defining a set of universal types of legal institutions, there was agreement that the following goals should be aimed at in establishing a vocabulary:

(i) The same institution, operation, or feature should as far as possible be referred to by one term and one term only.

(ii) If possible, a term should not be ambiguous in that it

---

[1] It has been argued most strongly by Bohannan, 1957. As stated in the *Preface*, Bohannan was unable to accept an invitation to attend the Seminar. For this point of view, see also, e.g. (i) Sonius, *passim*; (ii) Vansina, 1965, where it is stated that 'Kuba law is thus very different from any European legal system, and to try to define it in terms of European legal concepts is like trying to fit a Bantu grammar into a Latin model of grammatical categories, something that was actually done until descriptive linguistics taught us better'. H. and L. Kuper, the editors of the book in which Vansina's essay appeared, cite this statement and comment: '... In fact, Vansina is able to describe the Kuba system in terms of the concepts of Western jurisprudence' (in their 'Introduction', at p. 6).

relates to two distinct institutions, etc. (Thus some felt that the use of 'estate' meaning 'interest in land', and 'estate' meaning 'the property left by a deceased person', could be confusing (see below, pp. 45 f.); others argued that, unless an alternative term was proposed, the same word could be used with a distinguishing adjective or qualifying phrase unless the context made the connotation of 'estate' clear in each specific instance of its use).

(iii) The difference or points of discrimination between a set of related terms should be defined (e.g. between a right, power, privilege, or immunity),[1] so as to eliminate overlap in their reference.

(iv) The reader-hearer must not be misled by spurious references to other legal systems (hence, for instance, the risks of using 'trustee' in an English description of an African legal institution); but the investigator should examine how the multivocality of particular concepts was used by persons within a particular legal system (see Schapera's essay below on the fact that Tswana have one word for what in English is distinguished as 'right' and 'duty' so that he translates it as 'due', at p. 319).

(v) In establishing a comparative vocabulary, it would be preferable if any word selected in one language could be translated into equivalent words in closely related languages (as between English, French, etc.).

[1] See Hohfeld, 1917.

PART II PROCEDURES

V PROCEEDINGS AND EVIDENCE IN AFRICAN CUSTOMARY LAW

One might think that an indication of the quintessential characteristics of African traditional customary law might be found not in the rules of the different branches of the substantive law but in the ways in which disputes are tackled and settled. A similar approach might commend itself to the comparative lawyer who wanted to seize on and isolate the differences between English and French justice, and who found that, at the level of substantive rules, the two systems of law produced roughly similar answers to a given legal problem, but that their methods of arriving at such answers differed fundamentally. Problems arising from proceedings are raised in the essays by Ollennu, Epstein, Poirier, Shack, and van Velsen.

Among the characteristics frequently alleged as typifying traditional African judicial procedures are: simplicity and lack of formality; reliance on 'irrational' modes of proof and decision (Poirier draws attention to their survival in what he calls 'le droit secret'); the fact that the parties (and often the judges too) are normally involved in complex or multiplex relations[1] outside the court-forum, relations which existed before and continue after the actual appearance in court, and which largely determine the form that a judicial hearing takes; a commonsense as opposed to a legalistic approach to problem-solving; the underlying desire to promote reconciliation of the contesting parties, rather than merely to rule on the overt dispute which they have brought to court; and the role of religious and ritual beliefs and practices in determining legal responsibility.

[1] I.e. relations which persist through time and which serve multifarious interests, as compared with simplex relations, serving single interests (see for fuller definitions, van Velsen's essay below, p. 138).

There was virtually unanimous agreement with an exposition by Ollennu. He stressed that the very informality of proceedings in traditional courts achieved similar forensic ends to those achieved for developed courts by counsel and counsel's preparations of pleadings. This informality of procedure obtains in the mode in which litigants present their cases, in the manner of obtaining evidence, and in the role played by the court. It is usual to hear evidence from both litigants before requiring witnesses for the plaintiff to substantiate his case. Both parties are heard before witnesses are called in order to clarify and settle the issues and to determine on whom the onus lies, and hence who should first call witnesses in evidence of his claim. This procedure therefore serves the same purposes which pleadings, prepared by professional counsel, serve in superior European courts. Furthermore, since the plaintiff, lacking trained counsel's advice, may not be seised of the law, but perhaps merely feel that he has been badly treated, justice cannot be achieved unless he is allowed to speak about many things, which at first are apparently irrelevant, but which may later turn out to be crucial. The same observation applies to the other party's initial statement. In the absence of advance preparation and examination in court by counsel, litigants may not be able to present their grievances in coherent, logical, and relevant form. Here traditional judges play the role of counsel, as an English judge may do on behalf of a litigant who appears without benefit of counsel. And, again similarly to an English court, when traditional judges enter on judgment, they eliminate the irrelevant, and their arguments are couched in an accumulating logic leading to a verdict on the balance of probabilities in the light of the law. It is also necessary to remember that parties are responsible themselves for deciding what witnesses they require, while they lack experts to collect and evaluate evidence.

Traditional judges also play the role of counsel in cross-examining parties and witnesses. This has sometimes given rise to the mistaken idea among those used to Anglo-Saxon law trials, where the judges preside over an adversary contest between counsel, that in African courts there is a presumption of guilt. This presumption seems to arise wherever the judge's duty is himself to find out the truth, since it is only possible to check evidence under cross-examination by formulating questions *as if* the cross-examiner assumed the person to be lying.[1]

Ollennu further stated, following van Velsen's stress in his essay, that judges have to perform two duties: first, they have to determine who is right and who is wrong; and secondly, they have to lay down, in the light of that decision, consequential orders which ensure satisfaction for the parties and for the public. That is, in a small community they may have, as Epstein shows in his essay, to aim at redressive measures as well as, or in place of, penal sanctions. Attempts at reconciliation may follow as a dominant aim. But reconciliation is usually achieved when satisfaction is given to the aggrieved party and the wrongdoer is convinced of his error.

This type of procedure also influences the manner in which evidence is taken. It is the duty of the court, when it has heard all that parties and witnesses wish to say, to select that evidence which is relevant to the issues extracted from their statements. It is also clear from many reports that though little evidence is therefore ruled out initially as inadmissible, traditional judges did distinguish sharply between hearsay and primary evidence. As Shack shows in his essay, Gurage courts will not determine guilt and innocence only upon hearsay evidence: it must be corroborated by some independent primary evidence. Similarly, numerous reports show that traditional courts distinguish sharply between the firmness of evidence of eye-witnesses, and the difficulties which attend on determining guilt or liability by circumstantial evidence. We shall discuss below the use of oaths and ordeals.

Certain problems arise when cases come on appeal from local courts to superior courts. In Ghana it was customary for a relative to represent a party in proceedings in local courts, or to assist him in the conduct of his case. Unfortunately sometimes such a representative might give evidence as if it were the party himself speaking; on the principle of the hearsay rule, such evidence was usually excluded on appeal to the superior court, and if that were the only evidence in favour of the party's case, he was bound to lose on appeal, particularly where he was the plaintiff. On the other hand, the Supreme

[1] For a detailed description and discussion of this situation, see Gluckman, 1955, pp. 96, 360.

Court of Ghana held that where a local court admitted in evidence a record of a previous suit involving the parties with a person not appearing in the present case, it was right in doing so, for otherwise it might not have been able to understand the issues involved and a grave miscarriage of justice might have occurred, even though the documents would not have been admissible in the Supreme Court itself.[1]

VI THE NEW PERSONNEL OF LOCAL COURTS

The informality of local courts may not continue to be effective in securing justice when the judges are no longer selected from among the local community and are no longer conversant with the people, with customary law and daily practice, and with what litigants expect from their courts. If other types of persons, less knowledgeable and thus less interested in reconciling the parties, are appointed to these courts, the same looseness of procedure may not be conducive to justice and it may be necessary to lay down strict procedural rules (though in his essay van Velsen argues from American and European lower-level courts that this does not necessarily follow).

Ollennu's essay stresses that local courts under the colonial régimes obtained their jurisdiction under enabling jurisdiction which either recognized them or did not exclude them; and this position had continued with certain important changes under African independent states which had provided for the establishment of local courts.[2] The following discussion assumes this statutory position of local and customary courts as recognized in each African state.

The move to change the traditional personnel of these courts is supported on professional grounds. There is a demand for integration of the courts system as a whole, in order to constitute a single hierarchy, as well as for some unification and consolidation of the law, in the interests of the effective administration of justice and of national unity. The colonial régimes had instituted the control of these courts through appeal to higher courts with professional judges, and through supervision of

---

[1] *Ankrah* v. *Ankrah*, Civ. App. 117/64, 1966.
[2] See Allott (ed.), 1962 (2nd edition forthcoming), for the position in former British dependencies as of 1961; *Report of the Conference on Local Courts and Customary Law*, Dar es Salaam, 1964; Roberts, 1966.

their operation and records by various officials. Now African professional law officers and practitioners may feel that justice will be better achieved if all courts are staffed with adequately trained professional judges, so that every citizen is subject to the same law administered in the same way and with the same fundamental right of legal representation. McDowell stressed that these demands in Nigeria came largely from lawyers who were trained in Britain, and who often did not understand and were not sympathetic to customary law. He referred to the statement in Ollennu's essay that in view of changes in personnel of local courts and their lack of qualifications in Ghana, as well as the limited jurisdiction of these courts, 'it is evident that systematic development of the customary law can no longer depend upon the local courts; it can only depend upon the superior courts of the land . . .' (p. 118). We have already quoted Pauwels on the difficulties created by the drift of decisions on family law in Kinshasa courts, and he too considers (at p. 234) that trained lawyers should have the task of developing a better informed law. In fact, Ollennu argued that professional lawyers should be trained in customary law, a conclusion that was accepted as the ideal by the *Conference on Local Courts and Customary Law* held at Dar es Salaam in 1963. This implies that courses in customary law will have to be developed in African law schools, as is indeed happening. We note briefly that the increasing induction of young men into developing economies prevents them from sitting at customary court-hearings and 'arbitrations' where most of them used to learn the local law.

Finding professionally trained lawyers to act as judges and to represent the parties in local courts creates major problems. How many lawyers will be able to study the many systems of customary law which still exist in Africa, on top of their study of other branches of the law? Furthermore, Richardson's essay draws attention to the logistics of the problem. In Nigeria there were, when he wrote his essay, some one thousand barristers at work in the legal system; yet over 90 per cent of all cases were heard by the 1,500 local courts of the four regions. He estimates that the cost of professionalizing these courts would be towards £2,000,000 per annum.

It is little wonder that many at the Dar es Salaam *Conference* on *Local Courts and Customary Law* saw that work would have to continue with a non-professionalized system for some time, particularly in the fields of family and land law. In this connection, McDowell draws attention to a fact underlined in van Velsen's essay: 'It is as well in this context to remember that 97·5 per cent of all criminal charges in England are heard by lay justices . . .'

Nevertheless, whatever the difficulties in finding adequately trained lawyers to perform these tasks, political considerations may force out the traditional personnel. In many states chiefs and elders have been regarded as creatures who supported the colonial régime, and hence as unsuitable to retain their positions under independent democracy. Among the aspirations in the drive for independence was emphasis on election rather than succession to political position and office. The unity of a new nation is seen as threatened by continuing tribal affiliations with their traditional authorities. Some have suggested that there are further, deeper reasons for the taking away of judicial and other powers from traditional authorities. Officials of the colonial régimes drew their power from the metropolitan country they represented, and only to a limited extent therefore did they compete with chiefs and other African traditional authorities for the support of the general populace. The new African élites, both in the political parties and the bureaucracies, derive all their power from inside the State and its people, and hence are in rivalry with those traditional authorities. Furthermore, in the new situation of independence, the conflict between generations is exacerbated. Many of the young resent the authority of the elder generation, and the customary practices to which most of this generation adhere, and traditional authorities are identified with this older generation which allegedly obstructs progress. For all these reasons, in most states the traditional judiciary are now being deprived of their jurisdictions and their privileges to hear cases: but we stress that this is not universal.

This situation seems to contain three potential developments.

(1) Professional personnel is being produced at lower standards than those of the past. Practice here varies in several countries. For example, Tanzania, Malawi, and Zambia are holding six months' courses for magistrates who will sit in local

courts, sometimes with assessors drawn from the local areas. This would in a sense carry on procedures established in the colonial period, when officers had to sit with local assessors in both the British and French territories, when magistrates were encouraged by bonuses to learn local languages, and when interpreters would sometimes be used. There would be further raised the continuing problem of whether these local courts would have still to be supervised, and most of those involved in the practice of law felt this would be necessary. While McDowell considered that the Native Courts Inspectorate of Northern Nigeria had worked satisfactorily, by providing a method of challenging an allegedly bad decision more rapid than the normal judicial appeal channels, Ollennu, who drew on his wide judicial experience, felt that the control of local courts should be by the head of the judiciary, and not by the administration. He considered that powers of review should be vested in professional magistrates; while an inspectorate could check procedures, it was not in the interests of litigants or of justice to leave powers of revision to them.

(2) There are proposals in various states to codify and unify customary laws, so that no longer will each person carry with him his own personal law. This too was seen by the Seminar as a political, rather than a legal, problem, since for many African states unification of laws is a necessary ingredient of nation-building and mobilization for economic and social development. The policy in Ghana has been to integrate the laws, firstly by placing customary law on a parity with the general law, secondly by providing clear rules which specify which law to apply in any case of conflict (see now Ghana Courts Decree 1966, para. 64), and thirdly by promoting where possible the elimination of discordant laws, e.g. by drafting new unified legislation replacing former statutory, common, and customary law (see also above, pp. 13–14). As a contrast, Ghai reported for Tanzania that the Government had undertaken the devising of a unified system of personal law. The method adopted was to work out a modified restatement of personal customary law for the patrilineal tribes; a similar one was being prepared for the matrilineal tribes; eventually the two would be combined. Integration of the courts had been achieved in Tanganyika to the extent that there were now

no separate customary courts, although there was still some distinction in jurisdiction and function between the primary and other courts. This policy of integration of courts and law had a political inspiration, to contribute to nation-building, though it might involve overriding at some points the wishes and practices of various sections of the people.

Unfortunately, it was not clear to the Seminar how the law of patrilineal and matrilineal peoples could be unified (but see below, pp. 50–53). It did seem to the anthropologists, however, that there was some tendency for many systems to develop towards a common cognatic system of kinship, centring on the nuclear family, while extended kinship groups were weakening.

Ollennu reported that Ghana had wished partially to unify its marriage, divorce, and inheritance laws. The purpose was to bring together the customary, statutory, and Muslim laws of marriage. A commission had been appointed to find out what were the wishes of the people, but its report had not been published. A bill had been drafted to deal with this unification: it had been to Parliament three times, but representations by lawyers and other interested parties had led to its suspension early in 1964 and its reference to the Law Reform Committee. The opposition came from many sources, and, he felt, was not to the principle but to details. Several members of the Seminar pursued this point, arguing that each detailed proposal was likely to be opposed by those who felt they were oppressed by it.

Poirier, who had much experience with similar problems in Dahomey, Mauritania, and Madagascar, emphasized the difficulties, and (with Deschamps' support) stressed the necessity of adequate consultation with the public and study of its opinions in its different sections. In Mauritania younger people threatened a war if the right of a father to dispose of his daughter in marriage were maintained. If the public did not accept new laws, these would merely be recorded on paper while the people followed *le droit parallèle et le droit secret* (see his essay).

(3) A third potential development was that there would be a proliferation of moots and arbitrations outside the statutory system. If lay persons unacquainted with the customary law of an area, and possibly selected because they are *personae gratae* with the Government, sit in local courts, there seem to be two main possibilities. The first is that they will be subject to

the same pressures as operate in British magistrates' courts and American small-claims courts, and seek to administer a common-sense justice (see van Velsen's essay below), particularly if they are local people, or advised by local assessors. But, secondly, if they do not do so, as may happen either generally or in particular cases, there may well be a proliferation of family and village moots, and resort to 'arbitration' by those people who are still living in accordance with traditional law. Shack reports this situation among the Gurage of Ethiopia in the following terms (pp. 164–5): 'No Gurage can live outside the kinship network in Gurageland [as against urban areas]; and therefore no Gurage can live outside tribal law.' It could not be put more succinctly. McDowell similarly reported that the pagans in Northern Nigeria who are subject to Muslim judges will accept a decision only if the principles of pagan law are enforced and not Islamic law. They do not appeal; but they take no notice of a verdict based on Islamic law and settle the matter extra-judicially by their own modes of reconciliation. It would seem here—as anthropologists repeatedly stressed—that if the issue arose out of quarrels or dubious situations in a complex of ties between kinsmen and neighbours, with one person seeking clarification of status obligations in the whole complex, the decision in terms of Islamic law may not give even the winning party what he actually wants; and perforce he returns to some indigenous arbitrator(s) to achieve his purpose.

As Shack again describes for the Gurage, it will be possible for some persons to try to exploit both official and unofficial tribunals as he sees his advantage. But most members felt that community pressures, and the decisions of judges ethnically related to the litigants, might give satisfaction even to those who lost by their decisions; at least the judges would be working with the same norms as the disputants, and research had shown that this gave considerable satisfaction, since a man in these circumstances could be shown to be in the wrong by his own norms through his own words (see Epstein's report of cases in his essay).

What will official reaction be to such moots? The history of all new states suggests that where authority is being newly established it is likely to be jealous of independent 'jurisdictions' so that some governments may treat such unofficial tribunals as extra-legal, if not illegal (see Ollennu's essay, p. 111). Then these operations would move from being part of what Poirier calls '*le droit parallèle*' to '*le droit secret*'. Other governments may find it economical to allow certain types of cases to be handled by these customary procedures, providing they do not act in conflict with national law (e.g. witchcraft accusations, forced marriages, etc.), while different types of problems are handled by professional lawyers or 'social workers' within the domains of the new economy.

We have used 'arbitration' rather loosely above to cover many types of settlement. But the lawyers felt it important to distinguish between *arbitration*, where the parties agreed in advance to accept the verdict of the arbitrator, and what Ollennu called 'negotiations for a settlement' or 'promotion of reconciliation', and Allott 'conciliation', in which the award can only be binding on the parties if accepted by them. Allott further suggested that the term *adjudication* be reserved for situations where the jurisdiction of the person concerned comes from the law and not the parties to the dispute. All agreed that it would be best if awards in approved arbitrations should be reduced to writing and signed by arbitrator and parties, and possibly also accepted awards in conciliations (see Ollennu's essay, p. 119).

VII CODIFICATION AND RECORDING OF CUSTOMARY LAW[1]

Legislative intervention with customary law has taken many forms. The legislator strictly so called has repealed parts of the ancient law and codified or transformed other parts (as with the codification of laws in the francophonic African states). Penal law, the law of marriage and the family, and land law are some of the fields particularly affected. Law-making has also gone on in a more indirect and surreptitious fashion, through the guidance which administrative authorities have given, especially to native or customary courts. Lastly, of course, one must remember the capacity of customary law itself, and of those

---

[1] We are grateful to Deschamps and Pauwels for giving us written statements of their introductions to the discussions on these problems: we have drawn largely on them.

with the power of stating the law, such as chiefs, elders, and judges, to alter or extend its rules.

Codification in the African countries of the civil-law tradition (which include Ethiopia) has gone farthest in the making of a new, unified, systematic law. Different methods have, however, been followed to achieve this goal. In some states (e.g. Madagascar) codification has been preceded by a long and searching investigation of the local customary laws; in others (e.g. Ivory Coast and Ethiopia) codification has gone ahead without a full prior study of the local, and very diverse, customary laws. Codification, so far as it exists, has taken quite a different form in the common-law countries of Africa. After the initial deposit of codes (many of them derived from the codified law of British India), there has been little attempt in recent years to add to their number by any systematic codification of the civil law. Criminal law and the law of succession, contracts, evidence, procedure, and registration of title to land have been the fields where codification has been most comprehensively introduced. In recent years, however, several common-law countries have placed under investigation a particular branch of the law (as with marriage, divorce, and succession law in Ghana) with a view to producing a new law which would largely unify or integrate the previously diverse systems of written, customary, and religious laws. Little success has so far attended these initiatives. Rather more successful have been the attempts to restate in an authoritative form the customary laws of a given country (as has been done in Kenya, Malawi, Zambia, and Swaziland, *inter alios*). Here the object is not the preparation of a code but the furnishing to the courts of a guide to the applicable laws.

Pauwels pointed out that some of the legislation in African countries was of the programmatic kind, that is, concerned with establishing a pattern to which the conduct of members of the society might tend to conform as time went on, rather than setting up a system of rules of immediate, mandatory application. The Ethiopian Civil Code of 1960 was a striking example of this genre. As Deschamps pointed out, the 'coefficient of non-application' of such a code ran the risk of being high if it was not based on the detailed prior studies of anthropologists and jurists (but this view was contested by those who argued that in practice this was impossible, especially in such a country as Ethiopia, where the manpower was not available and the diversity of customs so great); if it failed to take sufficiently into account contemporary realities; and if it ignored the slow rate of development in the thinking of the people when set beside the rapidity of evolution of external circumstances.

'Code', it was clear from the discussions, is a word of many and contradictory meanings. It need not imply a unified law, though that is normally what is established by a code; and it can be applied in French (though not in English) to a collection of rules which are not binding as legislated law (such as handbooks of customary law). A code tends to deal systematically and comprehensively with the general principles of law in a certain field, but it may or may not descend to detailed rules. Codes may give the appearance of certainty without the reality, if either they are enacted in too broad language or they are not in practice observed or understood. The inflexibility of a code could be a disadvantage, especially in a rapidly changing society. Codification was a powerful weapon in the hands of government to shape the course of economic, political, and social development.

An equally contested question is whether, and if so how, the people affected by a change in the law should be consulted before any substantial alteration is made in the legal system. There are many groups of different kinds with different backgrounds and beliefs in any country. If there is no uniformity of view even within a group, owing to differential levels of education and economic progress, how in such circumstances (even if one got over the practical difficulty of organizing a sort of opinion poll in a country with poor communications) can a consensus emerge or be expressed, upon which a new unified law can be based? Anyhow, parliament, some argued, is the proper channel for the expression of public opinion, and should be used for the work of reviewing draft legislation. Against this one may say that it is precisely this lack of consensus, this lack of uniformity between communities of different laws, religions, and cultures, that makes the imposition of a uniform law such a doubtful and difficult operation.

VIII REASON AND THE OCCULT IN CUSTOMARY LAW

Both lawyers and anthropologists agreed that the ideas of 'reason' (not necessarily 'rationality') and of acting 'reasonably' (equally, not 'rationally') were highly important. Deschamps stressed that in Malagasy law there was the idea of *arina*, which was translatable as 'equilibrium' but which he would call 'reason'. *Arina* was opposed to the notion of *heluka*, twisting like a snake. Similar notions, stated in local languages, were cited by others. Shack stressed how the Sky-god chose the judicial site for the tribal federation's high court 'by burying the symbol of Gurage justice, "toor", next to his central shrine . . .' (below, p. 157). The central conception of 'reason' and what it constitutes is brought out clearly in Epstein's essay, where he cites a court's admonitions to a man guilty of frequent adulteries: 'You, fellow, you are a lunatic, you have no sense. It is time that you came to learn that a man of sense ought not to roam about as though he were a wild animal of the bush.' The frequent comparison of wrongdoers with animals by African, as by European, courts, indicates the critical significance of reason or sense in demarcating men from animals. But reason in men is associated with the rules, customs, and standards of the society concerned. Epstein therefore continues: '. . . one is entitled to expect of one's fellow-men that their behaviour will conform to certain standards: man enjoys the gift of intelligence (*amano*), and knows therefore that in his behaviour he must display manners and respect (*mucinshi*); insofar as one does not measure up to these expectations one's humanity (*ubuntu*) is diminished'.[1]

The purpose of education and initiation in Africa is frequently defined as to inculcate 'respect'. This refers to the observance of society's laws and conventions: 'reason' does not operate in a vacuum. Hence, to quote Epstein again as representing the views of the Seminar: if the importance of 'reason' implies that men should behave reasonably and respectfully, '. . . the character of "the reasonable man" in African law does not derive from the faculty of ratiocination alone, any more than does that of his English counterpart. He is a creature of custom and morality, as much as of reason'—

---
[1] The words in parentheses are in Bemba.

and Epstein proceeds to emphasize that 'in African thought he is above all a "whole" [*-tuntulu*] man' (pp. 297 f.).

Thus in the African view it is characteristic of men that they possess 'reason', socially defined; and courts will insist on this. It implies also that judges operate with reason in solving disputes. Van Velsen phrased the situation in a way acceptable to most participants: '. . . one finds as a general rule that once a dispute has been submitted to a court, the court is obliged to pronounce upon the matter, and if possible, not merely to determine the legal rights and wrongs but also to effect some conciliation between the parties. It is particularly in these situations (when conflicts have to be solved by *reason* within the framework of a limited number of *legal* rules, and not by reference to the supernatural), that courts employ the conception of "the reasonable man". This conception brings moral and social norms and practices and standards into the courtroom . . . and enables the study of *law* to move into the wider field of social control . . . Here the lawyer and the social anthropologist meet.' Ollennu suggested that these non-legal norms could in lawyers' terminology be phrased as 'the bringing in of "collateral" matters. They may at first appear irrelevant; but they must be accepted norms used as a guide by the court.'

The Seminar then discussed the relation of 'reason' to the use of oaths and ordeals, depending on what we shall call 'occult' powers—'occult' because they are hidden, and have to be brought to view by techniques like divination, or have to be left to work of themselves, unlike court procedures and other sanctions. Shack proposed that there are three situations where such beliefs and procedures operate:

(1) Where central executive and judicial power is not strong enough to enforce its wishes over the whole population involved, it is likely that the central power will be seen as supported by occult powers, and this support will extend to its judicial functions, in determining guilt and innocence; further dependence on occult support will apply particularly in cases where the contending parties before the judges are too strong for the judges to give a decision against one of them. These may then leave the test to occult powers, through oaths.

(2) Where, in any African society, the offence complained of is itself occult, as in a charge of witchcraft or sorcery.

(3) Where there is strong suspicion, but not definite proof. His essay shows that the Gurage clearly distinguish primary direct evidence and hearsay evidence, and evidence of eyewitnesses and circumstantial evidence, and decide cases on evidence. But the losing party may challenge the veracity or impartiality of even an eye-witness by requiring him to take an oath, each being supported by a variable number of kinsmen in a procedure akin to the medieval English compurgation.

He and van Velsen further argued that the effect of this situation is to shift some of the responsibility for determining the guilt off the judges; and they suggested that there are parallel practices in countries with sharp internal cleavages, as in countries which have a strong colour-bias that is in conflict with other basic principles of justice. The jury decision may relieve the judge of considerable responsibility.

They stressed further that, in all societies, courts are often faced with deciding issues that do not clearly fall within the framework of the 'legal', and which are inherently unsuitable for a forensic determination. These issues may be domestic or political. Such disputes cannot really be *solved*, said van Velsen, by a court's apportioning blame and establishing rights and wrongs. These disputes are inherent in the social system of the people concerned, and are, at best, amenable to *palliations* and not *solutions*. In such cases, judges may have to take into account not only the nature of the relationship between the parties but also the stated or unstated purpose of litigation, which may be to get a political decision out of what appears to be a domestic suit. Here was one possible source of variation in decisions given by customary courts. And 'here too there is greater scope for judges to express their personal, non-legal feelings about the case or the litigation'.

These situations commonly involve disputes in which each party claims under one of a number of valid principles, but the principles themselves are in radical conflict. Some anthropological studies have suggested that it is this conflict of equally valid principles which in Africa is associated with fears that occult forces are at work, including fears of witchcraft and sorcery. In such a type of situation judicial reason is helpless, and other modes of handling the crisis come into play. It is in similar situations in domestic and industrial and political relationships in Europe and America that we do not call on judges, but rather on specialist conciliators, or even the ballot box.

PART III CONCEPTIONS IN THE SUBSTANTIVE LAW

IX THE CONCEPTION OF LEGAL PERSONALITY

Is there a conception of a right- and duty-bearing unit in African legal systems, formulated in terms of claims on, and responsibility towards, others, and hence distinctive from conceptions of the individual personality as a whole?[1] The idea of such a unit would appear to be central to any legal system, since this comprises principles, rules, institutions, and procedures which specify and control the exterior relationships between fellow-members of a society. Classically these relationships have been conceived as effectively bilateral or multilateral, and as involving a corresponding duty-bearer for each right-holder. A right without a corresponding duty, or duty without a corresponding right, would be considered by jurists to be of imperfect obligation or unenforceable, and hence outside the legal system.

The discussion in Part I of this 'Introduction' of proceedings in trials indicates that at least in disputes within groups or networks of kin, 'a litigant comes before the judges not only as a right- and duty-bearing *persona*, but also as an individual involved in a complex of relations with many other persons', to quote Gluckman's summary statement on this point in his study of *The Judicial Process among the Barotse* (1955). That is, the court looks at what Radcliffe-Brown called his 'total social personality'. Gluckman concluded, nevertheless, that a closer examination of trials showed that though 'in administering the law the judges consider these total relationships, not only the relations between right- and duty-bearing units . . ., concepts of these units exist as nuclei for the substantive law'.[2] How, then, do Africans think about these units, whether explicitly or implicitly?

Allott's essay is concerned with this problem, and, working on law in former British territories, he asks whether Akan ideas

---

[1] For a good collection of analyses on this wider point, see Forde, 1954.
[2] At pp. 81 and 23. For fuller analysis, see p. 198 f.

about persons in, and at, law can be formulated in terms of English conceptions of 'the legal personality'.[1] There are important practical issues here, since English legal ideas have affected so greatly the development of customary law in superior courts manned by English, or English-trained African, judges and barristers. Some arise from what Allott called 'the "pseudo-problem" of corporate personality', which influenced judicial approaches to the question whether legal personality might be awarded to such typical customary institutions in Ghana as the 'stool' (chieftainship) and the 'family'. Accompanying this approach, there has been a tendency for judges in Ghana to force customary institutions into the conceptual framework of English law (e.g. to see the units of customary law as if they were akin to the relationships between English trustee and beneficiary, agent and principal, etc., as well as bringing in the doctrine of corporations as defined in English law). Allott himself judged some of these efforts to be misapplied parallelism; but the issue will obviously remain important because when at the Seminar he raised the doubt whether it would not be wiser to drop the whole conception of legal personality, other English-trained lawyers replied: 'How then do we deal with the facts?'[2]

In English law, legal persons comprise (i) natural persons, and (ii) juristic persons. Juristic persons must be corporations: these are, in English law again, either a corporation aggregate

---

[1] Editorial note.—His essay was introduced by a section on the English conceptions, and an indication of what he considered to be a broader theoretical, synthesizing manner of formulating the problems. This had to be excised for reasons of space, and it has been used in summary fashion in this section of the 'Introduction'.

[2] This discussion is in terms of the particular problems and conceptions arising from the English law about 'the legal personality'. Problems about the legal standing of African traditional groups and personages will arise where Roman–Dutch or the civil code law, both influenced by Roman law, are the law introduced into various regions of Africa, but there will not be the same search for 'legal personality'. In their *Roman Law and Common Law* (1952) Buckland and McNair wrote in their section on 'Juristic Personality' (pp. 54 f.): 'As to corporate personality we ought not to expect to find much difference between the Roman law and ours, since our theory of corporations seems to be mainly derived from medieval interpretations of Roman law. The Romans had no such word as *personalitas* and they did not use the word *persona* in the technical sense of "right- and duty-bearing unit". It had indeed begun to creep in among the orientals of the late Empire, but it does not appear in the *Corpus Juris*. A *persona* was simply a human being. A corporate body is never called a person, though it has legal capacities . . .'

(an artificial legal person consisting of a number of members who are natural persons), or a corporation sole (an artificial legal person consisting of one office-holder at a time in series of office-holders, and the personified office).

Practical questions arise about the attribution of rights and duties to corporations: what is meant by saying they own property, or are under a civil or criminal duty? Why should it lead to such absurdities in English law as that a company generally cannot rely on a contract entered into by a purported agent before the company was formed, since it was not a legal 'person' at the moment of contract? This seems to arise from the theory in English law, and even in general Western legal theory, that legal relationships exist between 'persons'. Judges in superior courts, and legislators influenced by English law, are likely to continue to have this approach built into them, so that it will continue to be an issue whether communities and/or their chieftainships, as well as leaders and indigenous political units of various sizes, such as villages, or sets of kinsfolk, can be treated as juristic persons. Allott suggests that the tests commonly applied to any customary 'institution' are: (i) can it sue or be sued in court; (ii) can (could) it hold and administer property; and (iii) in the changed circumstances of today, can it have land registered in its name?

Allott considers than when English law confers 'legal personality' on some form of association, it does so by an 'analogical fiction', which treats both corporations aggregate and corporations sole *as if* they were akin to natural persons. These fictions do of course express important social realities. In the English law a legal personality which is not that of a natural person is seen as an artificial person, and this influences its capacities, so that an agent cannot contract validly for a company before it has been formed. He considers that such a doctrine is not present in Akan law, because the Akan word *onipa*, meaning 'person', is never to his knowledge 'applied to any except a natural person'. However, Fortes has reported to the contrary: 'Ashanti say "one lineage is one blood" . . .; and again, that a lineage is "one person" (*nipa koro*). This is not a question of physiological theories but a way of stressing the corporate unity of the lineage.'[1] When reminded of this, Allott commented

[1] Fortes, 1950, p. 237.

that he himself had not met this usage, and that it appeared to be of metaphorical rather than legal significance. However, similar kinds of phrasing by members of communities and groups of kin have been reported from other parts of Africa, as well as elsewhere: besides 'we are one person', in patrilineal systems there are 'we are one blood', 'one bone', 'one penis', and in matrilineal systems, 'we are one womb', 'one breast'.

Whether this kind of usage is an analogical fiction or only of metaphorical significance, one would not expect its implications to be worked out in societies where the absence of jurists equipped with writing has rendered this explication difficult, as it may have been unnecessary where there were not formalized forensic procedures, and particularly where there were no pleadings by stylized 'writs'. Nevertheless, clearly African groups and their leaders have certain of the properties of a corporation, aggregate or sole, in English law: they can sue and be sued, and they can hold, administer, and benefit from property, as indeed Allott shows for Akan law.

Anthropologists have for some time discussed the powers, immunities, and claims, as well as the liabilities and responsibilities, of many African groups in terms of their being 'corporate'.[1] So have lawyers.[2] Allott himself concludes that it is reasonable to accept the use of the term 'corporate', where it can be shown that a group has a name; defined potential membership (by birth or adoption or by some other mode of recruitment); a defined structure and government; a symbol of identity; resort to concerted action; and durability; and where it is notionally attributed rights and duties as an entity in the traditional law. These criteria raised several difficulties for members of the Seminar, but all of these seemed to be soluble by proof of the facts in a specific case.

(i) The use of 'corporate' to refer to groups or associations raises difficulties in the absence of any specific written charters of establishment, which in European law have existed since classical and pre-feudal times. In Africa, these groups or associations either have a history of some period of independence, or

[1] See, e.g., Smith's essay herein, and also his discussion of how varying views of corporations in English and French law have affected the approach of their bearers to African institutions in his essay 'The Sociological Framework of Law' (1966).

[2] See, e.g., Mugerwa's and Ramolefe's essays herein.

they come into being, often out of already established social units, by processes which are sometimes marked by overt action, such as the setting up of independent habitations or shrines. There will be cases of uncertainty where it is difficult to determine whether a particular unit has achieved independence; but such uncertainty is characteristic of all legal problems. The indicia quoted from Allott can be used to test at what point in time a new corporate entity has been set up.

(ii) The indicia of corporateness may not always be clear, particularly where the term to describe important groups can be applied at various levels and in different contexts. The inherent ambiguity of such terms leads to situations where a man is considered a member of a group for one purpose but not for another. In this kind of situation legal issues may be inextricably interwoven with political issues. It seems certain that here, as with all problems of this kind, there are always borderline instances which do not meet all the criteria set up for the general idea of 'corporateness' in using 'corporation' comparatively without locating its provenance; but a useful concept for analysis should not be dropped because it does not cover every instance. Those responsible for settling an actual dispute can here, to quote Lord Justice Coleridge, only decide whether the particular case 'falls on the right or the wrong side of any reasonable line that might be drawn'. Indeed, English law faced with the same problems has had to speak of 'quasi-corporations'.

(iii) Forensic problems are also involved in the indicium that a corporation has a 'defined membership'. Forde said that while anthropologists use the same indicia for corporateness, there 'is a penumbra of quasi-members, enjoying *de facto* rights, so that the composition of such an aggregate might be ill-defined and uncertain. Thus in Yoruba lineages, which are theoretically agnatic in membership, claims through a woman are operative.'[1] In English law provision is made for ill-defined persons, such as that the people of the city of Chester have the right to walk across race-courses in the town, when who are Chester people is not clearly defined. The lawyers' answer here was that it is clear which the group is, though it is not always clear whether a particular individual belongs to the group. In

[1] See Lloyd, 1962.

short, a corporate group must have definable membership even if it be not precisely defined; others can be deemed to be potential members.

Even if one accepts that a general conception of corporateness is essential for description and analysis of African customary law, Allott in his essay is concerned to decide whether it is correct or sensible to bring such a group as an extended family or lineage under a rubric of the English law of corporations, particularly where it involves formulating the situation as if the property of the family were vested in the head of the family 'in trust' for other members as some English judges, and English-influenced African judges, did in the Gold Coast and have continued to do since this territory became independent as Ghana. He argues that subordinate members of such a group are more secure in their rights if they hold these as members of the group than if they hold them as moral or even legal burdens on the head of the group. Hence he reports with approval that the '"trustee–beneficiary" explanation is being abandoned in favour of the acceptance of the family as a customary corporation *sui generis*. The political stools have been treated similarly' (below, pp. 189–90). In short, if we are to discuss such groups as 'corporations', it must be clear that 'corporation' is here being used in its general connotation, without the technical increments of English law, or other introduced legal system.

If it is tempting for English-trained judges to view families as corporations aggregate, Allott considers the temptation to speak of stool chieftainships 'in English terms is even stronger, as the analogy with corporations sole is very close. Rights can be appurtenant to the stool, and exercised by the holder of the stool for the time being, just as with a bishopric in England.' But, he suggests, the analogy is more with a corporation aggregate such as a limited liability company, with the chief as chairman and managing director and his council as board of directors, while citizens are shareholders or members. It is presumably this combination of aggregate and sole qualities that makes the African corporation *sui generis*. That is, Allott thinks it useful for analytical purposes to use such specialized terms of English law as corporations aggregate and sole to show the differences and similarities in English and African law. Independently, Gluckman, as an anthropologist, described the

Barotse nation as 'a persisting arrangement of relations between a limited number of corporations aggregate and corporations sole, in some of which vest the powers and liabilities of certain corporations aggregate. The corporations sole are maintained in perpetuity in themselves and in relation to one another by the device of universal succession.'[1] The difference in these formulations may be due to real differences between West African systems, and some East, Central, and South African systems, to which Allott draws attention: in the latter regions there appears to be a clearer vesting of powers in the head of the group, who owes obligations to his dependants,[2] and this may be associated with the varying extent to which the private '*persona*' of the chief is submerged in political office in some systems as against others (see Allott below, p. 182).

Allott finds it more difficult to accord legal personality to the Akan ancestors as 'real landowners' (Rattray) or to spirits and deities as embodying various elements, and even ideas, among the Ibo (as Obi does). Again, Allott considers these are all, for legal purposes, 'analogical fictions'. In practice, there will always be a priest to act as 'effective agent' for a deity, while the so-called ultimate rights of Akan ancestors in land are no longer, if they ever were, exercised. He considers that thus one could treat similarly the deceased man who in leviratic marriage continues, as 'ghost-husband',[3] to be married to his widow, while some kinsman cohabits with her. The continued 'existence' of the dead man is again, Allott suggests, an 'analogical fiction', and the pro-husband acts as his effective agent.

Some of the anthropologists felt it was acceptable to regard priests as effective agents for deities, but that account had to be taken of restrictions imposed on their actions because they were dealing with property, etc., vested in 'spiritual beings'. Most anthropologists found it more difficult to accept the pro-husband as 'agent' for the ghost-husband: they considered it was better to split up the rights and responsibilities which vest

---

[1] 1965, p. 130, *circa*. Further problems in this connection are discussed below under 'Succession and Inheritance'.

[2] See Ramolefe on the position of the Sotho heir herein.

[3] Term first suggested by Evans-Pritchard in 1938. In some systems a woman can be married by a man to the name of a deceased unmarried kinsman, to 'raise seed', the dead man being the 'legal husband' as in leviratic marriage. See Ramolefe's essay herein on Sesotho institution of *kenela*.

Conceptions in the Substantive Law

in a living husband, and show that these are distributed among different 'persons'. The pro-husband exercises fully 'conjugal rights' (some call them 'uxorial rights') over the wife and bears conjugal responsibilities, in that he can claim the sexual and domestic services of the woman, and exercises normal husbandly authority over her: thus he can sue an adulterer, must represent her at court, can control and reprimand and beat her reasonably, and so forth, while on the other hand he must maintain her and grant her sexual claims equally with his own wives. He also exercises paternal rights over and bears paternal responsibilities for the children. These vest in him as pro-husband. What he does not exercise are what anthropologists call 'genetricial rights' (L. Bohannan), i.e. rights to claim the children as his own. He is their *genitor*, but not their *pater* (social father). The pro-husband acts for the deceased in begetting children and establishing genetricial rights over them. He also often controls the property of the deceased, and is responsible for it, during the minority of the woman's children, by whomsoever begotten. Since lawyers shy away from using 'trustee' here, he might be called 'caretaker' of this property as a more neutral word. But both claims on property and claims on office within the expanded kinship-group continue to devolve upon the woman's sons from the deceased husband and not from the pro-husband. Their position is determined by the genealogical position of the deceased man. The situation here is, of course, not dissimilar from calculations of rights to inherit in intestacy in Europe and America.

Thus the pro-husband has some capacity in exercising conjugal and caretaking rights, and here might be considered, on Allott's own argument about 'corporations' in these African systems, to have a legal personality *sui generis*. The dead man still exists for the determination of genetricial and thence property rights and duties.

Personality, Status and Capacity, and Persona

A person in law is an entity in whom certain rights and duties are vested. Where the rights of a natural person are considerably restricted (as in Africa with women, children in the womb, and newborn infants) it seems better to speak of restrictions on capacity, rather than absence of personality; and this seems to apply even to slaves, most servile strata, and strangers, who all have some rights, in the traditional law, save for the Masarwa among the Tswana. Personality has to be distinguished from *status*, which is generally viewed as a coherent agglomeration of a variety of specified rights and duties or capacities and incapacities; which relate either to a particular social function or the social functions generally of its possessor; whose incidents are determined not by choice of its possessor but by operation of law; which are generally imposed by law as the result of a given social or legal event (birth, adoption, appointment to office), and which in some instances may be voluntarily adopted (as by marriage); and finally, which mark out a category within the community of similar status holders. A person may possess more than one status at a time (e.g. be a husband and an alien) or his possession of a particular status may colour all his legal relationships (e.g. a slave or minor).

Capacity, on the other hand, is seen as specific to a given legal relationship: has X the capacity to marry, or to marry this particular woman? A capacity can therefore be discussed only when the legal purpose for which the question is posed is specified at the same time. It is in this sense that Allott in his essay speaks of 'restricted capacity' to do certain things.[1]

Though, as cited above (p. 39, fn. 2), it was only in the later Roman empire that *persona* ceased to denote a human being, and became restricted to a right- and duty-bearing unit, equivalent to what in English law would be called a legal person, lawyers discussing African law have denoted by *persona*, the total assemblage of legal rights, powers, duties, etc., which a given individual possesses at a given time, viewed as notionally detached from the being in whom they inhere. *Persona* and person in this approach are abstractions, taken from the real world but not realized in it in concrete form, yet a most convenient device for analysing a legal system. The conception of *persona* has been used in this sense particularly to assist with the description of certain African systems of what the Romans called 'universal succession', where the heir may be said to step into the legal shoes of the deceased.

Anthropologists considered that lawyers here had not clearly distinguished between the rights and duties attaching to a

---
[1] See also instances in Sesotho law as cited by Ramolefe herein.

person as a human being, and in a particular role or cluster of roles. In Central Africa they had followed Richards in speaking of *positional inheritance* or *succession*,[1] in order to emphasize the restriction that only part of the person's legal clothing is transferred to a single heir, which led Richards to use this phrase. But Gluckman has explicitly compared positional succession in African tribes with the Roman universal succession, by arguing that even in Rome universal succession was not succession to all the legal clothing (in Maine's phrasing) of a deceased. For if a man died while consul, his heir in the *familia* did not become consul. Gluckman cites and discusses in this connection reports on African systems where several positions of one deceased are distributed to different persons.[2] It might be helpful, therefore, in analysing in English the legal systems of Africa, if there were some neutral phrase to distinguish the cluster of legal rights and duties attaching to a person in one status, or legal relationship, from the total agglomeration focused on him as an individual. It may be confusing to use the Roman *persona*, as some lawyers and anthropologists have done, because of its wider connotations in early Roman law; and we have seen the difficulties that arise from the English use of 'personality'. We propose '*legal unit*' as a neutral neologism. 'Unit' can cover one individual and a number of individuals collectively, in specific relationship to some other(s). Then a 'legal unit' is any person, or set of persons, in themselves or acting in institutional position(s), that is the nucleus of a cluster of rights and duties defined by rules which are subject to external constraint, and which, through the backing of the accredited political organs of the social unit involved, are considered to have public legitimacy. The rules defining the rights and duties of a legal unit cannot be understood only in terms of the one-to-one relation between the persons concerned: those rules are part of a much larger body of rules similarly supported.[3]

[1] Richards first used the phrasing in her 'Mother-right among the Central Bantu' (1933), and it was thereafter adopted by many other anthropologists. Richards' latest development of the idea is in Richards, 1960.

[2] 1965, pp. 123–30.

[3] The elements of this definition follow closely Fortes's definition of 'jural rules', and many anthropologists would prefer to speak of a 'jural unit' rather than a 'legal unit'. See Fortes, 1969, Chapter V. Allott, and presumably other lawyers would agree, prefers 'legal' to 'jural'.

Legal units may be of different kinds, and we propose the following definitions:

(i) legal units of *status*, as in the core of rights and duties comprising a role such as husband or wife, or parent or child, or citizen or slave;

(ii) legal units of *transactors*, as in the core of rights and duties comprising the role of persons in commercial transactions (contracts), such as buyer and seller, pledgor and pledgee, landlord and tenant; here we speak of a *legal transactor*;

(iii) legal units inhering in the rights and duties of an office (the English corporation sole), to give us *legal office*;

(iv) legal units inhering in corporate groups (the English corporation aggregate) to give us *legal corporation*; and

(v) finally, there is the question of rights and duties inhering in associations of persons which are not corporate. Anthropologists classify these as groupings or categories of persons; and some of them might be deemed quasi-corporations in English law. For these we propose *legal association*.

X SUCCESSION AND INHERITANCE

The situation of kinship groups in Africa has been changing constantly, and some of the processes of change which we now see at work have operated for a long time. These groups have always been under pressure, and the necessity, to readjust their relationships internally. This readjustment has arisen from several causes. Above all, the uneven demographic growth of different segments or families within a group has produced the displacement of segments of the kinship group, claims for independence by those that have waxed in strength, and so forth. Every change has involved claims, superior and subordinate, over succession to and inheritance of property of all kinds. Individuals have also tried to assert independence of superior claims. The infusion of new types of property has always been important, but recent increases in the durability and the quantities of movables are likely continually to aggravate these processes of division, as are changing conceptions about kinship and other relationships, the development of new types of enterprise, desires to mortgage land, and so forth. Finally, there has been the introduction or strengthening of the powers of testators to make wills, under whatever restrictions. Thus radical changes are occurring in the total system of holding property, and of succeeding to positions or inheriting property. Ramolefe reports that Basotho heirs now would like their responsibility for liabilities to be restricted to the amount of the assets of an estate; in the terminology presented at the end of this section, they want 'beneficial' and not 'onerous' succession. 'Why should not an estate be declared insolvent?' asked Ramolefe.

This may well be introduced by legislation, or by decisions in customary or superior courts. Legislation is also establishing or extending the right to make wills. In some States legislation already provides that a portion of a man's property be set aside for the support of his widow and children, particularly when dealing with matrilineal systems, though it may be phrased as restricting the amount that can be devolved away from the matrilineal kin (e.g. in Malawi). Despite all these trends, issues of traditional succession and inheritance remain important, because very large parts of the population of Africa live in situations where traditional devolution of property prevails.

The first question is, what terms exist in particular African languages to describe: (1) successions to titles and property; (2) different categories of inheritors; and (3) the estate viewed as a fund or unit?

Many participants reported the use of the word 'eat' to describe both the process of succeeding to a title and the process of inheriting property, and several said that there was a word which might be translated as 'estate' in languages they knew. The word may cover both powers of administration, held during life or good conduct, and powers of beneficial enjoyment. That is, in some systems the successor selected has to administer the estate properly and meet his responsibilities; he is selected from a class of persons (by discretionary succession—see below) because of his seniority plus good conduct plus good character plus ability to administer, and a senior person lacking these other qualities can be passed over. The person selected does not inherit the property, since inheritance is the right of the family which appoints him to administer it. And an inefficient person or irresponsible person can be disinherited.[1] When a man is appointed thus, he should declare his own property, so that he can handle it separately, otherwise it merges with the family property. He enjoys the right to use some of the property.

The above accounts seemed to apply to many other systems. But if an estate was, and remains, the property of a kinship group or family, and the successor to its former holder administers it for the group even while he has beneficial enjoyment of it, can there be said to be 'inheritance' at all? Can a group be said to 'inherit' that which it already so-to-speak owns? Those who doubted whether this is sensible considered that it may be more accurate to speak instead of succession to the office of administering the main estate, and to reserve the word 'inheritance' for the successor's right to beneficial enjoyment and for the taking of particular items of property by various persons. It would then also be possible to speak of 'inheriting' newly created or earned property from a man, though in the next generation such property will in some systems be regarded as family property within that particular branch of the kinship group, property to the administration of which there is also succession. Here each set of property is confined to the descendants of the creator of that estate and it is excluded from the estates at higher level of the kinship group. Sections of the kinship group linked to it at higher levels cannot claim on that property unless all members of the branch have left or died. There are thus units of property at the different levels of the kinship group. But there are also systems where this differentiation into branches does not exist; and where at least in the past all property was regarded ultimately as a pool over which all kinsfolk of a specific kind or kinds had potential claims.[2]

Hence it may be important to distinguish different positions or legal units occupied by a successor:

(a) he enters into a position as head of a major group, and he bears the administrative responsibilities of that position as well as enjoying its assets;

(b) he may separately have special privileges on account

[1] Disinherison of an unsatisfactory heir is reported from several societies but may have had to be confirmed in some by action at law (see Ramolefe below).
[2] See, e.g., Colson, 1958, and also Poirier's 'circular inheritance' below.

of his incumbency of the headship of the group, as well as further responsibilities;

(*c*) he may separately also be head of one or more smaller incapsulated or 'nesting' branches of the group, with similar rights and responsibilities in each;

(*d*) he may remain still in the position of being an ordinary member of each of these several groups, enjoying his own rights and claims, and burdened with responsibilities within each.

What kinds of rights and powers has the successor in a bundle of rights over property vesting thus in a group, some of whose members are using part of the property? The lawyers considered that these rights are neither reversionary nor residuary, as they have often been described, since they exist concurrently with the rights of subordinate members over particular items, such as land (see below, pp. 55–59). The rights of superior positions continue all the time, though they are ascertainable only upon contingency, when they may have to be classified, e.g. after a death. They are political rather than property rights, administrative rights which are at once concurrent and contingent.

We have spoken of administering and administration, though some lawyers felt this might confuse the powers of a traditional successor with the technical meaning of 'administration of an estate under probate' in English law; and one suggested that 'caretaker' might here again be used. But most felt that 'administration' in its general sense was the most suitable term, in the way that one speaks of a government or civil service or chief administering; and that where confusion might arise 'administration under probate' was sufficient to clarify the situation.

In Africa many complexities arise from the fact that in traditional law different types of goods are distributed after a death to different categories of relatives and other persons. Edible property may be consumed by custom at the funeral. A title may pass to one kinsman or kinswoman, while associated property passes to another or others, and widows be taken by yet other kinsmen. It is important to state clearly the different kinds of interests involved and the various kinds of titles to those interests which pass to different successors or inheritors.

Hence in describing any particular system it may be necessary to distinguish between movable and immovable property, between durables and fungibles, and between different goods in each of these categories. In addition, it is important to consider succession to, and inheritance of, non-material privileges and claims to symbolic rights; and it was suggested that possibly the less the material property of society, the more important will be immaterial property marking the status of socially important legal units. Therefore it may be simplest to present the information about different forms of goods, and the way they pass, on a componential chart, setting out what rights held by a deceased are included or excluded in the property divided after death; how these rights devolve to various heirs, and the measure of freedom the deceased had over their devolution; and what are the powers of, and restrictions on, a guardian caring for particular items of property for a minor heir. An excellent example of such a chart is provided in Pospisil's account of 'Kapauku Papuan Laws of Inheritance' (1965, p. 181).

In view of the distribution of different types of goods frequently by different modes, systems cannot be characterized as entirely say 'patrilineal' or 'matrilineal', but for brevity they are conveniently referred to in terms of their dominant mode. Poirier proposed the following classification adopted by some French scholars:

(1) Horizontal inheritance, from brother to brother (in his opinion the most ancient African type).

(2) Vertical inheritance, from father to son, or vice versa, which he considered to be a more recent system (the Islamic and European systems are of this type).

(3) Oblique inheritance, characteristic of the matrilineal systems where devolution is from matrilineal uncle to uterine nephew (he considered that this also was very ancient).

(4) Circular inheritance, which is rather exceptional. Poirier has found it in Côte d'Ivoire, and in 'French-speaking' Central Africa. It is very complicated, and may be both patrilateral and matrilateral. Here certain goods (plantations allocated to a man during his lifetime, cattle, and some other goods) are not regarded as an individual's property. On his

Conceptions in the Substantive Law

death this property returns to the clan head, who keeps some, including enough to pay for the funeral; he then divides the rest among the deceased's collaterals, and not his descendants.

Poirier emphasized that he was well aware that each of these systems was complicated, as described above, because different types of goods were handled differently, but he felt that this classification sorted out the fundamental varieties of systems, both where the main heir is clearly defined in advance and where he is chosen from a specified group of collaterals as well as descendants.

It was noted with reference to (3) above, that while many speak of a movement from matriliny to patriliny, this is inaccurate. The movement is not from extended matrilineal inheritance to extended patrilineal inheritance involving the development of new unilineal kinship groups. It is rather a movement from matrilineal inheritance to the devolution of property from a man to his widow and children, i.e. conjugal and filial inheritance within a cognatic or omnilineal[1] system.

Another possible classification which summarizes one main characteristic of systems divides them by whether property on death is 'pooled' for redistribution or not. Poirier's 'circular succession' (4, above) is a pooling system; and 'pooling' seems also to be common in matrilineal systems, and patrilineal adelphic systems (Poirier's horizontal), while there may be a double pooling in double unilineal systems. Where property is pooled for distribution, succession also appears to be discretionary and elective, with a choice of successors. These systems contrast sharply with the systems where most of the property of a deceased has been allocated to different subordinate sections under his mastership, as among the Basotho described below by Ramolefe. Here succession is automatic for the successor to the main position of the deceased, and for successors to headship of each subordinate section, each successor replacing the deceased. This system has been characterized as 'the house-property complex' and it may be associated with the true levirate as against widow-inheritance (where the widow marries a kinsman of her husband in a new marriage), the

---

[1] Barnes's term to cover systems where property may devolve, and a successor be sought, in any line.

sororate, ghost-marriage, women marrying women, and other institutions. Hence this classification leads to a number of other problems which give an understanding of the interconnections of various sections of the law. In patrilineal systems marked by the house-property complex each wife in a polygynous household forms the centre of a set of property and is perhaps also the basis of a social title. Such systems attach women firmly to their husbands and are marked by a very low divorce rate. In adelphic patrilineal systems with succession from brother to brother and then to parallel cousins, in general the divorce rate may be higher, but it is still mostly lower than in matrilineal or cognatic (better omnilineal) systems. It seems also that in societies with the house-property complex, married women are regarded as the source of occult supernatural evil in several ways, including, where witchcraft beliefs exist, being suspected of witchcraft, possibly because property and position devolve from men to other men through women, so that struggles in the group focus on the status of wives. In the other patrilineal tribes, where redistribution and control of pooled property is directly in the power of men, and women seem to be vulnerable to charges of occult evil. In matrilineal systems, men in terms of their matrilineal relationships, men and women in their role as sisters, tend to be the focus of these occult fears.

The above discussion suggests that we might stipulate for convenience and clarity to confine 'succeed' and 'succession' to describe the process whereby there is an integral taking over of the responsibilities and liabilities of a jural unit. Succession thus involves the rearrangement of legal relationships, and reallocation of rights and duties of the new holder(s). It may be done by voluntary act (e.g. assignment of a contract, or resignation from office), or involuntarily (e.g. by death or bankruptcy), or by a compelled act (e.g. discharge of an unsatisfactory successor or official). Succession on death, or to office, are thus sub-cases of a wider series of legal actions.

'Inheritance', on the other hand, might then be reserved to describe a process by which both the successor to a deceased as a legal unit, as well as other persons, have claims on specific parts of the property of the deceased.

Despite the variety of systems in Africa, it would then be convenient and useful to discuss problems of succession with a

Conceptions in the Substantive Law

set of interdependent terms proposed by Allott to cover the varied processes discussed above:

A. SUCCESSION TO THE CATEGORIES OF ASSETS AND BURDENS

1. *Simple*	OR	1. *Complex*
Same mode for all categories		Different modes for different categories
2. *Singular*	OR	2. *Plural*
All categories, or all of one category, devolving on one person		Devolving on two or more persons

                        (a)   (b)

                      joint (taking on an inseparable or corporate title)   *divisory* (taking severally and individually)

3. *Automatic*	OR	3. *Discretionary or elective*
Successor automatically designated by law		Choice from several potential heirs

B. POSITION OF SUCCESSOR(S)

4. *Onerous succession*	OR	4. *Beneficial succession*
Responsibility for all liabilities, even in excess of assets		Liability limited to extent of assets
5. *Equivalent succession*	OR	5. *Limited succession*
Successor's title or interest equivalent with predecessor's		Successor's title or interest limited by newly created concurrent claims, powers, and privileges vested in others (e.g. the lineage; dependants of deceased)

C. POSITION OF PERSON SUCCEEDED TO

6. *Restricted distribution*	OR	6. *Dispositive distribution*
Unable to alter distribution as affected by concurrent claims or otherwise determined by law		Able to alter distribution either by disposition *inter vivos* or by testament

XI RIGHTS IN LAND

Vanderlinden's essay pursues a theme which has occupied much attention, the strength of the rights of individuals in land. He criticizes three authorities on African law who say that such rights do not exist. On the basis of definitions of 'ownership' in standard treatises on English, French, and Belgian law, and of definitions in Roman law, he examines nine ethnographic accounts of land-holding in various regions of Africa, and shows that individuals clearly have the rights to use and take the fruits of land they are working; and he finds in addition that they can dispose of the land freely, save that:

> (i) rights cannot be transferred to a stranger (save under a kind of usufruct—usufruct being in the original Roman law a claim to the fruits of land during lifetime, without altering

the nature of land), unless that stranger join the political community which has superior rights over the land, be it tribe, kinship group, village, or family; and

(ii) among Barotse and Tswana, as in all South-Central African tribes, land could not be sold traditionally, and could not under colonial régimes, because of policies establishing African Reserves.

Most importantly, these rights of the individual cannot be extinguished against his wishes; hence we can speak of these rights as '*perpétuel*'. The rights are transmissible then to fellow-members of the community, and they pass to an heir or successor on death. But the rights are sometimes restricted by the authorities, so we should distinguish between absolute and limited rights of disposal (*abusus absolu et abusus limité*). These rights can be called *propriété*, parallel to the term in French. Other land remains in the control of the community, and designated members can use it to pasture, to hunt, and to collect wild products. Concurrently the political community has rights of *souveraineté* over all land, though it (through its representatives) has also rights over specified parcels as *propriété*.

Vanderlinden argues that rights in Africa and rights in Europe are herein not dissimilar. While the Seminar endorsed his view of the strength of the individuals' rights it did not agree with him that these were similar to rights in Europe, not even in feudal times. Rather, it felt that the African complex of rights was *sui generis* like the jural corporations whose members had claims on the land. As described under succession, each parcel of land worked by an individual is subject also to concurrent contingent claims by superiors and subordinates. The Seminar therefore agreed, virtually unanimously, to adopt something like the framework advanced by Gluckman in his essay, with certain changes in terminology.

Vanderlinden's proposal that the rights of the political community be called *souveraineté* did not distinguish powers over land from other political powers. Hence some suggested *propriété éminente*, or eminent domain, derived from feudal terminology. Deschamps described how in Madagascar the power of the individual to dispose of land outside the tribe is blocked by the *propriété éminente* of the king, while within the tribe the individual can dispose of it freely. Whatever term is adopted here, the stress is on a holding downwards through a series of links of superordination and subordination. Developing an idea of Sheddick's,[1] Gluckman has spoken of primary, secondary, tertiary, and so on, 'estates of administration', to emphasize that the superior rights were rights to allocate land, to control its use, to restrict its disposal, etc. At the bottom of the hierarchy, where land was actually being used for some purpose, he spoke of 'an estate of production'. He argues that since a hierarchy is defined as 'ordered arrangement of items, elements and values in a graduated series' (*Oxford English Dictionary*), there can be a hierarchy of segments of kinship groups nesting within the largest, even where there is no chief. But series could be used in place of hierarchy.

The idea is implicit in Allott's essay on the Akan, because he speaks of adding a further tier to the interests in land, and also in a distinction Poirier made between *propriété éminente, le droit du seigneur*, and *le monopole du droit d'exploitation*.

The following endorsements and qualifications were made:

(i) As indicated above (pp. 50–51), one individual may occupy several positions within the hierarchy or series.

(ii) It is clear that there are two main sets of power which have to be distinguished, those to administer and control the land, contingently, though the powers are concurrent, vested in superior positions, and the rights of beneficial enjoyment in particular items of land vested in these positions and in subordinates.

(iii) Since these various rights coexist concurrently, some felt doubtful of allocating the title 'primary' to the most superior powers, as this implied superiority of the rights, as well as of the position. Gluckman now suggests the more neutral, clearly ordinal numbering, first, second, third, and so on. Numbering from the top downwards is preferable to numbering upwards, for though the latter procedure would stress the strength of individuals' rights, it would prevent a series being lengthened where an individual's land is divided among his heirs, but powers of administration vest in his successor. Numbering from

[1] *Land Tenure in Basutoland* (1954).

'first' could be translated into French as *premier, deuxième, troisième*, etc., with only *premier* conveying any sense of pre-eminence. If the chief, or largest political community, were said to hold the 'first estate' this could be seen as a landed attribute of sovereignty, and the rights of chiefs were, on the whole, similar to those of subordinate holders of administrative powers, so use of the same term would not be misleading. Allott agreed with numbering at the Seminar, but on reflection would prefer none, since he feels that 'superior' and 'dependent' are sufficient, provided that dependence on whom is clear, as well as superiority to what.

(iv) Some felt that the term 'estate' was too strong a term for the powers of administration. Gluckman said he selected it, following the authoritative studies of Cheshire on English land law and Radcliffe-Brown's important article on 'Patrilineal and Matrilineal Succession' (1935). 'Estate' has the advantage of exhibiting the connection of land-holding with status in the community, as citizen, villager, kinsman, dependant, and it was transmissible on death to successors to that status. A more neutral term, preferred by others, was 'interest', so one might speak of an 'interest of administration' or an 'interest of beneficial enjoyment', specifying interest in what.[1]

(v) Given acceptance of an hierarchy, some felt that the necessity to seek for an 'owner' of the land (in the way that the British Crown is described as 'owner' of all land) was eliminated. One could then see 'ownership' as applying to all rights held by anyone, with specification of the nature of the rights, these being an individual's or group's property. Others said it might be wiser to drop 'ownership' and 'owns' altogether, and to speak of 'X has a right to do Y'.

(vi) In addition, given the conception of a hierarchy, as against what was concluded above (p. 51), we may say that if all the rights or interests or estates exist concurrently and contingently, they nevertheless have 'residuary' or 'reversionary' elements; for contained within the concurrent rights of superior holders is the power to take over land in 'escheat' as

---

[1] Bentsi-Enchill, 1964, like Vanderlinden, speaks of sovereignty of the group which is politically independent, of 'allodial title' for the most superordinate interest in the land, and below that of 'proprietory occupancy' and 'beneficial ownership'. This terminology was not discussed at the Seminar.

bona vacantia because there are no longer appropriate persons at lower levels to continue to exercise subordinate rights.

Movables

The Seminar had not time to discuss holding of movables, but it noted that these are also held subject to claims of others related by status.

XII MARRIAGE AND AFFILIATION

1. *The Forms of Marriage and Marriage Payment*

We can reasonably translate as 'marriage' the word which members of all African societies use to distinguish certain unions between a man and a woman from other forms of union, whether licit or illicit. The recognized union gives rise to certain privileges and duties between spouses, their issue, and their families or guardians who may rank among the contracting parties. 'Real' as well as 'personal' rights are involved, since third parties are affected (a male adulterer, one who injures a spouse, one to whom a spouse owes a debt, and so forth).

Usually such a union is constituted between a man and a woman who are outside certain prohibited degrees of kinship or affinal relationship, but under polygamy a man may figure in several such unions. As we have seen, there are also 'marriages' which continue between a dead man and his widow, or a widower and a substitute for his dead wife (sororate), and an unwed woman can be married to an already dead man, while a woman can act as a man and marry another woman. Ramolefe describes all these forms of union among the Basotho. Among the Lele a woman can be married as wife to a village. Smith's essay herein describes how among the Kadara a wife can remain married to her 'primary' husband after she enters into a 'secondary' marriage with another husband. Among Ijaw and Northern Edo there are alternate marriage rights with high or low marriage payment.

It seems that Africans themselves consider and describe these forms of marriage as variants of the standard form of matrimonial relationship between a living man and woman. Hence these forms of marriage may be similarly regarded by the legal analyst. Therefore in setting out laws of marriage first it is necessary to state the criteria for a valid marriage of the recognized standard form, plus an additional statement giving the variants in other forms. Though lawyers might consider these analogical fictions, we have seen that the anthropologists would distinguish conjugal from genetricial rights and duties, as indeed was done in the Natal Native Code of 1896 which had to cover several of these variant forms.

Marriages which continue to unite a relict to a deceased spouse in levirate or sororate must be distinguished from new marriages where the survivor enters into a union with a kinsman (called widow-inheritance by anthropologists) or kinswoman (widower-inheritance) of the deceased. These forms in turn must be distinguished from the Central African custom whereby a kinsman or kinswoman of the deceased is required to cleanse a widow or widower respectively from the death in one ritual act of intercourse before remarriage is possible. To provide someone to do this is an onerous obligation of the deceased's kin.

Standard and variant marriages in Africa are established commonly by marriage-payment (bride-price, bride-wealth, '*dot*'), though sometimes there is labour-service, given by the bridegroom to his bride's guardian and kin. It is this institution which transfers the bride's uxorial services to the groom (and sometimes his kin) in all societies, and in patrilineal societies also transfers her genetricial services: thus it is this payment that is most commonly looked at as establishing and validating a marriage. Pauwels reports below that courts in Kinshasa will not grant the genitor *le droit de paternité* over his illegitimate child unless he has made the payment, and the same principle emerges from Smith's discussion of Kadara secondary marriage. African urban courts in what was Northern Rhodesia continued to look for this payment and the consent of the parties. We need hardly state that the marriage-payment is to establish clearly conjugal and genetricial rights, and does not place the woman in the position of chattel, serf, or slave to her husband. She has herself rights which involve duties for him.

The marriage-payment is also the mechanism which makes the variant forms of marriage possible. It can be given for a bride in the name of an already dead man, or by a woman for a bride, or by a village, and attaches the children to the legal husband, whosoever be the genitor, under a maxim phrased by the Zulu: 'cattle beget children'. In some tribes if a woman is divorced and remarries, the payment by the second husband gives him claims over children born in the preceding marriage (e.g. Kipsigis). Among peoples who stress this principle, the woman's husband can claim children clearly born in adultery, and the genitor is excluded as pater; but this rule is not general, though it is widely distributed (e.g. it does not exist among Lozi, Kikuyu, and Ganda). Schapera showed early that Shona marriages varied with the manner of payment or service,[1] and L. Bohannan has re-analysed the several forms of marriage found in Dahomey to show that the respective rights and duties of spouses, and claims on children, are determined by whether the marriage-payment has been transferred, or not, and how it was transferred.[2] Any statement of the law must therefore set out these principles clearly.

Despite the widespread importance of the marriage-payment, African courts administering so-called customary law have always had to face problems arising from long-standing unions between a man and a woman which have not been sanctioned by such a payment; and such unions are increasing, especially in the urban areas. Pauwels reported that, though cases arising from concubinage were barred in Kinshasa, as a matter of equity a man who had cohabited with a woman for a long time might be granted damages against an adulterer but he could not claim *le droit de paternité*. African urban courts in the former Northern Rhodesia acted similarly, though the question of paternal rights did not arise among the matrilineal tribes mainly involved. However, these problems are not confined to urban areas. Ramolefe's essay notes with regret a local court decision in Lesotho where it was held that each partner to such a long-standing concubinage should take what was bought with his or her own earnings; he feels that where a woman has borne children to a man and performed domestic services for a long time, she should be given half the joint goods of the household.

In such cases, African courts in deciding whether to grant a remedy may also take into account the observance of rights and duties between the partners and each other's family. Thus

[1] Schapera, 1929.   [2] Bohannan, 1949.

Ollennu cited a case from Ghana where a divorced man lived with two women and had children by them. After his death, the evidence showed that one woman and her family had performed obligations to the man's family at, for example, births, funerals, and annual feasts, while this had not happened with the other. The court held that he was married to the first woman, but not to the second. Thus courts continue to look at marriage as set in a wider set of kinship relationships; and this is indeed recognized in marriage-payment itself, since it has to be given to an accredited kinsman or kinswoman of the bride, implying consent to the marriage. Disputes may arise, especially in urban areas, over whether the recipient was an appropriate person.

Many problems arise in law out of the marriage-payment, besides questions of its return on divorce. In many tribes several payments have to be made; and, in addition, payments have to be made in order to set up a betrothal, and also as damages for seducing a virgin, so that there may be dispute over the function of a particular payment. It might be difficult in a woman's second 'marriage' to decide if a payment was refund of the marriage-payment or damages for adultery. Van Velsen reported, for instance, that the status of many unions among the Tonga of Malawi was extremely indefinite, so that it was difficult to tell whether a couple was married until a suit came to court; and then it might do so as the means of waging a political struggle. In many African societies, it was also common practice to leave part of the marriage-payment outstanding, because each marriage-payment was part of a network of 'debt' relationships which helped constitute the community's interrelationships.

The amount of the marriage-payment varies considerably from tribe to tribe, and within each tribe. Its 'value' obviously depends on the types and quantities of goods available, or the quantity of money in circulation; and it will be affected by the relative supplies of marriageable females as against males wishing to marry, which in turn depends on differences in the ages at which the sexes customarily marry. In crude terms it used to be argued that high marriage-payments stabilize marriage by making the woman's kin resist divorce because they do not wish to return the marriage-payment. It is probable that there is some such effect; but research indicates that high marriage-payments depend on stability of marriages rather than the other way round, since it seems that (despite a few exceptions) patrilineal systems with the house-property complex are marked by rare divorce, patrilineal systems with succession along a generational line, before the drop to the filial line, are marked by a somewhat higher rate of divorce, while divorce is most frequent in omnilineal and matrilineal systems. The institutions of leviratic and ghost marriages, and of the sororate, appear to be associated with the house-property patrilineal system; their effect is to prolong the union of the bearer of a set of children to one husband, beyond death itself.[1]

With the increase in money and the supply of more types of goods, the marriage-payment has continued to rise, and in general African women wish this institution to continue. We may note that it seems that the marriage-payment, commonly 'higher' in traditional patrilineal than in matrilineal or omnilineal systems, in urban areas moves towards a common norm for different classes; and there is some evidence that urban conditions are affecting marriages among all tribes in similar ways.[2] The discussion of the relation between these forms of marriage and forms of civil marriage or religious marriage falls outside our brief.

2. *The Establishment of Marriage*

We have already seen that customary courts may themselves be perplexed in deciding whether a particular union has been validly established. Ceremonies and feasts do not commonly seem to be essential requirements. It may be equally difficult to determine at what point a marriage came into being. For in many customary laws marriage is a process rather than a precise event, so that it is difficult to equate it with other forms of marriage in a modern African state, under which a man and woman are married at a particular moment by an accredited officer, subject to certain actions for annulment. A possible solution is to say that the critical point is when power to sue the woman's lover for damages passes to the alleged

---

[1] Gluckman, 1950. On a statistical validation of the above hypothesis, despite exceptions, see Mitchell, 1963.
[2] Ibid.

husband, and does not remain vested in her kin or a former husband. Thus in Ghana after betrothal a fiancé can sue the girl's lover, but only through her family; he can himself only bring suit when he and his 'wife' begin to cohabit. Is this typical?

It seems likely that all States will introduce compulsory registration of marriage as was long ago done in Natal; and it should be increasingly easier to do so with increasing literacy. Such registration should note whether a marriage is of the standard form or a variant, where these variants are not held to be contrary to good morals and public policy. Moreover, as Ramolefe stresses, persons may marry under more than one form of law, and registration noting how they marry would protect them in terms of the rights and duties they considered they were incurring when they married. Thus a wife entering a marriage under a monogamous law should not be put in a position where her husband can then marry another wife. Registration would not only clarify the point at which marriage is established but it will make simpler the investigation of property arrangements in disputes. Increasing mobility of the population aggravates the necessity for this step.

Registration would not, of course, eliminate disputes over long-term concubinages, but it would be a step towards simplifying a situation where variations in customs of the intermarrying people are numerous.

Betrothal. As noted, the indefiniteness of payments may confuse betrothal and marriage-payments, and between tribes there are variations about refund of betrothal gifts. Schapera reports (p. 326) that Tswana courts give what he calls 'special damages' to jilted girls; but, in general, customary law does not allow an action for damages flowing from breach of promise to marry, as generally tribal law does not admit consequential damages for breach of contract (below, pp. 76–77). The absence of such a suit in Ibo law has been held by a superior court to mitigate the damages awarded for the breach under English law.

3. *Dissolution of Marriage by Divorce*

It is as essential to know when a legal relationship like marriage is ended as to know when it is established. Were marriages to be compulsorily registered it would follow that divorces would also have to be registered, whether judicially decreed or not.

Some customary laws provided for divorce only by judicial dissolution, though here the husband might have the right to divorce his wife of his own will while she had to sue for divorce in court. Most systems also recognized extra-judicial dissolution. Whether this was done by will of the parties, or of one of them, or by arbitrators or a family meeting, it imported considerable flexibility into the law, both about whether a person was in fact divorced, and about the grounds, reasons, or motivations for the divorce. Smith discusses a particular instance of such difficulties, where the *idda* rule introduced a definite ending by divorce of the primary marriage of a woman which traditionally had remained in being.

In English law, proof of one of the specified grounds for divorce both entitles and requires the judge, in the absence of disabling circumstances, to grant divorce. Some members of the Seminar argued that formal grounds in this sense are not found in Africa, and that it might be better to speak of standard motivations, reasons, or justifications which induced judges or arbiters to agree to a divorce as against attempting a reconciliation of the parties. Other members of the Seminar acknowledged that customary law rarely compels a judge to grant a divorce, but they argued that even when a customary court took account of a whole series of dealings between the spouses and between each spouse and the kin of the other, nevertheless the spouse seeking divorce had to justify his or her action, and this justification, if in a standard form, might be regarded as a 'ground'. Save in tribes where divorce is very rare, however, breakdown of the marriage seems sufficient justification; and the court may consent to or advise a divorce because it fears that if compelled to remain together the parties will harm each other. That is, the court has its own grounds. However, it seems useful to state justifications generally advanced, in order to guide those who are concerned with administering marriages and divorces, even if the notion of such so-called 'grounds' has to be applied with care.

XIII INJURIES: LIABILITY AND RESPONSIBILITY

In French there is one word, *la responsabilité*, to cover notions delineated in English by the overlapping connotations of *liability* and *responsibility*. We shall use 'liability' to cover the obligation of a person to pay damages or make other redress to an injured party, and restrict 'responsibility' to describe whether the person so obliged is believed to have planned injury (i.e. was responsible). This stipulation accords with the usage among jurists, as is clear in Hart's use of the two words in his discussion of 'Punishment and the Elimination of Responsibility' (1962, at p. 20).

If we wish to determine whether there are general principles of liability and responsibility in particular African systems, and whether there are in different systems variations in these notions for which we would like to account, we have to study the sets of circumstances in which recompense is sought for injury in each system of law. There will, of course, be occasions when people consider that they have suffered injuries which are not recognized in law so that they cannot claim redress. The logic by which particular actionable 'injuries at law' are demarcated has to be elucidated. Here the essays in this book reflect differences of opinion more widely held.

Ibik begins from the threefold classification of wrongs in English law into crimes, torts (used by him interchangeably with delicts), and breaches of agreement (which he later names breaches of contract). He says no such distinctions are made in the native languages, but he does not consider this a valid objection for objective analysis. When Ibik did his research the central government had assumed responsibility for what were in its judgment crimes, and he found only one wrong he could classify thus. Setting fire to a house without dismantling it involves payment of a fine to the local authority, who alone can enforce it or remit it: in Ibik's phrasing there are echoes of Kenny's authoritative definition of a crime in terms of procedure, viz. that action on a crime once initiated can only be stopped, or pardon after conviction granted, by the Crown alone. Ibik then proceeds to distinguish torts from breaches of agreement on the ground that the latter are not actionable, though he shows that agreements are in fact actionable once there is performance by one party, be it only for recovery.

Epstein criticizes Elias's work on *The Nature of African Customary Law* (1956) because Elias also started (as Ibik here does) from the categories of English law, and not from African categories. Epstein considers that the categories of African customary law must first be spelled out, in terms of subsidiary as well as overall classifications. Thus his essay shows that if a Bemba woman is raped near people and is not heard calling for help, or does not immediately report the offence, it is assumed that she consented [i.e. evidentially it was not rape but adultery]. But if a man rapes a woman far from where people are, so she could not obtain help, it is assumed that she consented in fear of her life: 'Such an offence was indeed a thing of mystical ill omen . . . which defiled the country . . .; if it were not reported but was subsequently discovered, both parties were severely punished.' Epstein compares it with an 'abomination' in ancient Hebrew law. Presumably the husband still has his suit for damages. It would seem therefore that it is unwise to classify an action as either a crime or a tort or an abomination and thereby to assume that it does not fall also in one of the other categories. Here, as in English law, the community is insisting that its interests are involved, while not denying redress to the specific aggrieved party. In short, it seems wiser to classify private and public interests in wrongs in terms of the procedures brought to bear to rectify them, as is standard in jurisprudence; and to be aware that the same wrongdoing may provoke both private and public reaction (i.e. be in our terms delictual or tortious as well as criminal). The community always has some interest in wrongdoings not being committed, even though it may not intervene by providing facilities and pursuing rectification through its own officers: it does nevertheless tend to make it possible for the aggrieved party to seek redress with its help.[1] In societies without instituted courts, as Mugerwa's essay shows, this element of injury to the public interest affects the manner in which corporate groups may refuse to protect a wrongdoer in their ranks, if we take into

---

[1] Here, and below, thanks are owed to Professor Sally F. Moore, a trained lawyer and anthropologist, of the University of Southern California, for the clarification given in an article on 'Public and Private Law' (1969a).

account that repetition of wrongdoing is seen as injuring the group's interest in a way that a single wrongdoing does not.

Epstein's emphasis on the element of *abomination* in rape in the bush is an example of the general tendency of the law in societies with relatively simple technologies to see an occult power in many actions and events where the law of a modern industrialized society does not. With the differentiation of industrialized society, the secular courts do not take the same account of religious offences. In Britain blasphemy is still a crime but it is rarely prosecuted.

Reports on African customary law have not dealt well with liability for omissions to act so that another suffers damage, nor have they discussed adequately liability for damages caused by what we call negligence, inadvertence (failure to take due care), and accident. Ibik gives one case where omission to prevent another suffering harm created no liability. He also states that in Malawi a man is not liable to a visitor who freely enters and is injured by the collapse of a dilapidated house, under the defence that *volenti non fit injuria* (he who voluntarily enters a situation of peril has no suit for injury), a rule the Malawians share with Roman and modern Western law, and in Africa at least with Barotse law.[1] On the other hand, if the dilapidated house in its fall should damage a neighbour's house, the owner of the former is liable in damages. So too if a man in firing his dismantled house damages another's property. Here, at least, Malawian law recognizes a duty between neighbours, so to act as not to damage each other's property. Epstein reported, in his *Juridical Techniques and the Judicial Process* (1954), a similar case in a Zambian town of spreading fire, where the house-owner was held liable to his neighbour despite his plea, as a Barotse, that under Barotse law no suit lies for damage caused by fire or water.

Mugerwa's essay reports the clear development of the defence of 'accident' in Buganda. In general it appears that African customary law does take account of this as an excuse, though some liability may be enforced, while the law commonly holds persons liable for inadvertence and negligence.

Considerable research has shown that African law often defines the notion of liability in many situations within the

---

[1] See Gluckman, 1955, pp. 206, 252 n., 325.

context of specific social relationships of the parties concerned. The pattern of these relationships, particularly between groups, may be long established, and determine the nature of responsibility (or intention), as well as compelling acceptance of liability. Where two groups are at feud, an injury may be assumed to be deliberate when in fact it is not. In some cases the presumption of deliberate harmful intention is rebuttable, in others not. Where it is rebuttable, this may lead to readier acceptance of compensation in place of revenge. For whatever the responsibility in our stipulated sense, liability adheres. But where compensation is accepted on the basis that the damage was accidental, over time it may be remembered only that blood has been spilt, or other injury done and not avenged, in the pattern of constant feuding with its long tale of reciprocal injuries.

Failure to grasp the importance of the social context of relationships between injurer and injured can obscure the notion of liability in African customary law, and particularly the difference between individual and group liability. This is the theme of Mugerwa's essay. Individual liability may be enforced clearly within the ranks of a group. Injuries by a member of one group on a member of another group raises different standards. In polysegmentary societies there may be no authoritative means of settling disputes between opposed segments and hence there is resort to vengeance or self-help. Mugerwa argues that the fellows of the injurer will only support him against the injured man and his kin, if they are prepared 'to adopt the offence or liability created by the individual's action as falling on the group as a whole'. So a troublemaker may be abandoned, or not helped when he is injured. Even when the group thus accepts liability to the others, within its own ranks the wrongdoer must bear the main liability. Ibik reports from Malawi that in similar situations the head of the group can ask, but not compel, others than the wrongdoer to help, but he can impound the wrongdoer's property. Help from the other members sets up 'debts' to them from the wrongdoer.

The payment of compensation to the injured seems to be satisfactory for discharge of the obligation to repair the damage to public interests. Hence both Epstein and Mugerwa report that Africans disapprove of punishments of wrongdoers under which nothing accrues to those wronged.

In short, it is as misleading to pose an antithesis between individual and group liability as it is to pose an antithesis between individual and communal rights in land. We are not dealing with mutually exclusive categories: a person simultaneously occupies several legal units of status, in some of which he is a member of group(s). Through his membership of a group (or several groups), he acquires rights and responsibilities and liabilities: each group to which he belongs may have rights and responsibilities both to him directly, and through him to others.

The Seminar endorsed Epstein's argument in his essay that we should seek for certain basic assumptions about the nature of society, of human life, and of personality, that may underlie principles of liability in customary law. Epstein shows that where an assault, however justified in defence of a ward or however provoked by the other's own wrongdoing, commits irretrievable damage to another, the injured must be compensated. There is a deep concern with the human person whose wholeness or integrity must not be diminished. This is but one of many basic assumptions in each African customary legal system. These are akin to what Kohler called 'jural postulates'; and they are expressed not only in the rules of law but also in the manner in which these rules, together with rules of evidence and presumptions about causation, are brought to bear by courts on particular disputes. African legal systems seem to share many principles with one another, and even with European legal systems: but these principles are applied in different ways under the influence of basic assumptions. Many legal systems about which we have accurate historical information have retained certain rules of law through centuries: their application has changed with general social developments.

Careful analysis of how customary courts assess circumstantial evidence as warranting a finding for one or other party, may be most fruitful. While decisions on direct evidence are straightforward, basic assumptions may tip the balance of circumstantial evidence. A judge's use of metaphor, simile, and analogy will be revealing, as will be his reasoning when he seeks to find some means of emerging from an impasse where the strict rule of law runs against what he considers to be justice, or where he has to fill what Cardozo called 'a gap in the law', to meet a new type of situation. Here too we may profitably examine the sources of law as the judge scans them, and expounds his scanning, in search for the appropriate principle. Care is needed in detecting where assumptions are general, where sectional, and where individual. The dialogue between court and litigants is most rewarding for research. Having found the assumptions, our next task is to relate them to socio-economic conditions.

XIV AGREEMENTS AND TRANSACTIONS: CONTRACTS?

It is striking that the first twenty-two volumes of the series *Law in Africa*, from the well-known legal publishers Sweet and Maxwell of London, do not contain a treatise on the traditional law of contract. This is in despite of the fact that they concentrate only on two former British territories, Ghana and Nigeria, where, indeed, Africans were more fully involved in new forms of production and business than Africans elsewhere. We can deduce two things from this situation:

(1) The traditional law of contract was not as well developed as were the laws of family relationships, succession and inheritance, the constitution, and property. Here we emphasize again that the major co-operation in producing and exchanging goods and services was between kinsfolk and in-laws, i.e. in transactions between persons already related by status. Transactions establishing legal relations between strangers, as legal transactors, lay on the periphery of these status relationships. The trading that went on was mostly petty, in standardized transactions of barter, sale, loan, pledge, service of men and animals, agistment, with a few formless transactions. Even in the proto-cities of West Africa, the considerable trade was mainly confined to small markets, or large markets with many petty traders, though there were extensive credit arrangements involved in the long-established trade by Muslims in these regions. These credit arrangements continue, e.g. in the kola-nut and cattle trading still carried on largely by Hausa linked in terms of creed, ethnic origin, and even kinship.

(ii) The traditional law of contract has not raised many causes of action in superior courts, since it has not been applied in the numerous activities created by new productive and commercial enterprises in Africa. These have come under the introduced law of contract.[1]

Schapera found that 16 per cent of the cases he extracted from Tswana court records over many years dealt with contract, a relatively small proportion, since he includes as contracts disputes arising from agreements to marry. Both he and Ghai worked from brief records of this kind, supplemented by discussions with judges and other informants, and in Schapera's case by long-term observation of Tswana social life. Working on this kind of record raises difficulties already touched on: what importance can one attach to the brief and therefore necessarily incomplete judgment in a single case? Even where the record is taken down fully by an observer, what importance is to be attached to a judgment on a single case, where there is no full compilation of cases to assess it against? Where new issues arise, do decisions given by one judge or a few judges enable us to assess if there is a general trend? The difficulties are enhanced since disputes often arise from 'formless' contracts that have neither a ritual nor a ceremonial of contracting, nor an advance agreement on the terms. Both Ghai and Schapera acknowledge these difficulties in their essays.

1. Bare Promise and Bare Agreement

Following the wording of the Roman *nuda pacta*, Gluckman had stated that Barotse, and most tribal law, did not enforce bare agreements,[2] or bare promises. That is, if X promises to give Y £100, seriously enough, but Y makes no return undertaking, the promise is not enforceable at law, even in modern Anglo-American law. But a bare agreement in the sense of both parties making serious counter-offers is now enforceable, even without any performance: technically there must be consideration. In Roman law *nudum pactum*, a bare agreement, was not enforceable without some fulfilment. *Causa* was the grounds of agreement, and it had to be fulfilled in a material sense in early Roman law: hence possibly the *libripens* weighing his

[1] Hence our fullest reports in English on traditional law of contracts have come from anthropologists, rather than lawyers, notably Epstein, 1954, and Gluckman, 1965, Chapter VI.

[2] In English law, defined as 'an agreement made without consideration and upon which, unless it be under seal, no action will lie' (Osborne, *Concise Law Dictionary*).

copper. Therefore Maine stated that in early Roman law contracts were reciprocal conveyances of property. This implies that executory contracts, still to be fulfilled, were not enforced, and Epstein, Gluckman, Ghai, and Ibik found this to be the situation in the African legal systems they studied. Indeed, Mr. Justice Coker of Nigeria, who visited the Seminar, stated that: 'A feature of the customary law of Nigeria is that it emphasizes the distinction between executed and executory contracts, and the problem of execution as against formation. Customary law does not support that the real matter to be ascertained is the intention to take on oneself a legal obligation, whether it be described as *causa* or consideration, or "drink" [as in Ghana—see below].' And Poirier pointed out that African law here is like the law of the Middle Ages in Europe, when to sell a house the hinge of the door had to be transferred, or a piece of soil to transfer a parcel of land.

It is therefore necessary to look in some detail at the cases on which Schapera bases his statements that Tswana law differs here from the other systems reported. Some of the cases which he cites as being bare promises in contract which were enforced were suits in damages for cattle trespass and impregnation of an unmarried girl: the agreements were, in fact, admissions of 'delictual' liability, presumably taken by the court as evidence of liability and admitted assessment of damage. In one other case cited, a man induced a woman to marry on his admitted promise that he would not marry polygynously; and when he wanted to take a second wife, the court told him he must carry out his promise.[1] Since the woman had married on that understanding there had been considerable fulfilment on her side, and the Seminar agreed that the decision could hardly be described technically as enforcement of a 'bare promise'. It is more difficult to assess a case where A hired B to build a house and undertook to supply the bricks. B complained he could not start work because A had not kept his promise. A said he had told B there were no bricks, but that he would make them. 'Held: B should look for other work in the meantime, A was to call him when the bricks were ready, and two men were appointed "to watch the hut" ' (cited here from fuller

---

[1] The record of this case, like others cited in Schapera's essay below, is given somewhat more fully in Schapera, 1965, at pp. 142-3.

article, ibid., p. 143). The decision does not seem to order him to make the bricks, or to produce them by a certain date, while B is given no redress in the form of damages for loss of earnings and waste of time but is advised to find other work. At most the *implication* is that if A does make the bricks, B is entitled to be the builder and A should not employ another. This is scarcely authority on which to state that bare promises are enforced. On the other hand, Schapera (ibid., p. 152) does in the other article cite two cases where defendants were required to pay damages because they had not carried out undertakings. We are left to wonder whether in these cases the plaintiff had made some payment to the defendant in advance, though it does not seem so from the records, particularly the detailed judgment in one of the cases.

2. *Formation of Contract*

According to Ollennu, Akan and Fante law distinguishes between an agreement to enter into a contract and the contract itself: the mere request for, say, the loan of a bull, and mere consent, do not constitute an enforceable agreement. The consensus must be confirmed by the offer and acceptance of something, which is called a 'drink'. After the 'drink', the owner is obliged to lend the bull. Similarly, a 'drink' must confirm an agreement to agree to sell land: the 'drink' seals this agreement and details of the terms of contract are settled afterwards. This agreement to sell is different from transfer of the land, which involves religious elements in the form of a public declaration to the ancestors that the land has been granted. The transfer of money against the land does not transfer the land without the ceremony; performance of the ceremony transfers the land without the money being paid, a debt remaining between seller and buyer. Ceremonies are also necessary to effect contracts changing status. But when a cow is sold, it is transferred to the purchaser as soon as money is paid. It was noted that in many societies ceremonial transfer is necessary for land as distinct from movables.

It was agreed that an arrangement like the Ghanaian drink was common in Africa to seal a contract, as in Europe there are customs such as the clapping of hands or exchange of drinks to seal bargains. These arrangements provided evidence of intention to enter into serious legal relations, which is important in preliterate societies which have the possibility of formless contracts. But several participants argued that these arrangements were more than evidence, since Ghai, Gluckman, and Ollennu reported the refusal of courts to enforce an agreement even where the defendant admitted his undertaking. They argued that some movement of property was essential in many tribes, but possibly there was here variation in weighing such actions as evidence or as essential to found enforceable agreements.

Ghai reports that consensus (a meeting of minds) is essential for a contract to be valid in Kenya, and it is vitiated by mistake. But a court had rejected a plea that a contract was formed under duress as difficult to believe, and he had been told that drunkenness at the time of formation would not be allowed to void a contract. Moreover, while Gluckman had found among the Barotse that a contract was not enforced if it arose from an agreement contrary to public policy and good morals so that the rule was that in equal guilt the position of the defendant was stronger, Ghai considered that this rule was not compatible with the great concern of customary law 'to establish what belongs to whom and to restore it to him'. Hence he considered that while some of the Kenyan judges said that they would 'throw out cases involving illegal acts, others who denied that customary law was familiar with illegality as a vitiating, contractual factor . . . were probably nearer the truth'.

3. *The Effects of Contracts*

Here discussion focused on Gluckman's contention (loc. cit.) that among the Barotse and many other societies, contracts tended to be of the utmost good faith:

> (i) it was agreed that all African systems insist that where it is appropriate the transferor of goods must give warranty of title, and that a rightful owner can pursue goods and acquire them from an innocent acquirer;
> (ii) Gluckman in the 1940s had found in Barotse law the rule that the seller gave an implied undertaking to deliver sound goods at a fair price (i.e. *caveat vendor* rather than

caveat emptor) but in 1965 he was informed that for ten years the courts had changed the ruling to one by which buyers must test the goods and take responsibility for their condition. Schapera reported for the Tswana that goods must be delivered in sound condition at a fair price (see his other article, loc. cit., p. 146); but Ghai states that in Kenya there are few implied warranties and responsibility is with the buyer, though he cites no cases.

(iii) Ghai, Gluckman, and Schapera had found that risk remains with the seller until delivery, but increment is to the buyer; Ghai considers this is because 'there is retarded development of the concept of negligence as affecting risk . . .'.

Further research is required on all these points.

4. *Enforcement of Contracts*

Ghai considered that 'in no sense can it be said that African courts enforce contracts; what they do is to settle disputes arising out of a contract. More often than not, the courts will settle a dispute by cancelling the contract; they put the parties back in their original position, where this is possible.' Ibik also stressed that a disappointed purchaser has his money refunded if the seller sells elsewhere (as among the Barotse, save where a fishing-net is ordered, since only one net can be made in a season), while a farm labourer who neglects his work is not sued for damages caused by loss of crops but has to return his money and other perquisites. Ghai found one reluctant enforcement of specific performance, but Schapera records several from Tswana courts. African law here is akin to English law, whose courts rarely order specific performance, so they do not enforce the contract itself: but they compensate the plaintiff for his loss with damages as African courts do not (see below).

Schapera reports a case where a party was excused because it was impossible for him to fulfil the contract.

5. *Damages*

Schapera cites cases where courts awarded what he calls 'special damages', but the phrase is not used here with the technical meaning it has in English law (see his cited article, at p. 152). The Tswana seem here, as elsewhere, to be exceptional for Africa in allowing for damages or loss flowing from breach of contract. Failure to do this may be a major weakness of African law in its attempt to cope with new situations. Generally it was considered that 'debt' was a central concept in the African law of contract, and that it was unlikely to expand to cope with modern conditions. In the history of English law development was made with action in assumpsit rather than by action in debt, where assumpsit, originating in 1612, was 'a promise or contract, oral or in writing not sealed, founded upon a consideration; and an action to recover damages for breach or non-performance of such a contract'.

6. *Prescription of Actions*

No system in Africa seems to allow mere lapse of time to bar an action.

7. *Conclusion*

In brief, African traditional laws of contract show what Ghai calls a 'striking ability' to reach 'the person in possession of the goods in question', and therefore it protects only executed and not executory contracts. There are very rudimentary notions of privity of contract; but the customary law has experienced difficulty in classifying forms of actions; as well as in developing clear ideas on consensus, adequacy of consideration, mistake, negligence, and duress.

In these circumstances it seems that very few African legal systems had developed a clear conception or general model of contract. This is not surprising because even the Romans failed to do so until very late in their legal history. Schapera, however, considers that his evidence on 'the diversity of ways in which a single rule may be applied . . . [shows] that Tswana do have the idea of "contract" as such, and thus differ from the Barotse among whom, Gluckman says, "each transaction is regarded as a specific complex of rights and obligations, and there is no general model of contract" '. The Tswana have, since colonization at least, applied remedies, and possibly enforced agreements, in ways in which so far no other tribe has been reported to do; but there seems here to be some misunderstanding of what a 'general model of contract' is. With such a model, courts in approaching alleged understandings and agreements would look at whether there was a general offer and counter-offer with reciprocal acceptance, no defeasibility on various grounds, what was intended, and what remedies should be applied for breach. The Tswana do not in our judgment have such a model. This is not to deny that there are common 'ideas' present in each separate type of transaction, but they are not worked into a consistent set of principles.

BIBLIOGRAPHY

African Conference on Local Courts and Customary Law, proceedings of the Conference at Dar es Salaam, 1963. Geneva: H. Studer S.A.

Allott, A. N. (ed.)
(1962) *Judicial and Legal Systems in Africa*. London: Butterworth.

Bentsi-Enchill, K.
(1964) *Ghana Land Law*. London: Sweet and Maxwell.

Biebuyck, D. (ed.)
(1963) 'Introduction ' to *African Agrarian Systems*. London: Oxford University Press for the International African Institute.

Bohannan, L.
(1949) 'Dahomean Marriage: A Revaluation', *Africa*, xix, 4, pp. 273–86.

Bohannan, P. J.
(1957) *Justice and Judgment among the Tiv*. London: Oxford University Press for the International African Institute.

Buckland, W. W. and McNair, A. D.
(1952) *Roman Law and Common Law: A Comparison in Outline* (second edition revised by F. H. Lawson, 1st edition, 1936). Cambridge: Cambridge University Press.

Cheshire, G. C.
(1962) *The Modern Law of Real Property* (9th edition). London: Butterworth.

Colson, E.
(1958) *Marriage and the Family among the Plateau Tonga of Northern Rhodesia*. Manchester: Manchester University Press for the Rhodes–Livingstone Institute.

Elias, T. O.
(1956) *The Nature of African Customary Law*. Manchester: Manchester University Press.

Epstein, A. L.
(1954) *Juridical Techniques and the Judicial Process*. Rhodes–Livingstone Paper No. 23.

Forde, Daryll (ed.)
(1954) *African Worlds*. London: Oxford University Press for the International African Institute.

Fortes, M.
(1950) 'Kinship and Marriage among the Ashanti' in A. R. Radcliffe-Brown and C. D. Forde, editors, *African Systems of Kinship and Marriage*. London: Oxford University Press for the International African Institute.
(1969) *Kinship and the Social Order: The Legacy of Lewis Henry Morgan*. Chicago: University of Chicago Press.

Gluckman, M.
(1950) 'Kinship and Marriage among the Lozi of Northern Rhodesia and the Zulu of South Africa' in A. R. Radcliffe-Brown and Daryll Forde, editors, *African Systems of Kinship and Marriage*. London: Oxford University Press for the International African Institute.
(1955) *The Judicial Process among the Barotse of Northern Rhodesia*. Manchester: Manchester University Press (2nd enlarged edition, 1967).
(1965) *The Ideas in Barotse Jurisprudence*. New Haven: Yale University Press.

Hart, H. L. A.
  (1962) 'Punishment and the Elimination of Responsibility'. London: Athlone Press.
Hohfeld, W. N.
  (1917) 'Fundamental Legal Conceptions as Applied in Judicial Reasoning', *Yale Law Journal*, xxiii and xxiv, reprinted in book with same title, with other essays, edited W. W. Cook. New Haven: Yale University Press (1923).
Kenny, C. S.
  (1958) *Outlines of Criminal Law* (17th edition, by J. W. C. Turner). Cambridge: Cambridge University Press.
Kuper, H. and L. (eds.)
  (1966) 'Introduction' to *African Law: Adaptation and Development*. Los Angeles: University of California Press.
Lewis, I. M. (ed.)
  (1966) *Islam in Tropical Africa*. London: Oxford University Press for the International African Institute.
Lloyd, P. C.
  (1962) *Yoruba Land Law*. London: Oxford University Press for the Nigerian Institute of Social and Economic Research.
Maine, H. S.
  (1861) *Ancient Law*. London: Murray.
Mitchell, J. C.
  (1963) 'Marriage Stability and Social Structure in Bantu Africa' in *Proceedings of Sessions of the International Population Conference, New York, 1961*. London: International Population Union, ii, pp. 255–62.
Moore, S. F.
  (1969a) 'Public and Private Law' in M. Gluckman, editor, *Allocation of Responsibility*. Manchester: Manchester University Press.
  (1969b) 'Introduction, Part IV, Comparative Studies' in L. Nader, editor, *The Anthropology of Law*. Berkeley: University of California Press.
Pospisil, L.
  (1965) 'Kapauku Papuan Laws of Inheritance' in L. Nader, editor, *The Ethnography of Law*, Special Publication, *American Anthropologist*, vol. 67, No. 6, Part 2.
Radcliffe-Brown, A. R.
  (1935) 'Patrilineal and Matrilineal Succession', *Iowa Law Journal*, xx; reprinted in *Structure and Function in Primitive Society*. London: Cohen and West, 1962, pp. 32–48.
  (1950) 'Introduction' to A. R. Radcliffe-Brown and Daryll Forde, editors, *African Systems of Kinship and Marriage*. London: Oxford University Press for the International African Institute.
Richards, A. I.
  (1933) 'Mother-right in Central Africa' in E. E. Evans-Pritchard, R. Firth, B. Malinowski, and I. Schapera, editors, *Essays Presented to C. G. Seligman*. London: Kegan Paul, Trench, and Trubner.
  (1960) 'Social Mechanisms for the Transfer of Political Rights in Some African Tribes', *Journal of the Royal Anthropological Institute*, 90, pp. 175–90.
Roberts, T. L.
  (1966) *Judicial Organisation and Institutions of Contemporary West Africa*. New York: Institute of Public Administration.
Schapera, I.
  (1929) 'Matrilocal Marriage in Southern Rhodesia', *Man*, 29, pp. 113–17.
  (1938) *A Handbook of Tswana Law and Custom*. London: Oxford University Press for the International African Institute (2nd enlarged edition 1955).

Bibliography

(1965) 'Contract in Tswana Case Law', *Journal of African Law*, xi, pp. 142–53.

Sheddick, V.
  (1954) *Land Tenure in Basutoland*. London: H.M.S.O.

Smith, M. G.
  (1966) 'The Sociological Framework of Law' in H. and L. Kuper, editors, *African Law: Adaptation and Development*. Los Angeles: University of California Press.

Sonius, H. W. J.
  (1963) *Introduction to Aspects of Customary Land Law in Africa*. Leiden: Afrika Studiecentrum.

Vansina, J.
  (1965) 'A Traditional Legal System' in H. and L. Kuper, editors, *African Law: Adaptation and Development*. Los Angeles: University of California Press.

Résumé

PREMIÈRE PARTIE

I COMPOSITION DU SÉMINAIRE

Les juristes participant au Séminaire représentaient des systèmes juridiques codifiés, la *common law* anglaise et le droit romano-hollandais; en outre, les participants africains possédaient une expérience de la vie sous le régime du droit coutumier. Les ethnologues avaient tous une approche sociologique des phénomènes et cinq d'entre eux avaient également reçu une formation dans l'un des trois systèmes de droit mentionnés ci-dessus. Quelques uns des participants, outre le fait qu'ils poursuivaient des études théoriques, avaient été impliqués dans l'administration du droit, aussi bien sous le régime colonial britannique ou français, que sous celui de gouvernements africains indépendants. L'on peut espérer, en conséquence, que les idées présentées au Séminaire possèdent une représentativité raisonnablement large.

L'Introduction essaie de présenter les thèmes des études et d'un débat qui s'est poursuivi pendant dix jours. Ce débat fût consacré à des tentatives en vue de trouver une terminologie commune dans laquelle discuter les divers systèmes de droit coutumier rencontrés en Afrique et grâce à laquelle comparer ces systèmes.

Le rapport des débats fut préparé par les rédacteurs de *l'Introduction* et il est, en conséquence, nécessairement fondé sur les concepts du droit anglais et de l'ethnologie britannique. L'on peut néanmoins espérer que *l'Introduction* sera utile à des chercheurs de formation différente, qui pourraient souhaiter s'essayer à une analyse similaire.

II PROBLÈMES DE RECHERCHE ET DE MÉTHODE

Les juristes et les ethnologues étudiant le droit africain se fondent dans une grande mesure sur l'observation directe de la vie sociale journalière et de l'activité des tribunaux coutumiers, étant donné que cette pratique journalière et les décisions des tribunaux ne sont pas enregistrées par écrit de manière satisfaisante; cette approche est encore nécessaire en dépit d'une accumulation croissante de documents. En outre, le 'droit' n'est pas toujours aussi différencié d'autres types d'institutions qu'il l'est dans les sociétés plus développées technologiquement. Juristes et ethnologues sont d'accord pour insister sur le fait qu'il est essentiel pour l'analyse de posséder des témoignages écrits sur les procès en cours et sur les accords de nature juridique qui se produisent en dehors des tribunaux; ces méthodes de recherche sont présentées dans l'étude de Poirier.

Juristes et ethnologues travaillent en conséquent avec un matériau fort semblable, mais ils tendent à des fins théoriques différentes. Le juriste essaie d'isoler les principes généraux d'une branche du droit, de manière à assister les praticiens et les juges; en outre, il peut essayer de favoriser une unification plus grande du droit dans des buts aussi bien pratiques que théoriques. Il peut également examiner la répartition de divers principes de droit et essayer de mettre leur survenance en rapport avec les schémas sociaux et économiques. L'ethnologue a les mêmes objectifs. De plus, il étudie la place des conflits au sein de divers types de relations sociales et le fonctionnement des tribunaux par rapport à d'autres méthodes de résolution des conflits. Le juriste et l'ethnologue ont donc des tâches complémentaires.

III PROBLÈMES DE DÉFINITION: QU'EST-CE QUE LE DROIT COUTUMIER?

Le droit coutumier n'était pas immuable, même à l'époque pré-coloniale; durant cette période, il subit de temps à autres des changements considérables. Mais, ce sont naturellement l'avènement du régime colonial et l'apparition de la civilisation occidentale qui ont produit les changements les plus substantiels dans son contenu. Parfois, la lettre d'une règle juridique coutumière a été conservée, mais sa substance fondamentalement modifiée. Ceci constitue un problème caractéristique de tous les systèmes juridiques situés dans un contexte mouvant: l'adaptation constante des principes juridiques aux circonstances sociales nouvelles.

Lorsque l'on traite d'un droit qui n'est pas enregistré par écrit, les problèmes de recherche en sont aggravés. Si, en outre, le droit est incertain et se meut en réponse à des développements sociaux nouveaux, le chercheur, qui désire réétudier et réexprimer les principes du droit coutumier, est obligé de prendre en considération la nature des sources qu'il peut valablement consulter. Qui est à même d'exprimer le droit coutumier en vigueur? Le droit coutumier est-il celui suivi par les anciens traditionnels; ou celui décidé par ceux qui se tournent vers de nouveaux modes de vie?

La réponse à ces questions dépend de la tâche que s'est assignée l'investigateur. Pour des études académiques théoriques, le chercheur peut se complaire dans ces difficultés même qui sont cause de difficultés pour le praticien. Le juriste, qui a pour objectif d'aider le gouvernement et les praticiens dans leur dessein d'établir avec certitude le contenu du droit, peut seulement résoudre ces problèmes par une approche raisonnable, globale et pragmatique qui se base sur toutes les sources disponibles et définit les difficultés. Finalement, il est souvent nécessaire de légiférer en vue de clarifier la situation. Les problèmes de cette espèce se sont toujours posés aux juges des tribunaux supérieurs en Afrique lorsqu'ils avaient à appliquer le droit coutumier (dans la mesure où il n'était pas contraire aux principes de moralité et de justice naturelle); les juges français et britanniques siégeaient avec des assesseurs coutumiers pour les assister ou se documentaient d'une autre manière sur le contenu du droit coutumier. Au Ghana, depuis 1960, la législation prévoit que le droit coutumier n'est pas considéré comme un 'droit étranger' et que chaque tribunal est à même d'en établir le contenu. Au Ghana, comme ailleurs en Afrique tropicale, l'intégration des droits a été encouragée et elle aboutit à ce que tous les systèmes de droit, coutumiers et importés, soient dotés d'un statut égal. Là où il y a conflit entre ces différentes espèces de droit, le problème est résolu par un recours aux règles législatives qui gouvernent les conflits internes de droit; d'autres solutions adoptées dans des états d'Afrique indépendants sont également discutées dans les études présentées au Séminaire.

IV PROBLÈMES DE DESCRIPTION

On rencontre toujours de grandes difficultés lorsqu'il s'agit de traduire les concepts complexes d'un langage ou d'un système dans les mots d'un autre. En outre, l'étendue de la plupart des langues africaines est relativement restreinte, tandis que, dans un même état africain, coexistent souvent plusieurs langues. De plus, nombre de termes importants utilisés dans les systèmes juridiques sont particulièrement imprécis, ce qui cause des difficultés, même dans les systèmes où les chercheurs, avec l'aide de l'écriture, ont été à même de travailler et de raffiner l'usage d'un terme particulier.

Une approche verbale, qui soit aussi sophistiquée, doit encore être développée dans le domaine des langues africaines, de telle sorte que, pendant un certain temps, il semble que l'on doive continuer à décrire les institutions juridiques coutumières en utilisant le vocabulaire de la science juridique comparée ou en développant un langage neutre, qui couvrira, au moins, une partie des divers systèmes coutumiers.

Une combinaison de ces trois méthodes (développement d'un vocabulaire juridique local—recours aux termes généraux employés par les comparatistes—préparation d'une langue neutre de description) semble probablement la meilleure ligne de conduite à adopter; il ne semble en outre pas qu'une distortion sans espoir résulte de l'abandon de la terminologie propre à un système particulier. En effet l'usage des termes indigènes est susceptible de figer la recherche et la compréhension, à l'exception des cas où les institutions coutumières sont très inhabituelles ou particulièrement spécifiques. Mais, il y eut des différences d'opinion parmi les participants au sujet de l'utilisation de termes comme: droit, justice, droits et obligations, propriété, crime, contrat, délit, etc. . . . Gluckman, plus particulièrement, plaida pour l'utilisation de ces termes: il déclara qu'il avait délibérément utilisé le concept anglais de 'l'homme raisonnable' dans son analyse de la procédure judiciaire barotse, de manière à attirer l'attention sur les différences aussi bien que sur les similarités dans les concepts et leur utilisation. Il semble qu'en utilisant des définitions plus étroites et en évitant les ambiguïtés, il doive être possible de développer des vocabulaires comparés; une partie d'entre eux est présentée dans les sections suivantes.

DEUXIÈME PARTIE

ADMINISTRATION DE LA JUSTICE

V PROCÉDURES ET PREUVES EN DROIT COUTUMIER AFRICAIN

Les procédures judiciaires africaines sont caractérisées par leur simplicité et leur manque de formalisme; leur utilisation de mode de preuves irrationelles; le fait que les juges, les parties et les témoins peuvent être en rapport les uns avec les autres hors du procès; une attitude de bon sens dans la recherche des solutions; le désir de promouvoir la réconciliation; et le rôle de la religion et des rites dans la détermination des responsabilités.

Ainsi que le souligne Ollennu, le style élémentaire des procédures coutumières s'explique par le fait que les juges jouent le même rôle que les avocats dans d'autres systèmes: ils entendent les parties avant de convoquer les témoins, de manière à déterminer s'il y a lieu à procès et sur qui reposera la charge de la preuve; ils écoutent tout ce que les parties ont à dire, parce que celles-ci peuvent ne pas réaliser où gît le droit et que, par conséquent, il est impossible de dire d'avance quels éléments de leur déclaration présenteront ou non de l'importance. Pour cette raison, étant donné qu'ils conduisent l'examen contradictoire, qui, dans les tribunaux anglais, est confié aux avocats, il peut sembler, incorrectement d'ailleurs, qu'ils considèrent certaines personnes coupables; en effet les questions posées au cours de l'examen contradictoire peuvent seulement l'être lorsque l'on croit qu'une personne ment.

En outre, quand le tribunal essaie de réconcilier des parties qui se trouvent en relation permanente hors du procès, de nombreux faits peuvent avoir de l'importance, indépendamment des points de contestation qui ont directement rapport au procès. Cette apparence de préjugé, ainsi que les nombreux faits sans rapport avec la cause, sont éliminés quand le jugement est rendu.

Il y a deux étapes importantes dans le jugement. D'abord, les juges doivent décider qui a raison et qui a tort. Ensuite, ils doivent décider quelle injonction formuler à la suite de leur première décision ; l'étude de van Velsen traite abondamment de ces deux étapes de la procédure.

Il est clair que les tribunaux coutumiers dans leur ensemble se fondent sur des preuves pour justifier leur décision et préfèrent la preuve directe aux preuves circonstancielles, tandis qu'ils ne font pas confiance aux preuves par ouï-dire. Les modes de preuves irrationnels, comme les oracles et les serments, sont envisagés dans une autre partie de l'introduction.

VI PERSONNEL NOUVEAU DES COURS LOCALES

Les nouvelles cours locales (établies par la loi, elles succèdent aux tribunaux coutumiers de l'époque coloniale) ne sont plus présidées par des juges normalement titulaires de fonctions judiciaires dans le droit coutumier traditionnel. Une raison de ce changement est le désir de nombreux gouvernements africains de posséder un système national unique de tribunaux. Ce système unifié de tribunaux a l'avantage complémentaire de favoriser l'unification du droit coutumier et des autres droits sur une base nationale. Les principes selon lesquels toute personne doit être justiciable d'un même ensemble de tribunaux administrant le même droit à tous ; les juges de ces tribunaux doivent avoir reçu une formation juridique ; et chacun doit avoir le droit d'être représenté à chaque niveau de la hiérarchie judiciaire, sont généralement adoptés par les gouvernements africains modernes. Il y a souvent des motifs politiques derrière l'adoption de ces principes.

Si ces principes sont acceptés et si le droit coutumier est conservé, il est alors impératif que tous les juristes professionnels puissent être formés dans les divers droits coutumiers ou que des assesseurs siègent auprès des tribunaux, pour les conseiller sur le contenu du droit en vigueur.

Il semble qu'il y ait trois orientations possibles, si l'on considère une étape intermédiaire dans ce processus de réorganisation :

(1) la préparation d'un personnel aux qualifications professionnelles moins développées que celles que l'on désire sur un plan idéal ;

(2) une procédure de simplification, d'unification et de codification des droits coutumiers des différents systèmes de

manière à faciliter la tâche de formation et d'administration ; il existe toutefois des problèmes nombreux qui ne sont pas encore résolus et qui rendent cette procédure difficile ;

(3) si les tribunaux locaux équipés en personnel nouveau ne rendent pas une justice qui satisfasse les parties, il peut se produire une prolifération d'arbitrages et de tribunaux non-officiels existant parallèlement au système étatique. Poirier appelle ce phénomène 'le droit secret'; les gouvernements ne le considèrent pas favorablement et essaient de faire disparaître ces tribunaux parallèles.

VII CODIFICATION ET ENREGISTREMENT DU DROIT COUTUMIER

La codification en vue de produire un droit nouveau unifié et systématique s'est développée au maximum dans les pays influencés par la tradition continentale. Dans quelques états, elle a été effectuée sans étude préliminaire des types divers de droit coutumier; dans d'autres, une recherche initiale considérable a été entreprise. Dans certains pays qui suivent la tradition anglaise, les études de droit coutumier ont été faites dans l'intention de produire des manuels (conçus comme des sources persuasives plus qu'obligatoires), mais des efforts sont faits à présent par les autorités, dans de nombreux de ces pays, afin de préparer des descriptions systématiques, analytiques et globales de branches du droit coutumier.

Les codes se présentent sous des formes diverses: certains définissent des programmes de ce qui est désirable, plutôt qu'ils n'établissent des systèmes de règles obligatoires. Dans ces cas et pour diverses raisons, il est possible que ces codes ne puissent être appliqués de manière efficace. Le mot 'code' a, bien entendu, des significations nombreuses et contradictoires, plus particulièrement dans les manuels français (ceci ne semble pas être vrai dans les manuels anglais).

VIII RAISON ET OCCULTE EN DROIT COUTUMIER

Le droit coutumier semble basé sur une idée de la raison qui distingue, en principe, l'homme de l'animal; ceci apparaît dans de nombreux jugements où les coupables sont comparés à des animaux. L'homme bénéficie du don d'intelligence qui lui permet de se comporter avec dignité et décence et ainsi de présenter sa qualité d'*humanité*'; tel est le thème de l'étude d'Epstein. La 'raison' dans ce cas est définie socialement, puisque sa définition inclut le respect de la coutume, du droit et de la morale. Ceci conduit, ont estimé certains, à un concept de l'homme raisonnable qui serait fondamental en droit. Ce concept permet au juge de prendre en considération toute espèce de critère coutumier de conduite qui ne soit pas formulé explicitement dans les règles juridiques.

Les pratiques et les techniques occultes, tels les serments, les oracles et la divination ne sont utilisés que dans les cas où la raison humaine est inadéquate, et où les tribunaux n'ont pas de pouvoirs suffisament développés. Shack estime que ceci se produit là où les pouvoirs judiciaire et exécutif des autorités centrales ne sont pas à même de contrôler les échelons inférieurs de la hiérarchie administrative ou judiciaire; là où l'infraction en cause est elle-même occulte (comme dans les accusations de sorcellerie ou de magie); là où, enfin, il y a de fortes suspicions mais aucune preuve définitive.

Vues de l'extérieur, ces procédures transfèrent une partie de la responsabilité des épaules du juge sur le mode de preuve. Pour autant que ces procédures soient utilisées dans des sociétés où les clivages internes sont grands, elles ont une fonction similaire à l'usage d'un jury dans les pays qui sont divisés intérieurement (par exemple sur une base raciale ou de couleur).

Ces procédures fonctionnent également pour déterminer des solutions qui ne sont pas tellement juridiques que politiques et dans lesquelles un procès surgit sur la base de conflits tellement profonds, à l'intérieur d'un groupe de personnes, qu'il ne peut y avoir de solution au problème dans le cadre des rapports sociaux et qu'il est nécessaire de recourir à un palliatif.

TROISIÈME PARTIE

LES CONCEPTS EN DROIT SUBSTANTIF[1]

IX CONCEPT DE PERSONNALITÉ JURIDIQUE

Dans tout système juridique existe un concept central: celui de l'unité, titulaire de droits et d'obligations. C'est le concept de

[1] Le droit substantif (substantive law) s'oppose, en terminologie juridique anglaise, au droit adjectif (adjective law) qui concerne essentiellement les modes et techniques qui permettent l'exécution des droits et obligations tels que les définit le 'droit substantif'.

la personnalité juridique dans le droit anglais grâce auquel des groupes et d'autres ensembles sont considérés, par analogie, comme possédant la personnalité qui est celle d'une personne physique; on les appelle alors des personnes juridiques. Une conception similaire est appliquée à une fonction dont sont titulaires des personnes successives. Cette idée a influencé considérablement l'interprétation appliquée aux groupes et fonctions africaines et à d'autres entités par les juges formés au droit anglais. Allott discute dans son étude les difficultés auxquelles cette attitude conduit et estime qu'il vaut mieux considérer ces groupes et fonctions africains comme étant *sui generis*. Il présente une série de règles (reprises dans *l'Introduction*) grâce auxquelles des groupes peuvent être définis comme formant des entités juridiques et acquièrent donc la personnalité. En outre, accorder la personnalité juridique à des divinités ou à des esprits ancestraux ne peut être rien de plus, dans l'opinion d'Allott, qu'une fiction analogique qui est acceptable théoriquement, à la condition que l'on reconnaisse que tous les droits attribués à la personne juridique doivent en pratique être exercés par un agent humain effectif, par exemple, le prêtre pour la divinité, le vivant au nom des ancêtres, ou le remplaçant du mari à la place du mari mort dans un mariage résultant du lévirat.

Les ethnologues considèrent qu'il est inadéquat de décrire le remplaçant du mari comme étant l'agent effectif de son parent défunt dans le système du lévirat. Ils estiment qu'il vaut mieux définir cet état comme une situation dans laquelle divers droits et responsabilités sont transmis à différentes personnes. Le remplaçant du mari exerce des droits conjugaux (ou uxoriels) et supporte des responsabilités conjugales, tandis que les droits 'génétriciels' continuent à être attachés au mari mort, dans la mesure où la position sociale et les droits patrimoniaux des enfants du remplaçant du mari bénéficieront à ceux-ci, comme s'ils provenaient de l'homme mort.

Personnalité, statut et capacité, persona

Le statut est l'agglomérat cohérent d'une diversité de droits et d'obligations ou de capacités et d'incapacités qui sont imposées par le droit en fonction d'un évènement juridique déterminé (naissance, adoption, mariage, nomination) et qui caractérisent une catégorie de titulaires du même statut. La capacité, d'autre part, est spécifique à un rapport juridique particulier et peut seulement être discutée dans le contexte de ce rapport.

Quelques juristes ont utilisé le terme *persona* pour désigner l'assemblage total des droits et obligations qu'une personne particulière possède à un moment donné si on les considère comme détachés de leur possesseur. Le terme a été particulièrement utilisé pour faciliter la description de certains systèmes africains correspondant à ce que les Romains appelaient une 'succession universelle'; c'est le cas, où l'héritier prend la place du défunt. Mais les ethnologues ont considéré qu'il était essentiel d'insister sur le fait que les droits et obligations d'espèces différentes se groupent dans des agglomérats nombreux en fonction des rôles divers joués par l'individu. Ils ont, en conséquence, parlé d'héritage 'positionel' pour décrire ces systèmes de succession universelle.

L'utilisation du mot *persona* peut être source de confusion parce qu'il a différentes connotations, selon les périodes de l'histoire du droit romain. L'on propose, en conséquence, l'adoption d'un terme neutre, celui d'unité juridique, susceptible de recouvrir aussi bien un individu qu'une collectivité d'individus. Il sera alors également possible de distinguer divers types d'unité juridique (par exemple, des unités juridiques de statut telles qu'elles ont été définies plus haut (épouse, parent ou enfant, esclave ou homme libre), des unités juridiques de transactions (dans les transactions commerciales) ou encore, des unités juridiques rattachées à une fonction juridique.

X SUCCESSION

Il semble que, dans la plupart des systèmes africains, un successeur soit désigné à la fois pour administrer la propriété du défunt et en jouir. Mais peut-on parler de succession dans la mesure où la propriété appartient au groupe familial? Un groupe peut-il hériter de biens sur lesquels il a déjà des droits?

En outre, les positions de testateur et d'héritier se sont rapidement modifiées avec l'introduction de nouveaux titres de propriété, le développement de nouvelles espèces d'entreprises et l'introduction du droit de tester.

Il est nécessaire, à cet égard, de distinguer clairement entre les différentes unités juridiques dont le successeur fera partie en vue d'exercer ses droits, étant donné qu'il peut devenir responsable d'un groupe important, obtenir des privilèges particuliers en raison de cette fonction et, en même temps, être à la tête d'un groupe plus petit, compris dans un groupe plus large, tout en en étant simultanément un membre ordinaire. Les droits du successeur sont partiellement administratifs et ces droits existent concurremment avec les droits des unités subordonnés sur des parties de la propriété.

En Afrique, de nombreux problèmes complexes résultent du fait que différentes espèces de propriété sont attribuées à des héritiers différents et les informations à ce sujet seront présentées de la manière la plus adéquate sur un graphique montrant la destination de chaque élément de la succession. Malgré ces complexités, il doit être possible de décrire brièvement les modes dominants de succession. Poirier a suggéré une classification en systèmes de succession horizontale, verticale, oblique et circulaire, tous termes qui sont expliqués dans *l'Introduction*. D'autres ont suggéré une répartition majeure en systèmes dans lesquels on distingue les héritiers en fonction de catégories définies de biens et les systèmes dans lesquels il y a une mise en commun suivie d'une redistribution de l'ensemble des biens. Un graphique des termes susceptibles de convenir dans une discussion des différentes successions est présenté dans *l'Introduction*.

XI DROITS FONCIERS

L'étude de Vanderlinden défend l'idée que certains droits coutumiers individuels sur la terre peuvent être appelés des droits de propriété puisqu'ils couvrent aussi bien les droits de disposer de la terre que d'en prendre les fruits. Concurremment, la communauté politique détient les droits de souveraineté sur la terre, droits qui seront confiés aux autorités, tandis que ces autorités ont également des droits de propriété sur certaines parties spécifiques du pays. D'autres participants furent d'avis que les droits individuels rencontrés en Afrique ne sont toutefois pas semblables aux droits rencontrés en Europe. Ces droits furent considérés comme étant *sui generis*. Certains préférèrent adopter la suggestion proposée par Gluckman qui parle d'une hiérarchie ou d'une série de droits d'administration sur des éléments particuliers de terre, en partant du droit de la communauté ou de son chef politique pour aboutir au droit final du cultivateur, du pasteur ou du collecteur. Ces droits pouvant être qualifiés de droits de production ou d'exploitation. La discussion porta également sur l'intérêt de numéroter les séries de bas en haut, de manière à mettre l'accent sur la force des droits de l'individu ou de haut en bas de manière à étendre la série lorsqu'un élément particulier de terre utilisé par un homme est divisé entre ceux qui en dépendent. Dans une telle situation, les droits d'administration sur la terre peuvent être transférés au successeur de l'individu, allongeant ainsi la hiérarchie ou les séries. L'accent fut mis sur le fait que ces droits supérieurs sont réversibles, résiduels, concurrents et contingents selon les circonstances spécifiques.

XII MARIAGE ET FILIATION

1. *Formes du mariage et paiements matrimoniaux.* Parmi les unions possibles entre un homme et une femme, tous les systèmes africains semblent reconnaître certains types d'unions que l'on peut raisonnablement considérer comme étant des 'mariages'. Il semble que les africains eux-même considèrent d'autres unions, comme le lévirat ou le sororat, comme des variantes de cette forme standard. Ces unions sont généralement établies par le transfert de biens divers qui confèrent des droits conjugaux et 'génétriciels' au mari et parfois à sa parenté. L'étude de Pauwels discute la façon dont les tribunaux de la ville de Kinshasa insistent sur ce transfert, avant de conférer à un homme des droits de paternité sur les enfants nés d'une femme. Ce transfert distingue le mariage de toutes formes de concubinage. Mais, dans certains tribunaux, les concubinages à long terme obtiennent un statut particulier, notamment en ce qui concerne les droits sexuels du mari en cas d'adultère. Toutefois, les tribunaux prennent aussi en considération la manière dont les époux et leur parenté remplissent les uns à l'égard des autres certaines obligations réciproques. Le mariage est aussi souvent un rapport mettant en cause la parenté des époux, particulièrement en raison du fait qu'un parent de la fiancée doit accepter les valeurs. Le montant des valeurs varie de société à société et semble être mis en rapport, là où il existe des valeurs adéquates, avec

la stabilité du mariage. Mais il est possible que ce soit la stabilité du mariage qui permette le paiement de valeurs importantes plutôt que le contraire. La grande stabilité du mariage est à son tour reliée à la survenance de ce qui a été appelé dans les sociétés patrilinéaires un système de 'maison-propriété' (dans ce système chaque femme dans un ménage polygyne devient le noyau d'un élément de propriété attribué à ses fils).

2. *Conclusion du mariage.* Il est fort difficile de déterminer le moment où un mariage existe juridiquement et l'on pourrait peut-être considérer ce moment comme étant celui où le droit de poursuivre l'amant de la femme appartient au 'mari'. Il semble vraisemblable qu'un enregistrement croissant des mariages permettra de fixer ce point.

3. *Dissolution du mariage par divorce.* Lorsque les mariages seront enregistrés, les divorces le seront vraisemblablement aussi, ce qui résoudra de nombreux problèmes. Ceux-ci aparaissent particulièrement dans les systèmes où la dissolution du mariage peut s'accomplir sans une décision de justice.

XIII RESPONSABILITÉ QUASI-DÉLICTUELLE

Alors qu'il existe en France un seul mot 'responsabilité', l'anglais utilise le mot 'liability', qui peut être utilisé pour décrire l'obligation de compenser, et distingue ce mot de la 'responsabilité' qui se réfère à l'idée du dommage intentionnel. Dans de nombreux systèmes africains, l'accent est mis sur la 'liability' dans le sens ci-dessus, même dans les cas où le 'coupable' n'est pas responsable (dans le sens de: n'a pas l'intention de causer le dommage). '*Liability*' s'applique dans un nombre de contextes sociaux spécifiques, qui mettent en cause des relations particulières entre groupes.

Mais, l'on considère aussi que le groupe a la faculté d'accepter ou non cette '*liability*' pour une infraction commise par un de ses membres. Même s'il accepte la '*liability*' dans ses rapports avec le groupe qui a subi le dommage, il peut considérer le coupable comme 'responsable' (*liable*) à son égard, ou peut refuser de soutenir un récidiviste. Les responsabilités individuelles ou de groupes existent simultanément en fonction de relations différentes.

Des recherches plus approfondies sont nécessaires dans les divers systèmes de droit africain en ce qui concerne ces hypothèses de base; un point de départ est donné dans l'étude d'Epstein. Il semblerait que ces hypothèses se vérifieront (ou s'infirmeront) par une analyse approfondie de l'utilisation des analogies, des similitudes et des métaphores dans l'argumentation des tribunaux. Il est notamment important de considérer la manière dont les juges tranchent les affaires sur la base de preuves circonstancielles ou développent le droit pour rencontrer de nouvelles situations.

XIV CONTRATS

Le droits des contrats est l'une des branches les moins développées du droit coutumier; la plupart des transactions mettant en cause des biens et des services se produisent en effet à l'intérieur de la parenté. Dans ces circonstances, il est difficile de déterminer la façon dont se développe le droit des contrats en l'absence d'affaires soigneusement enregistrées, montrant les bases complètes des décisions.

1. *Simple promesse et simple accord.* La plupart des rapports suggèrent que les droits coutumiers africains ne conféraient pas force obligatoire à ce que les Romains appellent *nuda pacta*. Schapera, dans son étude, dit que les Tswana le font et que les décisions sur lesquelles il fonde son opinion ont été soigneusement analysées. Il semble également que le droit africain ne confère pas force obligatoire au simple accord exécutoire, mais seulement au contrat dans lequel il y a eu exécution partielle, généralement, sous la forme d'un transfert de propriété.

2. *Formation du contrat.* Dans quelques systèmes il doit y avoir au moins un acte pour que se forme le contrat, indépendamment de l'accord en vue de contracter; certains considèrent que l'accomplissement de cet acte a pour objet de fournir des preuves de l'existence du contrat. D'autres considèrent que les contrats n'étaient pas obligatoires (même dans les cas où les preuves étaient satisfaisantes) à moins qu'il n'y ait eu un transfert de propriété.

3. *Effets des contrats.* Il semble que le vendeur doive normalement avoir un titre valable par rapport au bien et qu'un propriétaire légitime puisse réclamer son bien dans les mains d'un acheteur innocent; que, dans quelques systèmes, les vendeurs doivent prendre l'engagement que les biens vendus sont exempts de tout vice; que le prix doit être raisonnable;

et généralement que le risque demeure avec le vendeur jusqu'à délivrance, du même que le croît passe à l'acheteur. Des recherches supplémentaires devraient certainement être faites sur ces divers points.

4. *Exécution du contrat*. Ghai a émis l'opinion que les tribunaux africains ne rendent pas les contrats obligatoires, mais règlent les conflits qui en résultent; en effet, très fréquemment, ils annuleront les contrats et restaureront la situation antérieure.

5. *Dommages—intérêts*. Dans la ligne des caractères qui viennent d'être mentionés le droit africain des contrats n'a pas développé l'idée d'octroyer des dommages-intérêts dans les cas de la perte résultant d'une rupture de contrat.

6. *Prescription de l'action*. L'écoulement du temps ne signifie généralement pas prescription de l'action.

7. *Conclusion*. Il semble, en conséquent, que les systèmes africains ne possèdent pas un modèle généralisé de contrat exécutoire, auquel adhèrent deux parties, qui puisse être, en conséquence, rendu exécutoire et dont la rupture puisse être compensée par l'octroi de dommages et intérêts. On peut enfin se demander si le droit africain des contrats peut se développer de manière adéquate de lui-même dans le contexte des nouveaux rapports juridiques gouvernant les entreprises.

SPECIAL STUDIES

I. L'Analyse des Espèces juridiques et l'Étude des Droits coutumiers africains
J. POIRIER

I INTRODUCTION

L'objet de la présente communication est l'étude des méthodes pouvant être utilisées, sur le terrain, pour la collecte et l'analyse des documents juridiques coutumiers encore saisissables par l'enquête directe. Certes, l'importance de la coutume ne cesse de décroître au bénéfice des droits modernes, codifiés ou non. Mais deux remarques permettent d'illustrer l'intérêt théorique et pratique de la coutume:

(i) l'irruption des droits nouveaux conçus à l'échelon central (Parlement, Ministère de la Justice), enfermant la coutume dans des sphères bien délimitées—en théorie—est une raison impérieuse de recueillir avant leur disparition les documents existant encore; il convient aussi, à plus forte raison, de recueillir les anciennes coutumes, aujourd'hui périmées, dont le souvenir est encore vivant; et

(ii) non seulement la coutume persiste en de nombreux domaines, mais on peut déjà noter qu'il se crée une *coutume nouvelle*, distincte du *droit écrit* théorique, et qui aménage ce droit en fonction des conditions sociales, des impératifs économiques, des traditions. Il existe une marge considérable entre le droit élaboré au niveau des pouvoirs législatif et exécutif, et l'*insertion* de ce droit dans la réalité concrète des sociétés villageoises; pour aménager ce droit et l'adapter au réel, une nouvelle coutume est en voie de création. Il est encore trop tôt pour apprécier correctement l'ampleur de celle-ci; mais c'est là un problème qu'il conviendra de suivre avec attention à l'avenir.

Comment, en pratique, faire la collecte des 'espèces' de droit coutumier, c'est-à-dire des cas concrets ayant fait ou non l'objet d'un litige ou d'une discussion? Nous entendons par espèce, dans le présent exposé, tout *document* coutumier saisi à l'occasion d'un fait concret, vécu: une succession, un conflit, réglé devant le tribunal ou devant l'arbitre, un divorce, etc...., un règlement pour l'irrigation discuté en conseil de village, etc.... Il s'agit donc essentiellement, non pas d'une tradition appréhendée au terme d'enquêtes par interview, mais d'une *dynamique juridique* emprimée par l'observation de la vie du groupe.

Nous passerons d'abord en revue les modalités de la coutume, plus variées qu'on ne le pense en général, pour étudier ensuite les méthodes de collecte.

II LES MODALITÉS DE L'IMPÉRATIF JURIDIQUE COUTUMIER

Une distinction s'impose entre le droit exotérique et le droit ésotérique. Au niveau du droit exotérique, c'est-à-dire non secret, ouvert au grand jour, nous avons affaire à deux impératifs: le droit coutumier 'officiel', si l'on peut dire, celui qui est admis par les pouvoirs publics, évoqué devant les tribunaux, la coutume, que nous pouvons appeler *officieuse*, encore moins connue que l'autre, et qui cependant semble être beaucoup plus importante, car c'est surtout elle qui est appliquée en fait; on la trouve au niveau des instances arbitrales, les intéressés préférant souvent ne pas recourir aux organismes officiels pour régler leurs litiges.

Le droit ésotérique pose des problèmes tout différents. Il n'agit pas dans le silence de la loi officielle, mais contre celle-ci; c'est un droit secret, interdit par les autorités administratives, et toujours contraire à l'ordre public; il concerne soit les modes de preuve (ordalies), soit la magie noire et la sorcellerie.

Nous avons donc trois plans à distinguer: le droit coutumier officiel, le droit parallèle, le droit secret.

(i) *Le Droit coutumier officiel*

En Afrique d'expression française, à l'exception peut-être de la République islamique mauritanienne, tous les pays ont entrepris un travail de codification—plus ou moins avancé selon les lieux—qui aboutira un jour à supprimer presque complètement, en théorie, le domaine d'application de la coutume, au bénéfice de la loi écrite; mais nous en sommes encore loin, et pour le moment, il n'existe que des textes spécialisés qui sont venus codifier tel ou tel domaine; la filiation, le nom, le domicile, le mariage. Ces textes reprennent une part du contenu de la coutume, part variable suivant le pays; mais dans tous ces cas, il ne s'agit plus de droit coutumier, lequel a disparu au bénéfice de la loi.

Au contraire, la coutume subsiste pour tous les domaines où un texte n'est pas encore intervenu, et ce sont les plus nombreux. Les tribunaux officiels se réfèrent normalement au droit coutumier, qu'ils appliquent d'ailleurs avec plus ou moins d'exactitude. Parfois, c'est la loi qui renvoie explicitement à la coutume à propos d'un texte particulier. Les difficultés sont nombreuses et l'application contemporaine de la tradition juridique orale par les nouvelles juridictions mérite une étude attentive, mais le problème abordé est différent.

Le pouvoir législatif, partout, est pris entre deux impératifs contradictoires: respecter la tradition pour ne pas heurter le sentiment de la majorité de la population, et, en sens contraire, la faire évoluer de manière à construire un droit moderne; on constate donc des hésitations, des reculs, ou parfois des essais de formules nouvelles qui s'expliquent par la persistance de l'attachement des Africains à leurs systèmes traditionnels. En ce sens, on signalera la méthode qui consiste à autoriser l'*option* entre le droit traditionnel et le droit moderne: le justiciable a la faculté de choisir l'appareil juridique sous l'empire duquel il a l'intention de contracter. Mais—et c'est là qu'apparaît la puissance de la coutume—c'est la solution traditionnelle qui est préférée; bien plus, quand la législation impose un système d'homologation de la coutume (en d'autres termes, qu'il valide la solution coutumière sous réserve d'une obligation d'enregistrement ultérieur), le justiciable contracte sous l'empire de la coutume, mais ne satisfait pas aux obligations d'homologation.

On constate que cette réserve va quelquefois très loin. A Madagascar par exemple, où la legislation a marqué une particulière prudence en réservant aux normes coutumières le maximum d'attention, le mariage peut être contracté de deux façons :

— ou bien au niveau du droit moderne, nouveau, devant l'officier de l'état civil,
— ou bien, quand les intéressés ont leur domicile sur le territoire d'une 'commune rurale' (c'est-à-dire en dehors des agglomérations urbaines), devant les autorités traditionnelles du *fokon'olona* (l'assemblée de village) pourvu qu'un représentant des pouvoirs publics soit présent et témoin; en pratique, ce représentant est le chef du village. Cette procédure est dite 'forme traditionnelle'; le représentant de l'autorité officielle enregistre le mariage et cet enregistrement est transmis à l'état civil.

Donc, en théorie, le système est souple et simple. La loi prévoit également en cas de divorce une procédure spéciale qui joue dans le cas où le mariage a été contracté dans la forme traditionnelle. Les conjoints peuvent porter leur différend devant une juridiction spéciale qui siège à l'échelon du village et qui est constituée ad hoc; cette juridiction est composée de quatre membres :

— un représentant du pouvoir exécutif, désigné par le sous-préfet ou le chef d'arrondissement (en général, le chef de canton),
— le maire de la commune rurale ou son adjoint,
— deux membres du village où les conjoints ont eu leur dernière résidence.

La juridiction siège au chef-lieu de la commune rurale et utilise une procédure très simplifiée.

Mais en pratique, on constate que les justiciables ne s'intéressent pas au système qui leur est proposé. Mariages et divorces continuent dans la très grande majorité des cas à être entièrement coutumiers. C'est dire à quel point il est difficile d'insérer le droit nouveau—même adapté de façon prudente—dans le milieu social; d'ailleurs, avec exemple malgache, nous sommes sortis du domaine de la coutume officielle, nous entrons dans celui du droit parallèle.

(*ii*) *Le Droit parallèle*

Il convient d'abord de s'entendre sur son importance réelle, car la question prête à discussion. Pendant la période coloniale, les tribunaux officiels n'ont réglé qu'une faible partie des litiges. Le problème est de savoir si cette proportion a augmenté ou diminué après l'indépendance, et l'apparition de juridictions 'nationales'. Il serait imprudent d'apporter une réponse générale, car la situation varie avec le pays en cause. Cependant, nous estimons qu'une observation attentive des faits permet de conclure qu'en de nombreuses régions, il y a eu non pas diminution, mais recrudescence de la justice arbitrale. Cette évolution est la conséquence de facteurs complexes; les juges, au moins en Afrique francophone après la suppression de l'indigénat, en 1946, se sont considérablement éloignés des justiciables (malgré la création de juridictions plus ou moins mobiles) et la situation, à l'heure actuelle, laisse encore beaucoup à désirer en ce sens; d'autre part, les antagonismes d'origine tribale, en Afrique Noire, compliquent beaucoup les choses et aboutissent à une certaine désaffection ou à une méfiance envers les organismes officiels; cette réserve s'accentue parfois en un véritable repli sur soi, très manifeste à Madagascar devant les pressions administratives qui, très légitimement, essaient d'encadrer solidement les populations pour la perception de l'impôt, l'établissement de l'état-civil, la modernisation des techniques agricoles et la lutte pour le développement; en réaction contre ces efforts, les populations tendent à s'adresser le moins possible aux représentants des pouvoirs publics. Certes, les déclarations officielles évitent de faire état de ces attitudes, qui sont sans doute transitoires, mais qui n'en existent pas moins. Ajoutons enfin que la substitution d'un nouveau droit à la coutume traditionnelle accentue encore la réserve exprimée par les justiciables.

Cette persistance—ou ce renouveau—de l'importance de l'arbitrage peuvent être considérés par exemple au Dahomey, au Cameroun, au Niger; il arrive que l'autorité publique le reconnaisse sans équivoque. Lors des enquêtes que nous avons faites au Dahomey entre 1959 et 1963, nous avons été frappé par l'insistance avec laquelle les sous-préfets et les chefs de canton soulignaient la fréquence du recours aux instances arbitrales, qui échappaient totalement à leur contrôle. De même, à Madagascar, lors du récent *Colloque du Droit Malgache*, organisé par le Ministre de la Justice en Octobre 1964, le Garde des Sceaux, M. Ramangasoavina, a mis très justement l'accent sur la place exacte qu'occupe le recours judiciaire dans le système des valeurs de la culture malgache: 'Dans la très vieille tradition malgache, le recours à la justice était un mal nécessaire, un remède ultime après de vaines tentatives de conciliation.' On ne pourrait mieux reconnaître que la voie de la justice officielle est par essence une voie anormale, exceptionnelle: une sorte d'appel auquel on a recours quand toutes les voies normales se sont formées. Cette conception a évident de quoi préoccuper les dirigeants.

La plupart du droit du mariage, de la succession et même du droit répressif est réglée par l'arbitrage, par le conseil de famille ou du village.[1] L'étendue de cette procédure et la réserve manifestée à l'égard du pouvoir sont démontrées au Madagascar, où les pouvoirs publics ont organisé une procédure d'arbitrage par les officiers de l'état-civil, qui n'a pratiquement jamais été appliquée.

(iii) Le Droit secret

Au-delà du droit parallèle, qui aboutit à perpétuer le règne de la coutume malgré les dispositions différentes de la loi, qui est connu, sinon par tous, du moins par la majorité du groupe, il existe un droit ésotérique, qui demeure tout imprégné de magie et de religion. Le droit parallèle est *juridique*, il concerne la filiation, le mariage, le régime de la propriété foncière, etc. . . .; il met en relation des hommes entre eux. Le droit secret, au contraire, se réfère toujours à une tierce partie, qui est une puissance du monde invisible: dieu, esprit, génie. Son approche est évidemment très délicate, pour deux raisons: d'abord, ce qui est sacré n'est pas facilement révélé au profane;

[1] Bien plus, on notera que les pouvoirs publics ont très pertinemment organisé une procédure d'arbitrage prévoyant un échelon antérieur à toute juridiction par le règlement des litiges survenant entre les habitants d'une même commune rurale; la conciliation est assurée par le maire et contrôlée par le sous-préfet. Or, cette procédure n'a pratiquement jamais été appliquée. Cet exemple est particulièrement expressif, car on mesure à partir de lui la profondeur de la réserve manifestée par les sociétés malgaches à l'égard de tout ce qui concerne le pouvoir: il a suffi que celui-ci veuille organiser l'arbitrage pour qu'on confonde aussitôt l'arbitrage et la justice, et qu'on refuse l'adhésion.

ensuite, sur un plan plus juridique, il est certain que la plus grande partie du droit secret est contraire à l'ordre public; les pratiques en cause sont donc punissables, et seraient poursuivies par les pouvoirs publics. Mais on peut distinguer deux niveaux distincts, selon que le droit est relié à la religion (ou à la magie bénéfique), ou à la magie maléfique.

Un premier ensemble de pratiques concerne la religion, la magie bénéfique ou la divination; il s'agit de procédures secrètes qui sont mises en œuvre dans tous les cas où l'on considère que la justice des hommes doit céder la place à une action de régulation ou de réparation sociales directement ordonnée ou organisée par les puissances invisibles; tous les modes de preuve ésotériques persistant en Afrique entrant dans ce domaine: la divination du coupable, les diverses ordalies (toutes ces pratiques contraires à l'ordre public, qui entraînent des poursuites judiciaires contre leurs auteurs), les réparations pour rupture d'interdit, forment l'essentiel de ce droit secret qui est aussi un droit *sacré*.

Mais il existe un second groupe de pratiques, relié à la magie noire; on sait que depuis la décolonisation, très généralement parlant, la magie est en progression aussi bien la sorcellerie que la magie bénéfique. Le droit secret de la magie se réfère non pas aux techniques internes de mise en œuvre, qui sont en principe inconnues des membres du groupe (car réservées aux seuls initiés), mais aux conditions d'insertion de ces techniques dans le corps social; la communauté, en effet, lutte contre les 'sorciers' qu'elle cherche à dépister, et lorsqu'elle a identifié l'un d'eux, elle applique alors un droit coutumier répressif parfaitement inconnu des autorités (et parfaitement 'illégal'). Ce droit secret est en somme un droit de la malédiction; à Madagascar par exemple, il régit toute la procédure qui tend à l'identification des sorciers et à leur mise en jugement.

Il existe d'ailleurs entre les deux niveaux un plan intermédiaire où classer les formes parfois subtiles selon lesquelles le groupe admet la collaboration des sociétés 'secrètes', des confréries, des sectes d'initiés, qui assurent parfois la police, font régner un certain ordre, assurent l'exécution de certaines sentences du chef. Souvent, ces confréries assument des fonctions ambivalentes qui relèvent aussi bien de la magie bénéfique (ou parfois de la religion) que de la sorcellerie. Mais ce qui nous intéresse ici, c'est de noter qu'elles ont une portée juridique; elles sont prises dans un réseau d'obligations et de prérogatives qui se situe entièrement en dehors du droit officiel.

III LES MODALITÉS DE L'ENQUÊTE

Nous espérons avoir nettement montré dans les lignes qui précèdent la réelle complexité des droits contemporains d'Afrique. Il n'y a pas un seul système, mais plusieurs ensembles interfèrent les uns les autres. L'enquête doit s'adapter à cette situation et se placer aux divers niveaux où l'on peut saisir la réalité juridique. Il est évident qu'elle sera d'autant plus délicate que le droit sera plus ésotérique. Nous avons maintenant à passer en revue les différentes situations concrètes où il est possible de saisir les manifestations de la coutume.

(i) *Les Dynamismes juridiques*

Une remarque préliminaire s'impose: il convient de définir la coutume, chaque fois que ce sera possible, à partir de faits positifs, observés sur le terrain, et non à partir de simples informations; c'est au moment du litige, du conflit, que le droit se révèle le mieux. On appréciera la différence qui existe le plus souvent entre l'énoncé théorique de la règle et la solution pratique apportée au conflit; le décalage observé éclairera sur la tendance, l'orientation de la coutume, que la seule enquête orale serait impuissante à faire apparaître; en effet, les intéressés demeurent attachés à la coutume et font état des solutions traditionnelles sans se rendre compte eux-mêmes que les *faits* sont parfois plus vite que les *règles*. On ne méconnaîtra d'ailleurs pas la possibilité de la superposition d'une triple norme:

(*a*) la coutume ancienne dont on se souvient, mais qu'on a cessé d'appliquer (exemple: sur le littoral de l'Ouest africain, les règles concernant le droit du premier exploitant en face des droits de 'propriété éminente' de tel village ou lignage);

(*b*) la coutume nouvelle adoptée devant la pression des nécessités économiques (on admettra par exemple que l'exploitant soit un étranger au groupe, mais il devra consentir à certains rituels et remettre certaines prestations; il ne pourra faire que des cultures vivrières et éviter les plantations d'arbres);

(c) la pratique réelle, suivie effectivement (les exploitants plantent des arbres, cocotiers ou palmiers à huile, et se créent ainsi une situation de fait qui devient génératrice de droit).

(ii) *La Collecte des 'Espèces': l'Enregistrement des Litiges judiciaires*
La situation matérielle des archives des divers ordres de juridictions africaines varie beaucoup selon le lieu; la bonne tenue des documents dépend aussi bien du président du Tribunal que du greffier ou secrétaire chargé de la rédaction.[1] La conservation des pièces est d'autre part assurée de façon très variable; dans certains tribunaux, les registres ou les feuilles les plus anciens sont dans un état critique: encre effacée, papier détérioré ou mangé par les insectes; c'est pourquoi nous avons proposé la centralisation systématique de toutes les archives à la capitale, où un service spécialisé aurait en charge leur gestion: on constate pratiquement que les demandes d'extraits d'état civil ou de jugement sont absentes en ce qui concerne les documents anciens et rares pour les documents récents; la centralisation au chef lieu faciliterait d'ailleurs la communication d'extraits.

L'exploitation des litiges peut être conduite sur un double plan, qualitatif et quantitatif. Pour cela, il est nécessaire d'adopter un modèle de fiche normalisée, faisant apparaître:

— les références de numérotage administratif, de temps, de lieu;
— les indications concernant les parties en cause;
— les circonstances de la cause;
— les débats;
— les motifs fondant la sentence;
— la décision intervenue.

Les dépositions des témoins apportent parfois des éléments originaux, mais l'intérêt de ces fiches est très variable: certains

[1] Rappelons qu'en dehors des documents écrits, il existe des archives matérielles auprès des juridictions répressives: les 'pièces à conviction' qui sont conservées par les Greffes. Il s'agit d'objets d'une grande variété: statuettes, fétiches, armes, végétaux, préparations magiques, amulettes et talismans divers. Des milliers d'objets sont ainsi conservés dans des conditions très précaires.

documents sont irremplaçables; la plupart, cependant, sont sans grand intérêt. Mais quelle que soit la valeur intrinsèque de ces documents, leur exploitation statistique apporte des renseignements très intéressants quant au nombre relatif des différentes catégories de conflits, quant à la qualité des parties en cause (selon l'origine ethnique ou géographique, le statut, le sexe, etc. . . .), quant à l'analyse interne des litiges enfin (pour le divorce par exemple: étude des demandeurs et des défendeurs, des causes invoquées, des circonstances; recherche des corrélations entre les divers éléments: sexe, statut, profession, origine ethnique, conjoncture économique, etc. . . .). Les 'accidents' juridiques peuvent ainsi être 'mis en situation', c'est-à-dire comparés aux divers phénomènes sociaux: des crises internes d'une société donnée, les tensions montant entre les générations, les déséquilibres démographiques, ont un retentissement juridique. La courbe des divorces et l'évolution de leurs causes, la nuptialité, l'âge au mariage, dépendent à la fois de la *sex ratio*, des migrations concernant l'exode rural, et de la situation économique; en ce qui concerne ce dernier point, il est certain par exemple que le taux du gage matrimonial ('dot'), là où il existe, est influencé à la fois par la structure démographique (nombre de femmes disponibles), par la 'propension' à la polygamie, et par l'importance des liquidités monétaires (dépendant elle-même de la conjoncture économique).

(iii) L'Enquête de Vérification

Nous voudrions attirer l'attention sur l'intérêt qui s'attache à une methode très rarement utilisée jusqu'ici: il s'agit pour l'enquêteur de *refaire l'instruction* du litige officiellement jugé, en interrogeant les parties en cause et les témoins. Bien entendu, cela n'est pas toujours possible et d'ailleurs, il n'est pas question de reprendre systématiquement tous les cas: ces enquêtes constituent de simples sondages concernant des litiges récemment jugés. Mais de tels recoupements sont très précieux: ils permettent de mesurer l'écart qui existe souvent entre le litige officiel et les vrais conflits. Sur le plan officiel, il y a un gauchissement de la réalité, des distorsions ou de mauvaises interprétations des faits; les échanges entre juges, témoins et parties ressemblent parfois à des dialogues de sourds. Les motivations les plus profondes peuvent n'être pas exposées, soit parce qu'on répugne à livrer au grand jour certains sentiments, soit parce que des malentendus ont surgi. D'autre part, dans une audience publique, chacun joue un rôle, celui de son personnage social. Ces enquêtes de vérification constituent donc un excellent test de la validité des débats officiels; elles permettent aussi d'aborder l'étude 'post-litem' des réactions au jugement émanant des parties et du groupe.

(iv) Analyse des Conflits parallèles

La justice arbitrale est souvent plus importante que la justice officielle. L'enquête ethnologique s'attachera à déterminer quels sont les organes qui assurent la conciliation, et reprendra les divers points abordés plus haut: parties en présence, circonstances de la cause, délibérations, références faites explicitement à la coutume, décision, suites éventuelles et réactions du groupe. Les organes, ou l'autorité (chef, prêtre, notable), qui font l'arbitrage, sont parfois des institutions ayant une existence administrative officielle, par exemple le *fokon'olona*, conseil du village, à Madagascar: nous avons alors le cas d'un organisme officiel assurant, en plus, une fonction officieuse.

Les conflits concernant la justice parallèle se prêtent aussi à une analyse statistique, et la comparaison des résultats de celle-ci avec les résultats concernant la justice officielle est très intéressante; elle montre quelles sortes de litiges sont portées devant l'une et l'autre des justices.

(v) Techniques d'Enregistrement

En dehors de la collecte directe des litiges faisant l'objet d'un conflit déclaré et des actes juridiques (contrats, accords, etc....), l'enquêteur aura intérêt à exploiter les diverses sources de renseignements: l'inventaire des proverbes et dictons se rapportant au droit ne sera pas négligé, mais d'autres sources d'information sont plus importantes:

— *Autobiographies juridiques:* le *récit de vie* d'un individu, qui reconstitue son existence juridique, est d'une valeur inestimable.

— *Discussion de groupe:* Elles sont concurremment employées pour la collecte des droits coutumiers (entreprise dans plusieurs pays africains comme préalable à la codification), mais elles sont rarement conduites de façon correcte; le groupe doit être de petite dimension (de 3 à 5 participants). Un problème très délicat concerne le *contrôle* de la discussion, car des impératifs contradictoires existent; la discussion devrait, en principe, se développer librement, sans intervention extérieure, et d'un autre côté, elle ne doit pas dévier et devenir hors-sujet. En pratique, l'enquêteur essaiera de concilier ces deux obligations: il sera présent, mais se fera oublier. On peut laisser la discussion libre ou contrôlée.

— *Enregistrement au magnétophone:* Il comporte de grands avantages et quelques inconvénients. Où on peut l'utiliser, c'est la vie même qui est préservée.

Summary

THE ANALYSIS OF JUDICIAL TYPES AND THE STUDY OF AFRICAN CUSTOMARY LAWS

This paper delineates methods of studying and collecting information on elements of customary law. We mean by this any documentation reporting a specific event, such as a succession, a divorce, a sale of land, etc.

I TYPES OF CUSTOMARY LEGAL RULES

There are two levels of customary law: one, exoteric, known by everyone in the group, and two, esoteric, always more or less secret. Three main categories have to be distinguished:

(i) official customary law, which continues to be very important. Either it has been recognized by the new statutory law, or persists in its own right since it still rules a very large part of the law of persons and property;

(ii) parallel law, which is far more important than is generally thought. Tribalism, suspicion of the central power, and the sanctity of traditional rules are some of the factors which maintain this non-official law that the people insist on observing. Justice by conciliation and arbitration, outside official jurisdiction, is still sought by many;

(iii) secret law, which is intimately involved with religion, divination, sorcery, and witchcraft. It has at least two aspects: the first concerns procedures in administering ordeals; the second concerns the regulation of conflicts with harmful magic (e.g. the use of sorcery).

II METHODS OF INVESTIGATION

The collection and the interpretation of customary law have to cover the three areas which have just been distinguished. A certain number of principles can be stressed to guide field investigation:

(i) we must try to expound customs from concrete cases, directly observed on the spot, and not only as given in informants' statements. It is on occasions of legal action under traditional law (e.g. the formation of a contract or a trial) that we can observe the customary law in its actual operation. We must take care to note divergences between theoretical rules and actual practice as well as digressions from the central issue;

(ii) the inventory of legal elements, derived from the archives of official courts, must be done with the use of standardized cards because a statistical analysis of litigation and research into correlations concerning the socio-economic environment are necessary. It is especially important to follow up recently judged cases by discussing them with the litigants involved;

(iii) among important procedures for the study and interpretation of cases are the use of elaborate records of individuals' histories in litigation and discussions of points of law with small groups (3–5 persons). Tape recordings should be made.

II. The Structure of African Judicial Authority and Problems of Evidence and Proof in Traditional Courts

N. A. OLLENNU

I INTRODUCTION

The local courts, variously called African Courts, Customary Courts, or Native Courts, in the African states formerly under British administration, derive their powers and jurisdiction as judicial bodies from statutes, and not from indigenous traditional authority. They differ in constitution, powers, and modes of instituting process, and execution of their decrees and orders, from the indigenous tribunals they have superseded, and approximate closely to a District Magistrate's Court in the English system. But they maintain the character of indigenous tribunals in that: (i) the cases cognizable are principally cases involving customary law; and (ii) their practice and procedure, including giving and receiving of evidence, are regulated in accordance with customary law, in both customary and non-customary cases.[1] E.g., a witness who, under English law, would be incompetent to give evidence of the traditions of a particular lineage because he is not in a direct line of descent, would be competent to do so if he belongs to a class of persons entitled by customary law to be told that tradition. This customary law is recognized even by the superior courts.[2] In an action involving a stool or other traditional office, the incumbent of the office gives evidence in the first person of events which happened in the times of a predecessor as if they occurred in his own time, since in African belief there is social identification of each holder with his ancestors and predecessors.[3]

[1] See, e.g., Courts Act, 1960 (C.A. 9g), Ghana, sec. 98 & sec. 103.
[2] See *Afrigie* v. *Dotwaah & anr.*, S.Ct., Civil Appeal No. 2964, 12 April 1965, unreported.   [3] See Busia, 1961, p. 73.

It does not mean that any form of hearsay evidence is admissible in a local court. Councillors in the local courts in the Ga state (comprising Accra, the capital) reject hearsay evidence with an old Ga proverb 'rumours wreck a nation' (*Ake ake le edzwaa mang*), implying that justice cannot be based on hearsay. Gluckman reports from Barotse this principle: 'A witness was told: What you heard with your ears, what you saw with your eyes, tell us. Hearing and seeing the quarrel are good. Do not tell us anything you have been told about the fight.'[1]

The local court will also admit any authentic document which may appear to it to be relevant to the issue before it, though that document will not be admissible in a superior court without strict proof.[2] But it should not admit an uncertified copy of a document without proof of its authenticity.[3]

It is further permissible for the local court, in its efforts to arrive at the truth, to put questions to the parties or witnesses, even though this savours of cross-examination and would be strongly disapproved if done by a judge in an English court. In African courts, this is considered natural and proper: it shows how the councillors are thinking during the process of the case,[4] and allows any party to try to correct views of the court about his case which he considers to be wrong.

II ARBITRATION

Yet, as stated, the indigenous tribunals, councils of chief or headman and elders, cannot properly be deemed ancestors of these modern local courts. Statutes creating these courts specifically prohibited the holding of any tribunal except as provided under them. This appears in the legal position of the local court in the judicial set-up of Ghana subsequent to the Native Jurisdiction Ordinance (1883, No. 5) and immediately prior to the coming into force of the Native Administration Ordinance (1927, No. 18). Branford Griffith, C.J., said of those

---

[1] Gluckman, 1955–6, vii, 1, p. 51, more fully discussed in Gluckman, 1955, Chapter III.

[2] *Asenso* v. *Nkyindwo* (1956) 1 W.A.L.R., p. 243; *Akomea & ors.* v. *Biei & ors.*, C.A., Civil Appeal No. 13/57, 19 May 1958, unreported.

[3] *Ntsin* v. *Ekutey & ors.* (1957) 3 W.A.L.R., p. 11.

[4] For an example of this practice, see Gluckman, 1955–6, (i) The Case of the Violent Councillor (1955), vii, 1, pp. 51, 53–54, more fully discussed in 1955, Chapter III.

tribunals recognized by the former Ordinance, as against those it did not recognize:

> ... *it merely regulates those of the Courts to which it applies*: it does not abolish and re-establish them, but, taking them as they stand with their customary constitution and customary procedure, it *merely cuts down some of the unlimited civil jurisdiction,* and provides for their further regulation; *but the Courts remain the Native common law Courts and are not the King's Courts* ... So far it has not been disputed that they exist and retain their powers, although within the British Dominions ... The reason that they do so exist is because they have been *recognised by the Sovereign,* not because they are King's Courts; their survival within the British Dominions is due only to implied recognition by the Crown. *In neither of the two Orders in Council is there any express reference to these Courts,* there is *only* IMPLIED RECOGNITION, and their continued existence is due to this implied recognition (Mutchi v. Annan & ors. (1907) Red. 211; 216–17. My italics).

And as to those it did not recognize, the learned Chief Justice said they continued to exist so long as they had not been specifically abolished.

Now the enactments which created the existing local courts have specifically abolished the indigenous courts; therefore no lawful local court can be held except as provided under the statute. But in each of these enactments the holding of arbitration under customary law is either expressly or implicitly exempted[1] so that arbitration under customary law continues to exist. Therefore in arbitration under customary law, unlike the local court, we have a continued existence of the indigenous judicial authority.

Some scholars have held the view that arbitration under customary law is merely an attempt to effect amicable settlement of a dispute between parties so as to bring about reconciliation, and that an award made by it becomes binding upon the parties only where both parties to the dispute accept it; those who belong to this school of thought take the view that it is an importation of English law into the customary law to hold that parties to a dispute can submit their dispute to arbitration with prior agreement to be bound by any decision which may be given. Thus Mark Wilson, C.J., said:

[1] See *Record of Proceedings: African Conference on Local Courts and Customary Law*, held at Dar es Salaam, Tanganyika, p. 17.

I have heard it argued that the concept of arbitration under native customary law set out in these cases [the cases of *Ayafie* v. *Banyea*, and *Mensah* v. *Takyiampong*; *Afayie* v. *Banyea* (1884) S.F.L.R. 38; *Mensah* v. *Takyiampong* (1940) 6 W.A.C.A. 118] is unduly reflective of English law and I have reason to believe (unfortunately on extraneous evidence) that in one respect at least it is not the law followed in many of the present-day Native Courts set up under local Ordinances. I understand that in their view of native customary law, an arbitration award is binding on the parties only if they agree to the decision; in other words *the essential thing is subsequent and not prior agreement to be bound by the award* [my italics]. It would also seem that by 'arbitration' native customary law originally meant a simple investigation of a dispute usually by a chief and his elders but sometimes even by a few individuals gathered together for the purpose, at which the parties to the dispute were heard and an attempt made by the more or less patient negotiation to reconcile opposing claims and to arrive at an agreed solution of the dispute acceptable to both parties. The dominant idea was to preserve peace and homogeneity of interest which was basically important in an African community. Since the essence of the procedure outlined above is the continuing consent of the participants, it would seem to be open to either party to withdraw from the proceedings at any stage.'[1]

The learned Chief Justice expressed similar views, though not in the same strong terms, in another judgment delivered by him on the same day in *Ankrah & ors.* v. *Dabra & anr.* (L.A. No. 93/53, 31 March 1954, *unreported*). However, being bound by judgments of higher courts,[2] he was compelled to hold in both cases that arbitration and negotiations for settlement are two separate and distinct proceedings, and that the proceedings in issue before him were negotiations for settlement. His decision in *Ankrah & ors.* v. *Dabra & anr.* was confirmed by the West African Court of Appeal ([1956] 1 W.A.L.R., 89).

Allott, who belongs to the same school as Sir Mark Wilson, argues that arbitration in the English sense does not exist under customary law, at least among the Akan of Ghana. He maintains that arbitration under customary law is an attempt at reconciliation, nothing more, and that an award made thereat

[1] *Djaka & ors.* v. *Amemadokpor & OB.*, L.A. No. 73/53, 31 March 1954, unreported.
[2] I.e. the West African Courts of Appeal in *Mensah* v. *Takyiampong* (*supra*) and the Privy Council in *Kwasi* v. *Larbi* (1953) A.C. 164 P.C., (1953) 13 W.A.C.A., p. 76.

is not binding unless proved to have been accepted by both parties. Thus commenting on the editorial notes in *Ankrah & ors.* v. *Dabra & anr.* (*supra*) based on cases like *Kwasi* v. *Larbi* (*supra*) and other cases, that 'native law and custom recognizes (although perhaps it does not clearly differentiate between) two types of customary extra-judicial procedure for the determination of disputes', namely, reference for adjudication on the merits with agreement *ab initio* to abide by the award, and reference to a mediator to seek a compromise arrangement, not necessarily on the merits, but what is acceptable to the parties, Allott submits 'that this dichotomy is a false one, and that customary arbitration merely varies in the degree to which the arbitrators attempt to impose their decision on the parties' and that 'it is generally contrary to customary ideas to commit oneself, before such proceedings begin, to accepting the decision of the arbitrators whatever it might be'.[1] After arguing all the cases then available on the subject he postulated:

(1) It is false to draw distinction between arbitrations and mere attempts to negotiate a settlement, since 'arbitration' (as the word is used in Akan custom) is an attempt at reconciliation, and the dichotomy does not exist.

(2) Only if an arbitration in the common-law sense is proved do the English rules with regard to withdrawing from the arbitration apply. In Akan custom either party is free to withdraw before the award is given.

(3) In Akan custom, again, it is submitted with respect that either party is entitled to withdraw until he has accepted the award. Until such time, either party has a *locus poenitentiae*. Acceptance of the award is indicated by the payment of *aseda* to the arbitrators.

(4) Before a doctrine contrary to Akan customary law has become consecrated through this series of cases a possible escape may be found in the closing dictum of the Privy Council in *Kwasi* v. *Larbi*, *supra*:

'... it is for the appellants to satisfy the Board that a right so contrary to the basic conception of arbitration is recognised by native customary law. In this they have failed.'

This would indicate that there was a burden of proof upon the appellants to prove the custom, that in this particular instance they failed to discharge the burden, that thereby the benefit of such a

[1] Allott, 1960, pp. 117, 134.

custom has been lost to them, but that it will not necessarily be lost to other litigants who manage to prove the customary law of arbitration with greater success. . . .

(5) There is no reason at all, with the greatest respect why customary arbitrations should not be accepted on their merits, without attempting to force them into the straitjacket of English law . . .[1]

Since in our opinion it is mainly in these ex-statutory-judicial proceedings that we find the successor to, or rather the continued assertion of, the indigenous tribunal of itself in the structure of modern judicial authority, it is necessary that we should make a brief examination of the indigenous judicial structure in order to arrive at the right conclusions as to the exact nature of arbitration under customary law.

Danquah's account of indigenous judicial and arbitral proceedings in his *Akan Laws and Customs* (1928, Chapter IV) provides very useful material on this point. [Editor's note:—I have summarized Ollennu's full analysis and citations, because of lack of space: page references in brackets are to Danquah.]

Every town or village has a tribunal in which the chief or subchief presides over captains and elders; and similar tribunals, *mutatis mutandis* in terms of the status of those who preside and who are members of the tribunal, exist at the level of subdivisions, and of each Akan state. Higher tribunals hear appeals from lower tribunals. In addition, there is a state council at the national level. Procedure is commenced by (*a*) oath, (*b*) summons, or (*c*) criminal 'indictment' (p. 66). All these tribunals were recognized by Ordinance in 1883 and later again in 1927.

Informal investigations, described as '*bo nkuro*', are held by the head and elders of a family, without such enacted jurisdiction, or by a chief *in camera*. These act as arbitrators (*Baguafo*). Their proceedings are almost exactly the same as those before a proper tribunal (p. 83), namely, judicial investigation on the merits, save that it is in an informal manner, and they end with judgment pronounced for one party or the other (p. 86).

During such a hearing, either party can swear the National Oath. The other can (*a*) then withdraw or cease to contest, and have judgment ordered against him. Or (*b*) he can proceed

[1] Allott, Chapter VI, 'Arbitral Proceedings in Customary Laws', pp. 117, 138.

without swearing, and the hearing will continue unless the first party swears to get the case before a proper tribunal. Or (c) he can reply to the oath; then the case has to go to a Chief's Tribunal since *Bagua* cannot hear an oath case (pp. 85–86). It is clear that a party to arbitration proceedings cannot resile: he can only have the case transferred to a proper tribunal.

An award in the arbitration proceedings can only be enforced by action in a court of competent jurisdiction. There the award is recognized as 'definite evidence of liability before competent witnesses' (p. 84): and it will support a plea for enforcement or bar a claim on identical issues.

Tribunals of this kind also exist in *asafo* companies, religious cults and communities (Christian and Muslim), and members of one tribe living among others, as well as families.[1]

Similar principles emerge from Banton's account of the development of councils of tribal headmen among groups of tribal migrants in Freetown, which were once given statutory recognition, and which continued to operate after that jurisdiction was withdrawn;[2] and from Schapera's account of the traditional judicial system in the Bechuanaland Protectorate.[3]

The essence of the proceedings before the *Bagua* arbitrators is that they decide who is right and who is wrong. Busia also reports '*fie asen*', 'family or domestic settlement', at which elders negotiate a compromise and persuade the parties to accept it, without going into the merits, as over a boundary dispute. Here an award can only be binding on the parties if accepted by both. It was described by Sir Mark Wilson, C.J., as an attempt by a chief and his elders or others to negotiate a settlement agreeable to both parties so as to obviate violence and the growth of bad feeling in a community. The essence of the situation is continuing consent of the parties, so that either may withdraw at any time or refuse to accept the award. They do not come as in other cases cited for adjudication on the merits of their dispute, but for negotiation of a settlement, which both should accept (*Ankrah and ors.* v. *Dabra and anr., supra*).

There are clearly two distinctive indigenous proceedings

---

[1] Allott, p. 86. Confirmed by Busia, 1961, pp. 67–68. Supplementary observations by Ollennu.
[2] Banton, 1954, p. 104.   [3] Schapera, 1940, pp. 63–64.

under customary law for extra-judicial determination of a dispute: (a) arbitration properly so called, which decides who is right and who is wrong, and (b) reconciliation or negotiations for a settlement. These have been fully described and distinguished in recent judgments of the Supreme Court of Ghana. Among other cases, in *Isifu* v. *Donkor*[1] it was shown that for an award of a valid arbitration to be binding:

> (i) the parties must have voluntarily submitted the dispute to the arbitrators to have it decided informally but on its merits, and there must be evidence that the full implications were explained to, and agreed to by, the parties;
> (ii) they must have agreed in advance to accept the award;
> (iii) the award must be arrived at not arbitrarily but after hearing both parties in a judicial manner;
> (iv) practice and procedure for the time being in the Native Court of Tribunal of the area must have been followed as nearly as possible; and
> (v) there should be publication of the award (taken from *Budu II* v. *Caesar & ors.*, *supra*).

It also shows that for an award of a negotiated settlement or a compromise to be binding upon the parties and to operate as estoppel against either of the parties, it must be shown that it was accepted by each of them. In such a case both parties give *aseda*, i.e. 'drink' in cash or kind at the conclusion to signify acceptance; while in proper arbitration the successful party alone pays '*Abene*', i.e. a judgment fee.

A typical example of the principle that proceedings in customary arbitration is trial informally but on the merits, is the illustration given by Danquah, of the trial of the debt case which one Kofe brought before a *Bagua* against Yao, who belonged to the same family or clan as he. Unhappily we must refer the reader to the text which we cannot cite for lack of space. The description makes it conclusive that the proceedings described, *Nkrobo*, before a *Bagua*, is judicial though informal, and not just reconciliatory.[2]

[1] S.Ct., Civil Appeal No. 78/62, 13 May 1963, unreported. Other case references are available from the author, editor, or the International African Institute.
[2] Danquah, 1928, pp. 84–85.

We have seen that as far as the structure of the pure African judicial system is concerned, the only vestige of it now extant can be traced to part of the procedure followed at trial in a local court, and in the latitude allowed for receipt of evidence in such a trial. All the indigenous African systems of judicial authority have been superseded and replaced by statutory authority. Again having regard to the fact that no special qualifications are required, as in the case of Ghana, for appointment of members of the local court, and also to the jurisdiction of a local court limited to minor personal suits and petty criminal cases, it is evident that systematic development of the customary law can no longer depend upon the local courts; it can only depend upon the superior courts of the land presided over by men learned and experienced in the law of the land—customary and non-customary, indigenous and introduced. Therefore the only institutions which now and in the future can be expected to reflect the indigenous African judicial authority are the arbitration and the negotiated settlement.

One of the main foundations of the indigenous extra-judicial proceedings was that the traditional executive authority was identical with the traditional judicial authority, or there was at least a strong link between those two authorities, and in modern days the moral obligations which the African continues to feel towards his traditional elders—the chief, and the heads of his family, of his *asafo* company group, of his church, and of any religious or other social organization to which he belongs, as well as the elders of these associations. With the divorce between the traditional authority and court membership, as Allott points out,[1] and with the present trend of change in African society which cannot be said to be strengthening family ties, it would appear that there is urgent need for some definite steps to be taken to ensure the preservation of the very useful, convenient, and less acrimonious process of settling disputes upon the merits and for giving encouragement to continuance of procedure in local courts, on lines similar to those of the customary law. Allott suggests legislation as a means of preserving the customary extra-judicial proceedings which he calls 'Arbitral proceedings', and offers a model legislation for it. He defines 'Arbitral proceedings' as:

[1] Allott, 1960, p. 144.

informal proceedings or negotiations out of court for the settlement of a dispute or the adjustment of claims as between the parties in accordance with customary law whether by reference to an arbiter or otherwise, but does not include an arbitration in accordance with English law under the Arbitration Ordinance.[1]

We strongly support Allott's suggestion for legislation with its emphasis that to support a valid arbitration under customary law there should be a written document signed by the parties to show they expressly agreed at or before the commencement of the proceedings, that a determination should in any event be binding upon them; we also support the view that the award should be reduced into writing and signed by the arbitrator. Those proposals are in keeping with the spirit of modern times when illiteracy is rapidly disappearing from African society. We further think that provision for enforcement of an arbitration award by a method additional to an action in court of competent jurisdiction is also desirable. Subject to these provisos, we think that an enactment which will make arbitral proceedings by customary law a statutory institution permissive merely of customary procedure, is undesirable, as its effect would be to wipe out the sole survivor of indigenous African judicial systems.

BIBLIOGRAPHY

Allott, A. N.
    (1960) *Essays in African Law*. London: Butterworth.
Banton, M.
    (1954) 'Tribal Headmen in Freetown', *Journal of African Administration*, vi, 3, p. 10.
Brooke, N. F.
    (1954) 'The Changing Character of Customary Courts', *Journal of African Administration*, vi, 2, pp. 67 f.
Busia, K. A.
    (1961) *The Position of the Chief in the Modern Political System of Ashanti*. London: Oxford University Press for the International African Institute.
Casely, Hayford
    (1903) *Gold Coast Native Institutions*. London: Sweet & Maxwell.
Danquah, J. B.
    (1928) *Gold Coast: Akan Laws and Customs and the Akim Abuakwa Constitution*. London: Routledge and Sons.
Gluckman, M.
    (1955) *The Judicial Process among the Barotse of Northern Rhodesia*. Manchester: Manchester University Press for the Rhodes–Livingstone Institute (republished, expanded, 1967).

[1] Allott, p. 146.

(1955–6) 'The Reasonable Man in Barotse Law', *Journal of African Administration*, vii, 2, pp. 51–55; vii, 3, pp. 127–31; viii, 2, pp. 101–5; viii, 3, pp. 151–6, reprinted in Gluckman, *Order and Rebellion in Tribal Africa*. London: Cohen and West (1962).

Record of Proceedings: African Conference on Local Courts and Customary Law, Dar-es-Salaam, Tanganyika, *1963*.

Report of Native Tribunal, Committee of Enquiry, Gold Coast, 1943. Accra: Government Printing Department.

Sarbah, J. M.
   (1897, 1904) *Fanti Customary Law*. London: William Clowes & Sons.
   (1904) *Fanti Law Report* (referred to as S.F.L.R.). London: William Clowes & Sons.
   (1906) *Fanti National Constitution*. London: William Clowes & Sons.

Schapera, I.
   (1940) 'The Ngwato of the Bechuanaland Protectorate' in *African Political Systems*, edited by M. Fortes and E. E. Evans-Pritchard. London: Oxford University Press for the International African Institute.

Tennent, J. R. M.
   (1961) 'Administration of Criminal Law in Some Kenya African Courts', *Journal of African Law*, v, 3, pp. 139 f.

Ward, W. E. F.
   (1958) *A History of Ghana*. London: Allen and Unwin (2nd revised edition).

White, C. M. N.
   (1964) 'The Changing Scope of Urban Native Courts in Northern Rhodesia', *Journal of African Law*, viii, 1, pp. 29 f.

Résumé

LA STRUCTURE DE L'AUTORITÉ JUDICIAIRE AFRICAINE ET LES PROBLÈMES DE LA PREUVE DANS LES GROUPES TRADITIONNELS

1. Les tribunaux locaux, connus dans quelques états africains sous le nom de tribunaux africains, tribunaux coutumiers ou tribunaux indigènes sont, à l'heure actuelle, créés par voie législative; ils ne se sont pas développés à partir des systèmes judiciaires indigènes précoloniaux. A des époques différentes, de nouveaux tribunaux locaux ont été créés pour en remplacer d'autres, avec des changements tels que l'expérience les rendaient nécessaires dans chaque société.

2. Il y a un élément commun à tous les tribunaux locaux: le droit qu'ils administrent est principalement le droit coutumier et ils ont le droit d'administrer n'importe quel autre droit auquel les parties en cause sont soumises dans un procès personnel. De nouveau, c'est un trait commun à tous les tribunaux locaux

soumis à la législation que la procédure doit être en accord avec le droit coutumier.

3. Lorsque le droit indigène et le droit introduit deviennent progressivement un, de manière à constituer un seul système de droit dans l'état, le développement futur du droit coutumier s'appuie sur les tribunaux supérieurs présidés par des juristes professionnels possédant beaucoup d'expérience et non plus par le tribunal local présidé par des hommes bons et justes mais qui ne possèdent pas nécessairement une connaissance spéciale du droit coutumier. Désormais, le devoir principal d'un tribunal local sera de faire des recherches sur des questions de fait; en conséquence, il est important que la procédure dans les tribunaux locaux continue à être souple dans l'usage coutumier de manière à permettre aux magistrats qui président de se former plus facilement une opinion sur la véracité des témoignages et de découvrir, sans trop de spéculations, la vérité.

4. Il y a deux procédés coutumiers extra-judiciaires distincts pour trancher les débats qui sont:

(i) l'arbitrage
(ii) les pourparlers en vue d'atteindre ou de promouvoir la réconciliation.

Ces deux procédés sont indigènes et sont employés pour trancher des débats entre membres de la même famille ou de la même organisation sociale (e.g. *asafo* ou groupe militaire, groupe religieux) ou même entre étrangers habitants la même localité (e.g. étrangers possédant des terrains contigus).

5. Les deux procédés, l'arbitrage et la réconciliation méritent d'être maintenus à cause des avantages spéciaux que chacun possède sur les démarches judiciaires formelles; chacun d'eux est plus simple, plus facile et plus prompt et évite l'acrimonie et l'animosité personnelles qui accompagnent habituellement les démarches judiciaires formelles; ces procédés par conséquent favorisent le bon voisinage.

6. Pour encourager l'emploi continu de ces procédés, dans l'avenir, spécialement dans les simples débats civils et dans les affaires criminelles telles que les blessures simples, les dispositions de la loi sur les tribunaux du Ghana et ees ordonnances créant les tribunaux d'autres états africains en vue de la pro-

motion de la réconciliation devraient être appliqués fréquemment par les tribunaux du pays.

7. Pour rencontrer les développements sociaux modernes, la soumission par les personnes de leurs litiges à l'un ou l'autre de ces procédés, devrait être mise par écrit de même que les décisions rendues; et en plus du procédé coutumier, il devrait y avoir un procédé de rechange pour renforcer la décision. Ce procédé pourrait être établi par un acte législatif; à cette exception près, on ne désire absolument pas une intervention législative qui soit en conflit avec le caractère traditionnel des institutions extra-judiciaires.

III. Whither Lay Justice in Africa?

S. S. RICHARDSON

The proceedings of the African Conference on Local Courts and Customary law held in Dar es Salaam in 1963 must be the first symposium on the subject reflecting the unfettered opinions of African jurists representing independent states. Both anglophone and francophone countries were represented and delegations were composed of distinguished judges, professional lawyers from the judicial and legal departments of the various governments, with some political leadership and, significantly enough, one or two administrators from those territories which had not achieved full independence from the Colonial power. Earlier conferences of this type have been dominated by the expatriate administrators who formerly exercised responsibility for the customary courts as part and parcel of the colonial system of provincial administration. Such professional intervention as was made by the bench and bar was concerned to state the customary law as a tolerated appendix to the received law of metropolitan origin acceptable only when suitably hedged about with repugnancy clauses and other devices to avoid conflict.

The high-water mark of this thinking was the Conference on the Future of the Law in Africa held in London in 1960 which forecast a spread of law in the English form in all fields except for the personal law throughout the English-speaking territories. Such was the capacity of such a body to rationalize from its own experience! In the former British territories at least there is already evidence that African scholars are intent upon research into the customary law of their countries and African judges and law officers are concerned to adapt the received law and to incorporate the indigenous law and custom into national systems of law with a decided African character. Inevitably the customary courts' system is being put on test by the professionals if only because of its lineage as an integral part of the British colonial system and because of its connections with tribalism, the chiefs, and traditional forms of government. The true issues are usually clouded by legislation prohibiting the professional representation of parties before local tribunals and a reluctance on the part of professionally qualified lawyers to accept appointment to a customary court bench.

Almost all cases involving the family law of Africans still depend upon the customary law and even the most sophisticated African lawyer linked professionally with his Inn of Court in London hesitates to marry or to die under English law or under a local statute based upon its principles. Similar considerations apply, although perhaps with less force, in the law of land tenure. While reform of the customary land law might well prove to be the concomitant of economic and social development in many African countries it is unlikely that the problem will be resolved by substituting a system of land tenure imported from a metropolitan country. The learned assembly in Dar es Salaam was broadly in agreement that the family law and the law of land tenure will continue to be governed or at least heavily influenced by the customary law. This conclusion is the more remarkable in that most of those participating in it were young professionals who as a class have been highly critical of the customary law and its administration. Face to face with the realities of power they now appear to be reconciled to the retention and development of the customary law as an essential African content of their legal systems except where it has never provided a substitute for the received law or in those fields, such as the criminal law, where its application was capricious and unacceptable for constitutional or other reasons in a modern state.

Discussion has been inconclusive as to whether an attempt should be made to integrate the customary law with the general law of the land or whether it should continue to be administered as a separate entity. Integration would necessarily mean its restatement and, ideally, a move towards achieving uniformity within the territory if the professional bar was to be able to work with it effectively as part of a national system. But, as had been earlier recognized at the London conference of 1960, diversity in the family law appears to be the politically acceptable norm in Africa and the interests of the state might be better served by not attempting to achieve uniformity in those fields where interference with the tenets of religion or with tribal and other local and ethnic affiliations might disrupt national unity. Conditions will clearly vary from country to country. Where substantial diversity prevails the capacity of the general practitioner to intervene effectively in the proceedings at first instance is obviously reduced. The substantive law and custom to be applied may be subject to variation from village to village and sometimes from family to family within the community. Where the law is regulated by the religion of the parties different customs may be applicable to individuals within the family group itself. A further complication is that it is frequently necessary to apply a procedure peculiar to the particular customary system if the court is to arrive at a full and acceptable decision. It is for this reason that some African countries have found it difficult to prescribe a standard civil procedure for use in the customary courts. While civil causes and matters arising on appeal from these courts are dealt with satisfactorily by the High Courts under a statutory procedure, considerable latitude in interpreting the procedure at first instance is usually admissible in a High Court subject to the operation of the repugnancy clauses. The intervention of the professional is practicable at this stage because the procedural framework and *modus operandi* of the High Court are designed to accommodate his method of pleading while evidence of the procedure adopted by the lower court is readily admitted if it is in issue. Circumstances in Northern Nigeria have imposed limitations even upon this formula since the *Shari'a* Court of Appeal exercises final jurisdiction in all cases involving Muslim personal law arising from the native courts and applies *Maliki* law subjectively and adjectively to the complete exclusion of legal representation by the professional bar. The decision to integrate the customary law with the general system or to maintain a separate and parallel system of customary courts is possibly therefore crucial in deciding the future of lay justice in any particular African legal system. Widespread concern is unquestionably being voiced by the new élites because legal representation of parties is not generally permissible in the customary courts and this feature of the system is frequently declared to be an abnegation of the fundamental human rights of citizens. The competence of laymen often illiterate and open to corruption to interpret and administer the customary law in the village courts in Africa is also generally challenged by the intelligentsia. It is therefore relevant to re-examine carefully the case upheld in Dar es Salaam for maintaining lay justice at least for the purpose of administering the native law and custom wherever it is the proper law of the cause.

At the Dar es Salaam conference the topic of legal representation of parties in customary courts produced a sharp conflict of opinion, but there was unanimous acceptance of a proposition that the ultimate objective of all African legal systems ought to be a fully professionalized magistracy. There may well be some argument about what some delegations considered to be the meaning of professionalism in this context. In Northern Nigeria, for instance, the special position of Islamic law would suggest that by the professional might be meant the properly qualified *Qadi*. The 'Magistracy' is also an institution open to various interpretations in various African countries. Where the jurisdiction of the magistrate is confined to criminal matters, there is no difficulty in the proposition. Where, however, the jurisdiction of the magistrate embraces all civil matters including jurisdiction over the family law, the proposition must presume the ultimate disappearance of customary courts altogether. Once the professionals had obtained acceptance of the proposition that the customary court and lay justice should ultimately disappear from the legal systems of Africa, the conference was able to state a defensive apologia in support of excluding professional legal representation of parties from the customary courts for the present. The requirements of an emotional commitment to abolition and the demands of reason for retention were thus reconciled. Qualification to the effect that the professional replacement of the lay justices would take a long time, also permitted the conference to advocate large-scale training programmes calculated to improve the staff of the customary courts and thus to allay criticism of their competence to an extent which might tend to prolong and even perpetuate their usefulness. A discussion on the subject of the appointment and dismissal of the staff of the customary courts produced the alternatives of vesting these powers in the Minister of Justice or in a Judicial Service

Commission or Chief Justice. Then, surprisingly, in view of the earlier conclusion on the establishment of a magisterial system the Conference decided that the ultimate objective should be to integrate the customary courts as an integral factor in an independent judiciary. Advocacy of advanced training programmes and a policy of integration suggest that some at least of the members of the conference contemplated a role for the customary court within the system indefinitely. This view may be more realistic than to accept a complete surrender to the takeover bid proposed by the professionals. It also harmonizes with the doubts of the common man about the efficacy of a purely professional system and the necessity for professional representation at all levels. While there is no dispute about the role of the Bench and bar in the upholding of human rights and the defence of persons accused of criminal offences, there is a detectable queasiness in the minds of most laymen whether in Africa or, for that matter, in England and the United States, over the capacity of the professional to clock up fees and spin out the issues in civil matters concerning the family law. In the less sophisticated areas this distrust can become intense as, for instance, in Hausaland where the saying *An yi mana lauya* is synonymous with a statement that the person has been cheated. Sharks and lawyers have been linked together metaphorically in many cultures and in many ages often in jest but always with the approbation of the public at large. The continued acceptability of the lay justice in England no doubt owes something to this attitude and to the acceptability of the judgment of one's peers in language and terms which are commonly understood—for an 'equitable' human approach rather than for a cold-blooded professional opinion. Here, too, lies the kernel of the fears of those who do not wish to see the passing of lay justice in Africa and who advocate a policy of achieving a marriage between the profession and the laymen in the lower courts as a happier solution to the problem.

It is interesting to note the criticisms directed with growing virulence at the lay magistracy in England. The lack of training, the inevitable variations in court procedure, the number of ineffective short-term imprisonments, the widely different sentences for similar offences, and occasionally allegations of political prejudice—all these matters are as much points of attack upon the system in England as in any newly independent country in Africa concerned with the future of the lay justice. Nevertheless the English system is cheap, and generally acceptable and is not open to the criticism that the employment of a stipendiary puts the liberty of the subject in the hands of one man without the countervailing power of a jury or a bench of 'sturdy local men whose sagacity is uncomplicated by any knowledge of the law of the professional'. Lord Gardiner is reported to be considering a compromise whereby the stipendiary magistrate will always be flanked by two laymen, thereby ensuring that the remoteness of the professional will always be tempered by lay knowledge and the amateur approach of the layman will always be balanced by the professional's specialized training.

The immediate difficulties facing the Lord Chancellor if he embarks upon such a policy also sound a familiar note to those acquainted with the problems of improving standards in the customary courts of Africa. Who will pay the cost and where will he find enough professional lawyers to act as stipendaries? Is there a case for such a middle-of-the-road approach in Africa which can satisfy at the same time the profession's legitimate desire to further the efficient administration of justice and the wish of the public for a cheap and popular forum for the settlement of their disputes?[1]

Professionalization of the customary courts or their substitution by professional magistrates must be ruled out as impossible of attainment in most of the African states within the foreseeable future. In Nigeria, for instance, the African bar is more strongly developed as a profession than anywhere else on the continent with almost a thousand barristers in practice or at work within the judicial and legal system. Yet it is estimated that over 90 per cent of the judicial work at first instance is handled by over 1,500 customary courts in the four Regions. This volume of work includes almost all causes and matters in the field of family law and land affecting Nigerians. Furthermore, although Western Nigeria has undertaken a significant experiment in professionalizing the customary

---

[1] The *Sunday Times*, London, 21 November 1965, p. 9. In Britain lay magistrates hear 97.5 per cent of the criminal indictments at first instance and approximately one in forty of the people in the country appear before them each year.

courts in recent years there is no evidence of any strong pressures from the bar to take up employment in the customary courts, since practice in the magistrates courts and the High Court or enlistment in the Regional or Federal Civil Service or political employment is generally regarded as being more prestigious.

While there may be underemployment there is no unemployment in the profession which might lead to enhancement in the attraction of work in the customary courts. Indeed, in Northern Nigeria, the Government does not appear to be attempting to induce members of the bar to work with the customary courts as a matter of policy but rather is relying upon parallel training programmes to produce large numbers of trained staff, especially for service in these courts on a semi-professional basis. Nor in Nigeria can material economies in the numbers of the courts be expected if full professionalization was achieved, since in the Northern Region there is still only one native court for an average of 29,000 inhabitants. In 1958, on the 1951 census figures there was one customary court to 13,590 with a declared policy of introducing professionals in Western Nigeria, while in Eastern Nigeria there was one customary court for 24,460.[1] These ratios must be materially worsened in all these Regions (the Mid-West now being excised from the former Western Region) by the 1963 census figures. Any substantial reduction in the number of courts would apparently reduce the judicial system's capacity to serve the community. Arrears would pile up and much work which now flows into the customary courts in the field of family law would presumably never be brought to court at all. If the policy was to instal a professional in each of the customary courts or in substitute for each court, then the Nigerian bar would need to be trebled to achieve this objective. If policy was further to make legal representation available in all these courts it might be realistic to expect a ninefold increase in the Nigerian bar. Optimistically the throughput of the Nigerian Universities might be contemplating four hundred law graduates a year. At present it is barely one hundred. In fact, unless the status of employment open to law graduates remains competitive with that of the other professions, the number of

[1] Keay and Richardson, 1966.

students entering law schools will not increase sharply. Further problems posed by language barriers, regional and tribal interests, the localized and highly specialized nature of the customary law or considerations of religion (particularly where Islamic law is concerned) would also mean that a high proportion of the profession would be unsuitable for employment in the customary courts system on grounds distinct from those of professional capacity. It is significant that where a degree of professionalization has been attempted in the Western Region, the population subjected to the experiment has been relatively homogeneous and the customary law for the most part uniform. Acceptance of custom as the basis of the family law in Nigeria necessarily commits governments to diversity of procedure and practice and a degree of localization of the staff and consequent immobility which would surely be irksome and restrictive to professional recruits to the judicial service. But such a complex of diverse systems of law means that governments must ensure that the manner of the staffing of the courts is accepted by those to whom the courts are administering, whether the system be based upon customary courts or upon a more formalized magisterial system.

It may be that a fairer picture of the magnitude of the problem in most of the former British territories in Africa is obtained by considering the logistics of professionalizing the customary courts in Northern Nigeria if the Government of Northern Nigeria would ever be induced to contemplate such a policy as acceptable or desirable. The present numerical strength of the Northern Nigeria bar is about fifty; practically all are absorbed in the Magistracy or the Attorney-General's chambers and there are vacancies to be filled in both departments. In 1965, 775 native courts were listed as established within the Native Authority estimates.[1] In addition there were thirteen Provincial Courts and a number of Area Courts established by the Ministry of Justice as native courts under the Native Courts Law. Some eight hundred professional lawyers would therefore be required to provide a professional for each court and possibly another eight hundred to provide reasonable opportunities of legal representation in such a large and diverse country.

[1] *Northern Nigeria Local Government Handbook, 1965*, pp. 76–77.

The total cost of judicial services provided by the Native Authorities in 1965 was £478,986 which was offset by revenue from the courts of £600,030.[1] The cost of salaries and allowances, etc., of eight hundred graduate employees at prevailing rates would be about £1,600,000 per annum and this cost would not include charges for capital works, assessors, registrars, clerical staff, and security which form a large part of the Native Authority figures and which would still be required. It might be accepted that the number of customary courts could be considerably reduced but it would be fallacious to assume that substantial savings of staff and time can be made by such rationalization. Would all this extra expense and reorganization be justified if the trained staff and the money could be found? The virtues of the present system are surely accessibility and the low costs of litigation at first instance. Throughout Nigeria, except for appeals to the *Shari'a* Court of Appeal in cases concerning the personal law of Muslims, legal representation is permissible on an appeal to the High Court which is of right from all decisions of the native or customary courts. No Nigerian has to travel far to find a customary court with jurisdiction over almost any cause or matter and especially for the disposal of family matters. The family law is administered by the customary courts to the evident satisfaction of almost all Nigerians at a speed and cost quite foreign to the professional courts. It is also apparent that where discontent with the system is developing, it is directed against the criminal jurisdiction of the customary courts and the problem might, therefore, be subject to a solution of divesting the courts of all or part of their powers in criminal cases without proceeding to the more radical and controversial issue of professionalizing the whole operation.

Despite these facts which are conclusive in excluding professionalization as an immediate solution to the problem, political pressures will continue to build up within the system if concessions are not made to the demand of the professionals for right of audience and for improvement of standards. A policy of *laisser faire* risks an explosion in the future which could sweep away the system with popular support and substitute in its place a system of professional justice with all the demerits

---

[1] Extracted from *Native Authority Estimates, Northern Nigeria 1965/66*.

from the public point of view which are observable in many societies so afflicted. Part-time training of laymen and increased professional supervision are valuable temporary palliatives to remedy the worst abuses. What is happening in the United Kingdom may, however, point the way to a longer-term solution. Earlier attempts at reform in England centred upon the introduction of the professional clerk to the justices and no doubt the system fails at times because the lay magistrates will simply not be guided by their clerk in making their judgments. Status problems within the profession and the attitudes of traditional office-holders would in any case exclude the possibility of experimenting with this approach in Africa. We are faced, therefore, with a requirement to examine the possibility of introducing professional presidents into the customary courts system as fast as the growth of the profession, public opinion, and the political leadership will permit. Progress in this direction will necessarily everywhere be slow and in many countries extremely cautious.

Precisely such an experiment is in motion in Western Nigeria with some measure of success but conditions there are particularly favourable. A large proportion of the Nigerian bar is of Western Nigerian origin. The customary law administered in family matters is relatively uniform and certain. The customary courts have adopted English type procedures and practice through the application of statutory and mandatory rules of court. Finally, the legal profession enjoys public respect and private practice is widely established in the Region. The wealth of experience behind the experiment is illustrated by the directive issued by the Minister of Justice to the Local Government Service Board responsible for making appointments to the customary courts. Persons with legal qualifications to be appointed as Presidents of the Grade A courts must have at least seven years post-call experience and of the Grade B courts five years experience. These requirements reflect exactly those prescribed by the Public Service Commission for the appointment of Senior Magistrates and Magistrates. Taking into account the numerical strength of the bar and the possibilities of its augmentation through the educational establishments, there can be few other countries in Africa where such standards could be set within the near future. Indeed, it is probably true to say that the high tide has been reached even in Western Nigeria. Fewer Western Nigerians are now likely to be admitted each year to the bar. Independence has opened up wider fields of employment and the Nigerian Universities are offering a variety of attractive courses leading to careers in less crowded professions.

The appointment of professional presidents in the customary courts voids all the classical arguments for the exclusion of professional legal representation. What evidence is available would suggest that in Western Nigeria the experiment is heading for success and that where professionals have been appointed the sting has gone from the political attack upon the customary courts system. The effect upon the development of Yoruba customary law remains to be seen. Will the essentially 'English' background of the profession so modify the custom that its application by the courts will no longer be the native law and custom as handed down by the traditional elders? The functions of the members of the courts are presumed to be those of interpreting the customary law to the professional president and of actively participating in the judgment. Will those members find it possible to discharge their functions and maintain the purity of the custom when the direction of the proceedings and the advocacy of the parties are essentially controlled by professionals educated in a foreign legal tradition? The probabilities must surely point to the repetition of the fate of Islamic law in India under the magisterial system established by the British. A highly respectable body of Anglo-Muhammadan law replaced the *Shari'a* throughout the former Indian Empire and attempts by the Pakistan Government and Law Commission to reinstate Islamic law are encountering formidable opposition.

Whenever Islamic law enters into the argument, as it frequently must in Africa, the Western Nigerian solution is unlikely to satisfy public opinion. The *Qadis* are essentially professionals in their own right usually intensively schooled and accustomed to sitting as sole judges in the cases brought to their courts. Western-trained professionals do not understand the procedure of the *Shari'a* Courts or the substance of the law administered therein. Predominantly Muslim populations will not accept readily the adulteration of their personal law and religion by the introduction into their courts of alien procedures. Appointment of a Western-trained lawyer as the President of a *Shari'a* Court or representation before such a court by members of the bar would be utterly incongruous in present circumstances. The admission of *Wakils* or legal practitioners specifically trained in the *Shari'a* and its application is, however, feasible, and has been achieved in the Sudan and a number of the African countries. The curriculum of the University Law Schools will have to undergo considerable change before the product would be considered as a possible substitute for the *Qadi*. Indeed, he would have to be a *Qadi* in his own right to be appointed to such a position and his other qualifications would be purely ancillary.

The misgivings of the intelligentsia and the profession may well have been allayed in respect of the customary courts in Western Nigeria, but time is needed to determine whether litigants are in fact better served by these new arrangements. If the cost of litigation rises sharply and the customary law becomes adulterated in the process there may well be a sharp reaction against professionalization. Fortunately, most of the rest of Africa must perforce wait in the wings as interested observers of the Western Nigeria experiment and can benefit from the experience gained there.

As the Dar es Salaam conference concluded, lay justice in Africa has by and large been reprieved for the present. It still remains to be seen whether improved training techniques, accurate restatement of the customary law, and the achievement of higher standards of probity can establish a case for the continuation of the customary court under lay control as a cheap and accessible system of justice subject to the supervision of the professional in the higher courts.

BIBLIOGRAPHY

African Conference on Local Courts and Customary Law—Record of Proceedings, 1963. Dar es Salaam.
Allott, A. N. (ed.)
   (1960) *Record of Proceedings of the Conference on the Future of Law in Africa.* London: Butterworth.
Native Authority Estimates, Northern Nigeria, 1965/66. Kaduna: Government Printer.
Northern Nigeria Local Government Handbook, 1965. Zaria: Gaskiya Corporation.

Keay, E. A. and Richardson, S. S.
(1966) *The Native and Customary Courts of Nigeria*. London: Sweet and Maxwell.
Statement by the Government of Northern Region of Nigeria on the Reorganization of the Legal and Government Systems of the Northern Region, 1958. Kaduna: Government Printer.
Statement by the Government of Northern Nigeria on further reforms of the Legal and Judical Systems of Northern Nigeria, 1962. Kaduna: Government Printer.

Résumé

L'AVENIR DE LA JUSTICE RENDUE PAR DES NON-JURISTES EN AFRIQUE

La contribution se propose de démontrer comment, dès l'indépendance, les administrateurs africains et les érudits ont mis en question le statut qu'ont accordé les régimes coloniaux aux tribunaux de droit coutumier. Le droit coutumier régit en effet encore une très grande partie du droit familial et du droit foncier, et même les juristes professionnels acceptent que cette situation continue. Par contre, on se rend compte que, vraisemblablement, le droit criminel sera modifié. En outre, des problèmes se sont présentés relativement à l'intégration ou au maintien de la diversité du droit familial. Plus grande est la diversité, moins il sera facile pour les avocats de profession d'agir dans ces domaines sauf dans les cours de cassation, et il y en a beaucoup parmi eux qui doutent de l'exactitude de ce fait.

L'auteur constate que pendant le cours d'une conférence à Dar es Salaam, en 1963, on a envisagé qu'un jour, la magistrature aurait un caractère entièrement professionnel; néanmoins, il est probable que des juges non-professionnels siégeront encore longtemps et qu'ils feront un jour partie intégrante de la magistrature. Il soutient que, dans un proche avenir, il ne sera pas possible de remplacer les magistrats non-professionnels par des magistrats de profession puisqu'il n'y a pas assez de juristes formés; en outre, ceux-ci ne montrent aucune envie de pratiquer dans les tribunaux de droit coutumier. Il existe des programmes spéciaux pour former des professionnels à ce genre de métier dans plusieurs pays. Mais la distribution des populations et les grandes distances exigent un grand nombre de tribunaux locaux, si on veut convenablement desservir la communauté. Les grandes différences de religion et de coutume entraînent aussi de grandes difficultés au point de vue de la formation rapide des cadres.

Enfin, donner au métier un caractère intégralement professionnel coûterait fort cher. Il se peut que la solution soit de nommer seulement des présidents de profession dans les tribunaux de droit coutumier. Des problèmes particuliers se posent aussi relativement aux tribunaux musulmans. L'expérience nigérienne suggère que le plus grand espoir pour l'avenir se trouve dans une amélioration des tribunaux de droit coutumier.

IV. Procedural Informality, Reconciliation, and False Comparisons

J. VAN VELSEN

I INTRODUCTION

Despite the large body of literature on African substantive law by professional and amateur anthropologists and by persons with legal training, there has been very little study of the actual operation of legal rules.[1] Epstein suggests that this is because of the apparent simplicity and lack of formality of proceedings and concentration on such things as oath and ordeal.[2] Ethnocentric opinions are commonly expressed. Moreover, much of the information is collected by interviews and posing hypothetical disputes, while the study of law in action requires intensive observation guided by comparative analytical concepts. Further, courts have to be studied as part of the wider problem of social control and the solution of disputes. Finally, I consider that most writers—including those with legal training—have an imperfect understanding of their own legal system with which, explicitly or implicitly, they tend to compare African legal systems. In Britain particularly the study of legal systems is still dominated by legal technicians, and there little attention is given to the roles of courts and judges in social life. Hence comparisons of these African systems with those of Britain are based on stereotyped and idealized notions of the latter, and hence highlight dissimilarities between the two sets of systems. Indeed, this contrast has itself hardened into a stereotype. I shall argue that this is false comparison, in which dissimilar data are treated as if they were similar.

As has often been stated, African societies traditionally have relatively simple technologies which do not allow a man to

---

[1] There are notable exceptions, e.g. the works of Bohannan, Epstein, Gluckman, and Gulliver quoted below.
[2] 1954, p. 1.

produce much over his subsistence requirements. There is little specialization or economic differentiation. With notable exceptions such as Rwanda, there are therefore no classes or categories with critically opposed economic or political interests, and there is a great degree of homogeneity in cultural values. Most interaction takes place in small areas in permanent relationships serving a variety of purposes. Following Gluckman,[1] I will call these 'multiplex' relationships in contrast with 'simplex' (what he calls 'single-interest') relationships. Simplex relationships do also occur. Within a multiplex relationship, a disturbance in, say, the political relationship is likely to affect the economic and domestic relationships. Where multiplex relationships prevail, judges and litigants, and the litigants among themselves, interact in relationships whose significance ranges beyond the transitoriness of the court or a particular dispute. Today they are disputing in court, tomorrow they may be collaborating in the same work-party. Frequently judges combine their judicial with administrative duties. Gluckman has pointed out that among the Barotse the judges try to prevent the breaking of such relationships so that the parties can continue to live together amicably; and therefore the courts tend to be reconciliating in such disputes. To do this, they have to broaden their inquiries to cover the total history of the relations between the parties, and not only the narrow legal issue raised by one of them. Hence the conception of 'relevance' is wide, because many facts affect the settlement of a dispute in multiplex relationships, while the conception of 'relevance' is narrower in simplex relationships.[2]

This sketch applies to rural, tribal ('traditional') situations and not to conditions in urban, industrial areas. The comparison usually made is one between the tribal legal system and the so-called 'Western' (or 'our') legal system. Here when making my own comparison I shall deal only with the Anglo-American common-law systems. These operate in highly industrialized societies with a market economy involving considerable specialization, and economic and political differentiation. There are classes with divergent economic and political interests, and hence there is heterogeneity rather than homogeneity. Simplex relationships are common. There are

[1] 1955, p. 19. [2] Ibid., p. 21.

Informality, Reconciliation, and False Comparisons 139

legal specialists with esoteric, technical knowledge; and in many courts judges, litigants, police, witnesses, etc., are usually not involved outside of the court with one another. Ideally, the judiciary and the executive are separated.

Writers have used this often stated contrast to present African tribal societies, and Britain and America, as polar opposites instead of a continuum. Indeed, there are striking differences in the incidence of multiplex as against simplex relationships. But multiplex relationships and other features of tribal life are found in industrialized societies also. There are also more similarities in the field of law (e.g. procedure) than most writers allow for. This is obscured by almost exclusive concentration in the British and American systems on the superior courts, ignoring the courts at the bottom of the hierarchy where we find the magistrates' courts, the Small Claims Courts, and so forth. Even writers such as Cardozo, Pound, Epstein, Gluckman, and Bohannan, who have treated the subject with greater sociological insight than most, make this error. Superior courts may be more important from the point of view of legal doctrine, but it seems to be generally accepted that the subordinate courts are more important as forums of dispute-settlement since the bulk of litigation starts and ends there. Thus Lloyd points out that 'the exceptionally high status of the judiciary in England is far more easily maintained by reason of the very small number of the higher judiciary . . . This exceptional situation is rendered possible by the large amount of judicial business conducted in England by lay benches of magistrates or by special tribunals.'[1]

II FLEXIBILITY OF PROCEDURE

The following case which I recorded in a court of lay magistrates in Manchester in 1956 shows some striking procedural similarities with what has been recorded in African courts.[2]

---

[1] Lloyd, 1964; see also Duhamel and Smith, 1959, p. 137: 'The Justices of the Peace . . . have, since feudal times, formed the backbone of the administration of justice'; and also Giles, 1949, p. 9.

[2] This case was the first I ever heard in an English magistrates' court and through it I discovered the wider prospects of the law outside the law reports and textbooks. Unfortunately I had no opportunity to investigate the social background—outside the court—of this case.

The Sailor and his 'Wife'

The undisputed facts of the case were that Beecham, a coloured sailor, had been living in concubinage with Dorothy Mandy, a White woman, for seven years until 1955 when she went to live with Taylor whom she married not long before the trial. Taylor was a Coloured friend of Beecham's. The other participants in the trial were: the two lay magistrates—a man and a woman; the court clerk, trained in law; and the solicitor representing Mrs. Taylor.

The solicitor told the court that in February 1956, Beecham had on three occasions threatened Mandy (as she then still was) with violence if she did not return to him; she was living with Taylor at the time. On one of the occasions Beecham was alleged to have threatened Mr. Taylor also. Mrs. Taylor gave the same story from the witness box. Beecham was then told by the court that he could cross-examine Mrs. Taylor. Instead of questioning her on the evidence she had given, Beecham kept asking her questions which had no direct bearing on the matter of the threats. For instance, he asked her whether she did not remember that day when he lent her 10s. The woman's solicitor intervened to ask when that event took place. On being told that that was the previous year he objected that the court did not want to hear what had happened the previous year but only matters relating to the threats. This happened several times: Beecham making statements—often in the form of questions —which were meant to show his concern and friendship for Dorothy Mandy and the solicitor rejecting them as irrelevant. Before she stood down Mrs. Taylor said that her husband was in court and could give supporting evidence.

When it was clear that Beecham would not cross-examine Mrs. Taylor, he was told by the chairman of the magistrates that he could give his own statement, either from the floor or under oath from the witness box. He opted for the former. From the way he reacted to the chairman's announcement I got the impression that Beecham's decision was not the result of a calculation of the relative tactical advantages. Rather, he seemed to consider it of minor importance where he gave his evidence from: he had his story and he was going to give that, wherever he stood. In his evidence Beecham told the court that Mrs. Taylor had told a pack of lies. In order to support this allegation he told several stories to show that she was a confirmed liar. Again, he kept harking back to the more distant past and, again, he was repeatedly told by the clerk that he should stick to the point at issue, namely the threats. Otherwise Beecham's evidence was meant to show how friendly he had always felt towards Mrs. Taylor (the loan of 10s. was but one of the background stories

Informality, Reconciliation, and False Comparisons 141

to prove this). Another part of his evidence was intended to show that he had never had any desire for violent revenge after she had left him for Mr. Taylor: 'If I had wanted to beat her why should I not have done so before? Why should I have waited until February [1956], more than half-a-year after she left me?'

The solicitor got up and drew the bench's attention to the fact that Beecham's evidence contained several attacks on the character of Mrs. Taylor and he, therefore, wondered whether he might be allowed to cross-examine Beecham even though he had not given his evidence on oath. The court clerk, answering for the court, pointed out that the bench was bound to give greater weight to the woman's evidence on oath and could ignore Beecham's evidence. The chairman did not allow the solicitor to cross-examine Beecham. The chairman next asked whether the complainant wanted to call Mr. Taylor as a witness. The solicitor answered that he did not intend to call him as he was not present on the occasions of the threats which were the subject of the trial; he, the solicitor, was not concerned with any threats uttered to Mr. Taylor, which was the only matter on which Mr. Taylor could give evidence.

The chairman then bent down to the clerk and asked him what sort of penalty the alleged offence carried. After receiving the clerk's answer he conferred in a whisper with the other magistrate and said that it was a question of one's word against the other's. They both agreed that they had their doubts regarding the veracity of the woman's story because the solicitor did not want to call Mr. Taylor. (I had been allowed to sit with the magistrates and could therefore hear their whispered conversation. I also discussed some points of the trial with them afterwards.) Prefacing the bench's decision the chairman remarked that they found it difficult to get down to the truth since the two stories were so conflicting and that if Beecham had threatened the woman as alleged—he did not want to say that he had—he would have committed a serious offence. He dismissed the case.

The first point to be noted in this case is the contrast between what one might call the 'common-sense justice' approach of the lay people (viz. the magistrates and the litigants) and the more technical, legal approach of the lawyers (viz. the court clerk and the solicitor). The magistrates ignored the lawyers' opinion regarding the greater weight of the woman's sworn evidence against Beecham's unsworn story. They also overruled the lawyers' technical objection to the 'irrelevancies' in Beecham's evidence, namely his desire to give the history of the dispute. In a discussion afterwards one of the magistrates told me that she thought that Beecham 'ought to be given a chance to tell some of the background facts because he obviously considered that a part of the dispute' and she added that legal chiché: 'Justice must not only . . . etc.' Thus the lay actors in this court saw the dispute in terms of a conflict in a personal relationship whereas the lawyers treated it rather as a breach of a legal rule. That the attitude of the bench in this case was not exceptional is clear from the following summary of magistrates' court procedure: '. . . magistrates normally show the greatest reluctance to cut short anyone concerned with the proceedings who desires to speak, however irrelevant or tedious his remarks . . . The result is that the court must struggle to do the work normally performed in other courts by solicitors, namely to listen to the whole story as it is poured out, to ignore what is irrelevant, and then to analyse the legal issues involved, and marshall the evidence. In order to cope with the usual volume of work in these circumstances, the procedure is less formal than in other courts . . . the magistrate attempts to reach a solution which acknowledges plain facts and meets the real problem causing the trouble.'[1]

To me the course of the Beecham–Taylor trial was most revealing: it was very reminiscent of what I had observed in African courts. It also seemed to contradict the current, oversimplified contrasts between African and 'our' procedures. To mention but one example, Hammond-Tooke[2] contrasts the informality and apparent nonchalance of Bhaca court procedure, its tolerance of irrelevant evidence and its preoccupation with 'restitution and a restoration of the social equilibrium' on the one hand and 'our own preoccupation with the niceties of legal procedure' on the other. This assumption might be

[1] Archer, 1956, pp. 109–10. See also Giles, 1949, p. 9, who writes about divorce cases: '. . . more often than not the parties come straight into [a magistrates'] court from the street. Their evidence has to be extracted there and then, whereas for the Divorce Court Judges it is carefully sifted in advance by solicitors who specialize in the work and is presented by experienced barristers.' And he says too of the magistrates' courts (p. 31): 'The common tendency is for the Clerk because of his constant preoccupation with legal forms and procedure to be too regardful of the letter of the law, and for magistrates impatient of restraints they do not understand to ride rough-shod over them in fulfilling what they consider to be the spirit of the law.'
[2] 1962, pp. 215–16.

true if all 'our' courts were superior courts. But the case described above and the quotations from Archer and Giles make it clear that the contrast is much less sharp when we compare African courts with inferior courts. This is as true in America as in Britain. For instance, Ploscowe[1] describes the inferior criminal courts of America as courts of 'grievances' which attempt 'to do substantial justice, without too much regard for the niceties of civil and criminal jurisdiction . . . and a sort of court of equity. It is the nearest approach to justice in the market-place of Oriental tradition.' As in the case of the English magistrates' courts, these inferior criminal courts, as the author points out, 'are the most important tribunals in the land, because they influence for better or for worse far more lives than any other court'.[2] Myers[3] writing on small claims courts in the District of Columbia, U.S.A., stresses their conciliatory aspects (see below) and their flexible procedure.[4]

III RECONCILIATION

Reconciliation is another feature which is supposed to characterize African court procedure in contrast to European procedure. Elias[5] and Gluckman[6] have pointed out that it would be wrong to make this contrast too sharp by assuming that a similar aim is not found in European law even if only in a semi-judicial form. Unfortunately, both authors, again, limit their comparison to superior courts, ignoring the expressly conciliatory functions of many inferior courts. For instance, in small claims courts in the District of Columbia, U.S.A., 'the trial judge, prior to trial, is required by statute to make an earnest effort to settle the controversy by conciliation'.[7]

This answers the question whether reconciliation is a feature

---

[1] 1953, p. 10. [2] Ibid., p. 12. [3] 1953, pp. 23–24.
[4] For similar conditions in German, Austrian, and Swiss courts, see Bedford, 1961, and also Feifer, 1964, on courts in Moscow. We noted earlier that Gluckman relates the Barotse judges' wide conception of evidence to the type of social relationships with which they deal. In a later work (1965b, p. 188) he writes that *a priori* one might expect that judges backed by powers of enforcement might be inclined to shorten the listening process in order to come to a decision more quickly—in other words, to narrow their conception of relevance. He adds that such an expectation could not be supported from his Barotse material. My foregoing data would not support such an expectation in relation to European courts either. [5] Elias, 1956, pp. 268 f.
[6] Gluckman, 1955, pp. 77–78. [7] Myers, 1953, p. 23.

of the European as well as the African judicial process. Another question is whether the aim and practice of reconciliation is as evident in the former as it is supposed to be in the latter. The following quotations are a necessarily limited selection from a large body of literature which stresses the great significance or even dominance of reconciliation in African judicial procedure. Lambert[1] writes with reference to the Kiambu District in Kenya: 'The judicial system of the European culture involves justice by decree and the granting of exclusive rights to an individual; the African system involves justice by agreement and the maintenance of social equilibrium.' Holleman similarly sees a sharp contrast and states that, both in the past and at the time of his writing, the Shona chiefs of Rhodesia 'would settle rather than decide, appease and reconcile rather than enforce'.[2] Bohannan, too, stresses that 'to determine a *modus vivendi*', to effect a mutually acceptable settlement between the litigants, is the aim of a Tiv court, but not 'to apply laws'.[3]

I share the views of Epstein[4] and Gluckman[5] that although reconciliation is an important value, it is not an 'ultimate, almost mystical, value' of African courts to which legal norms are sacrificed. However, the majority of writers on this topic would appear to start from the assumption that 'judgment by agreement' and 'judgment by decree' are mutually exclusive alternatives. And by concentrating on the conciliatory aspects of African courts, they tend to ignore the judges' task of applying laws. I suggest that this one-sided approach is related to the fact that the literature in this field generally pays inadequate attention to the different stages of the judicial process and thus fails to note at which stage it becomes possible or, indeed, imperative, to effect reconciliation. In general, writers identify reconciliation with the court's decision; they fail to distinguish in this respect between the *two* decisions any court anywhere must make, namely a decision as to the relevant facts and the appropriate legal rules to be applied (this is the judgment or verdict), and the decision as to the appropriate sanction for the judgment (this is the award or sentence).[6] For instance, I

[1] Quoted in Phillips, 1945, p. 65.
[2] 1950, pp. 53–54.
[3] 1957, pp. 19, 61–65, *et passim*.
[4] 1954, p. 2.
[5] 1955, p. 55.
[6] Epstein and Gluckman who, as quoted above, reject the mysticism of reconciliation and stress the necessity for a judicial decision, could have driven their

Informality, Reconciliation, and False Comparisons 145

quoted earlier Holleman saying of the Shona chiefs that they 'would settle rather than decide'. One is inclined to ask: decide *what?*—points of law or award? In addition, he expresses his view that instances of a Shona chief who 'summarily disposes a lot of cases per session by concise interpretation of the relevant points of law and snappy judgements' are likely to be 'innovations rather than renovations of Shona procedure'.[1] I doubt the validity of this view; I am sure that such an interpretation does take place and is bound to take place or otherwise there would be no *court* or *law*. In any case, 'snappy judgements' and 'concise interpretation' are not necessarily concomitants, nor does 'concise interpretation' necessarily exclude reconciliation, as is clear from the author's brief summary of Shona procedure later on. There it also becomes clear that the 'discussions and bargaining' over the amount of the compensation ('reconciliation'?) comes *after* one of the parties has been 'convinced that he has been wrong and that he must acknowledge his guilt and responsibility', in other words, after 'the relevant points of law' have been settled. Bohannan,[2] too, does not distinguish between a court's judgment and its subsequent sanctions. However, his case records plainly show that the courts do apply legal rules even in the face of strong protests from one of the parties (e.g. his cases 8 and 9), and that the Tiv courts' aim of a mutually acceptable settlement between the litigants refers to the courts sanctions rather than to their judgments. Thus in case 9 argument centred on the amount of the compensation to be paid by the accused. The owner of the stolen property was dissatisfied with the amount suggested by the court and 'shouted that the case was being decided "by force": that is, sufficient consideration had not been given to arriving at a settlement in which both parties could concur'. The facts of the case were not in question and it would appear that, apart from the accused himself, the general consensus among the members of the court and the public was that the accused's action approximated to theft. Similarly, Allott[3] relates a court's attempt 'to win the agreement of both sides' to the court's 'decision' in general.

---
points home more effectively if they had made the distinction between the two types of decision clear.
[1] Holleman, 1950, pp. 53–54.   [2] 1957.   [3] 1960, p. 68.

We should more clearly distinguish between the various stages of the African and any other judicial process. This would help to uncover the aims (and their realization) of the courts and also the role of the latter in social life. The first stage to be distinguished is the pre-trial stage. Courts are a means (only one of the means) of social control, aiming at preservation of peaceful co-existence of the members of a community despite divergent interests. This is not the truism it sounds—particularly with regard to the study of law and courts in Britain—if one considers that: 'In western (or at least English) legal procedure [which, one might add, is in some categories of courts largely in the hands of a highly specialized class of professional lawyers] litigation is often treated as a sort of game, with the judge as umpire holding the whistle, blowing when one party gets offside, and awarding the victory to the side which scores most goals.'[1]

In both African and European societies pressure tends to be applied to disputants to compromise over their disagreements and not to worsen and disrupt social relationships by going to court. This aspect has been studied in Africa, where there are useful accounts of moots by Beattie, Bohannan, Abrahams,[2] and others. These processes of pre-trial reconciliation have not been well studied in European systems, but it is known they are present (see, for instance, my quotations above from Gluckman and Elias, and from Myers). A specific example is in Emmett's description of a Welsh parish where 'informal methods such as friendly compromise, fear of public opinion, the need to co-operate and finally ostracism, keep most disputes between people out of court, and . . . make English justice only a final and extreme resort.'[3]

When a dispute does reach the court, it enters on a more formal stage of the judicial process viz. the judicial examination. Any court hears the litigants' stories, determines the legal points at issue, selects the appropriate legal rules and applies them to selected ('relevant') facts. Finally, the court must pronounce on the rights and the wrongs of the case, judging the acts of the litigants by the measure of certain legal norms. The court upholds the law in order to fulfil its task of regulating relationships. At this stage there is little room for reconciliation

[1] Allott, *loc. cit.*   [2] See bibliography.   [3] 1964, p. 89.

Informality, Reconciliation, and False Comparisons   147

because though legal rules may be bent (e.g. by interpretation) they cannot be ignored: the court is primarily concerned with interests lying beyond those of the litigants, i.e. the rights and interests of all persons who organize their lives on the assumption of the general and persistent validity of the rules which the court is called upon to defend. Reconciliation of the litigants may be attempted again at a later stage. Gluckman's statement that a Barotse court 'should not achieve a reconciliation without blaming those who have done wrong'[1] might be phrased as, 'no reconciliation without law', and would hold true for this stage of the judicial process in courts anywhere.

Pre-trial reconciliation may not be resorted to, or it may prove unsuccessful, for several reasons. Feeling may run too high, e.g. the particular dispute may be the culmination of a series of previous ones. Countervailing interests may be too weak to prevent recourse to court. Reconciliation may fail in multiplex relationships and is particularly likely to do so in simplex ones. Again, what may be at stake is not so much the redress for damages suffered, as a legal issue (or a non-legal issue in a legal guise) on which one of the parties (or both) requires a public pronouncement. I have argued elsewhere that the Tonga of Malawi, with their prevalence of multiplex relationships, may bring suits on interests which are capable of exact legal formulation (e.g. bride-wealth debts) to defend overlapping interests not so definable and not actionable in court (e.g. political claims).[2] The frequency of disputes which is such a striking feature of Tonga society, has often been noted in the literature and has usually been interpreted as a sign of social disintegration. Instead, it serves, like ritual and ceremonies elsewhere, to analyse and publicly reassert, personal relationships and rights. Thus, often the safeguarding of present and future interests is of prime importance and the sanctions demanded in the ostensible dispute secondary or even irrelevant. I was told of instances where those awarded damages refused them at home, or if already paid in court, returned them. Meek wrote in similar terms of the Ibo, where he said trials expressed public opinion and aired grievances, the litigant desiring public vindication rather than damages.[3]

[1] 1955, p. 22.   [2] van Velsen, 1964, pp. 125 f., 314–16, Case 18, *et passim*.
[3] 1937 (2nd edition, 1950), p. 342.

Since the (unstated) aim of litigation may be an authoritative and public statement of rights and wrongs, the desirability or possibility of effecting reconciliation out of court is not directly related to the incidence of multiplex relationships: just because two people are involved in multiplex relationships, a legal issue in one set of interests can be submitted to judgment in order to clarify non-legal issues in another set of interests; in these circumstances pre-trial reconciliation would defeat the purpose of the lawsuit. Analysis of reconciliation or its absence should, therefore, take into account not only the nature of the relationships between the litigants (and possibly the judge as well) but also the stated or unstated purpose of litigation.

After the judges have reinforced the legal norms another attempt may be made at reconciliation or other readjustments. This is the third stage in the judicial process, when the judges take their second decision, viz. what sanctions to attach to their first, legal, decision. While the first decision is the result of a process of logical reasoning, the decision on sanctions is less logical, more flexible, more overtly susceptible to considerations of expediency, more adaptable to non-legal desirabilities. Awards vary in similar cases in one court and between courts. There is greater scope for judges to express personal, non-legal feelings about the case or the litigants.

In England, judges often apply and defend the law during judicial examination, and then apply, at the third stage of the judicial process, only a token sanction, e.g. 1*d*. damages. Thus they express that on social, rather than legal, grounds, the case was a bad one without moral right, or that substantial damages would harm the litigants' relationship. Conversely, a severe sanction on a minor legal wrong expresses strong moral or political disapproval.

I have argued that in societies where multiplex relationships prevail (often referred to as 'small-scale' or 'face-to-face' societies), reconciliation is likely to be a conspicuous feature of the judicial process in order to prevent extensive damage to other activities of the disputants, and of persons closely associated with them. Where simplex relationships dominate, as, for instance, in the industrialized societies of Europe, reconciliation is less marked and few writers pay any attention to it. However, reconciliation may well be of greater significance than has generally been assumed. It has been said about the local administration of justice in Britain, that its 'whole essence . . . and the great value of the functions of justice are that they administer justice amongst people with whom they are acquainted and of whose lives and family history they know something'.[1]

On the other hand, one may not assume that in small-scale societies the pressure for reconciliation operates, or operates equally, in all courts. In societies with a hierarchy of courts reconciliation may be less important in the superior courts. In the first place, the very fact that a dispute has reached a superior court may be an indication that the parties want to 'fight it out' and are therefore less amenable to reconciliation. In the second place, the higher in the hierarchy the court, the less the judges are likely to be involved in the litigants' relationships and therefore the less likely they are to feel the pressure for reconciliation. Thus, Rattray writes of the Ashanti: 'The question of possible reconciliation of the parties—which . . . was such a marked feature of the lower unofficial tribunals—did not enter the province of the [higher] court.'[2]

To conclude, a comparative study of the incidence of reconciliation in the judicial process should go beyond the rather crude typology of multiplex small-scale societies and simplex industrialized societies; the differential incidence of reconciliation with regard to different types of court should also be investigated.

BIBLIOGRAPHY

Abrahams, R. G.
    (1965) 'Neighbourhood Organization: A Major Sub-System among the Northern Nyamwezi'. *Africa*, xxxv, 2, pp. 168–86.
Allott, A. N.
    (1960) *Essays in African Law*. London: Butterworth.
Archer, P.
    (1956) *The Queen's Courts*. Harmondsworth: Penguin Books.
Beattie, J. H. M.
    (1957) 'Informal Judicial Activity in Bunyoro'. *Journal of African Administration*, ix, 4, pp. 188–95.
Bedford, S.
    (1961) *The Faces of Justice*. London: Collins.
Bohannan, P. J.
    (1957) *Justice and Judgment among the Tiv*. London: Oxford University Press for the International African Institute.

[1] Quoted in Giles, 1949, p. 34.   1929, p. 388.

Duhamel, J. and Smith, J. D.
  (1959) *Some Pillars of English Law*. London: Pitman.
Elias, T. O.
  (1956) *The Nature of African Customary Law*. Manchester: Manchester University Press.
Emmett, I.
  (1964) *A North Wales Village*. London: Routledge and Kegan Paul.
Epstein, A. L.
  (1951) 'Some Aspects of the Conflict of Law and Urban Courts in Northern Rhodesia', *Rhodes–Livingstone Journal*, xii, pp. 28–40.
  (1954) *Juridical Techniques and the Judicial Process: A Study in African Customary Law*, Rhodes–Livingstone Paper No. 23.
Feifer, G.
  (1964) *Justice in Moscow*. London: The Bodley Head.
Giles, F. T.
  (1949) *The Magistrates' Courts*. Harmondsworth: Penguin Books.
Gluckman, M.
  (1955) *The Judicial Process among the Barotse of Northern Rhodesia*. Manchester: Manchester University Press for the Rhodes–Livingstone Institute (republished, expanded 1967).
  (1965a) *The Ideas in Barotse Jurisprudence*. New Haven and London: Yale University Press.
  (1965b) *Politics, Law and Ritual in Tribal Society*. Oxford: Blackwell.
Gulliver, P. H.
  (1963) *Social Control in an African Society*. London: Routledge and Kegan Paul.
Hammond-Tooke, W. D.
  (1962) *Bhaca Society*. Cape Town: Oxford University Press.
Holleman, J. F.
  (1950) 'An Anthropological Approach to Bantu Law (with special reference to Shona Law)', *Rhodes–Livingstone Journal*, x, pp. 51–64.
Lloyd, D.
  (1964) *The Idea of Law*. Harmondsworth: Penguin Books.
Meek, C. K.
  (1937) *Law and Authority in a Nigerian Tribe*. London: Oxford University Press (2nd edition, 1950).
Myers, F. H.
  (1953) 'The Small Claims Court in the District of Columbia', *The Annals of the American Academy of Political and Social Science*, vol. 287.
Phillips, A.
  (1945) *Report on Native Tribunals*. Nairobi: Government Printer.
Ploscowe, M.
  (1953) 'The Inferior Criminal Courts in Action', *The Annals of the American Academy of Political and Social Science*, vol. 287.
Rattray, R. S.
  (1929) *Ashanti Law and Constitution*. Oxford: Clarendon Press (republished 1956).
van Velsen, J.
  (1964) *The Politics of Kinship*. Manchester: Manchester University Press for the Rhodes–Livingstone Institute.

Résumé

FLEXIBILITÉ PROCÉDURALE, RÉCONCILIATION ET FAUSSES COMPARAISONS

Les comparaisons entre le droit africain d'une part et le droit occidental (ou le nôtre) d'autre part, prennent souvent la forme de contrastes tranchants entre le manque de formes dans la procédure du tribunal et une orientation générale vers la réconciliation des parties dans les sociétés africaines et la rigidité de la procédure et l'application stricte du droit dans les tribunaux occidentaux. Un auteur a résumé ce contraste dans les mots 'justice par accord' contre 'justice par décret'. Ma discussion explique que ce contraste est une grossière surcomplication qui s'est fixée en un stéréotype. Ceci est le résultat d'une incompréhension du procès judiciaire dans les deux sociétés, l'africaine et l'occidentale.

En ce qui concerne cette dernière, l'attention de la littérature et des hommes de loi est attirée presque entièrement par les tribunaux supérieurs. On ne connait presque rien de la procédure quotidienne (il en va de même pour les règles idéales prescrites par la procédure). Or, c'est seulement dans les tribunaux qu'on peut rencontrer les parallèles les plus étroits avec la procédure des tribunaux africains. Il y a des indications que les tribunaux inférieurs dans les sociétés occidentales cherchent aussi à rendre la justice suivant l'esprit du droit plutôt qu'à la lettre. Autrement dit, beaucoup de comparaisons sont fausses parce que la procédure occidentale est assimilée à celle des tribunaux supérieurs.

En ce qui concerne la procédure dans les tribunaux africains, la tendance dans la littérature est d'accentuer le but de réconciliation des tribunaux africains. A part quelques exceptions, on ne paie pas assez d'attention au fait que ces tribunaux s'inquiètent en même temps de soutenir et de défendre des normes juridiques. S'ils ne le faisaient pas, il n'y aurait ni droit, ni tribunaux. C'est seulement à des étapes définies dans le procès que le but de réconciliation des tribunaux doit être proéminent. J'ai donc discuté l'importance de distinguer les différentes étapes du procès en fonction du devoir principal et du but des tribunaux au cours de ces différentes étapes: premièrement, essais de réconciliation avant le procès; secondairement, examen judiciaire des faits et sélection des normes légales appropriées aboutissant à la première décision du tribunal, le jugement; et finalement, la deuxième décision du tribunal en ce qui concerne les sanctions légalement ou socialement désirables pour son jugement.

Ayant ainsi séparé le problème en parties plus faciles à traiter, nous serons dans une meilleure position pour comparer la procédure dans différentes sociétés. Nous trouverons probablement qu'il y a plus de similitudes entre les pratiques procédurales dans les sociétés africaines et occidentales qu'il n'est communément assumé.

V. Guilt and Innocence: Problem and Method in the Gurage Judicial System

WILLIAM A. SHACK

I INTRODUCTION

In the main, social anthropologists and legally trained scholars developed serious concerns about customary African judicial methods long after European law, Native Authorities, and established courts had modified, if not entirely replaced, most traditional procedures by which African courts formerly ascertained guilt. In the strict sense of the term, these African courts were no longer *traditional*; European and Islamic overrule had radically curtailed the traditional powers and jurisdiction of African courts in dealing with crimes and delicts. Generally these changes in the judicial function of native tribunals followed a similar pattern nearly everywhere in former colonial Africa, but the position of customary courts in some, though not all, tribal societies in Ethiopia provide an exceptional case in point. For a half century or more the judicial system of the Gurage tribe, which I describe here, has retained its traditional structure and authority despite the imposition by the Ethiopian Government of formal courts for the administration of its tribal districts.[1] However, it lies outside the scope of this discussion of Gurage judicial methods to detail the several historical and political factors which account for the side-by-side existence of antithetical legal systems, traditional and modern, throughout the many tribal districts of Ethiopia. Here I can only call attention to the sociological importance of understanding this phenomena as it relates to the broader problem of the flexibility and adaptability of traditional

[1] The data used in preparing this paper were gathered while carrying out field research among the Western Gurage tribes in South-west Ethiopia in 1957–9, and in 1963–5 under National Institutes of Health Research Grants Nos. MH-07141-03. I gratefully acknowledge the assistance of Ato Gabru Gebre-Wold in the translation of Gurage legal terms and juridical concepts.

African courts of law under conditions of political and legal change.[1]

An analysis of Gurage judicial method makes evident the fact that Gurage legal concepts cannot be discussed without reference to Gurage religious concepts. Clearly, religion, and its related conception of moral righteousness, underpins the Gurage legal system, and this close correspondence between religion and law finds expression, in one way, through the variety of notions Gurage hold concerning right and wrong behaviour. I have discussed elsewhere[2] the intertwining of the secular and religious norms and values of Gurage society which penetrate the realm of Gurage law; and here I contend that these concepts form an ideological as well as juridical construct against which Gurage courts decide on matters of guilt and innocence. However, as background to the discussion of judicial procedures in Gurage courts of law, it is worthwhile to illustrate briefly this interrelatedness between religion and law by way of reference to the development of their judicial court system.

Gurage historical traditions establish the beginning of law and government with the founding of their judicial 'high court' (*yägoka*). This development of a centralized judicial system, underpinned by the core religious institutions, was an essential element in the process of formation of a 'segmentary state' which took place during the 1840s.[3] It followed after the political ambitions of the Chaha Gurage tribe to exert its domination over the whole congeries through conquest had failed, and the Chaha then reverted to a policy of peaceful coalescence. By welcoming representatives of the major deities, *Waq*, the 'sky god', and *Božä*, the 'thunder god', and encouraging them to relocate their central shrines on Chaha territory, the ritual dignitaries, in turn, sanctioned all five judgeships[4] of the Gurage high court as an hereditary right of the politically

---

[1] See, e.g., Kuper and Kuper, 1965.

[2] Shack, 1966.

[3] The tribes of Chaha, Muher, Ezha, Gyeto, Ennemor, Aklil, and Walani-Woriro, comprise the political grouping known as the 'seven Gurage houses', or '*säbat bet Gurage*'.

[4] The increase from five to seven judges in the High Court was made after 1889, to accommodate the Aklil and Walani-Woriro tribes, who joined up with the original five 'houses'.

dominant Mogämänä clan of Chaha. This interplay between religious and judicial institutions in the structure of the Gurage authority system characterizes the society as being more centralized ritually than it is politically.[1]

II GURAGE JUDICIAL STRUCTURE AND PROCESS

Gurage judicial process is based on an hierarchy of legal assemblies which reflect the segmentary structure of Gurage political organization; but the law of *säbat bet* Gurage—*qʷəčä* —is the basis for all adjudication. At the lowest levels of territorial–lineage segmentation are village, clan, and tribal courts, without hereditary judges; at the opposite extreme stands the intertribal High Court *yägoka*, represented by a permanent council of judgeship. Gurage lower courts are of the *yäqaya danä* (village), the *yätəb danä* (clan), and the *yägän danä* ('tribe' or 'country'). Lower courts can be further distinguished from the High Court in that disputants appearing before lower courts are always of the same lineage, clan, or tribe, and that the issues concerned are civil wrongs. All lower courts except those of the village are vested with coercive powers to enforce their judgments, exercising this right, if need be, in all cases that are not appealed to the High Court. The clan chief sits as 'head' of clan and tribal courts which consist of the disputants, the village headman, elders representing both sides, and the body of informal judges, *yäsäwä danä*, who actually conduct the trial, and upon whose advice the chief relies in reaching a decision.

Judges do not hold permanent, let alone hereditary, positions; their appointment to conduct a particular hearing is reached by the mutual agreement of both disputants. This often involves considerable haggling, since the elder kinsmen of each contestant offer advice on selecting judges and they usually have conflicting opinions which the principals take into consideration before final choices are made. Men elected to serve as judge (*danä*) have earned the title because they possess expert knowledge of Gurage law, a long experience in arbitration, and a reputation for reaching wise and just decisions. Judges are sometimes referred to as *äbʷakʸar*, 'wise men', a term usually reserved for 'wizards' (sorcerers and diviners). For, like

[1] Shack, 1967b.

wizards, judges are also credited with possessing unusual powers to 'see things', a quality lacking in ordinary men, which in the judicial context means the ability to detect legal irregularities in court procedure that if allowed to pass unnoticed might seriously damage a claimant's case. Hence a few men with the highest reputation in certain aspects of Gurage law, such as land tenure, contract, or debt, appear more frequently in the role of judge than do others who lack such attributes. So also the composition of clan and tribal courts, usually an odd number of judges, three or five, is important in Gurage concepts about judicial checks and balances, especially in deliberation and passing judgment. Although the possibility of the court reaching a biased judgment is lessened, legal and moral responsibility is placed on the disputants to accept the lower court's ruling unless the decision is appealed to the High Court.

Clan and tribal courts are empowered to exact penalties up to $Et.1000.00 (about £143) in awarding damages for the following civil offences: attempted burglary, theft, slander, personal injury resulting from aggravated assault or by accident, including the loss of or impairment of the use of limbs, sight, or hearing, and wilful destruction of property, except by arson. In cases of personal injury a plaintiff can be awarded $Et.1000.00 for the loss of each body member. But Gurage judicial authority failed to monopolize completely the use of force, and in cases of personal injury resort to self-help as retaliatory action is always liable to occur. A situation that begins as a private wrong can easily turn into a criminal matter if one of the disputants or his kinsmen attempts to settle the issue through retaliation, and loss of life or destruction of property through arson is suffered by the opposing party or his kinsmen. The reconciliation of parties set apart by the blood feud (*bado*) and the awarding of compensation (*yäsäda*), are functions of the High Court which, in addition, serves as an appeal court against the judgment handed down in civil cases in a senior court. In the customary form of appealing, the principal stands before the court (which convenes in the village of the chief in front of the sacred *zəgba*-tree where communal rituals are periodically performed) and, with a great display of anger, shouts loudly, 'Let the High Court hear the case,' 'Let the sky-god (*Waq*) decide.'

That the Gurage High Court, as well as the sacred area where it convenes, are called by the same term—*yägoka*—is one indication of the relationship between Gurage ideas concerning supernatural punishment and law in their concepts of justice. One myth concerning the origin of the High Court credits the sky-god with having chosen the judicial site for the High Court by burying the symbol of Gurage justice, '*ṭoor*', next to the central shrine of *Boẓä*, the 'thunder god', who, it is held, presides supernaturally over the High Court, whenever that court is in session. Thus judgment handed down is believed to be permeated with morality, ritually sanctioned, and the deliberation of the High Court judges is conducted with full awareness of the ritual consequences of supernatural punishment imposed when those entrusted with justice misuse it. Not only are the legal and religious aspects of Gurage law given concrete form through the High Court but the indemnities awarded by the High Court also express the enormity of criminal offences brought before it. The court imposes the maximum penalty of $Et.2000.00 (£286) on the guilty party, as compensation to victims of arson, adultery, manslaughter, homicide, or attempted homicide.

In Gurage legal reasoning these misdeeds are both secular and religious crimes for two reasons. First, murder, arson, and adultery are heinous acts, an affront against the highest values of society which individuals will defend by fighting, and which, if this defence leads to death, kinsmen of the dead will avenge. Second, these are all sacrilegious offences against the deities from whom Gurage seek ritual protection from *Boẓä* for their life and property. Criminal offences, like inter-clan and inter-tribal civil disputes are potentially disruptive of the bonds of clan and tribal solidarity which the network of kinship and economic relations attempts to maintain. Disputes arising over criminal wrongs proliferate easily and may involve lineages and clans in feuding, making it more difficult to restore peace. In utilizing its coercive powers to reconcile disputing parties, and to award compensation to the injured and to enforce payment, the High Court also attempts to 'dry the blood' (*däm watərq*) between the former contestants, after which normal social relations are expected to be resumed. The High Court relies indirectly upon the diffuse moral sanctions embodied in kinship and clanship relationships to support its efforts to restore peace, harmony, and goodwill, and ultimately upon primary supernatural sanctions of the deities who support Gurage law.

Before turning to the problems and methods of adducing evidence in Gurage courts, I mention briefly the most common form of court in which Gurage participate. This is the informal village court called *yäqaya danä*, frequently convened to settle minor disputes between Gurage of the same village or neighbouring villages.[1] A breach of peace might have been caused by borrowing a neighbour's goods without permission; by accidental damage to house property, fencing, crops, or livestock; by simple assaults which do not result in serious or permanent injury; or by striking a neighbour's child without good reason. Disputes of this nature are settled merely by intervention of the village headman (*qoro*), elders, and a few witnesses; and the judgment of the headman who presides over the court, based on 'village law' (*sera*), is made in consultation with the elders. The only sanction at the disposal of the headman to enforce his ruling is the combined moral support of the villagers, for village courts lack authority to impose fines of either money or goods. After peace has been restored through reparation or public apology, the convention of passing coffee, *ṭallä*-beer, *ensete*-bread, and roasted grains takes place; for when disputants can sit to drink coffee and eat *ensete* together, the act symbolically implies that the enmity previously existing between them has ended.

III GUILT AND INNOCENCE

A man who has suffered an injury will accuse another on suspicion alone, and he or his kinsmen will seek a court hearing. Failure to respond to a summons issued on behalf of the court by the headman in the company of appointed elders is taken as an admission of guilt, the accused and his clansmen then being liable to pay compensation. If there is insufficient evidence to support the plaintiff's charges in court, he can issue a challenge to the defendant to 'satisfy him'; that is, he demands that the defendant swear a ritual oath (*mwəris*) of innocence, to

---

[1] Disputes between families of different lineages living in the same village are settled by the local judge (*yäqaya danä*) unless his verdict is appealed.

utter which falsely can bring on a man incurable ritual illnesses that affect him and his succeeding generations. The burden of asserting innocence is extended further to kinsmen of the accused. They can free him from the charge of wrongdoing by agreeing to undergo the *abʷätəb* oath, that is, swearing the 'father's clan'. This form of oathing assumes two variations depending upon the genealogical depth of the defendant's clan: (i) accused from a major, 'old' clan must present twelve kinsmen directly related genealogically to the fifth ascending generation of his father; (ii) accused from a 'minor' clan (*wät*) must present twelve kinsmen directly related genealogically to the seventh ascending generation of his father. Since clansmen are at all times expected to defend fellow-members wrongly accused of misdeeds, which they commonly do, a defendant who is unsuccessful in satisfying the court with testimony adduced ritually from kinsmen is considered guilty.

Oathing may be resorted to in both civil and criminal cases whenever there is insufficient evidence to condemn the accused and the plaintiff's allegations rest solely on weak grounds of suspicion. Ritual oathing has a double-edged function in the Gurage judicial process of determining guilt or innocence: it makes manifest the moral and economic liability of the oath of 'the father's clan', under which men assume the liability for the misconduct of kinsmen; it limits the possibility of presenting perjured evidence since the threat of supernatural punishment ultimately affects all living clansmen and future descendants as well. Suspicion is rife among the Gurage and there are many court cases in which the plaintiff demands to be 'satisfied'. But allegations of wrongdoing based solely on suspicion tend to be curbed by the legal right of Gurage to bring countercharges of slander (*qänema*), even though the accusation failed to receive judicial support owing to a lack of evidence; to 'clear the name' is of equal importance in Gurage notions of justice. Moral retribution can be made either by public apology in the presence of the court or, if obstinacy makes the former plaintiff persist in his charge, by paying compensation of money and cattle.

In Gurage courts witnesses are always called upon to testify in cases of slander, attempted arson, burglary, and homicide. Hearsay evidence is admissible, but it is not sufficient grounds for the courts to arrive at a judgment of guilty. To obtain substantial evidence against the accused, especially in cases of theft and assault, the plaintiff will often engage a *čakämä*, 'one who tells' (a diviner), to seek out the suspect, the goods, or both. Once he has discovered the suspect or goods, the diviner informs the victim who, together with armed kinsmen, descends on the suspect and publicly announces the accusation. Later the diviner appears in court as witness against the defence. With many Gurage today living outside the tribal district working at wage labour, it is not unusual for a victim to engage a diviner to search after a culprit who has sought escape from local authority by means of the thin veil of anonymity urban areas provide.

In criminal cases the High Court convenes only after establishing a modicum of peace between the kin groups of the principals. When murder has taken place and the offender is publicly known or later discovered, he, along with all adult male lineal kin of three ascending generations, must accept banishment from the clan/tribal district until compensation is paid. Refuge may be sought in any clan/tribal district other than that of the criminal's cognatic kin, or that in which the murder was committed. If this fails and a blood feud erupts, no compensation is paid when the criminal or one of his kinsmen is caught and executed, nor for property damaged in the mêlée. During the several months which usually lapse between public announcement of the crime and convening the High Court, the headman and elder clansmen of the offender, acting as go-betweens, attempt to negotiate a peace settlement by offering cattle to the victim's kinsmen. Cattle symbolically represent blood-money, an admission of liability. Nowadays blood-money is not legal compensation, however; it remains a survival of former times when cattle were offered as recompense for a loss of life in feuding, before money was introduced in Gurageland. Today the High Court awards the victim's closest male kin one *wädärä*[1] of land confiscated from the criminal, including all crops, and $Et.1500.00 of which his clansmen assume part of the liability for payment. If the criminal owns less than one *wädärä*, kinsmen of the victim claim the entire land-holding;

---

[1] The customary unit of land inherited by each son is one *wädärä*, about 48 square yards. A person convicted of homicide is legally deprived of land ownership; by extension, a loss of status but not tribal citizenship.

in addition, they receive compensation of $Et.2000.00, and a two-year banishment is imposed on the guilty party; a landless criminal pays compensation of $Et.2000.00, and remains banished until the award is settled. In all judgments where compensation is awarded, one-third or one-half of the amount of the award is claimed by the court to be 'left for the elders', i.e. for the judges who presided over the case.

Provocation leading to homicide in incidents of theft, arson, attempted murder, and adultery, where the criminal is caught *in flagrante delicto*, are the only exonerating circumstances; the High Court convenes in such cases to 'clear the name' of the accused. In distinguishing between accidental death and wanton homicide, the circumstances under which death occurred are considered by the High Court in its deliberations and judgment. Death caused by a 'will-not-kill thing' (i.e. an object which is not normally considered as liable to cause death, such as a stone or stick, but which if improperly or carelessly handled will do so) is distinguished from death caused when the accused had no direct contact with the victim, having neither 'seen' nor 'touched' him, as in killing by accident while hunting. In the first instance retribution amounts to $Et.1000.00, in the latter $Et.500.00, the elders receiving one-half of the award in both cases. Retaliation frequently occurs in cases of accidental death; but if the accused or one of his kinsmen is killed in vengeance, his group is supported by the law. The loss of life through vengeance after judgment has been passed in court is considered an act of aggravated violence; the High Court levies the maximum fine to which the criminal and his clansmen are liable for compensation.

The pronouncement of judgment in Gurage courts expresses the majority will of the assembly (*nəbʷär*). When the judges retire to consider their verdict they weigh carefully the evidence of witnesses, and of members of the audience who have volunteered information, in the light of the relative strength of arguments presented by the litigants. Witnesses are the primary source of information in both civil and criminal cases, the court giving their testimony highest regard. But the integrity of witnesses can be challenged if the litigant demands that a ritual oath be taken before presenting their testimony. In High Court hearings issues of fact are always examined in detail by *yàzànga säb*, the 'people of law', men who habitually attend High Court sessions, acting as informal judges, checking court procedures, sorting out fact from hearsay, but also providing the contestants with a means of assurance, by seeing to it that their trial is properly conducted. Interested members of the assembly may also demand to be heard, giving opinions regarding the testimony presented and the verdict at which the court ought to arrive. Apart from each litigant (*yämäraks säb*) influencing the court's verdict by personal testimony and supporting witnesses, the favourable outcome of the case depends greatly upon knowledge of Gurage legal procedure and the ability of the litigant to express his argument in the style and language of the court. Through the system of legal representation, a person lacking eloquence and clarity of exposition can strengthen his case by engaging a professional 'champion-at-law' (*maro*), or a kinsman skilled in legal matters, to plead his cause.

Ideally and in practice Gurage judges are expected to maintain absolute impartiality and aloofness, and in practice they seem to do so. They interfere in the trial only to correct some irregularity or to guide the case, but seldom, if ever, to direct cross-examination. While the majority opinion of the assembly influences their judgment, the council of judges, *yämsaya danä*,[1] are not bound by its views, legally or morally. This fiction of independent judgment is suggested further in the name by which the court members are known. *Yämsaya* literally means 'those who straighten the crooked case', the deliberation of the judges being likened to cutting rough wood with a saw, rendering the edges clean, the surface smooth. And the numerical composition of *yämsaya danä* adds to this fiction; for the 'odd' judge of the council of seven acts as chairman, casting the final vote to reach a majority decision if there should arise a judicial deadlock. Where considerable quarrelling has taken place during the trial, making a decision more difficult to reach, the judges may invite one or more members from the assembly to rehearse for them particular disputable facts of testimony. At clan and tribal courts learned elders counsel the chief; the 'people of law' advise the High Court judges.

[1] In their judicial role, High Court judges are termed *yämsaya danä*; in their legislative role *yäqʷəṭa danä*, literally, 'makers of law'.

Judgment handed down at the High Court is final and not subject to legal appeal. But when an accused feels he has suffered an unjust condemnation, he may petition the ritual arbiter of blood feuds, *wäg*, to 'justify', rather than revoke the High Court's ruling. The ritual arbiter performs a peace-making sacrifice only to redress doubts of justice; in such cases both parties partake in the sacrificial feast, an act which signifies acceptance of the court's verdict, approved by the deities who support Gurage law. The High Court's decision is seldom, if ever, defied after the ritual arbiter restores peace, but open defiance can take place if the sacrifice has not been performed. If the guilty party or his kinsmen refuse to pay the fine or compensation, or to make restitution as decreed, the verdict will be enforced. The court then appoints an armed force to confiscate the criminal's property, and, in former times, a defiant criminal would be apprehended and brought before the High Court for execution. When *yägoka* has to impose its judgment by resorting to coercive power, the guilty party henceforth is deprived of all legal rights in the whole Gurage grouping; if involved subsequently in a dispute where the verdict would obviously be in his favour, legal redress cannot be obtained through the judicial system. In the execution of judgment and enforcement of regulations Gurage courts are supported by social sanctions of ridicule, opprobrium, and ostracism, and ultimately by ritual sanctions brought to bear by the judges invoking the deities to spell a lasting curse on the recalcitrant offender against public peace.

IV THE JUDICIAL SYSTEM IN THE PROCESS OF CHANGE

Prior to the enactment of the Criminal Code of 1930, the ancient Ethiopian religio-legal code of the Fetha Negast, the 'laws of the King', was the legal instrument of the military administration, which was established under Emperor Menilek II in 1889 to rule over Gurageland and other tribal districts. Under the Administration of Justice Proclamation of 1942, government courts were instituted throughout the Districts to replace the judicial authority of the District Governor (Malkanya) who, prior to the Act, could convene informal courts to settle disputes between local tribesmen.[1] Since 1942,

---
[1] Perham, 1947, pp. 138–59.

two judicial systems have existed in theory, though not always in practice, in Gurageland: (i) traditional courts, with which I have been concerned in this paper, where Gurage customary law is the basis of adjudication in disputes ranging from torts to crimes; and (ii) government courts which have functioned for about one decade only, with the council of the highest district court, the *Awradja Gizat*, constituted of three non-Gurage judges, one of whom, the Governor of the tribal district, presides over tribunals.[1] Judgment in government courts is based on the Ethiopian Penal Code of 1957.

Gurage courts, unlike those of the Barotse[2] and Tiv,[3] for example, are not legally recognized by the Government who authorize only their appointed courts to adjudicate on disputes in Gurageland and elsewhere in Ethiopia.

Thus it is legally possible for an avaricious Gurage to exploit the two judicial systems; no legal or political sanctions are contained within the corpus of Gurage law which can restrain principals in a government court, if either party is dissatisfied with the judgment based on customary law. But the threat of severing kinship ties, together with public ridicule, can be formidable sanctions, restraining individuals who might attempt to manipulate the Government against the traditional courts for personal gain.

Gurage appear before government courts mainly because of infractions of 'government law', within the sphere of tribal administration, such as failing to pay tax, or keeping peace. Gurage courts deal principally with disputes which arise out of the network of kinship, economic and social rights and duties existing between all Gurage who claim tribal citizenship, even migrants who reside abroad for long periods. In the daily exercising of their rights and performance of their duties, infractions of Gurage law inevitably occur, but Gurage consider it the duty of their traditional courts, not the duty of government courts, to readjust social relations between tribesmen. No Gurage can live outside the kinship network in Gurageland; and therefore no Gurage can live outside tribal law.

Even so, the traditional Gurage judicial system is gradually being weakened as an increasing number of Gurage now look

[1] Marien, 1954, p. 73.
[2] Gluckman, 1955.
[3] Bohannan, 1957.

Guilt and Innocence 165

to government courts for legal redress. This trend in the past decade represents not a loss of faith in Gurage courts. On the contrary, government courts have shown a lack of resistance to chicanery, bribery, and corruption, thus creating conditions whereby known offenders can be exonerated from guilt. In this way, government courts have introduced a 'legal' mechanism for escaping punishment,[1] thereby lessening the burden of moral and ritual liabilities formerly placed on clansmen to swear oaths in doubtful support of wrongdoers.

The Gurage judicial system itself contains elements of change. For the Gurage High Court, like the High Court (*kuta*) of the Lozi, is also 'an ecclesiastical chapter, as well as a court cabinet, civil service, and parliament'.[2] It thus acts as a modernizing influence, legislating new laws and modifying old ones to meet changing social and economic conditions. In its legislative capacity, the Gurage High Court has enacted laws against the payment of bride-wealth as a necessary condition of marriage; it changed the former redemption for loss of life in feuds from blood-money in cattle to cash when Ethiopian currency became the standard for monetary transactions in Gurageland; and, as the economic prosperity of Gurage increased, it raised the limitations of legal awards in civil and criminal judgments to accord with present standards.

In spite of locally introduced factors which tend to slow up erosion of the traditional Gurage judicial system, such external factors as migration, and the effects of urbanization and education of young Gurage, work against the preservation of the High Court. Few young men today have the desire to remain in the village or to participate actively in keeping the old court system alive, especially when their primary social and economic interests are centred in the towns. And here they come under different systems of law and authority.[3] Equally so, almost all of the hereditary judgeships in the High Court, as well as the ritual offices, will soon pass to men who have acquired some

---

[1] The position of government courts in this regard represents a partial return to the days before the Gurage High Court was established, when self-help in seeking redress rested primarily upon the armed strength of supporting kinsmen. Today, an offender with sufficient financial resources to prolong a hearing by repeated continuances might eventually be exonerated, and the verdict of the court will, if need be, receive armed backing from local government authorities.

[2] Gluckman, 1955, p. 265.   [3] Shack, 1967a.

formal education and have experienced town life. It is conceivable that some men will relinquish their rights to traditional offices and opt for the quasi-security which employment in town temporarily provides. But the extent to which those who accept judgeships bring into their offices both the good and bad features of urban society will profoundly influence the traditional Gurage judicial system.

BIBLIOGRAPHY

Bohannan, P. J.
 (1957) *Justice and Judgment Among the Tiv*. London and New York: Oxford University Press for the International African Institute.

Gluckman, M.
 (1955) *The Judicial Process Among the Barotse of Northern Rhodesia*. Manchester: Manchester University Press for the Rhodes-Livingstone Institute.

Kuper, H. and Kuper, L. (eds.)
 (1965) *African Law: Adaptation and Development*. Berkeley: University of California Press.

Marien, M.
 (1954) *The Ethiopian Empire Federation and Laws*. Rotterdam: Royal Netherlands Printing and Lithographing Company.

Perham, M.
 (1947) *The Government of Ethiopia*. London: Faber & Faber.

Shack, W. A.
 (1966) *The Gurage*. London and New York: Oxford University Press for the International African Institute.
 (1967a) 'Urban Tribalism and the Cultural process of Urbanization in Ethiopia' in A. W. Southall and E. Bruner, editors, *Urban Anthropology*. Chicago: Aldine Press.
 (1967b) 'On Gurage Judicial Structure and African Political Theory', *Journal of Ethiopian Studies*, v, pp. 89–101.

Résumé

DE LA CULPABILITÉ ET DE L'INNOCENCE:
PROBLÈME ET MÉTHODE DANS LE SYSTÈME
JUDICIAIRE DES GURAGE

La structure judiciaire des Gurage reflète les principes segmentaires autour desquels le système politique est organisé. Au pivot du système embrassant le village, la tribu et les relations judiciaire entre tribus, se tient le tribunal de grande instance, qui, outre ses fonctions législatives et judiciaires, est aussi une cour de cassation. Tous les débats entre les tribus, civils ou criminels, aussi bien que les offenses criminelles (assassinat, incendie par malveillance, adultère) y sont traités; les tribunaux de petite instance sont autorisés à entendre seulement les offenses civiles, le tribunal du village seul, manquant des pouvoirs coercitifs pour faire exécuter ses jugements.

La charge de rejeter des accusations repose sur l'accusé. Les parents peuvent soutenir ses prétentions d'innocence en se soumettant à une épreuve. Si l'accusé n'obtient pas le soutien d'un parent, le tribunal interprète cela comme une preuve de culpabilité.

La suspicion seule est une base suffisante pour porter une accusation. Mais un abus possible de ce principe tend à être réprimé par le droit sous forme d'une action en diffamation si l'accusation ne parvient pas à entraîner la conviction du tribunal. On demande toujours des témoins pour témoigner dans les procès; l'ouï-dire est admis, mais celui-ci n'est pas la seule base sur laquelle le jugement est fondé. Dans les cas d'homicide, les seules circonstances à décharge sont, la capture criminel *in flagrante delicto*: le tribunal se réunit alors pour acquitter l'accusé.

On fait toujours une distinction entre mort accidentelle et homicide volontaire. Le tribunal, par un jugement final, exprime la volonté de la majorité de l'assemblée qui est formée des témoins, des parents soutenant les plaideurs, des interrogateurs professionnels, des spectateurs intéressés. La décision du tribunal peut être souvent influenceé par la nature de l'argument qu'un représentant peut produire au nom de son client. Les juges maintiennent la fiction de l'indépendance et bien qu'il ne soient pas tenus par l'opinion de l'assemblée, celle-ci est prise en considération quand ils en arrivent au jugement final. La décision du tribunal de grande instance n'est pas soumise à l'appel, mais on peut demander un arbitre rituel pour accomplir un sacrifice au nom de la personne insatisfaite, ce qui signifie que la décision du tribunal est supportée par le rite. Si le tribunal est obliger d'imposer sa règle en ayant recours au pouvoir coercitif, on prive alors la personne coupable de tous droits dans la tribu.

Depuis 1942, les tribunaux traditionnels des Gurage ont fonctionné à côté des tribunaux gouvernementaux qui sont présidés par des juges non-gurages, dont les décisions sont fondées sur les préceptes juridiques modernes. Les tribunaux gurages ne sont pas reconnus légalement par le gouvernement; la plupart des Gurage s'adressaient dans le passé, aux tribunaux traditionnels, où le droit coutumier est appliqué, mais un nombre croissant profite maintenant des tribunaux gouvernementaux. Ceci et des facteurs tels que l'émigration, l'urbanisation et l'éducation de la jeunesse gurage, détruisent la structure du système judiciaire traditionnel.

VI. La première Codification africaine: Madagascar 1828–81

H. DESCHAMPS

Le droit malgache traditionnel reposait sur la coutume des ancêtres (*fomban-drazana*), à fondement religieux. A côté du *zanahary* (Dieu), les ancêtres étaient supposés vivre dans le tombeau et veiller à la bonne marche de l'ordre qu'ils avaient établi, punissant ou récompensant leurs descendants selon que la coutume était ou non observée. Le mot *fomba* (coutume) vient de *omba*: ce qui couvre, qui protège; c'est l'ordre des choses, du monde, qui protège tant qu'il n'est pas violé. La notion de tabou (*fady*) est à la fois religieuse et sociale; le meurtre, l'inceste, l'entrée d'un vivant dans le tombeau en dehors des cérémonies sont également des crimes. La faute (*ota*) est la violation d'un tabou, une sorte de sacrilège. La sanction est d'ordre religieux (calamités collectives ou personnelles, maladies, stérilité des femmes ou du bétail, mauvaises récoltes, etc.). Mais il est possible d'apaiser les ancêtres et de détourner leur colère par des offrandes ou des sacrifices de bœufs.

Ce système primitif, limité à la famille ou au clan, dont le patriarche est le prêtre, se transforma, dans les temps modernes surtout aux XVIIe et XVIIIe siècles, dans les régions où des royaumes étendus prirent naissance, tels les royaumes Antemoro au Sud-Est, Sakalava dans l'Ouest, Betsileo et Merina dans le Centre. On passait de petites sociétès, facilement surveillées et de conscience uniforme, à des ensembles plus vastes où les individus étaient plus libres de leurs mouvements, les rapports plus complexes, l'autorité plus lointaine. Dès lors, sans perdre sa base religieuse, le système se transforma. Les sanctions religieuses, évitables par des sacrifices bovins, furent partiellement remplacées par des *amendes* en bœufs payées au roi, lui-même personnage sacré, dieu-visible (*andriamanitra hita-maso*). Le tabou devient un délit pénal sans perdre tout à fait son caractère de sacrilège. A la coutume des ancêtres s'ajoute, comme source de droit, la loi (*lalàna*), c'est-à-dire les commandements (*didy*) du roi. De 1787 à 1810 un grand souverain, *Andrianampoinimerina*, donne ainsi, par ses Kabary (discours) puissamment imagés, un ensemble de règles nouvelles au royaume Merina; elles ont pour but l'organisation de l'Etat, qui est une nouveauté; mais aussi elles modifient sur certains points la coutume ancestrale.

La politique extérieure de ce roi n'aura pas des conséquences moindres. Il réalise l'unité des Merina, qui n'avait jamais été complète et, par l'intimidation ou la contrainte, il soumet les peuples voisins, notamment les Betsileo. Les rois soumis deviennent 'ses enfants', c'est-à-dire ses vassaux. En mourant, il lègue à son fils *Ramada 1er*, son testament politique: '*la mer sera la limite de ma rizière*', c'est-à-dire: de mon royaume. Radama exécute sa volonté: de 1810 à 1828 il soumet la plus grande partie des peuples de l'île. Sa femme et successeur, *Ranavalona 1ère* consolidera ces annexions sans les étendre. Ainsi, jusqu'à la conquête francaise (1895) subsistent plusieurs catégories de peuples malgaches: 1.—Les Merina (sensiblement la province actuelle de Tananarive). 2.—Les peuples d'administration merina, où les chefs locaux ont perdu leur importance au profit des gouverneurs envoyés de Tananarive (tels les Betsileo de la province de Fianarantsoa, et les peuples de la province de Tamatave). 3.—Les peuples simplement vassaux, ayant conservé leur organisation et leurs souverains, sous la surveillance effective des gouverneurs et des garnisons merina (tels les peuples du Sud-Est et du Nord-Ouest). 4.—Les peuples restés indépendants, occupant des régions éloignées et ingrates, de pénétration difficile, organisés en petites chefferies turbulentes et belliqueuses.

Cette distinction de fait amène une distinction de droit. Le Royaume de Madagascar n'est pas monolithique. Outre la catégorie 4, la catégorie 3 conserve ses coutumes; il en est encore ainsi, très largement quoique moins nettement, de la catégorie 2; seuls les Merina (catégorie 1) auront un droit uniforme.

C'est là une situation qui n'apparaît guère dans les textes et qui ne crée pas de conflits pour diverses raisons: (1°) Les coutumes malgaches, comme la langue, sont assez semblables d'un bout à l'autre de l'île, avec des différences assez minimes,

La première Codification africaine: Madagascar 1828–81 171

tout au moins au début du XIXe siècle; (2°) les chefs locaux ont gardé leurs pouvoirs de juridiction, sauf recours aux gouverneurs merina pour les causes pénales les plus graves; (3°) certaines règles générales d'organisation sont prescrites pour l'ensemble du royaume, afin d'en accroître la cohésion et de régler les situations entre les peuples; c'est, en partie, l'objet des *codes*.

Les prescriptions d'Andrianampoinimerina avaient été observées de son vivant et conservées par la tradition orale. Sous le règne de Radama 1er, en 1820, arrivèrent des missionnaires protestants anglais qui proposèrent d'écrire le malgache phonétiquement en caractères latins. Radama accepta, en adoptant les consonnes anglaises et les voyelles francaises (1823). Les missionnaires avaient surtout en vue la traduction de la Bible. Mais, dès 1826, les lois nouvelles étaient affichées à la porte du Palais. En 1828 étaient diffusées aux gouverneurs de provinces les Instructions connues sous le nom de *Code de Ranavalona 1ère*.

Divisé en 48 articles, il constitue avant tout un code pénal. Andrianampoinimerina avait énuméré 12 crimes punis de mort: neuf concernaient la révolte ou les atteintes à l'autorité du souverain, le dixième était la sorcellerie maléfique, le onzième le meurtre, le douzième le vol (tout au moins les vols les plus importants: vol au tombeau, effraction, vol de riz, vol de boeufs, enlèvement de personnes). Ce chiffre de 12, ayant un caractère sacré, fut respecté par la Reine, bien qu'elle supprimât le vol de cette liste; on le remplaça en répétant sous une autre forme le crime de révolte. Le poison d'épreuve (*tanguin*), auquel Andrianampoinimerina attachait une grande valeur, était conservé, et la Reine en usa largement. Les femmes et enfants des condamnés étaient réduits en esclavage, leurs biens confisqués. Des différences pour certaines sanctions étaient prévues selon les castes. Les délits étaient punis d'amendes en boeufs et en piastres (pièces de 5 F en argent); les insolvables pouvaient être vendus comme esclaves. Etaient punis de confiscation et d'esclavage, entre autres, l'acte sexuel commis avec des esclaves ou avec des vaches, l'adultère si le mari entre temps était mort à la guerre (on considérait que cet acte avait été la cause de sa mort). Est puni d'une amende celui qui enterre un sorcier la tête à l'Est (comme tout le monde,

Le sorcier devait être placé la tête au Sud). Conformément aux prescriptions d'Andrianampoinimerina, celui qui a pris, en passant, des vivres dans un champ en les consommant sur place n'est pas considéré comme coupable.

Le but du code est donc avant tout d'établir fermement l'autorité royale et de faire punir, par ses fonctionnaires, les crimes et délits, dont l'importance dans la mentalité du temps apparaît avec la gravité des peines. Le passage d'un système de sanctions religieuses à un système d'amendes est achevé. Il s'y ajoute la confiscation de biens et la réduction en esclavage pour la famille : le crime capital est donc un sacrilège. La défense de l'ordre social est en même temps une défense de l'ordre du monde; le tanguin est le jugement de Dieu et des ancêtres.

La disposition finale du Code marque bien le souci politique qui l'anime et son sentiment du possible : les sanctions édictées ne sont valables telles quelles que dans la région centrale de l'île (l'Imerina, le pays des Merina). Dans les provinces les peines sont réduites de moitié. Les coupables de crimes capitaux eux-mêmes ne doivent pas être exécutés sur place, mais envoyés à Tananarive où il sera statué sur leur sort. Il s'agit évidemment d'amadouer les populations soumises, en évitant de les soulever par des sanctions trop dures.

Aucune allusion n'est faite par le code au droit civil. Celui-ci est constitué par la coutume de chaque peuple, bien connue de tous; les contestations sont soumises aux patriarches de famille ou aux anciens du clan suivant leur importance. Ce sont des affaires privées, en dehors du domaine public. L'Etat n'a ni la possibilité ni le désir d'intervenir en l'espèce. Nul ne pourrait sans sacrilège toucher à la coutume des ancêtres; le danger serait à la fois social et religieux. La vengeance des invisibles ne tarderait pas.

A l'époque où meurt Ranavalona 1ère (1861), les coutumes juridiques n'ont donc guère été adultérées. Les premiers essais de christianisation ont été réprimés. Le droit malgache traditionnel est encore à l'état pur, surtout dans les provinces.

Le système de parenté est patrilinéaire, mais la parenté maternelle n'est pas sans conséquences. Le souci primordial est d'assurer la continuité du culte des ancêtres; faute d'enfant mâle on en adopte un. La père de famille est prêtre domestique; il peut rejeter un enfant coupable; il est souverain 'entre ses portes et ses fenêtres'; il peut disposer de ses biens sans restriction. Les clans (*foko*) sont encore les groupements sociaux et politiques de base. Chez les peuples organisés en royaumes, les clans sont répartis en castes hiérachisées. En Imerina, depuis Andrianampoinimerina, des groupements territoriaux (*fokon'olona*: gens des villages) ont reçu les pouvoirs judiciaires de base; des divisions administratives (*toko*) se superposent aux clans; des envoyés du roi (les *Vadin-tany*: époux de la terre) parcourent le pays et veillent aussi bien à l'ordre public qu'à la justice. Depuis l'avènement de la Reine, les chefs des clans du Nord, d'où est sortie la monarchie reconstituée, sont les conseillers royaux, représentant la caste Hova (hommes libres à peau claire) auprès du souverain, émanation de la caste noble (*Andriana*).

La personnalité n'est atteinte par l'individu que peu à peu: 1ère coupe de cheveux, circoncision, nom (individuel) qui change plusieurs fois. Elle n'est pleinement acquise que par le chef de famille. La femme est prêtée à la famille du mari, qui peut la répudier. Il existe des mariages à temps. La polygamie est fréquente, ainsi que les fiançailles d'enfants et l'héritage de la veuve par le frère (lévirat). Le tombeau est le centre de culte; les funérailles et autres cérémonies mortuaires exigent le sacrifice d'un grand nombre de bœufs.

Autour des rois, notamment chez les Merina, s'est développé un cérémonial religieux, avec la fête du bain (*fandroana*) et les talismans royaux (que les chrétiens appellent 'les idoles').

La propriété collective des clans sur la terre a été, en Imerina, transcendée par Andrianampoinimerina, déclarant: 'La terre est à moi' et la redistribuant à ses sujets 'pour que chacun puisse satisfaire la faim de son ventre'; l'impôt (en nature) représente une sorte de location payée au roi. La création d'une rizière (par un membre du clan) confère le droit d'usage et d'aliénation de celui-ci, sauf aux étrangers. La brousse non cultivée (terres *lava volo*: aux longs cheveux) peut être utilisée par les membres de la collectivité. Les tombeaux et le terrain qui les entourent sont inaliénables.

Il n'y a pas de communauté matrimoniale, sauf chez les Merina où Andrianampoinimerina a prescrit que les biens acquis pendant le mariage seraient communs et partagés par tiers (*Kitay telo andalana*: trois petits tas de bois à brûler mis en rang). Les successions suivent des règles très différentes suivant les peuples et les castes. Des biens (*Ko-drazana*: pour les ancêtres) peuvent être constitués en fondation inaliénable pour l'entretien des tombeaux et les cérémonies mortuaires. Les contrats étaient passés autrefois entre familles ou entre membres du même clan, avec assistance de nombreux témoins et érection d'une pierre levée (*orim-bato*). Mais la diffusion des marchés et la circulation accrue avec l'élargissement du royaume ont augmenté les échanges, devenus moins solennels mais reposant sur un certain nombre de règles coutumières et de délais de repentir. Le prêt suppose remise d'un gage. La rareté de la monnaie rend l'usure énorme (10% par mois).

Dans l'ensemble le système traditionnel subsiste, fondé sur la famille, le clan, la collectivité de village. Mais le changement d'échelle avec l'extension du royaume et la mobilité nouvelle, crée de nouvelles perspectives auxquelles l'organisation politique et pénale, seule encore esquissée, ne suffit pas à répondre. La crise va éclater à la mort de Ranavalona 1ère, qui s'était efforcée, par l'isolement extérieur et la contrainte intérieure, de maintenir les coutumes ancestrales.

Radama II (1861–3), fils et successeur de Ranavalona 1ère, ouvre brusquement le royaume à toutes les innovations étrangères. Son code, cependant, n'innove guère, sauf par la suppression du tanguin et par celle de la peine de mort que remplacent les fers (très lourds) et la marque au front. La réduction des peines est maintenue pour les provinces; de plus, si les coutumes locales prévoient des peines différentes, il conviendra de s'en inspirer.

Le code de *Rasoherina* (1863–8) rétablit la peine de mort, sans autre changement notable.

Le règne de *Ranavalona II* (1868–83) sera au contraire celui des réformes, décidées par son Premier Ministre et époux, *Rainilaiarivony*, de caste Hova, qui comprend la nécessité d'une certaine adaption au monde moderne pour consolider le royaume. En Septembre 1868 est promulgué (et, pour la première fois imprimé) le *Code des 101 articles*. Les dispositions générales, placées en tête, proclament la liberté religieuse, déclarent qu'aucune parcelle du territoire, 'fût-elle comme un seul grain de riz', ne passera aux mains des étrangers, et posent comme justification du droit pénal le principe du retour (*tody*) des fautes contre leur auteur, 'ses propres actes se retournent contre lui', principe profondément ancré dans la conscience malgache, source de crainte et d'inhibition. Les innovations sont encore faibles: la privation de liberté pour les femmes et les enfants des condamnés à mort n'intervient plus que pour non-dénonciation du crime; la traite des esclaves est interdite; de nombreux articles punissent les abus d'autorité des fonctionnaires et la concussion des magistrats; quelques dispositions civiles, concernant les modalités des testaments et les ventes à réméré, apparaissent timidement.

En février 1869 la Reine et le P. M. se convertissent au protestantisme qui devient Eglise d'Etat. Les conversions, plus ou moins spontanées, deviennent légion. L'influence des missionnaires anglais grandit, alors que des conflits se dessinent avec la France, où des groupes de pression poussent à la conquête de l'île. Dès lors Rainilaiarivony entreprend de réformer la structure du gouvernement et le système législatif, pour que son pays fasse figure d'Etat moderne. Le 29 mars 1881 sont proclamés, d'une part la formation d'un Ministère (qui n'aura guère d'efficacité) et, d'autre part, le *Code des 305 articles*, qui sera le dernier état de la législation malgache et restera en application même après la conquête francaise.

La Reine place son royaume 'sous la protection de Dieu' et, tout en invoquant la tradition, indique la nécessité des réformes: 'L'expérience et le savoir accomplissent ici des progrès au niveau desquels il faut placer l'organisation des affaires de l'Etat.' Pour la première fois il est proclamé que 'la loi est la même pour tous'. Le Code est divisé en 5 titres et 38 chapitres.

Les peines sont plus diversifiées: à côté des amendes et de la mort, sanctions anciennes, sont consacrés les fers, et on voit, pour les délits mineurs (vols de menu bétail ou de cultures), apparaître la prison. Les 12 grands crimes restent les différents aspects de la révolte contre l'Etat et le meurtre. Des interdictions nouvelles sont édictées: commerce des esclaves, avortement, cruauté contre les animaux, incendie de forêt (contrairement à la technique culturale traditionnelle du *tavy*), écrits pornographiques, vente de médicaments sans licence, culture du pavot, fabrication et vente de l'alcool; les enfants devront fréquenter l'école de 8 à 16 ans.

Mais l'innovation essentielle, c'est l'intervention dans le domaine de la coutume; non qu'on ait cessé de révérer les ancêtres, mais on a désormais la protection directe de Dieu et l'enseignement du christianisme, qui condamne certaines pratiques ancestrales. D'où l'aspect à la fois civil et pénal des nouvelles dispositions: interdiction de la polygamie, des fiançailles forcées, du lévirat, de la répudiation, de la vente des terres aux étrangers, des prêts usuraires. Les modalités des testaments et des remboursements de créances (source fréquente de procès) sont fixées. De nombreuses mesures administratives viennent compléter et renforcer cet ensemble: institution des registres administratifs (*bokimpanjakana*) tenant lieu à la fois d'état-civil et de notariat, prescriptions aux *antily* (fonctionnaires placés dans les villages), aux magistrats, aux *fokon'olona*; assistance obligatoire aux vieux parents, aux enfants abandonnés (signe d'une désintégration de la vieille société communautaire); limitation des droits des féodaux.

Les missionnaires catholiques de cette époque ont accusé leurs collègues protestants d'avoir inspiré ce code. Sans aucun doute le christianisme et même l'esprit missionnaire sont présents dans nombre de dispositions. Mais le caractère autoritaire et ombrageux de Rainilaiarivony n'aurait certainement pas admis d'éminence grise. D'ailleurs la présentation un peu désordonnée du code, aussi bien que certaines de ses dispositions (maintien de peines lourdes contre les adultères si le mari meurt en expédition; interdiction des mariages entre les castes; règlementation de l'esclavage) indiquent nettement que les rédacteurs sont bien des Malgaches, sujets de Ranavalona II, et non des Anglais victoriens.

Aussi bien deux articles, qui clôturent la partie juridique du Code, sont-ils expressifs à cet égard:

'263.—Les lois et coutumes anciennes, et jusqu'à ce jour observées, alors même qu'elles ne figureraient pas parmi les présentes, restent en vigueur et doivent être appliquées à l'égal des lois écrites réunies dans le présent code.

'264.—Les prières à Dieu ne sont pas obligatoires, car vous êtes tous ses créatures.'

Ainsi s'affirme le souci du P. M. de réformer hardiment sur certains points, mais avec toute la prudence nécessaire pour que l'œuvre ne soit pas compromise, ni le royaume ébranlé. La coutume des ancêtres subsiste dans son ensemble et l'application des dispositions nouvelles ne touchera guère que l'Imerina, déjà amplement christianisée, donc préparée à les recevoir. Un code spécial, en 118 articles, a été proclamé en 1873 pour les Betsileo. Dans les pays vassaux les coutumes locales subsistent sans changement; elles seront maintenues sous le régime français; la polygamie a subsisté dans le Sud jusqu'à nos jours dans les moeurs; elle avait simplement cessé d'avoir des effets légaux; de même l'état-civil n'a-t-il été effectivement appliqué à l'île entière qu'à une époque récente; l'obligation scolaire n'atteint encore que la moitié des enfants.

Ainsi se manifeste, dès ce début malgache, un caractère essentiel de la codification africaine: elle vise à être, *non la constatation du droit existant, mais un idéal et un instrument de transformation dans le sens du monde moderne.* La toute-puissance des gouvernements issus de la décolonisation leur permet d'entreprendre cette révolution. Elle ne peut réussir qu'à condition de ne pas vouloir s'imposer brutalement et uniformément, et d'observer la patience et la confiance dans l'évolution dont la reine Ranavalona et son Premier Ministre leur ont donné, il y a déjà bien longtemps, le premier modèle.

Summary

THE FIRST AFRICAN CODIFICATION: MADAGASCAR 1828–81

Malagasy custom, based on the ancestor cult, and limited to small clannish societies, must have been filled in by legislation, when, from the seventeenth century on, the kingdoms enlarged their political horizons. The most important of these kingdoms was, at the end of the eighteenth century, that of the Merinas, which in the nineteenth century annexed two-thirds of the island, taking the name of 'Kingdom of Madagascar'.

After the oral legislation of the important King Andrianampoinimerina, wide and full of images, there appeared from 1828 on, written codes whose provisions were exclusively penal. The customs of the ancestors were sacred, and it was considered sacrilegious to alter anything. It was only in 1869, after the conversion of the Queen to Christianity, that the codes, still discreetly, began to deal with civil law, especially in the 'Code of the 305 Articles' (1881).

This legislation, containing penal sanctions, is a kind of programme rather than a statement of existing law. So the dispositions are careful: those customs not expressly altered are maintained. The code only applies in its entirety in the central province, which was easily controlled. There was reliance upon time and on example to spread the influence of the new dispositions. This code, largely maintained under French rule, is today giving way to a new juridical approach.

VII. Legal Personality in African Law
A. N. ALLOTT

I INTRODUCTION[1]

Where English law insists that legal relations must be at least bilateral, African customary law appears to permit the existence of single-ended legal relations, such as, for instance, the alleged vesting of rights in property in a deity or the ancestors. This might be taken to indicate a completely different approach to the analysis of legal obligations. African law is not dominated by procedural considerations, as is English law. It may not have as exact a means as is provided by incorporation in English law for registering the creation of a new legal person. It is, therefore, instructive to see how far the three tests which one would employ in English law to decide who has legal personality, and what such legal personality implies, are applicable to African legal institutions. The first of such tests is more general and abstract; the second and third are more particular and concrete. They are:

(i) Who (i.e. what human or other being, collection or group of beings, entity, thing, force, or idea) can figure as a member of a legal relationship?

(ii) Who can sue or be sued in a court or other dispute proceeding?

(iii) Who can hold or benefit from property in his or her own name?

In applying these tests, we must recognize the formidable theoretical obstacles in our path. As to the first and most general test or question, we must decide how far to accept

[1] The research upon which this report is based was mainly conducted, as far as Ghana is concerned, in the period 1949–51 in the Fante, Ashanti, Akim, and Assin areas of Ghana, by means of oral inquiry from chiefs, elders, councillors, and linguists, and the reading of the record books of native courts in the areas visited. [Editorial note: Originally this essay was introduced by a section on 'The concept of legal personality': this has been transferred to the 'Introduction' at p. 38.]

appearances as betokening reality, i.e. statements by 'informants' or the assumptions of the customary legal system as decisively representing the law. Direct or indirect information tells us that, for instance, in Ibo law:

> ... Physical phenomenon, pyschological forces and even purely abstract conceptions are deified by the Ibo mind and accorded legal personality ... they all are accorded legal personality in that they can acquire, enjoy and transfer property rights and interests as freely and fully as natural persons.[1]

And for Ghana customary law:

> The title to property owned by a group such as the family or clan, the village community or state or *oman* or stool is vested *not* in any member of the collectivity, but in the group regarded as a unit ... [2]

And in 'ghost-marriage' in Nuer law:

> It is the dead man, to whose name the wife is married (by his kinsman acting on his behalf), who is considered the legal father of the children.[3]

The recognition of non-natural, including supernatural, entities as in some way participating in the legal order; the importance of social and political groups and communities; the perpetuation of legal personality after death—these are just three of the problems typical of African law and for which English law, or European-based comparative law, apparently offers no ready solutions or explanations.

Apart from the recognition of legal personality where English and other European laws might be tempted to withhold it, we also have the possible problem of the non-recognition of legal personality where English law accords it. At its broadest, this point involves a consideration of whether African customary laws typically recognized individual legal personality at all, or whether—as some have represented it—African law was a law of groups and not of individuals. More narrowly, we have to ask ourselves whether there is any special class of the population —minors, women, strangers, slaves, or serfs—who are denied personality in customary law. In so doing, we must remember

[1] Obi, 1963, pp. 25–26. [2] Bentsi-Enchill, 1964, p. 41. [3] Howell, 1954, p. 74.

the uncertain boundary between personality and capacity. Restrictions on the legal *persona* may, perhaps, be more aptly described as deficiencies in capacity rather than as absence of personality.

The second test was a procedural one: who can sue or be sued? In applying this test to customary laws, we must first of all consider whether it is appropriate for a legal system which lacked a written procedure and hence many of the verbal niceties of modern legal systems. Two special problems come up here. The first derives from the frequent involvement in legal disputes of the families or kinship groups of the original disputants. This has even led some commentators to argue that traditional customary law cases were between families or kin-groups rather than individuals. We shall have to consider how far this explanation is justified when we come to look at the structure and legal functioning of family groups generally. But we can note here that very often there is an original complainant and an original wrongdoer in customary law, even if the complaint is taken up on his or her behalf by his or her family or guardian; and even if another person, or group of persons, may generally or in particular cases (as with respect to women, children, and formerly slaves) be answerable for a wrong committed by one in his charge.

The second problem in connection with the same test is to determine who is suing or being sued. This is particularly difficult in cases where a family or guardian is involved, but it also arises where a community, or to speak more exactly either the person holding authority in that community (e.g. the chief) or representative members of the community, may purport to take part in legal proceedings. This problem also arises in connection with the enjoyment of rights in property. Once one recognizes that agency on behalf of a juristic legal person (as with the priest of a deity in Ibo law, or with the employee of a limited company in English law) is possible, or that representative actions on behalf of a community may be taken to bind and benefit the so-called community as a whole, then there is no logical or legal limit to the number and types of juristic persons who can be recognized under a given system of law. A criminal prosecution in the name of a fictitious entity, the 'Crown', in England is then no more and no less mysterious than the expiation ceremonies connected with a homicide in Ibo law, conducted in the name of Ala, the land deity.[1]

The third test, that of who can hold or benefit from property, is of value not because it gives a definitive answer to the question of who has legal personality in a given system but because it illustrates the general approach to property rights in that system. Thus one can compare West African laws, on the one hand (Akan,[2] Yoruba,[3] Ibo,[4] etc.), in which a family or local group is conceived of as holding land 'in its own name', and various Southern, Central, and East African laws (e.g. Venda,[5] Tswana,[6] Luo[7]), where the accounts, reflecting the understanding of the people themselves, picture family or household land as 'vested' in the head of household, etc., but subject to legal or moral obligations to provide for his junior relatives or dependants. In so far as there is a regional difference in Africa, this is just as likely to be due to the fact that land cases in West Africa constantly reached the superior courts, whereas in East and Central Africa they rarely if ever did so, as to any intrinsic difference in the customary laws. Even if the attribution of legal personality is differently made, the practical results may be much the same in the two kinds of system; divergence may appear, however, through contact with novel circumstances: reinterpretation of the customary laws by non-customary authorities, and the reaction of indigenous property systems to new economic possibilities, may provide an opportunity for differential development of the system. In such cases, a property system in which the 'family' is expressed to be the ultimate corporate proprietor will preserve the rights of lesser members more effectively than one where their rights are conceived of as a legal, equitable, or even worse, a purely moral, burden on the proprietorship of the head of the group.

The discussion of the property rights of families brings out a fundamental theoretical point for our understanding of so-called legal personality, viz. that personality is an attribution, express or implicit, of the legal system. In so far as natural persons are concerned, attribution of legal personality means

[1] Cf. Meek, 1937, pp. 208 ff.
[2] Cf. Allott, 1954.
[3] Cf. Lloyd, 1962, esp. pp. 76 *et seq.*
[4] Obi, op. cit., *passim*.
[5] van Warmelo, 1949, esp. pp. 851 ff.
[6] Schapera, 2nd edition, 1955, pp. 195 *et seq.*
[7] Cf. Wilson, 1961, esp. pp. 76–77.

that the legal system recognizes the participation by individuals of that class or description in legal relationships. A legal system can—e.g. in connection with slaves or other groups considered sub-human—refuse recognition to individuals as being right-holders; to that extent, such individuals can be described as lacking legal personality (though inspection often discloses that they are still duty-bearers, and moreover that actually, as with the slave's *peculium*, or potentially, as with emancipation, the individual may acquire some legal rights).

Recognition of an individual as a legal person is usually the corollary of his recognition as a human being. The model for individual legal personality is provided by natural personality. Similarly, the recognition of artificial legal personality is by extension from the recognition of natural personality. It is here that many juriprudential discussions—for example, those which ask whether corporations 'really' have personality—have gone astray. Juristic personality is *attributed*, and it is attributed *by analogy* with human personality. The personification of natural forces and the recognition of group personality do not imply a total (and hence necessarily absurd) identification between such entities and natural persons; they mean that for certain limited purposes the legal system and those who operate it treat the entity *as if* it possessed legal personality. Thus, in the instances already given, Ibo law will accept the agent of a deity as being an agent *for someone*; Akan law will permit someone claiming to speak for a 'family' to initiate legal proceedings; Nuer law will recognize that the wife in a ghost-marriage is lawfully married to her dead husband. In each case we have an analogical fiction. In each case both law and common sense recognize the limits of the fiction: the Ibo deity must be represented by a priest; the living members of the Akan family are collectively entitled to bind the dead members and those who are yet to be born; the wife in a Nuer ghost-marriage enjoys normal relations with a pro-husband who performs all the usual marital offices which the ghost-husband is incapable of doing.

To call the attribution of juristic personality to non-natural entities an analogical fiction may seem to imply that all this is a game or pretence, a denial of reality on the part of the legal system. This would be a travesty of the true position. The attribution of personality is a *device* used to implement a mental or social reality. The family members feel solidarity, both with one another and with their departed ancestors, which they wish to express in unity of action. The deity is conceived of as a real person, though of a different order of reality from persons on earth. The departed husband may have died, but he is not socially non-existent. In the same way a limited liability company such as Imperial Chemical Industries, the Crown, or the University of London do not 'exist'; but we behave, for limited purposes, as if they did.

II PERSONS IN AFRICAN LAW: THE INDIVIDUAL

Absence of Personality

Are there any classes of human being who are denied personality in African law? There are many classes with restricted legal capacity (minors, women, strangers); but it is difficult to find any class of individuals entirely lacking both rights and duties under the law.

Slaves. The obvious group to begin with are slaves. However depressed their status, they were rarely rightless. More usually they could acquire limited rights in property, and even marry. In some societies (e.g. Hausa) they could become generals or administrators; in some they could buy their freedom. Injuries to a slave were often injuries to, and actionable by, his master. Often the slave might have no legal protection against his master, but in some societies this was not so.[1]

Servile strata. The depressed Bairu peasantry in the Hima kingdoms of East Africa were not rightless. Only the Sarwa of Bechuanaland seem at one time to have been denied recognition as right-holding human beings under Tswana law.

Strangers. Non-members of the tribe or other maximal political unit were usually accorded recognition as legal persons, except perhaps in time of war or continuing hostility. Often, of course, a stranger would have more limited rights than a member of the community, especially to acquire interests in land; but this was merely a diminution in capacity, not a denial of personality.

New-born infants. In several systems (e.g. Ashanti) a baby does

[1] E.g. in Ashanti: cf. Rattray, 1929, p. 38.

not acquire human, and hence legal, personality at birth. Some ceremony, e.g. that of naming, may be required to establish its status as a 'person'.

Acquisition of Personality

The conclusion, then, is that—excepting infants *en ventre sa mère* and the new-born—human beings acquire legal personality at or soon after birth. Typically this personality may be limited, or more exactly legal capacity may be restricted, until the minor becomes of age, marries, leaves home, or otherwise attains majority (if he ever does so). Slaves who become emancipated may win a similar enlargement of capacity.

Cessation of Personality

Legal personality may be withdrawn exceptionally, as by banishment or outlawry; or lost permanently or temporarily through mental defect, as with lunacy and drunkenness, or (formerly) through enslavement. It is when we come to consider the effect of death on legal personality that we meet a problem of interpretation. Thus in Ashanti law, according to Rattray,[1]

The *samanfo*, the spirits of the departed forebears of the clan [= matrilineal lineage], are the real landowners.

And

The Ashanti owner has to account in full and be subject not only to the control of councillors, clansmen, and family, but finally ... in virtue of his spiritual trusteeship, to the dead.[2]

Is this picturesque language expressive of legal reality? Or is it merely a poetical way of conveying the feeling that the living hold land 'in trust' for the departed and those who are yet to come (the same feeling that the Benchers of an Inn of Court might have for the property and traditions of their Inn)? Now quite clearly in traditional Ashanti belief departed relatives were felt to be in touch with the world of the living; the ritual of pouring libations was one outward sign of this communication. Equally, as in other parts of Africa, the living were careful to placate the spirits of their ancestors before doing

[1] Rattray, 1923, p. 216.　　[2] Ibid., pp. 228–9.

anything with the land originally acquired by those ancestors. But if we look at the functioning legal system, what part do we find that the ancestors play in the control over and derivation of benefit from the land?

The answer is, practically none. Rattray's own account of Ashanti land tenure (curtailed and full of gaps though it is) indicates that: (i) a subject allocated land for farming out of unallocated stool land had to give the chief 'a sheep' each year for the '*Samanfo*' (spirit ancestors);[1] (ii) the spirits did not have to be informed if individually occupied land were mortgaged;[2] (iii) if a senior wing chief sold some of his stool land, 'the *Samanfo* were informed'.[3] And that is all.

I quote Rattray to begin with because he offers us an account of the traditional pre-European law. Any account of Ashanti land law in the twentieth century (e.g. that derived from my own researches) would reveal even less mention of the ancestors' role in the functioning land law. This role is very different from that of living, functioning, interest-holders. To begin with, it is entirely passive. Secondly, the requirement is no more than that of keeping the ancestors informed of certain land transactions of major importance. Thirdly, it is the living who decide what is to be done with the land, and who derive enjoyment from it. I conclude that to call the ancestors 'legal persons' and to declare them the 'true owners' of the land may express sentiments felt on some occasions by Ashanti, but is literally meaningless, i.e. without function in the law.

Is the same true of the Nuer ghost-husband? Again his role is purely passive; again it is the living who decide what is to be done and who derive benefit from the arrangement:

> The man who marries a wife to the name of his dead kinsman is father in all roles and is in every respect the husband of the woman except in the strictly legal sense.[4]

III PERSONS IN AFRICAN LAW: GROUPS AND COMMUNITIES

The discussion in general jurisprudence of the nature and indicia of legal personality has centred on the personality of

---

[1] Rattray, 1929, p. 350.
[2] Ibid., p. 357.
[3] Ibid., p. 358.
[4] Howell, 1954, p. 74.

corporations. African customary laws are typically laws of, or based on, groups and communities, social and political. The study of group-personality in African law is thus inescapably the most important task both from the jurisprudence and from the more narrowly African points of view.

Many different kinds of African groups and communities have been declared by alien observers to have legal personality, or at least to be 'corporate'. Since there is usually in customary law no system of incorporation, no formal process of grant of personality or dedication, it is not as easy to pick out the artificial legal persons as it might be in English law. But perhaps it may be possible to pick out a 'charter' of corporate personality in a broader sociological sense, some act or symbol or process which identifies groups with legal personality. Charters in this sense can be found in African law. Thus—taking examples only from Akan law in Ghana—we can pick out for the two main types of legal person, the political stool and the family, certain indicia of personality or separate identity:

(i) *Name*. The stool or the family (lineage) has a name. The political stool-name is normally either the name of a place, within or over which the stool exercises jurisdiction, e.g. the Mampong Stool, or the name of an office or position, e.g. Adonten Stool. The matrilineal family is usually named from its clan and the place in which the clan-segment is found: 'Yego Family of Apaa Quarters of Nyakrom'.

(ii) *Defined membership*. The subjects of a stool fall into two categories: (*a*) the vast majority, who are subjects by reason of birth into one of the matrilineal families subject to or members of the stool; (*b*) a minority who are expressly accepted into membership by the stool-holder. The members of an Akan matrilineal family are precisely defined through their acknowledgement of a common *abusuapanin* or lineage head and through their participation in family rituals, their contributions to funeral expenses, etc.

(iii) *Defined structure and government*. A stool is held by a chief or other ruler with defined powers. His accession and possible destoolment are marked by precise ceremonies. Similarly a lineage or family has a defined structure of government; those with authority in the family are precisely picked out by the law;

family meetings of a formal kind provide the opportunity for the ascertainment of the common will of the family members.

(iv) *Symbol of identity.* A so-called stool is itself a symbol of identity, identifying a particular *oman* or political unit. The authority of the stool, conceived of as an entity, is symbolized by the physical stool which the holder for the time being notionally occupies. (The parallel with the Crown in England is extremely close.) Similarly each family may have a stool occupied by its head; the family burial ground also symbolizes family unity and separateness.

(v) *Concerted action.* Members of the group—stool or family—habitually act together, either generally or for some specific purpose, in a concerted fashion. There is a machinery for determining the general will of the group; action so decided on is taken in the name of the group.

(vi) *Attribution of rights and duties to the entity.* Both the members of a particular group, and the legal system generally, attribute certain rights and duties to the group as if it were a separate entity. The stool or the family is said to hold land—'stool land' or 'family land'; the stool or the family takes part in legal proceedings in its own name. In the ancient law the family was held, and held itself, collectively responsible for the misdeeds of its members. This detachment of the entity from its members does not go to the extent, however, in the traditional law of identifying or classifying the family as a legal, still less a natural person. The family exists as an entity in a separate order, the order of groups from that of individuals and the same is true of the stool. Linguistically one can remark that the Akan word *onipa*, meaning 'person', is never (to my knowledge) applied to any except a natural person. A family or a stool could not be called *onipa*. (And the same is probably true in other African languages: cf. Venda *mutu*, for example.)

(vii) *Durability.* 'Permanency' (the term used by Lloyd[1] in writing of the Yoruba) would appear to be too strong a word to use here. It is noticeable that the family is not, and is not viewed as, a transient collection of human beings who happen to find themselves associated at one moment in their existence. Rather is the family thought of as a group with a history (which can be and is recited); and it is the same with the stool. On the

[1] Lloyd, 1962, p. 32.

other hand, families and stools can disappear in time (at least in theory).

The English-based legal system in the Gold Coast, later Ghana, has had some difficulty in analysing and assimilating these traditional institutions in terms of the English law of corporations. It is not possible in this paper to discuss this analysis in detail; but we may note that the general law of Ghana recognizes stools and families as legal persons, capable of holding property in their own names, of acting as plaintiffs and defendants in legal proceedings, etc. Some judges have been tempted to describe the family as if the property of the family were vested in the head of the family 'in trust' for the other members; but this trustee–beneficiary explanation is now being abandoned in favour of the acceptance of the family as a customary corporation which is *sui generis*. The political stools have been treated similarly. Here the temptation to describe the institution in English terms is even stronger, as the analogy with corporations sole is very close. Rights can be appurtenant to the stool, and exercised by the holder of the stool for the time being, just as with a bishopric in England.

But this analysis understates the plural element in the stool. Firstly, the stool embodies and represents the *oman*, or political collectivity, the body of citizens or subjects. Secondly, customary law does not normally permit the chief or stool-holder to manage the affairs of the stool on his own: he is obliged to consult with and act through his council of subordinate chiefs and elders. The analogy is therefore much more with a corporation aggregate such as a limited liability company in English law—with the citizens as the shareholders or members, the chief in council as the board of directors, and the chief himself as chairman and managing director—than with a corporation sole.

Many other types of groups and communities, including various sorts of kinship or family groupings, have legal significance in African law generally. The extent to which they are viewed, whether by the people themselves or by external observers, as 'persons' in the law varies enormously. Among such groups are *villages* (or local residential communities); *age-groups* and other forms of age-association; *societies* (many of them secret, and often with specific social functions, especially in the sphere of law and order); *work-associations*, guilds, partnerships, etc. Space forbids discussion of all these in detail here; but a brief comment on two types of grouping found in Akan law will clarify the issues.

The Village Community

Sarbah,[1] perhaps influenced by the writings of Sir Henry Maine on Indian village communities, felt that the village community was the basis of Fante land tenure. After explaining the process by which an original settler in virgin territory cleared land, occupied it with his family, and became the ancestor in the female line through his sisters of the village headman or *odekuro*, he goes on to say:

> Land in possession of the founder of the village is family stool property. Land cleared and occupied by subsequent settlers who have joined the founder is the property of the subsequent settlers. Land acquired by the founder and settlers together is held by the village community, and becomes attached to the stool of the person for the time being head of the village. All the inhabitants of the village have each of them a proportionate share in such lands as common property, without any possession or title to distinct portions.

Historically this description is doubtless accurate; juristically the interpretation is seriously misleading. Since Sarbah's words were adopted by certain native courts and then by the superior courts in British times,[2] it is of great importance to qualify or correct them.

My own researches (based on oral inquiry and case records)[3] showed that villages were in Akan law the basis of local exploitation of land, as one might expect. The claim to use land as of right was based primarily on membership of a village community, and secondarily on membership of the appropriate larger political unit (indigenous 'state' or division). This entitlement extended only to (i) the taking into cultivation or occupation ('appropriation' is a suitable word here) of virgin land within the sphere of control of the village community,

[1] Cf. Sarbah, 1906, pp. 6 f.
[2] Cf. *Boadu* v. *Fosu* (1942) 8 W.A.C.A. 187 (in the West African Court of Appeal).
[3] Cf. Allott, 1954, esp. at pp. 129 f.

and (ii) participation in the exploitation in common of certain natural resources within the village area (e.g. collection of firewood, drawing of water from streams). Much of the so-called village lands are in fact appropriated by families or individuals, leaving merely a residual claim in the community on the one hand (a power of land control) and in the several members of the community on the other (e.g. a right of passage). Sarbah's mention of land 'attached to the stool' of the village headman should be reinterpreted as 'powers of land-control vested in the stool-holder for the time being on behalf of the village community'; the villagers do *not* have a proportionate share in such lands. Distinguishing the appropriated and unappropriated lands of the village, one may say that: (*a*) a particular family or individual (or sometimes more than one individual) has a separate, exclusive interest of use and benefit in the particular land it has appropriated, with—as noted above—a very restricted power of land control vested in the village head in council, representing the community interest as a collectivity, and very restricted common rights vested in the village members severally; and (*b*) as for unappropriated land, the community power of land control—exercised again through the village head—is far more extensive, including a power of partial or total alienation, while the individual villagers have in the unappropriated lands both a common right to appropriate land for farming, and common rights of use equivalent to easements and profits in English law: in other words, by exercising his prior common right to appropriate, a villager can acquire 'possession or title' (I prefer to say an 'interest') to a distinct portion of the village lands. What is so characteristic of African systems of land tenure is that the effect of his so doing is to add a further tier to the hierarchy of interests already subsisting in that particular land.

I conclude that a happier way of describing the village community in Akan law is to mention that the village head, as stool-holder, is the agent and representative of a customary legal entity, the stool, which has both plural (cf. corporations aggregate) and singular (cf. corporations sole) characteristics. The stool itself represents the village community, whose representatives sit on the council which advises the stool-holder, and together with him administer the affairs of the stool. The rights of the individual village members are of at least three kinds: (i) a joint, undifferentiated right to participate in the affairs of the stool/community; (ii) common rights to exploit the resources of the community in a non-exclusive manner, but severally and for their individual benefit; (iii) individual rights derived in part from their exercise of their common rights, e.g. through appropriation of unoccupied land or forest produce, such rights being exclusive as against other villagers, but incapable of excluding the land-control powers of the community and its superior political authorities. The village community might thus be termed, not a legal person, but rather an entity with legal significance and legal organs.

Partnerships

Akan law recognizes various forms of joint exploitation of natural resources. Two brothers may combine to clear and plant land; they then become in effect joint owners of the resulting interest. A more specialized form of partnership is found in the Fante fishing communities along the coast, where the unit is the fishing canoe and its crew. Unfortunately I have not yet had the opportunity to examine the legal structure of such fishing partnerships in detail, but my information indicates that they are well worth studying from the legal point of view. What seems clear is that neither the boat nor the team is viewed as a legal entity or person; this, then, is an intermediate form of legal organization between the *ad hoc* collaborators on the one hand, and the closely knit 'corporate' group on the other.

BIBLIOGRAPHY

Allott, A. N.
   (1954) *Akan Law of Property* (unpublished).
Bentsi-Enchill, K.
   (1964) *Ghana Land Law*. London: Sweet and Maxwell.
Howell, P. P.
   (1954) *A Manual of Nuer Law*. London: Oxford University Press for the International African Institute.
Lloyd, P. C.
   (1962) *Yoruba Land Law*. London: Oxford University Press for the Nigerian Institute of Social and Economic Research.
Meek, C. K.
   (1937) *Law and Authority in a Nigerian Tribe*. London: Oxford University Press.

Obi, S. N. C.
  (1963) *The Ibo Law of Property*. London: Butterworth.
Rattray, R. S.
  (1923) *Ashanti*. Oxford: Clarendon Press.
  (1929) *Ashanti Law and Constitution*. Oxford: Clarendon Press.
Sarbah, J. H.
  (1906) *Fanti National Constitution*. London: Clowes & Sons.
Schapera, I.
  (1938) *A Handbook of Tswana Law and Custom*. London: Oxford University Press for the International African Institute (2nd edition, 1955).
van Warmelo, N. J.
  (1949) *Venda Law: Part 4, Inheritance*. Pretoria: Government Printer.
Wilson, Gordon
  (1961) *Luo Customary Law and Marriage Laws and Customs*. Nairobi: Government Printer.

Résumé

LA PERSONNALITÉ JURIDIQUE DANS LE DROIT AFRICAIN

I LE CONCEPT DE LA PERSONNALITÉ JURIDIQUE

En général, les droits et les devoirs, dans un système juridique donné, sont considérés comme étant exercés entre 'personnes'. Est-ce vrai en droit africain?

Trois critères principaux sont employés pour isoler les personnes juridiques dans un système:

(i) qui peut se présenter en tant que membre d'une parenté juridique?
(ii) qui peut poursuivre et être poursuivi en justice?
(iii) qui peut être propriétaire?

Il y a des obstacles théoriques à l'usage de tels critères dans le droit coutumier africain. Quelques droits africains semblent accorder la personnalité à des phénomènes 'praeternaturels', à des groupes sociaux et politiques variés et à des personnes décédées. Des groupes interviennent (ou intervenaient) directement dans des instances affectant leurs membres; une procédure non écrite peut ne pas spécifier avec précision qui sont les personnes dans de telles instances. Les systèmes concernant les biens familiaux sont articulés et conçus différemment dans les différents droits africains. On doit se souvenir que la personnalité juridique est attribuée dans un système juridique donné par analogie avec des personnes naturelles; il n'y a aucune limite théorique à l'attribution d'une telle personnalité, que ce soit à une divinité ou à un groupe, spécialement si le système définit que les 'personnes' peuvent agir par l'intermédiaire de mandataires. La personnalité juridique est attribuée par une 'fiction analogique' mais ce moyen exprime une réalité psychologique ou sociale.

II LES PERSONNES DANS LE DROIT AFRICAIN: L'INDIVIDU

Dans le droit africain, les êtres vivants acquièrent généralement la personnalité juridique à la naissance ou peu après, mais peuvent avoir une capacité temporairement restreinte (par exemple les mineurs) ou restreinte d'une façon permanente (par exemple les femmes et les esclaves). Bien que la personnalité, par définition, se termine à la mort, ceci n'est pas vrai dans les systèmes où les 'ancêtres' sont considérés comme contrôlant la terre familiale (comme chez les Ashanti) ou où le 'mariage fantôme' est reconnu (comme chez les Nuer). Le compte rendu de Rattray au sujet du droit familial des Ashanti est rejeté en tant qu'il implique que les esprits des ancêtres disparus sont 'de vrais propriétaires'.

III LES PERSONNES DANS LE DROIT AFRICAIN: GROUPES ET COMMUNAUTÉS

Plusieurs sortes de groupes et de communautés africains ont été déclarés avoir une personnalité légale. Puisqu'il n'existe généralement aucun système de personnalisation, on doit chercher des indices de personnalité. Les deux principaux types de personne juridique dans le droit akan, le siège politique et la famille, sont caractérisés par: (i) un nom, (ii) des membres définis, (iii) une structure définie et un gouvernement, (iv) des symboles de leur identité, (v) une action concertée de leurs membres, (vi) l'attribution des droits et devoirs à l'entité, (vii) la durée.

La tentation d'assimiler ces institutions à celles du droit anglais est forte; des juges au Ghana (Côte d'Or) ont décrit le bien familial dans le cadre du rapport entre le 'trustee' et le bénéficiaire, et le siège comme une entité unique. Mais il est suggéré qu'il est préférable de reconnaître ceux-ci comme des êtres juridiques qui sont *sui generis*, bien que présentant des analogies avec le droit anglais.

Le droit africain reconnait généralement beaucoup d'autres sortes de groupes et associations: villages, groupes d'âge, sociétés, associations de travail, etc. . . . Deux parmi ceux-ci sont brièvement discutés en rapport avec le droit akan. Une distinction devrait être faite entre les terrains appropriés et inappropriés dans la limite du village; les droits communautaires (exercés par l'intermédiaire au chef du village et du conseil représentant les villageois) et les droits communs des villageois dans les terrains appropriés sont très restreints; et les droits des villageois sur la terre devraient être différenciés en droits conjoints, communs et individuels. La communauté du village peut être décrite comme un être avec une signification juridique et des organes juridiques plutôt que comme une personne juridique.

VIII. Sesotho Marriage, Guardianship, and the Customary-Law Heir

A. M. R. RAMOLEFE

My interest in customary law in general and heirship in particular derives from factors over which I had no control. At University, law degree students were obliged to study either *Bantu law* or the *South African native law*. None of these had ever appealed to me and, in fact, until I enrolled at the University of Natal, I had always prayed that mine should never be the misfortune of having 'to waste my time' reading 'a system of conventions' which 'only baaskap South Africa was committed for political reasons to entrench'. Be my and my peoples' feelings what they will in this regard, and having little choice in the matter, I opted for the much wider *Bantu law* which embraces *Native law* and the customary laws practised in states north of the Limpopo. Within a year I passed this course, with my interest in its many contradictions aflame.

Midway through my degree studies, my father died. Responsibility came my way in a flood. Wherever that dear soul would have officiated, wherever his word would have spelt amen, wherever he it was who would have paid the bill—there I found myself firmly planted in his shoes. In vain I resisted, insisting throughout that burdens laid on me should match the benefits he had left me—no less, no more. I saw as the only way out of my dilemma precise knowledge of what my position as heir entailed. I had to content myself with waiting till I had completed my degree before I could initiate this inquiry.

I finished my studies, returned to Lesotho, and found a friend in the then Judicial Adviser to Lesotho Customary Courts, Mr. Tsepo Mohaleroe, who had me made Registrar. In this post, and as the Senior Field Officer, Mr. Mohaleroe left to me the regular inspection of court work and the giving of advice where it was meet. Court staff, on the other hand, expected me to be a kind of walking encyclopaedia on Custom. Mindful of my limitations I nevertheless decided I would try to master the Customary Law. Besides, was this not the chance I had always craved to map the boundaries of my rights and duties as my father's legal successor?

On my return from the London University's 1964 *Colloquium on African Law* I took on the duties of Customary Law Commissioner, that is, I became the chairman of the Panel for the Restatement of Sesotho Law and Custom. Customary law is now my devoted study, not because I willed it so, nor because I am one with those who bleat: 'Let the natives develop along their own lines', but because up in the Maluti Mountains, and in several pockets of lowland-dwellers, Custom is very much still *the* law and no amount of contempt for it by others can alter this fact.

Sesotho law and custom is largely unwritten. Part of it in written form is *The Laws of Lerotholi* or 'The Lerotholi Code' which, first produced in or about 1903, was amended in 1922 by the then purely advisory National Council of Basutoland. Gleanings of Custom can also be found in the writings of early Paris Evangelical Missionaries and those of anthropologists. Books by South Africans on Customary Practices among the Basotho are unreliable, dealing largely, as they do, with caricatures of concepts known to and used by the Basotho of Lesotho.

Whether or not any practice qualifies to be regarded as Custom hinges largely on its consonance with justice. In the scale of justice many rules formerly mistaken for law have turned out rejects. Justice is, therefore, one of the yardsticks against which we measure practices said to have the force of law. Having said this much I now proceed to deal with certain familial statuses, following as best I can the outline on my paper. And, as there is much overlapping between the content of each of these statuses and the rights and duties of the heir, a slow picture of the heir will emerge in the process.

The term 'child' in customary law takes in unmarried issue of both sexes, whether legitimate or not, and can apply to married women and widows in certain cases as I shall endeavour to show.

Children or minors have no *locus standi in judicio*. Sued civilly they must be assisted by their legal guardians. Whatever damages are payable for their delicts bind their natural guardians and such other guardians as can be shown by satisfactory proof that though they are not natural guardians they ought to be bound on the score of their having been recipients of the fruits of the wrongdoer's labours. It would appear, however, that in the cases falling within the latter category the burdens would be made commensurate with the benefits. The guardian takes all the child's earnings and may use these to discharge obligations imposed by the child's erring ways. A delict committed before the minor attained majority through matrimony binds the guardian. But justice would allow that where the guardian had been 'excused' execution, process issues against the tortfeasor himself.

Minors who have no natural guardians can, it appears, have a *curator ad litem*, usually a paternal uncle, appointed to cure a minor's want of capacity in the courts. An incorrigible ward can be disowned and from then onwards, provided he ceases to take the benefits flowing from such ward, the guardian may escape liability stemming from such ward's misdeeds.

Every child has the right to claim maintenance in the forms of food, clothing, shelter, and necessary medical expenses. With the absence of compulsory education it does seem that no Mosotho child has a legal right to be put through school.

Bohali (bride-wealth, sci. dowry) for a male ward's first wife is provided by the guardian, and the receiver of the girl's bride-wealth must produce the trousseau.

Posthumous issue (issue *in utero* at deceased's death and children born of approved cohabitation with widows after the death of the head of the family, that is children born of a lawful *kenela*, seed-raising, relationship) are legitimate and are owed the rights I have already outlined. All illegitimate issue are attached to their mother's brothers and sisters and their rights flow from their maternal grandfather or his legal successor.

The children of a *lefielo* (a servant-wife) claim all their rights from their mother's 'husband'. A *lefielo*, or broom, is a woman married by a bride's parents who goes with the bride to her new matrimonial home to work as her servant. This practice was confined to the rich and the chiefs who were not always happy to see their married daughters work. The bride is regarded as the 'husband' of the broom. The 'husband' looks to her own husband for the keep of the *lefielo* and 'its' children who must be begotten by the husband. In extreme cases resort can be had by the 'husband' (i.e. the bride) to her parents.

The children of a *ngoetsi*, a woman married by the man for attachment to a particular house as a shadow wife, rank next in importance to the children of the main wife in the house. Note that the other and ordinary meaning of *ngoetsi* is daughter-in-law.

A *seantlo*, a wife's blood relation who is married to step into the shoes of a deceased married elder sister, bears children of the full blood just as are issue of a *ngoetsi*. While on this point it can be stated that only a *seantlo* and a *ngoetsi* can *kenela* (lawfully inherit) all the matrimonial rights of a deceased wife and that no other 'wives' can. It is on the ground that it failed to take account of this rule that the case of *Maseela* v. *Maseela*, in which judgment was handed down on 2 March 1954 by the learned Chief Justice, Sir Harold Willan, C.M.G., M.C., is rejected as of no authority.

The duties which fetter the head of the family devolve upon the heir at the former's death. With these come also such rights as reposed in the deceased during his lifetime. Purely personal rights, such as the deceased's right to the widows' beds, do not pass to the heir.

So much for minors in general. Female minors or women stand in a context somewhat different from the males. At marriage they pass from the *potestas* of their natural guardians to that of their husbands. I incline to the view, expressed obiter by Lansdown, J., in *Bereng Griffiths* v. *'M'Antsebo Seeiso Griffith*. *H.C.T.L.R.* 1926–53 at 57D, that today it can be shown that certain widows, divorcées, and women of independent means have become emancipated in certain spheres of life. In the majority of cases, however, women are still classed as children and may appear in court only when duly assisted by their husbands. Be that as it may, where a woman appears in court alone claiming enforcement of a right residing in her absent husband or guardian and claiming mere agency, I can hardly see her non-suited; for were women to be denied a hearing, no matter how peculiar the case might be, it would mean that even interdicts would be beyond their reach—those speedy remedies resorted to by people unjustly despoiled.

The question has yet to be decided what happens where a woman after committing a tort *stante matrimonio* divorces the husband against whom a judgment in respect of the wrong has already been given. In my view, according as the divorce results from the husband's conduct or not, justice would probably bind him, otherwise the woman or whosoever becomes her next guardian would be bound.

The rights of women married in a monogamous union and others tied together in a polygamous union are alike except in a few details. In a polygamous 'marriage' the senior wife is owed the duty of respect by the junior wives; she is consulted when it is proposed to marry a shadow wife (*ngoetsi*), or where it is necessary to find another woman to bear children for her, in case she herself is barren. The wife in a monogamous union also is consulted in these two cases. Finally, a senior wife can become the heir's guardian and the controller and administrator of her deceased husband's unallocated property, about which more in due course.

According to two cases decided by the High Court (CIV/A/6/62: *Ralienyane Lekaota* v. *'M'Amoselantja R Lekaota*, and CIV/A/1/64: *Molungoa Bolei Khatala* v. *Francina Bolei Khatala*) the wife in a monogamous union cannot claim that she is entitled to the control of the deceased husband's estate on the ground that being the only wife she forms one 'house' and, therefore, that all that her husband died possessed of is allocated to her house. Their Lordships decided that she formed no house in as much as, so their Lordships said, there had not been an overt act by deceased in his lifetime from which such allocation could be inferred. I shall say more about these decisions later; presently, however, let me attempt a synopsis of the status of widows.

The Lerotholi Code in Section 11 gives as heir in Lesotho the first male child of the first-married wife and that, if there be no male issue in the first house, then the first-born child of the next-married wife in succession shall be the heir. The senior widow succeeds where there is no male issue, but custom requires her to consult the relatives of her deceased husband who are her proper advisers. The senior widow may also act as the heir's 'regent' where such heir is a minor (see the *Bereng Griffith* case referred to above).

A senior wife who takes as heir inherits all the unallocated property of the estate which she is obliged by custom to use with the other widow(s) of her late husband, and to share it with male issue of such widow(s) according to the order in which their mother(s) were married. She inherits this property together with its attendant *vinculae* just as if she were a male heir herself. The question of what moiety shall be set aside for the support of such widow(s) shall be decided by the paternal uncles of the principal heir, i.e. usually the first son of the first-married wife, and such other relatives as by custom have the right to be heard in this connection. Besides unallocated property, she keeps all the property which has been allocated to her own house. Of this latter property she has both the control and the use. The remainder of her house property passes to the principal heir upon her death, which the principal heir must use to maintain dependants of the deceased widow's house. In disposing of the property of her house the widow shall seek the prior consent of her guardian. In the instance under review the principal heir may be the father of the deceased husband or his brother(s).

Where the heir is a minor, his guardian and the administrator of the estate, who may be, as we have already seen, the senior widow herself, is required to keep a written record of her administration which shall lie open to inspection by the paternal uncles and such others as share this their right. In addition, the prior consent of these people is requisite for the guardian of the heir and administrator of the estate to part with any of the assets.

If in a house, other than that from which the principal heir comes, the widow has male issue who is still a minor, such widow shall have both the control and the use of all the property appropriated to her house. At her death the remainder of this property devolves upon her eldest male child who must share such property with his junior brothers or, if her eldest son attains his majority before her death, she is divested of control in favour of this son. The phrase 'reached majority' seems to indicate age rather than emancipation through marriage.

In dealing with this property over which during her son's

minority she has control and use—a use that is not like usufruct as she can actually make inroads into the substance—the widow would have to consult her guardian. At this point it might be appropriate to turn to a statement George Tlali Moshoeshoe made in 1873 to the Cape of Good Hope *Commission on the Laws and Customs of the Basotho*.

In his evidence Mr. Moshoeshoe told the *Commission* that the eldest son in each house inherits all the property allocated by his late father to that son's mother's house. He then goes on to say that the eldest son 'is only acting for his mother who has charge of all her deceased's husband's property during her lifetime belonging to her house but at her death it then devolves upon the eldest son of the house'. *The Lerotholi Code* in *Section 14 (3)*, however, says on this point: the widow shall have the control and the use of the estate during the heir's minority. He takes over control on attaining his majority. It would appear that even her use from this moment onwards hinges upon whether this son and his junior brothers wish, with the concurrence of their paternal uncles, to enforce their right to share such property. I am the first to admit that both *The Lerotholi Code* and the Report of the 1873 Commission are mere guides which have no statutory authority so that one may use the one as well as the other. Be that as it may, practice seems to have bent in favour of *The Lerotholi Code* provision, but personally I consider Mr. Moshoeshoe's view better law. (See my comments below on *Lekaota*'s case.)

A widow can claim that a portion of the property that is not allocated be set aside for her maintenance. Where during this lifetime the husband had allocated but not distributed certain property to his house(s), the allotment is confirmed by his death and cannot be upset 'provided the heir according to Basuto custom has not been deprived of the greater part of his father's estate'. It seems that a widow has one or both of the following heirs to contend with after her husband's death: in respect of unallocated property she is faced by the heir, the principal heir; as far as her house property is concerned, she has to give way to her son's right of control. If she has no son, she retains control and use, and the residue passes to the principal heir at her death. This heir must use it to maintain dependants of the widow's house.

I have already referred to the decisions in *Lekaota*'s and *Khatala*'s cases which state that a wife married monogamously does not form a 'house'. With this proposition I respectfully disagree. I assert, as does the Judicial Commissioner's Court, that where a man has married only one wife the question of allocation does not arise. To make the quest is the work of supererogation. In a monogamous union there cannot be any floating or unallocated property. All of it belongs and can belong only to the one 'house' the woman and her children represent. It would be inequitable to regard a wife and her children as forming a 'house' only where her husband is a polygamist. An unfortunate halo round a dying practice! Religion, which has had its hand in improving customary practices, would frown at the suggestion. I submit that the solitary wife forms a house. And here is how Stafford and Franklin in their *Principles of Native Law* define a 'house':

'House' means the family and property, rights and status, which commence with, attach to and arise out of the customary union of *any* [my italics] woman or the marriage of *any* woman [again my italics].

There is in my view no passage in any judgment of our High Court which, in conflict with both *The Lerotholi Code* and the 1873 Commission's Report, so unfairly extends the heir's rights and materially encourages the diminution of a widow's rights as does the last sentence in the following extract from *Lekaota*'s case:

Where there is male issue such interest as a widow has by Basotho Law and Custom in unallocated movables including cattle remains *unaffected* [my italics] by the death *per se* of her husband so that, save that the heir takes the place of the deceased husband in regard to the control of such property, no such widow is by reason of the husband's death beneficiary for life or otherwise of such property except as provided by the said law 13. [She can ask for some to be set aside for support—A. M. R. Ramolefe.] I [the judge] might perhaps mention that my Assessors in their advice add to this, by way of example, that in consequence of the death not affecting, as hereinbefore stated, such interest of such widow in such property, ordinary household effects and such like should not be removed by the heir from the family home during the lifetime of the widow.

The widow's rights do not inhere in crockery and bedding only. The heir may not remove any of the unallocated property as the widow's right to 'use' and 'consultation' whenever the heir wishes to deal with the property in any manner might be lost were such property to be taken away from her sight. An even greater objection is that heirs could, with impunity, swoop down hawk-like after their father's death and drive all before them leaving the widows and other dependants only with such china as may still be serviceable at their father's death. Surely, if her interest in unallocated property remains unaffected by her husband's death, a proposition I endorse, then there can be no question of removal of anything especially if we accept the statement that the only change is that of control passing from her husband to her son or the heir.

It is a disturbing trend that with money coming more and more to take the place of cattle, sheep, and goats, our courts still seem to look for 'ear marks' even in estates consisting only of cash. There is not sufficient boldness to accept a new medium and, guided only by justice, even if this means jettisoning part of *The Lerotholi Code*, to evolve new rules, equitable rules, of succession. The reluctance of the courts to define the word 'control' in relation to the heir's right has caused many a widow's heart to break. The oft-stated fear that left with the estate the widow would probably hand it to other men is unfounded. After all an amorous widow or one who remarries loses her right for all time to the property left by her former husband.

Finally, and before I go on to look at other aspects of the heir's rights and duties, a word about a peculiar man–woman relationship. This is where particular women merely ally themselves to particular men in a 'conjugal' relationship that is not legal marriage. What are the rights of the parties here *inter se*? And what is their status? Both remain unmarried and are minors. Problems concerning their property arise firstly, where the union is terminated by either party, or, secondly, after the consort's death. A local court seised of a suit after the parties had parted ruled that the man take what he had bought with his earnings and, so too the woman. It seems that it would accord with justice that where the woman had borne the man illegitimate issue and had then served as cook, housewife, and nurse in the joint household for the court to order a fifty–fifty sharing of the joint property thus doing simple justice between man and woman in unions which are unfortunate, which should be discouraged, but which are only too common among Africans, including Basotho, in South African cities.

If, after her consort has died, the woman should claim as follows: 'I admit X was not my husband, but further I claim that ours was a universal partnership, sharing profit and loss', and such a woman can prove her contribution in labour and in goods or property, which way would justice tilt? In most cases our customary courts have shied away from the problem and have sent the woman empty-handed away.

While discussing the status of others above, much has been revealed of the content of heirship, which is a status in Sesotho Law and Custom. Standing as he does, *in loco parentis* to all deceased's former wards, the various claims others had had on the head of the family, the *paterfamilias*, are inherited by the heir, as we have already stated. In monogamous and polygamous unions the heir is the first male child of the first-married wife or, if there is no male issue in the first house, then the first-born male child of the next-married wife in succession shall be heir. Failing an heir in any house, the senior widow becomes heir but custom requires that she consult the relatives of her deceased husband who are her proper advisers. The heir inherits property that cannot be shown to have been appropriated to any one house and is required to use this with the widows and to share it with his junior brothers. In illicit unions, or what has often been called man–woman partnerships, the heir remains the parent of the man, if he was not married and had no children before he 'contracted' the union, and in the case of the woman her parents.

The *paterfamilias* is entitled to disinherit the heir in the rare case of an heir who is out and out wayward and disrespectful to the *pater*. It appears that an announcement in the presence of relatives, especially the paternal uncles, is essential. On the other hand, the heir also has a right to refuse to accede. But there is no recorded instance of this ever having happened in Lesotho. Even though the liabilities exceed the assets in the estate, the memory of the departed and their power to procure for a successor luck or ill-luck may, alone, be the factor which has militated against repudiation. Besides, the status 'heir' is one that is not altogether uncoveted because of the sphere of influence and authority it gives one.

At the death of the head of the family the assets in his estate are not realized. All the heir does is to call upon debtors to pay their dues, except long-term debtors such as those who owe *bohali* (bride-wealth). Creditors, except long-term, are also paid or undertakings made to discharge their debts. Brothers and sisters of the full- or half-blood take equally and the heir takes the *bohali* of the girls but passes it to the house from which each of these girls comes because, as the saying goes, 'houses do not eat each other', meaning that what is paid for these girls is allocated to their mothers' houses. The heir is the natural guardian of all illegitimate issue born to women who were the deceased's wards.

In his 'administration' of the estate the heir is accountable only to the widow(s) with whom he must consult and jointly use the property left. The paternal uncles keep a discreet supervisory distance and step in where disputes develop between the heir and the widow(s) and others of his father's dependants. An heir's regent, on the other hand, must keep a written record of the assets in the estate and of his or her administration. The record lies open for inspection by the paternal uncles and others to whom custom concedes this right. The regent may not part with any part of the property unless such alienation has been approved beforehand by the paternal uncles. Having said so much, can we liken the heir's position to that of a residual legatee or a fiduciary or a usufructuary?

In respect of unallocated property, he looks in part like a fiduciary and a usufructuary. Because the estate is not realized, and even potential debts, and the heir's duty to find the dowry for his junior brothers, and future assets, such as dowry hoped to be paid for his sisters, are counted as part of the estate, there cannot be talk of a residue. The heir administers the property left by the deceased in trust for the deceased's family and is entitled to take a portion himself: he uses the estate with the widows and shares it with his junior brothers according to the rank in which their mothers were married.

Is there any discernible change in the traditional concept of heir? There are rumblings on two fronts both of which call for reform. Heirs would like to have the benefits they receive match the burdens. Disproportion which results in the heir's own property falling to clear the deceased's death is not only a real hardship but is also seen as unfair. Why cannot a deceased estate be said to be insolvent if its liabilities exceed its assets? The other group that is agitating for a change is widows. Why must an heir be given the character of an all-devouring monster? Why must he not merely supervise the estate of which the widow will be usufructuary? Better still, why should not the right to dispose of property *inter vivos* be put beyond the reach of the *Lerotholi* rule which says that such disposition will be valid only if 'the heir according to Basotho custom has not been deprived of the greater part of his father's estate'? These, then, are fresh stirrings in this sphere and only the Legislature or the Courts, if they accept *The Lerotholi Code* and the 1873 Commission's Report as mere guides to custom, can improve what is today largely a heart-breaking set of rules: the rules of heirship and succession in Sesotho Law and Custom. Perhaps what needs to be done is to give parties to a marriage a choice of declaring at the time they marry, either that their marriage shall be in accordance with Roman–Dutch law principles, meaning that civil law proprietary consequences will follow; or to choose the potentially polygamous marriage of Sesotho law and custom. And the time has come to scrap Colonial-day survivals such as *Section 3 (b)* of *The Administration of Estates' Proclamation, No. 19 of 1935*, which provides that the Proclamation shall not apply to estates of Africans, which shall continue to be administered 'in accordance with the prevailing African law and custom in the Territory', with the proviso that such law and custom is not to apply 'to the estates of Africans who have been shown to the satisfaction of the Master to have abandoned tribal custom and adopted a European mode of life, and who, if married, have married under European Law'.

BIBLIOGRAPHY

Cape of Good Hope Government
    (1873) *Report and Evidence of Commission on Native Laws and Customs of the Basuto.* Cape Town: Saul Solomon.
Stafford, W. G. and Franklin, E.
    (1950) *Principles of Native Law and the Natal Code.* Pietermaritzburg: Shuter and Shooter.

Résumé

LE MARIAGE, LA TUTELLE ET LA QUALITÉ D'HÉRITIER
CHEZ LES SOTHO

Dans cette étude, la position de l'héritier dans le droit coutumier des Sotho est discutée en fonction d'un nombre de statuts familiaux qui se recouvrent, dans une certaine mesure. Ceux-ci comprennent le statut des mineurs et des femmes. En ce qui concerne ces dernières, certaines différences spéciales ont été créés par nombre de jugements du Tribunal de Grande Instance. Quelques uns de ceux-ci établissent par exemple qu'une femme mariée selon le système monogame, ne fait pas partie d'un 'ménage'; cette proposition conduit à des restrictions considérables dans un cadre moderne.

Dans les unions monogames et polygames, l'héritier est le premier enfant mâle de la femme épousée en premier lieu ou, s'il n'y a pas d'enfant mâle issu du premier mariage, le premier enfant mâle de la femme épousée ensuite. S'il n'y a pas d'héritier dans le ménage, la veuve ainée devient héritière mais la coutume demande que celle-ci consulte la famille du mari décédé qui deviennent ses conseillers. L'héritière hérite des biens dont on ne peut démontrer qu'ils ont été appropriés à un seul ménage et elle doit s'en servir avec les veuves et les partager avec les frères cadets du défunt.

Dans son administration de la propriété, l'héritier est seulement responsable vis-à-vis de la (ou des) veuves qu'il doit consulter et avec lesquelles il doit employer conjointement la propriété laissée. Les oncles paternels exercent à distance une supervision discrète et interviennent quand des conflits s'élèvent entre l'héritier et la veuve ou entre d'autres parents de son père. Un 'régent d'héritier' doit garder par écrit un état de l'actif de la propriété et de son administration. Ce rapport est ouvert pour inspection aux oncles paternels et aux autres personnes à qui la coutume accorde ce droit. Le 'régent' ne doit se séparer d'aucune partie de la propriété à moins qu'une telle aliénation ait été approuvée auparavant par les oncles paternels.

Les demandes de réforme du droit sesotho des successions en considèrent deux aspects. Les héritiers aimeraient que les bénéfices qu'ils reçoivent s'équilibrent avec les charges. La disproportion qui frappe les biens propres de l'héritier, qui ne peut régler la succession du défunt n'est pas seulement un vrai fardeau mais elle semble aussi injuste. Deuxièmement, il y a eu de l'agitation en ce qui concerne les veuves. Pourquoi donne-t-on à l'héritier le visage d'un monstre qui dévore tout? Pourquoi ne doit-il pas tout simplement superviser la propriété dont la veuve sera l'usufruitière?

IX. *Idda* and Secondary Marriage Among the Northern Kadara

M. G. SMITH

I INTRODUCTION

The Kadara are one of many 'pagan' tribes in the southern half of Zaria Province whose traditional institutions of marriage excluded divorce.[1] In 1934 the Muhammadan practice of *Idda*, described below, was imposed on these tribes by laws of the Zaria Native Authority and the British Provincial Administration. In this paper I wish to discuss some effects of this new rule as observed among the Northern Kadara in 1950 and 1959.[2] In this respect the present essay is a brief study in the conflict of laws. It should also show how an internally consistent structure of interlocking and ramifying rights may react to the introduction of an alien element when the conditions prerequisite for its reorganization are lacking.

Ideally, we should compare these Kadara reactions with parallel responses in other societies affected by the *Idda* rule. This comparison has been made with the Kagoro, but it cannot be presented here.[3] Briefly, after a period of confused reactions, Kagoro, who are politically united and autonomous, resolved the problems that *Idda* presented by institutionalizing a new set of marriage rules and procedures, which were devised to conserve their basic units of social organization, while eliminating the traditional form of secondary marriage. Lacking

[1] Smith, *The Social Structure of the Northern Kadara* (unpublished MS) (1951); 'Secondary Marriage in Northern Nigeria', (1953). These give a general account of the people.

[2] In March–April 1950 I spent six weeks with the Kadara of Kajuru district while holding a studentship from the Colonial Social Science Research Council. In April 1959 I revisited Kufana for a few days while attached to the Nigerian Institute of Social and Economic Research. To both these bodies grateful acknowledgements are due.

[3] *Secondary Marriage and Social Change: A Comparative Analysis* (unpublished MS) (1960).

political unity and internal autonomy, Kadara cannot develop a common policy on this matter, but are obliged to respond to their situation as individuals, lineages, or communities. In consequence, within their context of legal conflict, Kadara cannot resolve the problems which arise from the opposing interests of these different levels of social organization in a uniform manner.

Idda is a period of continence lasting three months which Maliki law requires before a free woman may remarry after leaving her husband.[1] In the Muslim Hausa courts of Northern Zaria, divorce is granted only on completion of *Idda*, which the court prescribes after failing to reconcile the couple. Since Muslim law forbids women to remarry without first obtaining a divorce, the Muslim courts must administer *Idda* before granting a divorce.

In 1934 a Kadara pagan court was established to administer their matrimonial cases. Its members were the Kadara village heads and it administered tribal law as well as the new *Idda* rule. For some years the court met at Kufana, the largest Kadara village in the district. It was then moved to Kajuru Town, where the District Head, who convened it for one week monthly, provided executive supervision and support through his Native Administration police. When the Kajuru District Council was set up in 1954, each Kadara village area was represented on it by its chief and two elected delegates, the Council meeting under the presidency of the Sarkin Chief of Kajuru. As Kadara comprise the majority of the district population, they provided the majority of the council members; but the council was ethnically mixed, and remained under Hausa control. It was not a tribal council.

Until 1954, fines for failure to observe the *Idda* regulation were set at 15*s*. for the erring wife and 25*s*. for her new husband. In 1955 these rates were increased by the Kajura district council to £3 for the woman and £6 for the man. At the same time the woman's father became liable to a fine of £4 if his complicity was established. Between 1955 and 1959, only two fathers were fined for this offence.

Within their village areas, Kadara are grouped into distinct communities, which are further divided into localized ritual aggregates (*ategburu*) each containing two or more patrilineages

[1] Ruxton, 1916.

(*ute*), who conduct their rituals together and constitute a separate ward. Lineages belonging to the same *ategburu* need not be linked by agnatic kinship, although this is common. Lineages form the primary segments of the ritual groups which are the major units of community organization; and each *ute* is itself divided into a number of minor lineages settled in separate compounds, known as *aban*. Compounds are further segmented into family households, known as *engau* (pl. *ungau*). All units at each level of organization have their most senior men as ritual heads; but administrative leadership of the lineage and of ritual groups is generally vested in an active man of middle age, selected by the lineage elders. In the old days, ritual group divisions of the local age-sets (*ufro*) served as fighting units; today they are called out for the larger hunts.

Kadara marriage is virilocal and normally patrilocal. Marriage between all cognates is expressly tabooed. Tribal law sanctions three forms of marriage (*uballe*): primary marriage, secondary marriage, and widow-inheritance. Primary marriage (*ario*) is preceded by a lengthy betrothal (*teshi*), during which the groom's kinsmen perform labour services for twelve years at annually increasing rates. With certain fixed gifts of grain, salt, mats, and hoes, this constitutes the standard bride-wealth at first marriage. Secondary marriage (*aherezam*) presupposes the woman's earlier marriage and the assent of her father or guardian and bride-wealth consists mainly in standard gifts of beer. Widow-inheritance (*alelalako*) is obligatory for primary and secondary wives alike, widows being allowed to select a spouse from their dead husband's agnates, in the hope that they will then settle.

Under tribal law, secondary marriage was subject to the following rules: (i) It was prohibited within each community. Formerly this was the village area or group of attached settlements; but since 1950 each settlement has come to be treated as a separate community. (ii) It was prohibited between all branches of a common lineage or clan, wheresoever located. (iii) Unmarried maidens could not be taken as secondary brides. Kadara placed no value on pre-marital chastity, the children conceived or borne by girls before marriage belonging to their primary husbands, who were then obliged to ratify their claims by traditional prestations to their fathers-in-law.

(iv) Secondary marriage required the approval of the woman's father or his surrogate. (v) On moving from one husband to another, a woman was required to present proofs of menstruation to her senior kinswomen at her next three periods, failing which the deserted husband claimed the next child as his. (vi) Relations of primary and secondary marriage are mutually exclusive. Men call those whose daughters they marry '*azaimi*'; those whose wives they abduct, '*aformi*'. The abducted wife always belongs by birth to a lineage with which her abductor's agnates maintain *azaimi* relations. He is thus in some sense entitled to seek her as a wife. *Aformi* relations, which are laden with tensions and dispute, were prohibited within each community; and traditionally all first marriages took place within these communities, following infant betrothals. (vii) A woman's abscondment terminates her cohabitation, but not the marriage. Wives may rejoin their deserted husbands permanently or on visits (*abusan*) of varying length, during which marital relations are resumed with the consent of the woman's other spouse, without any further transfers of bride-wealth. Absent wives are summoned by their dead husband's lineage kin for inheritance. (viii) A woman's first husband has an unqualified claim to all her issue before she leaves his home; but he is required to validate these claims by substantial gifts of beer to her father after the birth of the child, and by similar triennial gifts until the third child is born. Secondary husbands, in their turn, are also required to make these gifts. (ix) Under tribal law a husband could not claim return of bride-wealth once his wives had borne him a child, whether it survived or not. Claims for return of bride-wealth had no place in traditional practice, being inconsistent with secondary marriage and with lineage relations. Such practice would empower individuals to claim for themselves the value of services provided by their lineage kin. By so doing it would allow men to surrender claims to their children and to discontinue the residual rights that their lineages held in their wives. Finally, under Kadara norms, any issue of unions terminated in this way would trace descent from its mother's father, in opposition to the patrilineal mode of Kadara society.

Under tribal law, primary and secondary husbands enjoy identical rights in their wives on marriage. Besides exclusive domestic and sexual rights for the duration of their cohabitation, these men have primary claims to all the issue borne by their wives during cohabitation, unless paternity is disputed by a preceding spouse. The woman's father retains substantial control over his daughter's marriages, and at fixed intervals receives set gifts from her cohabitating spouse. Normally, eligible suitors solicit the father's approval before abducting the woman; and even when women are 'taken away by force' (that is, without the father's prior consent), tribal law prescribes that the abductor should at once transfer the prestations requisite for secondary marriage. Though the parties directly involved in these relations are individuals, the relations which regulate their respective obligations and rights are corporate ones, holding between the lineages to which they belong. The tribal law of secondary marriage is set deep in a framework of corporate patrilineages which hold and transfer rights in women as daughters, wives, mothers, and widows in ways that reinforce their autonomy and interdependence equally. Under this régime, a father-in-law held a strong position, being responsible for directing his daughter's unions in conformity with lineage interests and the network of its marriage relations. In arranging or entering marriages, and in disputing paternity or inheriting widows, individuals exercise personal capacities which are allocated to them on grounds of kinship status within the corporate framework of tribal law.[1]

As just described, this law excludes divorce. The marriage never dies, however long or often cohabitation has been broken. The husband could not dismiss his wife; and as a jural minor, she was not legally liable for her acts. Even when absconding freely with her lovers, a woman is said to have been 'taken away by force'.

II CASE MATERIAL

Under the *Idda* regulation of 1934, both parties to unions not preceded by observance of *Idda* were held to have committed a 'criminal' offence and were liable to fines. In 1955 the woman's father became liable to a fine if his complicity was proved. The original law neither provided women who intended to leave their husbands with opportunities to register in advance

[1] Gurvitch, 1947.

for *Idda*, nor did it establish any machinery for comprehensive report of these offences. Instead, it left aggrieved parties to report individual complaints. Thus although the *Idda* law made the traditional practice of secondary marriage an offence at law, it neither proscribed such unions formally nor did it explicitly institute divorce on completion of *Idda*. The ostensible aim of the *Idda* law was to reduce paternity disputes by eliminating their principal cause; and, under it, women were free to move between two or more husbands as they pleased, provided that they performed *Idda* on each transfer. The law did not prescribe what should be done if a woman undergoing *Idda* was found to be pregnant. Again, if the court fined an offending couple for failure to observe *Idda*, payment secured their release unless the deserted husband pressed further complaints. By the same token, payment of these court fines legalized the unions of offending couples. However, since unreported 'offences' escaped the law, the traditional forms of secondary marriage persisted, though liable to court sanctions whenever reported.

From 1934 the Kadara tribal court was primarily occupied with matrimonial issues. Between May 1947 and December 1949, 50 per cent of the 'criminal' pleas and 86 per cent of the civil suits brought before it arose out of matrimonial affairs. Of civil cases, 63·7 per cent were paternity suits, and 16 (15·6 per cent) were claims for refund of bride-wealth.[1] Of 90 'criminal' suits heard between 24 February 1957 and March 1959, 27 (30 per cent) were for failure to observe *Idda*, as against 29·2 per cent ten years before. Of 34 civil suits tried between 10 March 1956 and 31 December 1958, 7 were claims for bride-wealth and 20 (59 per cent) were paternity suits.[2] Since paternity suits should be absent under effective enforcement of *Idda*, these data indicate the substantial failure of the new law to eliminate those traditional practices of secondary marriage which produce these uncertainties.

[1] Smith, *The Social Structure of Northern Kadara* (1951, unpublished), p. 35.

[2] As for 1947–9, cases recorded in the court books were classified and tabulated by the writer; but not all court records were available for the second period, and the cases classified here are only a part of the total heard by the court during this period. On the assumption that the records made available to me contain a representative sample of the cases heard at court, the proportions falling in differing categories may be usually compared with those obtaining ten years before.

In April 1959 I compiled marital records covering the period since April 1950 for 179 married men in 42 compounds at Kufana. Of these, 19 (10·5 per cent), though formerly married, were wifeless in 1959; 116 (65 per cent) then had one wife each; 38 (21·5 per cent) had two, 5 (2·8 per cent) had three, and one had four wives. Men who had never married were excluded from this survey. The 160 husbands in these 42 compounds had a total of 211 resident wives, of whom 155 were primary wives acquired by betrothal, 70 of these having married before 1950, and 85 thereafter. Of the remaining 56 resident wives, 48 were secondary wives acquired from other villages, and 8 had been inherited. In addition, between 1950 and 1959 these 179 men had lost a total of 30 wives to other villages. Excluding some deaths, in April 1959 these 179 men had 241 wives, resident or absent, of whom 109 (45 per cent) had absconded at least once between 1950 and 1959, 48 to join them, 30 to leave, and 31 to rejoin them after one or more adventures. Of their 155 primary wives, 124 (80 per cent) had not absconded. Only one of these 179 men had asked the court for a divorce; and he was a pioneer.

To determine how *Idda* applies, it is necessary to analyse the movements of these 109 mobile wives, paying special attention to the role of the court. In the following table which sets out these data, the total number of entries slightly exceeds the number of women involved, since some cases evoked two or more types of action, and are represented accordingly. Adopting Kufana as our reference point, women are classified as 'gains' when moving into the village on marriage, as 'losses' when moving away.

Table I

Action Taken on the Abscondment of 109 Woman

Type of action taken	Kufana Gains	Losses	Total
Woman's restoration by her parents once	3	12	15
Woman's restoration by her parents twice	7	4	11
No parental restoration, no legal action	40	23	63
Legal action, one suit	8	13	21
Legal action, two suits	3	2	5
Total	61	54	115

The total number of women involved is 109 since six of these cases were taken to court following the woman's unsuccessful restoration by her father. Only in 26 of those 109 marriages (23.8 per cent) did the matter go to court on any issue. Under traditional practice, husbands generally appeal to their wife's father immediately the wife departs; and even when the woman's father makes no attempt to restore her, in rather more than half the examples (63 or 58 per cent) the deserted husband makes no complaint to the court. Evidently many men prefer customary procedures to those of the court.

To compare the effectiveness of 'legal' and 'customary' modes of action in these situations, I summarize the data for 84 women who had deserted their primary husbands, classifying these cases by the woman's movement to or from Kufana, and by the use or avoidance of court procedures.

Table II
Women's Movements under Legal and Customary Procedures

Effect	Kufana gains Custom	Kufana gains Legal	Kufana gains All	Kufana losses Custom	Kufana losses Legal	Kufana losses All	Total	Handled customarily
Woman returns to primary H	10	2	12	15	5	20	32	25
Woman stays with secondary H	25	8	33	7	4	11	44	32
Woman goes to a third H	2	1	3	—	2	2	5	2
Woman moves between first 2 Hs	1	—	1	—	1	1	2	1
Woman remains with her parents	1	—	1	—	—	—	1	1
Total	39	11	50	22	12	34	84	61

Legal and customary procedures offer deserted primary husbands equal chances of recovering their wives, 30.2 and 29.8 per cent respectively. However, nearly three-fourths of these movements are not reported to court, despite, or perhaps because of, recent increases in the fines levied for failure to observe *Idda*.

In 1955 the Kajuru District Council authorized the Kadara court to issue dated certificates to women on their completion of *Idda*, and also to permit those women who planned to leave their husbands to register for *Idda* in advance. In 1955, 19 women took advantage of this new facility before changing husbands; in 1956, 22; in 1957, 16; and in 1958, 13. Evidently few Kadara women are inclined to undertake observance of

Idda before changing husbands. The new facility is not a striking success. It merely adds yet another alternative to the increasingly varied procedures by which Kadara women enter new unions.

III ANALYSIS

What are the structural correlates of these ambiguous distributions? Clearly traditional procedures of secondary marriage persist with their harvest of paternity disputes; but the status of these unions is progressively obscured by successive amendments to the *Idda* rule. A deserted husband may complain to court that his wife has not observed *Idda* on her departure. The court first inquires into the conduct of the woman's father. If he is innocent, the court fines the woman £3 and her new husband £6. The deserted husband usually pays his wife's fine immediately, thereby asserting his legal responsibility for her as her husband. In this way plaintiffs appeal to court to announce their claims to absconded wives, often years after the woman's departure, when the performance of *Idda* is usually pointless. Only the deserted husband may report his wife for failure to observe *Idda*, and if he does not pay her consequent fine, it is understood that he will shortly return to court to claim refund of bride-wealth. When a man suspects that his absconding wife is already pregnant, he normally requires the court to enforce her observance of *Idda*, thereby seeking to assert his future paternity claim. Failing this, he may still claim paternity after the child is born.

Observance of *Idda* is not held to constitute divorce, though under the new law it is prerequisite for subsequent marriages. Only when bride-wealth has been reclaimed and refunded does the former marriage cease. Under tribal law, as mentioned above, this exceptional event was regarded as annulment, and any issue of the union reverted to the wife's natal lineage. Under the *Idda* law, return of bride-wealth constitutes divorce, the woman's ex-husband retaining the children as his. None the less, in some cases the husband may seek refund of bride-wealth from the girl's father directly or through the local village chief, without proceeding to court. Since this course of action forfeits his claim to the children under tribal law, only those men whose wives have borne no issue normally adopt it. The majority of deserted husbands are still restrained by the pressure of their lineage obligations. Where bride-wealth is informally reclaimed, the wife's father is obliged to demand it from his daughter's current husband; and whether settled at court or outside, the transaction terminates the first marriage and capitalizes the later marriage whether *Idda* has been observed or not.

The *Idda* rule has had important indirect effects at two levels, the personal and the corporate. It has taken effect by altering the balance and form of personal liabilities and rights which formerly prevailed under tribal law, and by obscuring the validity of these liabilities and rights where this derives from traditional procedures. Under *Idda* as administered by the court, women have ceased to be jural minors, and are now directly responsible for their failure to observe *Idda*. In those cases where both husbands refuse to pay a woman's fine, she may be sent to jail; and, if she has persistently disobeyed her father, he will not come to her aid. Fathers have also lost their formerly unchallenged jurisdiction over their daughter's marriages and fertility. So long as a woman's various husbands negotiate their claims upon her out of court, her father preserves the form of his original right, and administers paternity suits to her issue, where these arise; but at best these paternal rights are now conditional. Where paternity disputes are brought to court, traditional authority ceases, and if they take the form of complaints for failure to observe *Idda*, the woman's father may then himself be liable to fine. Deserted husbands may require *Idda* or reclaim their bride-wealth.

After many years some Kadara women undertake *Idda* before changing husbands, but most still do not; and while some husbands report their wives' departure to the court, to secure observance of *Idda*, most do not. Either course of action by husband or wife lends itself to ambiguous interpretations by the other. A deserted husband may regard his wife's observance of *Idda* before joining another man as evidence of intent to return, or as evidence of the opposite. The wife may treat her husband's demand for the observance of *Idda* in similar ways. Sons-in-law now have various legal tools to use against their fathers-in-law; but these legal actions do not increase their security as husbands. Relations between a man and his daughters' husbands are equally unstable.

Paternity is still a fertile subject of dispute, since observance of *Idda* is very poorly supervised. Following court fines and orders, *Idda* is often begun, to be abandoned shortly after. Few deserted husbands then summon their wives to court a second time, since by so doing they render themselves liable to pay her second fine. A man's rights *in uxorem* are now no wider or more secure than formerly. Since these rights are now subject to two conflicting legal systems, tribal law based on corporate lineages, and court law sanctioned by the state, they may in fact be less secure.

The *Idda* rule has had its most important indirect effects at the level of corporate organization. Under the law, women may remarry as they please following performance of *Idda*. The court, administering this Muhammadan rule, has not yet found a way to forbid those marriages which violate traditional proscriptions, since these latter form no part of the Islamic order which the Kadara court is required to observe by its Hausa superiors. In consequence, traditional prohibitions against secondary marriage within communities and ritual groups are increasingly broken. Widows, having completed their mourning periods, may refuse inheritance, as happened in Kufana in 1956. Such events transform *azaimi* relations of solidarity between the lineages of a community into the institutionalized antagonism of *aformi*.

By permitting unrestricted 'remarriage', the *Idda* rule transfers full initiative to arrange such unions from the parental generation, who represent lineage, ritual group, and community interests, to the generation of the spouses themselves. The rule accordingly permits and supports breaches of the tribal law that once served to integrate relations of secondary marriage with the requisites of Kadara corporate organization. Unrestricted 'remarriage' exposes the traditional forms of corporate groupings on which the society still depends for its cohesion and order to progressive dissolution under the internal conflicts and strains which perennially attach to *aformi* relations between antagonistic lineages.

Secondary marriage persists as the typical form of later union among Kadara; but its validity is now obscured under the superordinate law. Alongside the traditional structure of secondary marriage and in competition with it, 'remarriage' has emerged as a new form in consequence of the *Idda* rule; and under the law as administered by the court, 'remarriage' eludes those traditional proscriptions that formerly regulated secondary marriage. The bases and relations of Kadara corporate groups, traditionally insulated from antagonistic *aformi* relations by mechanisms which restricted the alternative modes of marriage to mutually exclusive social spheres, are progressively compromised; the differing forms of prestation for primary and secondary marriage are assimilated; and the personal rights and liabilities of women, their fathers, and their rival husbands, remain obscure and ambiguous, even after submission to court.

The traditional structure and distribution of individual liability and right have been disturbed by the introduction of an alien structure with very different presumptions and implications. The two systems of law, tribal and alien, coexist in conflict, although each has partly absorbed the other into itself, by dislocating some of its rival's institutional connections.

BIBLIOGRAPHY

Gurvitch, G.
  (1947) *The Sociology of Law*. London: Routledge and Kegan Paul.
Ruxton, F. H.
  (1916) *Maliki Law*. London: Luzac.
Smith, M. G.
  (1951) *The Social Structure of the Northern Kadara* (unpublished MS).
  (1953) 'Secondary Marriage in Northern Nigeria', *Africa*, xxiii. 4, pp. 298–323.
  (1960) *Secondary Marriage and Social Change: A Comparative Analysis* (unpublished MS).

Résumé

IDDA ET LE MARIAGE SECONDAIRE CHEZ LES KADARA DU NORD

Ce résumé essaie de décrire les effets directs et indirects d'une loi qui prescrit l'observation de l'*Idda* par les femmes de Kadara lorsqu'elles delaissent leur mari pour un autre. L'*Idda* est la periode de 3 mois d'abstinence que les épouses doivent observer dans le droit musulman sous la surveillance des tribunaux avant le divorce.

Outre le premier mariage, les Kadara pratiquent l'héritage de la veuve, et le mariage secondaire. Les Kadara sont groupés en patrilignages localisés et exogames (*erute*, sing. *ute*). Le mariage (*uballe*) est virilocal. Les veuves sont adoptées par le patrilignage de leur mari.

Le mariage secondaire était une sorte de remariage, qui donnait au mari secondaire les droits exclusifs aussi longtemps que durait la cohabitation avec la femme, sans pour cela abroger les précédents mariages de la femme. Une femme pouvait avoir autant de maris secondaires qu'elle désirait, mais elle ne pouvait cohabiter qu'avec un seul à la fois, et selon la tradition ces maris devaient être choisis dans autant de communautés différentes. En bref, le départ de l'épouse terminait la cohabitation mais non le mariage. Les femmes étaient libres de retourner auprès de leur mari en permanence, ou en visites formelles (*abusan*) pour des périods établies, renouant dans l'intervalle leurs relations rompues avec leur mari.

Sous la loi Kadara, pour résoudre les réclamations de paternité, une épouse, abandonnant son mari, doit montrer des preuves de menstruation à ses parentes pendant trois périodes successives; mais les discussions de paternité sont communes. Le père de l'épouse traditionellement décidait qui était le père d'un enfant.

Sous la loi nouvelle de l'*Idda* il y a maintenant une obscurité considérable au sujet de l'état et de la validité des droits et des responsabilités individuels en tant que maris, femmes, pères ou beau-pères, sous ce conflit continuel des règles et procèdures légales. Tandis que les droits dérivant de la loi tribale du mariage secondaire peuvent être réglés de nouveau par la cour, la cour peut aussi légaliser indirectement les infractions de la loi tribale.

En légalisant les 'remariages', sans ces restrictions traditionelles par lesquels les Kadara abritaient leurs groupes fondamentaux des effets désagréants du mariage secondaire, la loi de l'*Idda* administrée par la cour jusqu'en 1959 a progressivement affaibli les communautés de Kadara, les groupes rituels, et les lignages. Etant donné que les lignages auparavant se servaient du mariage secondaire pour affirmer cette construction collective, le 'remariage' et le divorce, sous la nouvelle loi de la cour renverse cette même construction collective avec sa distribution logique de sanctions, de responsabilités et de droits.

X. Legitimation of Children in Customary Law in Kinshasa[1]

J. M. PAUWELS

I INTRODUCTION

The Congo is ruled by a dualistic system of law and courts: so-called written-law courts apply largely French-type law,[2] and so-called customary or native courts apply the law of numerous indigenous peoples in urban, as well as rural, areas. There are more than twenty customary courts of the first instance (*tribunaux de centre*) in Kinshasa, and one court of appeal (*tribunal de ville*) for which certain matters are also reserved, including legitimation cases.

Changes in customary law, occurring everywhere, are most marked in large towns. Kinshasa is not situated in the territory of a single powerful tribe, and its customary-law judges apply the personal law of the parties in some matters with embryonic conflict rules. Most matters have been handled by a new uniform law strongly influenced by French law and ideas. It is called '*la coutume évoluée de Kinshasa*'.[3] Legitimation of illegitimate children falls under it, and is tried only by the central court. It is one of several examples showing considerable acculturation.

The distinction between legitimate and illegitimate children is fundamental in European law. In both French and English law only children begotten or born in lawful wedlock automatically enter into the prescribed rights and duties attaching to the status of children vis-à-vis parents. Illegitimate children traditionally had no recognized juridical link of affiliation to

---

[1] [Editorial note.—Rather than reduce the text of this paper, footnote references to case numbers and to details of provisions of statutory provisions have been eliminated. These are available from the author, the editor, and the International African Institute.]

[2] Almost all Congolese are still, even after independence, ruled in family matters by customary, and not by legislated, law (see Pauwels, 1964).

[3] Hence I speak of customary law, though it is 'judge-made law'.

their father and/or mother. The Code Napoléon provided for an improvement in their status: they could be legitimated by the subsequent marriage of their parents, and alternatively could be affiliated to either or both by *reconnaisance*, voluntary or compulsory (*recherche de paternité* under strictly limited conditions). Affiliation to supply a general status to an illegitimate child is unknown in English law, though it can nowadays acquire some rights with regard to its mother and can be legitimated under a statute of 1926.

French law did not allow *reconnaissance* or *légitimation*, and English law denied legitimation, to a child conceived in adultery by its mother, or begotten in adultery by its father. In Britain, since the 1926 Act, such a child can be adopted, and a 1959 statute allows it to be legitimated by subsequent marriage. French law has long admitted legitimation of such a child under certain conditions;[1] and in Belgium a recent statute has slightly mitigated the severity of the prohibition. But Congolese written law, unmodified, maintains this prohibition.[2]

An exhaustive analysis of traditional Congolese rules about illegitimacy might reveal great diversity, so it is difficult to give a summary statement. But it seems that an illegitimate child in general did not suffer inferior status, though it might not be assured the protection of its father's kin-group. Subsequent marriage in all customary legal systems legitimated such a child, and an adulterine child was apparently not excepted. Affiliation outside of marriage does not seem to have existed in most customary systems, and has been introduced under the influence of Western law.

II SITUATIONS AND MODES OF LEGITIMATION

The customary law of Kinshasa knows the concepts of *enfant légitime, enfant naturel, enfant adultérin, enfant légitimé* (although the latter term is not used). As the law of Kinshasa is unwritten, the scope of the notions concerning illegitimate birth are best studied through cases of legitimation, affiliation, and guardianship.

[1] Legitimation of a child adulterine *a matre* who has not been disowned by the mother's husband is still difficult.

[2] Belgian civil code, articles 331, 331 bis, 334 (Act of 10 February 1958); Congolese civil code, articles 201, 206, and 211.

The father of an illegitimate child may claim what is called the *droit de paternité* over his child when he marries the child's mother (legitimation action); the mother of an illegitimate child may claim what is called the *droit de maternité* over her child (affiliation action); a person who is neither the father nor the mother of an illegitimate child, but in most cases a member of his kin-group, may claim what is called the *droit de tutelle* over the child (guardianship action). Affiliation cases brought by the mother are extremely rare; guardianship cases concerning illegitimate children are mostly settled according to the general principles of kinship law. Only legitimation cases will be considered here.

If the illegitimate child's father marries the mother of the child, he is entitled to claim the *droit de paternité* over the child. Two ways to obtain this right are open to him: either he recognizes (*reconnaît*, i.e. voluntarily establishes the affiliation) his child in the act of registration of his customary marriage, or, if he omits to do this, he can claim, in court, the *droit de paternité*, after the marriage is contracted.

By either procedure, the child, who up to then was illegitimate, is legitimated. A personal link of filiation between the father and his child is thus established, with the effect of conferring on both of them the status of respectively legitimate parent and legitimate offspring.

We are entitled to characterize this granting of the *droit de paternité* as 'legitimation', thus referring to a concept of European law. Legitimation here has nothing to do with the question of which clan or lineage the child belongs to; individuals of matrilineal origin acquire the *droit de paternité* as well as fathers whose personal custom is of a patrilineal type.

The granting of the *droit de paternité* entitles the originally illegitimate father to exercise the authority of father (*la puissance paternelle*), i.e. he is in the situation held by the husband with respect to the children born of his wife in wedlock. What is very important is his right to child bounties. In practice, most legitimation cases are brought in court in order to establish a title to those family allowances. Another incentive to introduce legitimation suits is the need to prove that children, seeking admittance to a school in Kinshasa, are taken care of by a responsible parent.

A typical legitimation case goes like this: the husband, acting as plaintiff, claims the *droit de paternité* over his son or daughter, born before his marriage with the defendant, at present his wife, who expresses her consent that her husband should acquire the right of fatherhood. If the court is convinced that the parties are married (e.g. it will hear testimony from the father or the uncle of the wife who received bride-wealth) and that the representative of the wife's kin-group consents to the granting of the right, then the court will grant the claim, quoting one of its formal clauses:

> vu la coutume qui accorde le droit de paternité sur l'enfant né avant le mariage coutumier, quand la dot est versée après.

The *droit de paternité* will be granted by a Kinshasa customary court, only if a number of conditions are fulfilled.

(*a*) The claimant has to be the physiological father (genitor) of the child. A husband could not obtain the right of fatherhood over a child, brought into his household by his wife, but whose father is a third person, even if the husband maintains the child or promises to do so. But under these circumstances, the court would grant him the guardianship.

(*b*) The father of the child has to marry the mother of the child. Paternal rights are not granted, nowadays, outside marriage.

(*c*) The legitimation of children born in adultery is prohibited at present.

The conditions enunciated under (*b*) and (*c*) are sufficiently important to justify separate examination (see below).

(*d*) Legitimation can only take place if the '*ayant droit coutumier*', customary chief of the kin-group of the child, agrees to it. The need for this consent was stressed in older cases, and indirectly appears in the care displayed by the court to acquire the consent of the customary head of the family of the children.[1] But it seems that no refusals to grant the right of fatherhood have occurred in recent times, and it is submitted that the dismissal of a claim to the *droit de paternité* on the ground that

[1] In one case among patrilineal Ngombe, consent given by wife's cousin, her father having died; in one among matrilineal Kongo, consent given by mother's sister.

the customary family head of the child is unwilling to cede his rights over the illegitimate child, would be unconstitutional under article 12 of the Congolese Constitution of 24 June 1967.

As the granting or the refusal of the *droit de paternité* depends on the existence of a valid (customary) marriage between the child's mother and his father, the main problem to be solved by the court is often to determine whether the parties are actually married, i.e. in practice, whether bride-wealth has been paid. The refusal of courts to recognize a customary marriage without bride-wealth is an aspect of the uniform urban law.

The Ejection of Paternal Affiliation from Kinshasa Custom

During the 1950s the customary courts of Kinshasa (then Leopoldville) granted the *droit de paternité* to the illegitimate father even if he did not marry the mother of the illegitimate child, if he could do so according to his personal custom. So it was decided that a matrilineal Yombe (sub-group of the Kongo) could not obtain the affiliation of his illegitimate child outside wedlock, whereas it was admitted that Luba, Tetela, and Songye (all patrilineal tribes) could affiliate their illegitimate children according to their personal custom, provided they paid a sum, called *bukoleshi* in Luba, to the representative of the child's kin-group.

Until 1956 the courts agreed to apply the personal customs of the parties in affiliation matters. Then, for some reason, it was felt that a uniform solution for all inhabitants of Kinshasa should be adopted, and this solution was sought in 1957. The question whether affiliation outside marriage should be admitted in Kinshasa was debated in the Social Commission of the *Conseil de Cité*.[1]

I must stress that the only problem was the affiliation of an illegitimate child to his father: the right of the mother to claim the establishment of the link of filiation with her illegitimate child has never been questioned.

The opinion of the members of the Social Commission was divided. It appeared that most judges (all customary judges

[1] In the colonial period this council was composed of representatives of the African population, including all judges of customary courts. It was consultative. It was dissolved in 1957 when Leopoldville was changed from a '*cité indigène*' to a '*ville*'.

were *de jure* members of the *Conseil de Cité*) were opposed to the general granting of affiliation independently of marriage, influenced as they were by their tribal origin: the majority were matrilineal Kongo, whose customary law does not allow affiliation with the father outside marriage. In the report of the *Commission Sociale* we read:

> Au tour des juges, ils s'opposent énergiquement à cette question. Ils croient que ce serait un préjudice pour le mariage coutumier; les jeunes ne seraient plus tentés à se marier et ce serait une cause de plusieurs divorces dans les ménages Bakongo dont ils défendent la coutume.

In other terms, orderly sexual intercourse did not constitute a sufficient incentive for marriage; the acquisition of rights over children had to be kept an exclusive privilege to married people, lest the institution of marriage be seriously undermined.

Other members, on the other hand, alarmed by the increase in juvenile delinquency, due partly to the fact that numerous illegitimate children lived in Kinshasa without the protection and the guidance of a male parent, were in favour of extending the possibility of paternal affiliation.

The European president of the commission summed up the two positions thus:

> Les Congolais aiment les enfants. Il faut les reconnaître. Il faut préserver également le mariage coutumier, sinon les jeunes n'auraient aucun intérêt à se marier.

A compromise was reached. The commission, refusing to '*renverser brutalement les coutumes*', which meant that it took the view of the majority of the judges, disliking affiliation outside wedlock, expressed the wish that the customary courts should grant the *droit de garde* to the illegitimate father, although not the *droit de paternité*, unless he married the child's mother.

Whereas the *droit de paternité* entitles its beneficiary to the authority of father, the *droit de garde*, in the terminology of the Kinshasa customary courts, entitles only to custody. This right concerns only physical custody and residence; and it gives no right to family allowances.

The result of this change in the law was that *reconnaissance*, *droit de paternité* outside marriage, disappeared altogether from the law of Kinshasa. The persistent opposition of the judges to it was one of the reasons. Invited to apply a uniform law, they were not willing to apply rules contrary to the personal law of the majority of them. On the other hand, the concept of *droit de garde* was not clearly defined, and as it gave no right to social advantages, it was of no particular interest to the fathers of illegitimate children. Moreover, this concession to the customs of certain patrilineal inhabitants of the city became totally worthless when it was decided, in 1958, that the courts would not hear any more cases on *droit de garde*, these being left to communal administrations.

We conclude that the influence of Western law had not been strong enough to be introduced into Kinshasa law of affiliation outside wedlock. Against the combined action of matrilineal and other judges who did not know this institution from their personal customs, and of the impact of *moral* conceptions of Western origin, viz. the protection of regular marriage against concubinage, Western law had to yield.

The Granting of the Droit de Paternité *to the Father of a Child Born in Adultery*

Two quite different situations have to be considered here, the first being that of a child born of parents living in concubinage, of which one at least was married at the time of his begetting or birth. These are the real adulterine children. A second problem has to be examined, since Congolese law provides that polygamous marriages are void: this is the problem of the child born in customary wedlock, in case the marriage of his parents is void under the provisions of the *décret* of 4 April 1950.

(i) *Children Born in Adulterous Concubinage*

During the fifties the legitimation of adulterine children was admitted by the customary courts of Kinshasa. No distinction was being made between children adulterine *a matre* (and eventually *a patre* too) and children adulterine *a patre*, except for the fact that the first category could only be legitimated by their father if disowning by mother's husband preceded it. The only restriction was that pure affiliation was not admitted, but with the disappearance of affiliation this restriction would have lost its importance.

In two law review articles, Mr. Petit, then president of the *tribunal de territoire* of Kinshasa, defended this view.[1] One should not forget that this solution, the possibility of legitimation of adulterine children, constituted at that time in the eyes of written-law lawyers a most shocking thing. Such legitimation was considered as completely contrary to the public policy of a Western-type law (*ordre public interne*) and they were inclined to consider that the same principle should be introduced in customary law by the technique of *ordre public universel*, the Congolese equivalent of the repugnancy clause.

He commented favourably on a decision of the *tribunal de centre* delivered in 1954, in which the *droit de paternité* to a child, adulterine *a matre*, was conferred on his father, after the mother was divorced from her first husband and had married the father of the child. Mr. Petit insisted on the fact that the affiliation was not established during the existence of the first marriage, which made the link between father and child adulterine:

il importe donc, de préciser d'une manière restrictive, qu'est contraire a l'ordre public, la coutume qui admettrait la reconnaissance de l'enfant adultérin en cours de mariage.

The *décret* organizing the customary courts provides that the judgments of these courts may be annulled (*procédure d'annulation*) by the *tribunal de District* (until 1959 by the *tribunal de Parquet*), for several reasons, among others the application by a customary court of a custom repugnant to natural justice, etc. (more exactly 'contraire à l'ordre public universel', according to Congolese legislation).

It seems that the *tribunal de Parquet* considered that the practice of legitimating adulterine children, adopted by the Kinshasa customary courts, was contrary to those universal principles of civilization, and forced the native judges (including the European president of the *tribunal de territoire*) to abandon it:

La légitimation d'enfants adultérins est admise par la coutume; le Tribunal de Parquet considère que cette coutume est contraire à l'ordre public; le Tribunal de territoire a toujours refusé de se ranger à cette opinion. Les législations occidentales tendent du

[1] Petit, 1955a and 1955b.

reste actuellement à un adoucissement de la situation de l'enfant adultérin.[1]

From 1956 onwards, legitimation (*a fortiori* affiliation independently from marriage) has been considered forbidden by the customary judges of Kinshasa. This rule has been incorporated as a positive norm in the local custom, and is being applied regardless of the tribal origin of the parties.

Decisions of the post-independence era prove that judges generally stick to this rule, although deviations mitigating the principle occur.[2]

(ii) *Children Adulterine as a Result of the* Décret *on Polygyny*

The *décret* of 4 April 1950 declares void all polygynous unions concluded after 1 January 1951.[3] A polygynous husband is considered as living in concubinage with his second, third, etc., wife. Although polygyny has thus been banned from Congolese law for more than fifteen years, its practice in this country is far from dying out; perhaps the number of polygynous households is even increasing since the Congo's accession to independence. Some Congolese without doubt feel that the *décret* annulling polygyny was forced upon them and consider it to be an unpopular measure. Yet recent decisions of the *tribunal de ville* show that the Congolese judges are still willing to apply the statute, although the solutions adopted in some more intricate cases suggest that the rule forbidding the legitimation of children born in adultery is not deeply rooted in their minds.

Here is an example of strict application of the *décret*: *Tribunal de ville* 20.748/11 (5 May 1964). The plaintiff was the polygynous husband of two wives. He had taken the second wife with the authorization of the first. He claimed the *droit de paternité* over the two children born of his second wife. The first wife, present at the court, supported his claim. But the court recalled

---

[1] From a report of the service of native affairs and labour, 1956. Unhappily the older archives of the *tribunal de parquet* are not available so that the judges' reasoning cannot be traced. But the quoted passage indicates that the judge invoked the repugnancy conception of *ordre public universel*.

[2] A married man who lived apart from his wife and who had introduced a suit for divorce had a child by a concubine whom he married after his first wife had obtained a divorce. He was granted the right of paternity.

[3] Information about this enactment is in Phillips, 1953, pp. 190 f.

to them the existence of the *décret* on polygyny. As a result the husband's claim was dismissed. Although he was not entitled to the *droit de paternité*, the court conferred on him the *droit de garde* of his children, as long as he would take care of them.[1]

It has to be mentioned that at least some among the judges admit exceptions to this rule. We shall illustrate this new attitude by one case, *Tribunal de Ville* 18.014/11 (14 January 1963)[2] in which the court adopted a solution which constituted an innovation to the established rule forbidding legitimation of adulterine children. But in this case, it must be acknowledged, the facts were very particular. The wife's bigamy was only technical, and the court found it necessary to soften the hardship of a procedural rule of Kinshasa customary law. A woman's husband had disappeared, after escaping from jail. She lived with another man, and gave birth to a child. Later on the second man paid bride-wealth for her (her first bride-wealth was never returned), so that, according to custom, he considered himself to be her husband. They had four more children. The second husband wanted to acquire the *droit de paternité* with respect to his five children. No divorce of the first marriage had been pronounced because the Kinshasa customary courts are opposed to proceedings by default, and pronounce divorces by default only if the defendant spouse has been absent for ten years. This rule combined with the other rule, prohibiting the legitimation of adulterine children, led in this instance to an inequitable result. The conflict was resolved in a way that, if not logical, seemed at least equitable to the judges: they refused to legitimate the first child, born before the second bride-wealth had been paid, but they agreed to legitimate the four following children, born after the payment of the bride-wealth.

III SOURCES OF CUSTOMARY LAW IN KINSHASA[3]

European law has influenced totally affiliation and legitimation, which though not conceptions without equivalents in customary law, have been applied in alien ways to all parties regardless

---
[1] When this decision was made, the *droit de garde* did not entitle its beneficiary to family allowances. The situation is different under a 1965 *décret* on hiring and services. I do not think that the judges have yet taken advantage of this change.

[2] Published in *Revue Juridique du Congo*, 1964, p. 218, with a note by Pauwels.

[3] [Editorial note.—This section has been summarized from a longer version by Mr. Pauwels.]

of their tribal origins. By direct legislation (the ban on polygyny, which is unlikely to be abolished by the Congolese legislature even if it is disapproved of by many people), and through the influence of indirect legislation (family and other allowances, etc.), and through the control exercised by European court-presidents over African judges and assessors, a uniform body of law applicable to all Africans in the city was elaborated. This applied particularly to the treatment of illegitimate children: though Africans were not ruled by the civil code, the Europeans looked to its provisions and held certain African customs to be against '*ordre public interne ou universel*'. These favoured paternal authority as against that of the mother's brother under matriliny leading to the notion of '*le droit de paternité*'. On the other hand, lawful families were to be protected against polygyny and concubinage. Concubinage suits were banned from the courts.

In this background, urban custom innovates mainly by:

(*a*) The refusal to admit simple affiliation outside marriage even if permitted by the personal law of the parties. It is notable that this refusal does not shock African judges, whatever their tribal origin. The test of marriage is, as traditionally, the payment of bride-wealth. (*b*) The ejection of the adulterine child from the family founded by its parents, unless accepted by the husband of an adulterous mother. This rule seems not to be followed in all cases. The distinction between adulterine and simple illegitimate children seems more alien to the judges than the first deviation from traditional law. It does not have the clear traditional indication provided by bride-wealth or a legitimation fee to support it.

This partial reception of French-type law has been somewhat harmful to the status of the illegitimate child in that he has no claim against his proven genitor, as he would have in France. He is entitled to all the rights of an ordinary member in his mother's kin-group.

In some respects, this European influence corresponds with certain aspects of traditional law, principally in the institution of legitimation, its grant to the biological father, subject to recognition by the woman's husband. But in addition the consent of the head of the mother's kin-group is required. Surprisingly, the judges do not require that compensation be paid to the child's kin as a further condition, though doubtless this affects the amount of bride-wealth.

The whole problem of the status of illegitimate children needs to be considered carefully by the Africans subject to it, for it is regrettable that it should be left to a largely unconscious adaptation to provisions of social legislation, rather than to a coherent family policy which would combine respect for traditional rules with their adaptation to new needs. The presidents of the courts do their best, but lacking training in both customary and written law, they hesitate in the face of the need for innovations. The young lawyers now graduating from the universities will have to face this stimulating, but most difficult, task.

BIBLIOGRAPHY

Pauwels, J.
(1964) 'Le droit coutumier et la constitution du Congo', *Études Congolaises*, vii, 9, pp. 1–26.

Petit, M.
(1955a) 'A propos d'un jugement—Reconnaissance d'enfant adultérin', *Journal des Tribunaux*. Brussels, vi, pp. 47–48.
(1955b) 'La reconnaissance d'enfant adultérin et l'ordre public', *Journal des Tribunaux*. Brussels, vi, pp. 171–2.

Phillips, A.
(1953) *A Survey of African Marriage and Family Life*. London: Oxford University Press for the International African Institute.

Résumé

LA LÉGITIMATION D'ENFANTS NATURELS DANS LE DROIT COUTUMIER DE KINSHASA

La contribution traite de cas jugés par le tribunal de ville de Kinshasa concernant la filiation illégitime. Il y est constaté que ce tribunal accorde actuellement le 'droit de paternité' (qui correspond *grosso modo* à la légitimation) au père de l'enfant qui a épousé la mère de celui-ci, sauf en cas de filiation adultérine. Les juges n'appliquent toutefois plus dans toute sa rigueur la prohibition visant les enfants adultérins, vestige de l'époque coloniale. Ils continuent cependant à appliquer dans ce contexte le décret du 4 avril 1950 déclarant nulle la polygamie. La reconnaissance de l'enfant naturel par son père sans mariage subséquent des parents n'est pas admise; la jurisprudence tient encore, en ce domaine, à une règle établie en 1957. Par contre, la mère de l'enfant naturel se voit attribuer le 'droit de maternité' (correspondant à la reconnaissance maternelle).

Des conclusions sont formulées dans la troisième partie. Le droit coutumier de Kinshasa est marqué par l'influence du droit occidental. Cette influence s'est fait sentir, d'une part, à travers l'activité des juges européens qui ont élaboré le droit de Kinshasa avant 1960, et d'autre part par l'intervention de la législation écrite (le décret sur la polygynie et la législation sociale). Comme ce droit coutumier, en fait un droit jurisprudentiel, est largement uniforme, la distance qui le sépare du droit traditionnel est encore plus marquée. L'étude de l'évolution du droit coutumier de Kinshasa concernant la légitimation démontre que ceux qui sont à l'origine de ce droit ont été inspiré plus par le désir de protéger le mariage monogamique régulier ainsi que les prérogatives du père, que par le souci de préserver les structures de parenté traditionnelles.

XI. Réflexions sur l'Existence du Concept de Propriété immobilière individuelle dans les Droits africains traditionnels

J. VANDERLINDEN

Dans trois ouvrages récents consacrés au droit traditionnel, respectivement de l'ensemble de l'Afrique, de l'une de ses grandes régions et de l'un des pays qui la composent, différents auteurs semblent admettre, de manière plus ou moins nette, l'inexistence du concept de propriété immobilière individuelle parmi les catégories juridiques propres aux habitants de ces diverses aires géographiques.

A l'échelle de la République démocratique du Congo d'abord, Antoine Sohier, dans son *Traité élémentaire de Droit coutumier du Congo belge*,[1] déclare que: 'Il faut, pensons-nous distinguer entre le groupe, la communauté clanique ou tribale, qui avait la propriété des terres, et les parentèles ou les individus, qui ne possédaient pas un tel droit, mais possédaient simplement des droits sociaux vis-à-vis du groupe, en vertu desquels ils pouvaient occuper les terres de celui-ci ou y exercer certaines prérogatives. Ainsi la propriété individuelle paraît ne pas avoir existé (on en trouve cependant des traces semble-t-il), mais bien la propriété collective.'

De même, quoique de manière moins nette (sans doute l'étendue des territoires en cause doit-elle inciter à la prudence), André-P. Robert, dans son *Évolution des coutumes de l'Ouest africain et la législation française*,[2] souligne soit que 'la terre n'appartient à personne parce qu'elle s'appartient à elle-même' (cette affirmation, indépendamment du problème qui nous occupe, est en soi extrêmement contestable sur le plan juridique), que 'l'homme est un simple usufruitier', qu'enfin il ne peut être question, dans le chef de l'habitant de ces régions,

[1] 1954, p. 142.   [2] 1955, pp. 111–14.

Le Concept de Propriété immobilière individuelle

que d'une possession collective et hiérarchique, précaire et intransmissible.

Enfin, passant à une échelle géographique plus large encore, T. Olawale Elias, dans *The Nature of African Customary Law*,[1] déclare: 'Thus whereas the radical title to the land remains with the family or the community, the individual can have, at any rate in theory, a right only to its use. In other words, the ownership is that of the group, and the individual member has mere possession.'

Avant de discuter ces propositions, il est nécessaire de préciser ce qu'il faut entendre par propriété ou *ownership* dans l'esprit de ces juristes belge, français et nigérien (quoique T. O. Elias prenne soin de préciser qu'il emploie le second de ces termes 'in [its] ordinary English [sense]'.[2]

En consultant deux dictionnaires juridiques usuels, ceux de Capitant et de Jowitt,[3] nous constatons que, pour le premier, la propriété est le 'droit d'user, jouir et disposer d'une chose d'une manière exclusive et absolue sous les restrictions établies par la loi', et, pour le second, 'the most extensive right allowed by law to a person, of dealing with a thing to the exclusion of all other persons, or of all except one or more specified persons'.

De leur côté des traités généraux de droit comme ceux de Dekkers, de Ripert et Boulanger, ou de Stephens (pris, comme les dictionnaires précités a titre strictement exemplatif)[4] mettront en évidence le fait que la propriété est:

— un droit étendu voire le plus étendu des droits ou même un droit absolu (quoique ce dernier terme prête aisément le flanc à la critique) que l'on ramène le plus souvent à l'*usus*, *abusus* et *fructus* du droit romain, le titulaire pouvant faire à l'égard du droit ou de l'objet sur lequel il porte tout ce qu'il ne lui est pas interdit de faire;

— un droit exclusif de son titulaire qui ne le partage avec

---

[1] 1956, p. 163.
[2] Ibid., note 1, où la phrase est au pluriel, s'appliquant aussi à 'possession'.
[3] Capitant, 1930, p. 392; et Jowitt, 1959, II, pp. 1283-4.
[4] Dekkers, 1954-5, I, pp. 513-14; Ripert et Boulanger, 1949-51, I, pp. 920-4; et Stephen, 1950, I, pp. 425-6, quoique ce dernier ouvrage envisage essentiellement le propriété des meubles en raison des caractères extrêmement particuliers du régime immobilier anglais.

aucune autre personne juridique si on excepte le cas de la co-propriété;

— un droit perpétuel, en ce sens qu'aucune durée ne lui est assignée et qu'il se transmet de propriétaire en propriétaire aussi longtemps que l'objet sur lequel il porte existe.

En outre, il est clair que, pour tous ces auteurs, le droit de propriété est un droit appartenant à la catégorie des droits dits civils, c'est-à-dire, des droits dont peut normalement être titulaire tout individu.

Toutefois l'État, formé par l'ensemble des individus qui en sont membres, est susceptible d'être titulaire de ce droit. L'État, comme l'individu, peut être propriétaire, mais nous laisserons ce point de côté pour l'instant car la propriété individuelle est notre seul centre d'intérêt immédiat.

Enfin, les notions que nous venons de décrire s'appliquent en droit français et belge tout le moins, de manière indiscutable tant aux meubles qu'aux immeubles. Nous concentrerons toutefois nos efforts sur la seule propriété immobilière. Il ne semble pas en effet que les mêmes problèmes se posent quant à l'existence de la propriété mobilière individuelle dans les droits africains traditionnels: elle semble être généralement admise.

On peut donc en conclure que lorsqu'Elias, Robert et Sohier emploient le mot propriété, ils ont à l'esprit une réalité juridique relativement semblable qui correspond à un usage courant[1] dans leurs sociétés respectives.

La question qui se pose alors est de savoir dans quelle mesure ce faisceau de droits se ramenant à un droit absolu (ou du moins au droit le plus étendu qui se puisse concevoir dans la société en cause), faisceau exclusif et perpétuel par ailleurs est inconnu, du moins au niveau des individus, dans les sociétés africaines traditionnelles. Pour y répondre, nous procéderons à l'analyse d'une dizaine de systèmes fonciers traditionnels dont nous possédons des descriptions suffisamment précises; nous prendrons ces exemples respectivement au Congo, en Afrique de l'Ouest et dans d'autres régions de l'Afrique enfin.

Considérons tout d'abord le fait que le droit de propriété

---

[1] Il est évident que les théoriciens du droit de propriété pourraient être amenés à définir différemment la notion, mais on peut supposer que faute de s'y référer explicitement. nos auteurs adoptent des sens usuels du mot.

peut être considéré comme un faisceau de droits qui semblent pouvoir tous se ramener à trois droits plus simples (mais complexes eux aussi), le droit d'usage, le droit de jouissance des fruits et le droit de disposition (*usus*, *fructus* et *abusus*).

Il faut remarquer immédiatement à cet égard que le droit d'usage et celui de jouissance des fruits, s'il ne s'agissait que d'eux, ne poseraient pas de problème dans le cadre de cette étude. En effet, Sohier[1] mentionne, au premier rang des droits sociaux dont sont titulaires les individus, celui d'utilisation des terres aux fins d'habitation et de culture (*l'usus*) et, précédemment[2] le fait que les fruits de la terre appartiennent à celui qui les a faits siens par un travail quelconque. Robert, de son côté,[3] parle de l'individu vivant en Afrique de l'Ouest comme d'un usufruitier, donc un titulaire de l'*usus* et du *fructus*. Elias, enfin,[4] traite de droits plus étendus que ceux de l'usufruitier allant même jusqu'à parler de pouvoir de disposition dans le chef de l'individu alors qu'il condamne par ailleurs sans équivoque l'existence dans son chef d'un droit de propriété. Ce droit à l'usage de la terre et aux fruits résultant de cet usage se retrouve par ailleurs chez tous les groupes étudiés à titre d'exemples.[5]

Le problème essentiel semble donc être celui du troisième élément constitutif du droit de propriété: le droit d'*abusus*, de disposition. Mais que faut-il entendre exactement par ce terme latin? Tout d'abord sans doute, dans un sens strictement matériel, mais qui n'a que peu d'applications en matière d'immeubles, le pouvoir de destruction de l'objet sur lequel porte le droit de propriété. Mais aussi, et cette acception du mot est bien plus intéressante pour l'analyse qui nous occupe, le pouvoir de renoncer librement au droit que l'on exerce sur l'objet du droit que ce soit entre vifs ou à cause de mort, à titre onéreux ou gratuit. Le propriétaire, titulaire de l'*abusus*, peut renoncer quand il lui plaît, comme il lui plaît et à l'égard de qui il lui plaît à tous ou à une partie des droits qu'il possède sur l'objet du droit. Ceci distingue sa situation de celle dans laquelle se trouverait toute autre personne qui aurait sur la chose

---

[1] Sohier, 1954, p. 145.   [2] Ibid., p. 140.
[3] Robert, 1955, p. 111.   [4] Elias, 1956, p. 165.
[5] Voir notamment Malengreau, 1939, p. 18 ff.; Vansina, 1956, pp. 908-14; Vanderlinden, 1960, p. 600; Obi, 1963, pp. 60-62; Pogucki, 1955, pp. 25-17; Schapera, 1955, pp. 207-13.

d'autres droits que ceux du propriétaire (l'usufructuaire, par exemple).[1]

Voyons donc ce qu'il en est dans une dizaine de groupes africains.

Chez les Kongo tout d'abord, l'analyse de Malengreau[2] commence par éliminer la possibilité pour l'individu d'être propriétaire du sol et par ne reconnaître que la seule propriété des meubles, fusent-ils immeubles par incorporation aux yeux du Code civil belge ou français (il est alors question de cases construites sur un endroit défriché de plantations, etc. . . . .). Cette constatation semble résulter du fait que 'toute parcelle abandonnée sans esprit de retour par celui qui l'occupait, fait retour au patrimoine territorial des membres de la communauté; ceux-ci peuvent en disposer de nouveau'.

Il semble donc qu'une fois qu'un individu a acquis des droits sur une parcelle, que celle-ci soit à l'usage de culture ou d'habitation, il ait certainement le droit d'en user et d'en jouir, étant notamment entièrement maître de l'affectation à donner à chaque élément de terre qu'il a compris dans son domaine (ainsi les terres consacrées à l'habitation peuvent devenir terrains de culture, les terres de culture être mises en jachères, et même certaines terres de jachère être utilisées pour l'installation de l'habitat). En outre, au moment qu'il lui conviendra de choisir l'individu décidera de renoncer à ses droits sur la terre, il en disposera au profit de la communauté et perdra dès lors de sa seule et propre volonté les droits qu'il avait acquis précédemment.

L'hypothèse d'une éventuelle cession de la terre, que ce soit à titre onéreux ou gratuit, entre vifs ou à cause de mort, à d'autres membres de la communauté considérés individuellement, n'est pas mentionnée par Malengreau et il faudrait donc en déduire qu'elle est impossible. Le problème est alors, sur le plan de la définition du concept, de savoir si, lorsque l'individu ne peut apparemment disposer de ses droits qu'au seul bénéfice de la collectivité, la notion de propriété est nécessairement absente.

Remarquons immédiatement que, dans un système juridique

[1] La destruction de l'objet est d'ailleurs une forme de renonciation à ses droits par l'élimination de ce sur quoi ils portent.
[2] Malengreau, 1939, p. 18 ff., et surtout 24.

comme celui de la Belgique ou de la France, les biens sans maître appartiennent à l'État donc à la collectivité qu'ils soient meubles ou immeubles (art. 713 du Code civil). Or le Kongo, qui abandonne sans esprit de retour une parcelle de terre, la transforme en fait en bien sans maître et ce bien sans maître retourne à la collectivité. Cette constatation ramène la solution de notre problème à la réponse à une seule question: est-il réellement exclu, en société Kongo traditionnelle, sur le plan du droit et non sur celui des faits, qu'un individu transfère à un autre individu les droits dont il serait titulaire sur la terre? Cette question doit malheureusement demeurer sans réponse faute de données scientifiques à son sujet, mais il faudrait en tout cas souligner immédiatement la dichotomie qui est susceptible d'exister entre les faits et le droit à cet égard. En effet, dans une société vouée à l'économie de subsistance ou à une économie de marché réduite, dans laquelle en outre la location d'immeubles ou de main d'œuvre est chose inconnue (chaque chef de famille est à la tête d'une unité de production autonome proportionnée à ses besoins et aux resources dont il dispose pour l'exploiter), on voit mal un individu accroître la surface de terres sur lesquelles il est susceptible d'exercer des droits, puisqu'en fait il serait incapable soit de trouver des personnes intéressées par cette location, soit d'exercer ses droits avec l'assistance d'une main d'œuvre louée. On pourrait donc dire que, si la cession de droits sur des immeubles n'apparaît pas dans la pratique, elle est néamoins possible sur le plan des principes du droit. Et si rien ne vient confirmer pareille hypothèse, la question reste posée puisqu'aussi bien aucun élément ne semble avoir été fourni jusqu'à présent établissant de manière définitive l'absence totale de transactions ayant la terre pour objet en société kongo traditionnelle.

Chez les Kuba, Vansina[1] déclare d'emblée que toute 'terre défrichée devient propriété personnelle de celui qui l'a mise en valeur' et aussi que l'annonce de l'intention de défricher faite en public suffit à établir le droit de propriété. Et, de nouveau, il semble que ce soit de la volonté seule du défricheur que dépende l'extinction de ses droits sur la terre: en effet, ses droits ne s'éteindront qu'au jour où il laissera la jachère se développer de telle façon que l'on pourra en conclure à un

[1] Vansina, 1956, p. 911 ff.

abandon de ses droits sur la terre. Il existe donc ici une présomption d'abandon, mais elle ne jouera que si le titulaire du droit de propriété la laisse jouer.

Chez les Zande[1] enfin, nous avons eu l'occasion de montrer dans une étude précédente que sur toute terre à laquelle il avait incorporé, sous quelque forme que ce soit, son activité (ce que nous avions appelé la terre travaillée) l'individu possédait un droit absolu qui se traduisait par l'usage dans son chef du mot *ira*. Nous avions également dit qu'il nous avait été impossible d'analyser dans toutes ses connotations ce droit complexe, mais qu'en tout cas il faisait de l'individu zande le véritable maître ou, mieux, dans le contexte qui est le nôtre aujourd'hui, le véritable propriétaire de la terre travaillée. Comme dans les deux exemples que nous venons d'étudier nous pouvions dire que la décision d'éteindre ses droits sur la terre travaillée était du seul ressort de l'individu. Mais, en outre il lui était possible d'éteindre ces droits en les transmettant à autrui, que ce soit à cause de mort ou entre vifs; nous avions toutefois souligné combien en pratique semblables transmissions étaient rares en raison des données de fait propres à la société zande (tout individu est un agriculteur pratiquant une stricte activité de subsistance dans un pays où il existe des terres de qualité moyenne en abondance).

Enfin, rien ne venait limiter ce droit absolu de l'individu si ce n'est l'obligation, de nature publique et non plus privée cette fois, de respecter l'autorité politique du lieu où il avait décidé de s'établir et de faire usage de la terre que ce soit pour y installer son habitat ou en tirer sa subsistance.

[Note de l'éditeur.—L'auteur cite ici Obi sur les Ibo,[2] Pogucki sur les Adangme du Ghana,[3] Fréchou sur les Peuls du Fouta Djalon,[4] Gluckman sur les Barotse,[5] Wagner sur les Logoli,[6] et Schapera sur les Tswana,[7] pour les peuples de l'Afrique occidentale, centrale, orientale et du Sud, pour démontrer l'existence de principes pareils à ceux décrits ci-dessus en

---

[1] Vanderlinden, 1960, pp. 580–1 et 592–8.
[2] Obi, 1963, voir notamment, pp. 52–67.
[3] Pogucki, 1955, p. 13 et p. 32 ff.
[4] Fréchou, 1965, voir notamment, pp. 450–60.
[5] Gluckman, 1965, voir, pp. 84–86.
[6] Wagner, 1956, voir II, pp. 75–100.
[7] Schapera, 1953, pp. 195–213.

ce qui concerne le droit foncier de ces populations; il y a quelques différences, notamment la défense de la vente des terres chez les Barotse et les Tswana. Ces citations ont été coupées, faute d'espace.]

Le deuxième caractère du droit de propriété est que celui-ci est un droit exclusif de celui qui en est titulaire. En effet, soit implicitement, soit explicitement, la plupart des auteurs indiquent que les droits sur la terre que nous venons de mentionner sont bien exercés par l'individu qui en est titulaire et par lui seul.[1]

Le troisième caractère du droit de propriété veut que celui-ci soit perpétuel en ce sens qu'il est impossible à un individu de cesser d'en être titulaire par le simple non-exercice de son droit. Il semble que ce caractère ne doive pas non plus donner lieu à discussion en ce qui concerne les exemples que nous avons étudiés. En effet, la plupart des auteurs[2] mentionnent expressément le fait que le non-usage des droits sur la terre n'entraîne pas l'extinction de ceux-ci dans le chef de l'individu qui en est titulaire. Seul, l'abandon volontaire et définitif (qui est en fait une aliénation à une personne indéterminée) est susceptible d'éteindre les droits que possède l'individu sur la terre. Il est donc bien possible de parler de ces droits comme étant perpétuels.

Il semblerait donc, dans la mesure où notre analyse est correcte (nous supposons bien entendu que les données de base que nous avons utilisées le sont elles-mêmes), que l'*abusus*, l'exclusivité et la perpétuité en tant qu'éléments caractéristiques de ce faisceau de droits que nous avons appelé la propriété, puissent exister dans certains systèmes africains traditionnels, et qu'en outre cette propriété puisse exister dans le chef d'individus. Nous serions ainsi amené à dire, au contraire des auteurs cités au début de cette communication, que le droit de propriété immobilière individuelle existe en droit congolais, ouest-africain et même africain, ceci ne voulant toutefois pas dire que ce droit existe dans toutes les sociétés vivant dans les mêmes limites géographiques. Notre objet n'est pas de procéder à

[1] Voir notamment, Fréchou, 1965, p. 416; Schapera, 1955, p. 205; Gluckman, 1965, p. 83; Pogucki, 1955, p. 13, note 44; Obi, 1963, p. 62; Vansina, 1956, p. 911.
[2] Voir notamment, Malengreau, 1939, p. 23; Vansina, 1956, p. 911; Vanderlinden, 1960, p. 594; Obi, 1963, pp. 64-65; Pogucki, 1955, p. 21; Schapera, 1955, p. 204.

une généralisation absolue, mais plutôt de mettre en question une autre généralisation. Ce premier point étant établi, nous voudrions poursuivre notre analyse en rapprochant, dans les diverses sociétés que nous avons prises comme exemples, les droits exclusifs des individus de ceux qui sont exercés par la communauté toute entière à titre collectif sur les terres n'ayant pas fait l'objet d'une appropriation individuelle.

Mais avant de procéder à cette analyse, il est nécessaire d'encore souligner combien les conclusions ci-dessus dépendent du sens exact donné à la notion d'*abusus*. En fait il faudrait distinguer, au sein de l'*abusus*, une véritable hiérarchie de concepts selon la manière dont s'effectue le transfert des droits et aussi, peut-être, envisager la nature des personnes au bénéfice desquelles le transfert peut s'effectuer. Il faudrait également prendre soigneusement en considération la nature des terres sur lesquelles l'*abusus* est susceptible de s'exercer.

Dans le premier cas, il semble que le droit de disposition soit général (si on excepte bien entendu le cas des Kongo) s'il s'exerce à cause de mort et à titre gratuit (cette deuxième condition étant, semble-t-il, implicite lorsque le transfert s'effectue à cause de mort). A un deuxième degré, on trouverait le pouvoir de disposer entre vifs à titre gratuit, qui est également connu de tous les groupes étudiés, mais il serait parfaitement possible de rencontrer des systèmes dans lesquels seule la transmission à cause de mort serait possible. Enfin, à un troisième degré, la transmission entre vifs est possible aussi bien à titre gratuit qu'a titre onéreux (c'est le cas des Kuba, des Zande, des Ibo, des Adangme, des Peul, des Logoli, mais pas des Barotse ou des Tswana). Ce n'est qu'à ce dernier stade peut-être que l'*abusus* africain coïnciderait avec son homologue européen.

Dans le deuxième cas, le transfert des droits au bénéfice de la communauté est toujours possible ; celui au bénéfice d'un de ses membres également, mais la situation change dès qu'il s'agit d'un étranger. On rencontre en effet des sociétés dans lesquelles l'étranger qui désire conserver sa qualité d'étranger, est exclu du bénéfice des transactions immobilières ; mais ceci n'a rien d'irréconciliable avec certaines sociétés européennes ou l'État interdit également (ou a interdit) le transfert d'immeubles à des étrangers pour des raisons de politique économique.

Le Concept de Propriété immobilière individuelle 245

Enfin, il est clair que dans de nombreuses sociétés africaines certaines terres, de par leur nature, restent en dehors du circuit économique. En ce sens la quantité d'objets sur lesquels l'*abusus* est susceptible de porter est plus restreinte, mais le concept n'en existe pas moins.

Les droits collectifs que possèdent les individus semblent pouvoir en fait se ramener à un véritable droit d'usufruit[1] en ce sens qu'il s'agit des droits d'usage (au sens le plus large du terme) et de jouissance des fruits de cette partie du domaine foncier qui ne fait pas l'objet d'appropriation individuelle ou familiale. Ainsi, rencontre-t-on le plus souvent le droit de pacage (pour le petit et gros bétail), le droit de chasse (en tout cas pour les petits animaux), le droit de prélever (dans les limites des besoins personnels de chacun) de l'eau, du bois, de la terre, voire même dans certains cas des denrées plus précieuses comme du sel, enfin, le droit de libre circulation, tous ces droits étant reconnus à tous les membres du groupe social indistinctement et chacun d'eux étant à même de les exercer librement sur le domaine collectif. Et il faut souligner que ce domaine foncier reçoit dans de nombreux droits une appellation qui lui est propre et qui le distingue des autres terres; ce sera le *nsi* des Kongo, le *sende* des Zande, l'*oluangereka* des Logoli. C'est ce que personnellement, dans notre analyse de la société Zande, nous avions appelé la terre brute en ce sens que personne n'y avait encore incorporé son activité.

Cette notion d'une terre échappant à l'exploitation individuelle pour être réservée à l'usage de la communauté n'est certes pas étrangère aux droits européens. On la retrouve d'abord au niveau de certaines communes rurales qui ont hérité de l'histoire, des prés, des bois, voire des sources qui sont soustraits à l'exploitation exclusive d'un individu et réservés à la collectivité qui s'y fournit en bois, y fait paître son bétail et s'y approvisionne en eau; ces cas deviennent sans doute de plus en plus rare aujourd'hui, mais ils existent toujours et nous sommes alors confrontés avec une situation très proche de la réalité africaine traditionnelle.

[1] L'utilisation du mot *usufruit* ne nous semble toutefois pas souhaitable dans la mesure où ce qui est dit plus bas au sujet de propriété et de souveraineté est fondé. En effet, si on désire doter d'une terminologie propre les concepts de droit privé et de droit public, il est peut-être difficile d'admettre l'usufruit comme un démembrement de la souveraineté.

A un échelon plus complexe, il est nécessaire de mentionner les innombrables portions du domaine public qui sont mises par les différents pouvoirs publics à la disposition des individus. Que ce soit sous la forme de réseau routier, de parcs publics, de littoral, (pour ne citer que quelques exemples) l'autorité politique des États modernes reconnait aux individus un droit d'usage de ces parties de son domaine. Bien entendu les développements de l'économie moderne, et plus particulièrement en Europe de l'Ouest, du capitalisme, ont contribué à diminuer considérablement cette portion du sol national laissée au libre usage des individus. En outre, pour des raisons tendant généralement à assurer une meilleure conservation ou un usage plus rationnel de ces espaces publics, une réglementation abondante a le plus souvent été édictée. Mais, malgré ce cadre réglementaire, on peut considérer que nous nous trouvons là dans une situation fondamentalement identique à celle rencontrée dans les sociétés africaines traditionnelles.

Sur ces terres brutes, un contrôle, variable selon les groupes, est généralement exercé par l'autorité sociale, politique ou foncière locale. C'est à elle qu'il appartient de vérifier si l'exercice des droits d'usufruit de chaque membre de la communauté s'effectue bien dans les limites qui lui sont fixées (l'une des limites semble être que l'exercice de ce droit doive toujours dépendre étroitement des besoins de l'individu et ne puisse être le point de départ d'une activité économique lucrative).[1] De la même façon il semble que ce soit aux autorités du groupe social que soit reconnu le privilège exclusif de disposer éventuellement des terres collectives du groupe. Certes, pareille notion est rare en pratique, les groupes sociaux étant fortement attachés aux terres sur lesquelles ils vivent. Il n'empêche que le principe de la libre disposition des droits sur la terre brute est reconnu en de nombreux endroits dans le chef de l'autorité socio-politique. Dans certains cas d'ailleurs ce droit absolu de l'autorité sera caractérisé par l'usage d'un terme identique à celui qui caractérise le droit le plus étendu de l'individu sur les terres qui sont les siennes. Ainsi le chef

[1] Il semble en effet inconcevable qu'un individu puisse organiser à son seul bénéfice l'exploitation systématique du territoire collectif. Il est certain que la large tolérance dont font souvent preuve les autorités socio-politiques en ce qui concerne l'usage de la terre brute par les individus ne s'explique que par le fait que ceux-ci restent dans les limites strictes de la satisfaction de leurs besoins.

zande sera-t-il *ira sende*, maître ou propriétaire de la terre brute tout comme le zande sera *ira kporo*, maître de son habitat ou *ira bino*, maître de son champ. De même Gluckman dans son analyse des concepts Barotse, semble montrer que le terme *mung'a* peut être appliqué à diverses personnes (chefs ou sujets) titulaires de droits relativement identiques sur des entités foncières distinctes.

Il en va de même dans de nombreuses sociétés européennes où l'autorité politique (le plus souvent le Parlement) est investie non seulement du pouvoir de règlementer l'utilisation du domaine public, mais aussi du pouvoir de modifier les limites du territoire national, c'est-à-dire en fait, éventuellement, de celui d'en céder des parties à un autre État. Ceci est sans doute aussi rare que dans les sociétés africaines, mais trouve par exemple son application dans les cas, relativement fréquents ceux-ci, de rectifications de frontières où l'une partie cède une portion de son territoire à l'autre et vice-versa pour assurer un tracé plus régulier des limites les séparant.

Considérant maintenant les problèmes de terminologie, nous voyons que Gluckman qualifie le chef Barotse d'*owner*, donnant au terme de *mung'a* une connotation de droit civil plutôt que de droit public.[1]

Nous préférerions quant à nous parler de *maître* et de *maîtrise*, s'il est indispensable de traduire des termes comme *ira* ou *mung'a* par un même mot dans les langues européennes. Nous croyons toutefois que ce n'est pas là une nécessité absolue et qu'il serait sans doute préférable d'utiliser les termes *souveraineté* quand il s'agit des pouvoirs des autorités socio-politiques et *propriété* quand il s'agit des droits des particuliers. En effet, dans nos droits, la pratique s'est installée de faire disparaître du vocabulaire juridique la nécessité d'une référence au statut socio-politique pour pouvoir déterminer la nature exacte des droits les plus étendus qu'exercent sur la terre soit les individus, soit les autorités politiques et sociales; dans le cas des premiers, on parlera toujours de propriété, dans celui des seconds, de souveraineté, étant par ailleurs bien entendu que ces termes concernent toujours également des notions de terre qui sont nettement distinctes l'une de l'autre. Dans le cas des individus et de leur propriété, il sera question surtout de la terre à usage

---

[1] Gluckman, 1965, pp. 79 et 140.

économique, tandis que dans le cas de l'État et de sa souveraineté, il sera question de la terre en tant que territoire national. Bien entendu, les développements contemporains de l'activité économique de l'État ont fait apparaître la distinction entre le domaine public de l'État et son domaine privé, ce dernier étant considéré, sous réserve des règles qui lui sont propres, comme un bien sur lequel l'État exerce des droits identiques au propriétaire individuel. Il est donc nécessaire de corriger la déclaration précédente en disant qu'il pourra aussi être question de propriété de l'État sur les biens de son domaine privé, le terme de souveraineté étant conservé pour le domaine public.

On pourrait alors dire, comparant la situation du Barotse ou du Zande avec celle du Belge ou du Français, que les uns comme les autres sont propriétaires de leurs terres tandis que les détenteurs de l'autorité socio-politique de ces groupes africains sont les souverains du territoire de leurs communautés, tout comme l'État belge ou français est souverain en ce qui concerne son territoire national. Sur leurs terres respectives, les individus auront tous les droits du propriétaire, tandis qu'ils n'auront sur le territoire national ou de la communauté qu'un droit d'usufruit plus ou moins étendu selon les circonstances de fait propres à chaque société.[1]

Par rapport à ces derniers territoires, le droit le plus étendu, comprenant l'*usus*, l'*abusus* et le *fructus*, droit exclusif et perpétuel du souverain, appartiendra à l'État ou aux titulaires de l'autorité socio-politique.

En conclusion, il semble que l'écart souligné par de nombreux africanistes entre les conceptions africaines et européennes de la propriété immobilière ne soit ni aussi important, ni aussi généralisé que d'aucuns se plaisent à le dire fréquemment. Certes les sociétés africaines ne semblent pas avoir atteint, dans de nombreux cas, un stade comparable à celui atteint par les sociétés européennes sur la voie de l'individualisme. Ceci se reflètera, sur le plan du concept de propriété, par un sens restrictif de la nation d'*abusus*, le pouvoir de disposition de l'individu étant susceptible d'être limité par certaines modalités, par la nature des terres en cause ou par la personnalité des bénéficiaires de la disposition. Mais il ne semble pas que ces restrictions soient suffisantes pour faire disparaître la

---

[1] Voir la remarque en note 1, p. 245, sur l'utilisation du terme *usufruit*.

nation du droit d'*abusus*, et par conséquent la notion de droit de propriété, dans le chef de l'individu.

Ceci étant dit, il n'en demeure pas moins que, sur le plan de la terminologie, l'usage généralisé du terme propriété ne parait pas souhaitable. Tout d'abord il semble particulièrement inadéquat lorsqu'il est nécessaire de décrire les pouvoirs des autorités socio-politiques; celui de souveraineté parait plus indiqué. En outre une approche plus analytique du concept de propriété semble souhaitable sur le plan de l'analyse exact de l'*abusus*. Il semble nécessaire de faire la distinction entre l'*abusus* absolu (caractéristique de nos droits occidentaux) qui comprend le droit de disposition entre vifs ou à cause de mort, à titre gracieux ou onéreux et d'autres *abusus* qui ne comprendraient qu'une partie de ce droit. Il est certain que la compréhension entre comparatistes pourrait être facilitée s'il pouvait être fait référence dans chaque cas à une idée précise telle que *abusus absolu* et *abusus limité à la disposition entre vifs à titre gratuit*, ou *à la disposition à cause de mort*, étant admis que la disposition entre vifs à titre onéreux entraine les deux autres et que la disposition à cause de mort à titre onéreux semble exclue, du moins provisoirement.

Enfin, il n'est sans doute pas inutile de souligner que toute comparaison entre systèmes juridiques sur le plan du droit immobilier suppose la définition exacte dans chaque cas de trois éléments: le titulaire du droit, l'objet du droit et la nature du droit. Faute de délimiter chacun d'eux avec suffisamment de précision (celle-ci n'excluant pas les tentatives de conceptualisation de manière à permettre la rencontre des idées propres à chaque système), toute comparaison entre systèmes fonciers est vouée à l'imprécision et à l'approximation.

BIBLIOGRAPHY

Capitant, H.
  (1930) *Vocabulaire juridique*. Paris: Les Presses universitaires de France.
Dekkers, R.
  (1954-5) *Précis de droit civil belge*, 3 vols. Bruxelles: Bruylant.
Elias, T. O.
  (1956) *The Nature of African Customary Law*. Manchester: Manchester University Press.
Fréchou, J.
  (1965) 'Le régime foncier dans la région des Timbi (Fouta Dialon)', *Etudes de droit africain et malgache*, Jean Poirier, editor. Paris: Cujas. 407-502.

Gluckman, M.
(1965) *The Ideas in Barotse Jurisprudence*. New Haven and London: Yale University Press.
Jowitt, W. A. J.
(1959) *The Dictionary of English Law*. London: Sweet and Maxwell.
Malengreau, G.
(1939) 'Le régime foncier dans la société indigène—Le Bas-Congo', *Congo*, ii, 1–46.
Obi, S.
(1963) *The Ibo Law of Property*. London: Butterworth.
Pogucki, R.
(1955) *Report on Land Tenure in Adangme Province*. Accra: Government Printer.
Ripert, G. and Boulanger, J. (eds.)
(1949–51) *Traité élémentaire de droit civil de Planiol*, 3 vols. Paris: Librairie générale de Droit et de Jurisprudence (later edition, 1950–2).
Robert, A.-P.
(1955) *Évolution des coutumes de l'ouest africain et la législation française*. Paris: Éd. l'Encyclopédie d'Outre-Mer.
Schapera, I.
(1938) *A Handbook of Tswana Law and Custom*. London: Oxford University Press for the International African Institute (2nd edition, 1955).
Sohier, A.
(1954) *Traité élémentaire de droit coutumier de Conge Belge*. Bruxelles: Larcier.
Stephen, H. J.
(1950) *Commentaries on the Laws of England*, 4 vols. London: Butterworth (21st edition).
Vanderlinden, J.
(1960) 'Principes de droit foncier zande', *Revue de l'Institut de Sociologie*, 3, 557–610.
Vansina, J.
(1956) 'Le régime foncier dans la société kuba', *Zaire*, X, 9, November, 899–926.
Wagner, G.
(1956) *The Bantu of North Kavirondo*, vol. 2. London: Oxford University Press for the International African Institute.

Summary

REFLECTIONS ON THE EXISTENCE OF A CONCEPT OF INDIVIDUAL LAND PROPERTY IN AFRICAN TRADITIONAL LAW

This communication proposes questioning the assertion which is often made that the concept of individual land property is unknown in traditional African societies. After defining the meaning of the word 'property', this meaning is compared with the statements of various jurists and anthropologists about a dozen traditional African societies, namely, the Kongo, Kuba, Zande, Adangme, Ibo, Peul, Logoli, Barotse, and Tswana.

The conclusion drawn from this comparison is that the

concept of individual property exists in these societies. Moreover, it is concluded that this concept deals with a well-defined kind of plots of land, those used by the individual, and that a relatively identical conception is found, affecting the territory occupied by the whole of ethnic group, in the property of the chief of the socio-political authority governing the group. Finally, the differentiation of these concepts in traditional African societies is only apparent if one brings together the title-holders and the objects of the land rights, while in European societies the distinction is made directly at a conceptual level without such a coalescence.

XII. Property Rights and Status in African Traditional Law[1]

M. GLUCKMAN

I LAND TENURE: GROUP AND INDIVIDUAL RIGHTS

Widespread sharing of produce is the rule in tribal societies. Some early Western observers therefore concluded that they were 'communistic', and that individual rights in land and other goods did not exist. There is implicit in this judgment a false antithesis between 'communistic' and 'individualistic', arising from the way in which we say that a person or a group 'owns' a piece of land or some item of property. We are speaking loosely when we use this sort of phrasing: what is owned in fact is a claim to have power to do certain things with the land or property, to possess immunities against the encroachment of others on one's rights in them, and to exercise certain privileges in respect of them. But in addition other persons may have certain rights, claims, powers, privileges, and immunities in respect of the same land or property. Hence, when we say that a particular group of kinsmen owns land, we are also saying that all the members of that group have claims to exercise certain rights over that land—maybe equally with one another, maybe varying with their status. The incidence of rights over land varies with the technology of the tribe concerned, from those who live by hunting and collecting wild products to those who have elaborate systems of agriculture. Even when, as in hunting tribes, each member of the tribe has the right to hunt freely over the extent of the tribe's territory, this reduces to a right of every individual to hunt without let and hindrance from others; and this particular right to hunt freely may exist among agriculturists whose arable land is allocated specifically to smaller groups and to individuals within the tribe. Rights of

[1] A fuller justification of the argument of this essay exists in Chapters III–IV of my *The Ideas in Barotse Jurisprudence* (1965), with many bibliographical references.

Property Rights and Status in African Traditional Law 253

this kind can vary with the methods of exploiting the land: thus hunting with bow and spear may be free, while particular groups may own rights to hold game drives or to set game-nets in particular areas.

Similar variations occur in the use of pasturage among herders. There may be areas where rights to graze stock are free, in the sense that any member of the tribe may exercise such rights, while rights to use particular areas around waterholes are restricted. In Bechuanaland no man may own grazing land, which is open to all members of the tribe, but the chief in practice gives rights to men to graze their cattle in particular places and will protect them against trespassers. In that arid land the main problem is shortage of water: and rights to water are granted by the chief especially when a man has sunk a water-hole (Schapera). In most tribes with a mixed husbandry, cattle graze freely on the crop stalks in anyone's fields, though if cattle stray into the fields before harvesting, suit for damages lies.

The position among agriculturalists is more complicated; but in Africa land-tenure laws seem to fall into a general pattern, of which the Lozi (Barotse) tribe who dwell in the great floodplain of the Upper Zambezi River are strikingly representative.[1] Because the river floods every year during the summer rains the people have to build their small villages on mounds in the plain which will stand above the waters. Even from these they move at the height of the flood to temporary villages on the margins of the plain. Each village on its mound is the centre of a number of pockets of arable land, scattered over the main expanse of uncultivable land in the plain and variously affected by flood-waters or by rainfall. The village is also the centre of sites suitable for fishing.

Ultimately the Lozi consider that all the land, and its products, belong to the nation through the king. Though one right of Lozi citizenship, to which all men who are accepted as subjects are entitled, is a right to building and to arable land and a right to use public lands for grazing and fishing, it is by the king's bounty that his subjects live on and by the land. Commoners think of themselves as permanently indebted to the king for the land on which they live and its wild and domestic-

[1] I write of the situation as I observed it in the 1940s.

ated products which sustain them. The Lozi say this is why they gave tribute and service to the king and still give gifts. Since tribute was abolished by agreement with the British Government the king has had to purchase many of his necessities from his people, and this is the standard by which the Lozi assess their present poverty.

The king is thus the 'owner' of Loziland and its cattle and wild products, in the sense that he ultimately claims rights over all land. These rights entitle him to demand allegiance from anyone who wants to settle on the land; he has the power to distribute to people any land which has not been allocated by him or any of his predecessors; he has a right to ask subjects to give him land which they are using, but he cannot dispossess them; he has the right to claim any land (or other good) which has been abandoned or for which family heirs cannot be traced; he has the power to control where men are allowed to build their homes; he has the right through his appropriate councils to pass laws about the holding and use of land; and he can expropriate land for public services, subject to giving the holders other land.

To balance his rights and powers, the king is under duty to do certain things with the land. He is obliged to give every subject land to live on and land to cultivate, and he must allow every subject to fish in public waters, to hunt game and birds, to gather wild fruits, and to use the clay, iron ore, grasses, reeds, and trees with which the Lozi make their pots, utensils, mats, baskets, weapons, implements, nets and traps, furniture, huts, medicines. The king must protect all subjects against trespassers or anyone attempting to prevent them from exercising their rights. Once the king has given land for cultivation, or a fishing site, the subject has in it rights which are protected against all comers including the king himself. Should he desire the land, either for his own use or to give to another, he must ask for it: 'The king is also a beggar.'

In practice, the ruling king has not granted most of the land to its present holders: they were given their rights by his predecessors, in some cases under a tradition reaching back to legendary times. The king should not interfere with these past dispositions of land, and his own courts protect his subjects against any attempt he may make to do so. The major distri-

Property Rights and Status in African Traditional Law 255

bution of land is to the villages on the mounds, and it is vested in the title of each village's headman. Whenever land is given to a man he acknowledges the gift by giving the royal salute to the palace of the king, or to the king sitting in council. When a headman of a village dies and his heir is installed, the latter gives the same royal salute and to this are referred the continuing rights of his title to control the land allocated to it.

A headman thus gets from the king rights to administer this land, not to work all of it. The headman in his turn is obliged to give sufficient land, if it is available, to all heads of households in the village, including himself; and each head of a household can take his own share to cultivate but must distribute lots among all his dependants. These rights to claim some of the land attached to a village inhere in membership of the village, and Lozi insist that, by their law, if a man (or woman) leaves the village he loses his rights in the land. Nevertheless, one frequently finds people who are not resident in the village but are working its land. This they do under another law: all kinsmen, in all lines, of the main family group of a village are entitled to make use of its wealth, provided that there is more than sufficient land for the members resident in the village. This was made clear in a case where a bad-tempered headman drove his villagers away. When his son succeeded to the headmanship he found himself head of a relatively empty village. Sons of two of his sisters who resided in other villages were working fish dams which had been allotted to their mothers by the dead headman. The new headman sued to have them ordered either to move to reside with him or to return these dams to him. This case put the judges in a moral dilemma: for while they were reluctant to find for the headman because he was behaving ungenerously by wishing to expropriate from the family property kinsmen who had done no wrong to him, they appreciated that were they to find against him they would be upsetting a basic rule of land-holding—that land is vested in the headman's control as representative of the resident villagers. In a Lozi court, judgment proceeds from the most junior of the many judges to the most senior. The judges wavered in their decision: some ruled the headman was entitled to expel his kinsmen but urged him not to, while others ruled that he could not expel them. Eventually the head of the court found a brilliant solution to the dilemma: clearly the dams belonged to (expressed in Lozi by a possessive prefix to the headman's name) the headman and this law could not be varied against him because he was ungenerous; but the court could invoke its powers to discharge an unsatisfactory headman. He threatened that unless the headman were generous and allowed his nephews to use the fish dams, the court would discharge him and find a more generous man to be headman. This case brings out clearly that rights to control the land vest not in an individual but in the title of headmanship. It emphasizes a point of great importance: we must continually differentiate between a society as a structure of social positions (titles) and as a structure of relationships between incumbents of these positions.

This example of land-holding in a large African kingdom emphasizes firstly that in kingdoms of this kind we are not dealing with 'feudal-type' states, as is often loosely alleged. Despite their common insistence on personal allegiances between lords and underlings, which is one of the main characteristics of both a tribal and a feudal system, rights to land are quite different in the two types of state. The right of all subjects to claim sufficient land, as an inherent attribute of citizenship, marked the political systems of the Ancient Germans and Celts, and not the land-tenure system of feudalism. Under feudalism a vassal entered into a special contract with his immediate lord in which he gave service of a demarcated kind in return for control over land and those attached to it. No one in those times could go to the king and demand land as of right, as men could do in Africa. Nor in African systems were there the means to build castles in which lords could live a different style of life from that of their underlings. All men also carried the same simple weapons, from king to meanest soldier (spear, club, bow-and-arrow, and hide-shield). No knights superior in armour on horseback formed a class of chivalry.

Secondly, this system of land-holding was an essential part of the organization of social relations from the king downwards through the political units of villages, into the hierarchy of kinship relationships. The king may be called 'owner of the land' only as trustee or steward for the nation. He granted what I call a primary estate of rights of administration to all titles of heads of villages, including himself in his capacity as head of many villages. Each head of a village then broke his estate into secondary estates with rights of administration which he allotted to the heads of households in the village, including himself. These holders of secondary estates might allocate tertiary estates of this kind to dependent heads of household, but usually secondary estates were broken up and allocated in parcels of land to be worked as arable or as fishing sites by the holders, including the administrator of the secondary estate of administration. Thus at the bottom of the series there is an 'estate of production'. Land-holding in these tribes is thus an inherent attribute not only of citizenship but also of each social position in the total political and kinship hierarchy.

Each parcel of land was therefore not communally owned but was subject to a series of retreating or reversionary[1] rights from the final user up to the king. And every one of these rights was effective. If a user of land—a holder of an estate of production— left the village, the land reverted to the holder of the secondary estate of administration of which he was a member; and if the secondary holder in turn left, his estate reverted to the primary holder of the estate of administration; and only if he, and all who might replace him, departed from the area, was the king as ultimate owner of all land entitled to claim the whole estate. All these rights are not only valid in African law but they have also been recognized by British courts. In a Nigerian case in 1930 where land was required for public purposes, the British Privy Council held that the individual African holders were entitled to compensation, and the chiefs only to compensation for their reversionary[2] rights. This was a major recognition of African law and showed a change of outlook from the time when the same Council held that only the Ndebele king and not individual subjects had rights in land, which hence could all accrue to the conquering British South Africa Company.

In short, if we are to understand the use of land as a unit of production in these tribal societies we have to appreciate that it is too simple to talk of them as marked by either communism or individualism. Clearly land, as it is ultimately cultivated, is worked by individuals with secure and protected rights, but

[1] The discussions brought out that the rights were not 'reversionary' only, since they subsist all the time.
[2] See preceding footnote.

representatives of their family, of their village, and of the nation have claims on the land. No superior can arbitrarily oust a junior from his holding, and the heir of each junior enters on succession into this holding. What the junior cannot do is dispose of the land to any outsider or invite an outsider to come and use the land without consulting his superiors, up to that point in the social structure where the invitee ceases to be an outsider. That is, a junior inside a secondary estate cannot give land to a villager from outside the group which has rights in that particular estate unless he secures the approval of the secondary estate-holder; that secondary holder must consult the primary holder, the village headman, before he thus invites on to his land someone from outside the village; and a village headman must consult the king before he accepts into his village someone who is not a subject of the king. Correspondingly, a superior holder cannot force an outsider on the holder of a junior estate, without the latter agreeing.

The terminology I am using here may sound complicated, but I have adopted it for comparative analysis for two reasons. First, there is no suitable terminology extant in European languages or in African languages in general. Many writers use various terms from European languages, but all have connotations quite different from those involved in tribal tenure. 'Possession' is too weak a term, since it does not emphasize the strength of the rights owned by the holders of the land. 'Usufruct', defined by the *Oxford English Dictionary* as a 'right of enjoying the use and advantages of another's property short of destruction or waste of the substance', is often used. The dictionary definition also does not cover the strength of rights of African holders; and those who use the word, with the meaning to enjoy the fruits, similarly fail to recognize this strength. The land is not 'another's property'. Moreover, in Roman law a grant of 'usufruct' was for use of fruits during the holder's lifetime, not transmissible to heirs, as African land-holding is. Second, since there was no suitable term available it seemed sensible to find a terminology which described the rights and duties involved and the manner in which they inhere in status itself: status as a citizen, status as a villager, and status as a dependant in a family. Each status gives rights to claim land in the appropriate estate. 'Estate' is a term deriving from status. 'Administration' and 'production' describe the rights involved at different levels of 'status'.

One term can be used for all levels of the hierarchy, since the rights and duties obtaining between adjacent holders in the series are identical: the junior must give support and respectful allegiance to the senior, who must give support and land to the junior. In addition, however, each junior holder in the series owes his duties to all seniors, and he can be expelled from all his estates up to that held by the senior whom he offends. A young man working land can be expelled from the village if he offends the headman, and from the kingdom if he offends the king sufficiently.

This system of land-holding can be worked out among almost all the tribal peoples of whom I know, though some of them, in West Africa and South-East Asia, in more recent times began to allow pledging and sale of land, rights which are excluded in most of Negro Africa because of the ultimate reversionary[1] rights of the chief, or the reversionary[1] rights of the tribal community as a whole in those tribes which do not have chiefs. The hierarchy of estates may appear as a delegation of the primary estate of administration from king or paramount chief to district chiefs, then from them to sub-district chiefs, then to ward-heads, then to village headmen, as among Basuto and Zulu. It is least clearly marked where land is plentiful, as among the Bemba of Northern Rhodesia. Its main effect, seen even there, is that as citizenship gives a right to claim land, so if one enters on the use of land, this founds a claim by holders of superior estates to demand one's allegiance.

II RIGHTS IN CHATTELS

We shall shortly see that tribal law emphasizes individual appropriation of produce and manufactured goods, and the dominant rights which this gives a man or woman over these. But no one owns a food or chattel absolutely, because his kinsfolk and even outsiders may have claims upon it which he has difficulty in denying. The extreme form of a claim of this kind is seen in the Lozi institution of *kufunda*, which is defined in the standard Lozi dictionary as a 'legal theft'. *Kufunda* allowed any kinsman or kinswoman of a Lozi to take anything

[1] See preceding footnotes.

S

belonging to the latter, without exposing himself or herself to the charge of stealing which would be levied against outsiders. The Lozi attached such importance to this privilege of kinship that when their king and council signed a treaty to come under the protection of the British South Africa Company they specifically stated in it that *kufunda* was to be allowed and not to be liable to prosecution. Many years later the king ruled it to be theft, but I never heard of anyone prosecuting a kinsman for it, though I knew of families that suffered severely under the depredations of ne'er-do-wells. They accepted the depredations, even if with a lot of grumbling. Eventually one family sued in the king's court to have a man of this sort declared no longer to be a kinsman of theirs: while he was kin they felt they could not deny him this privilege; if he ceased to be a kinsman he lost the privilege. The court agreed. *Kufunda* in this large African tribe corresponds closely with what Firth calls 'forced exchanges' in the small island of Tikopia in Oceania. These are extreme forms of a rule which is very common, though the privilege may be restricted to particular categories of kinsfolk.

In cattle-owning tribes it is almost impossible to work out who is the 'real' owner of cattle in a herd, for most cattle are also subject to claims by others for various reasons. I illustrate this situation again from the Lozi. When a Lozi girl marries as an ostensible virgin her bridegroom presents two beasts to her kin. He pays the first beast to make the girl his wife, the second is for her untouched fertility. Should he divorce her and she has not conceived, he is entitled to recover the second beast handed over with its progeny. This is, therefore, called 'the beast of herding', i.e. the bride's kin merely herd it for the husband until he has impregnated their 'daughter'. They have the right to hold it and to sue for it, against the world including the groom, but it is not theirs: it is still the husband's, though he cannot claim it without divorcing his wife.

The husband's obligations are discharged provided he receives her from, and gives cattle to, an apparently accredited guardian with whom she is living, whether this guardian be of her paternal or her maternal kin. Whichever side of her family receives the two beasts should give one to the other. Within each of these groups, if the recipient slaughters the beast, he should divide the meat among his kin. Different kinsmen are entitled to specific portions of the beast: the bride, for instance, gets the tongue, 'for is she not the owner of the beast since she brought it to the village?'

If a bride is not a virgin, only one beast is given. If it is killed by the person who receives it, he should share the meat with the bride's kin on both sides according to fixed rules. If the beast is kept to breed, say by the father of the bride, he must give the mother's family the first and then all alternate calves. Thus he owns the beast but not all its offspring.

Courts will enforce all these claims by the bride's mother's family against the father's, or vice versa: but claims within each family are not enforceable at law; they are moral claims only, since kin should not sue one another. But any kinsman who feels he was neglected could reject responsibility if the spouses or their children ran into difficulty. He would say: 'I know nothing of this marriage.'

The rules for distribution of the marriage-cattle—which I have given in simple form—show how a chattel, like land, may be subject to a cluster of rights held by different persons in terms of their relationships within the network of kinship ties. In fact, their rights to claim on the marriage-cattle define their kinship relationships to the central parties. If they are not given their shares, this denies their kinship: hence they state they did not know of the marriage. The law of property is again intricately intertwined with the law of status. It means that to understand the holding of property, we must investigate the system of status relationships; and to describe the system of status relationships, we must deal constantly with relationships to property.

III IDEAS OF PROPERTY AND THE SOCIAL SENTIMENTS OF STATUS

Even among ourselves this is to some extent true. To describe family relations, we have to bring in the provision of goods and services by parents for children. If parents do not provide these they are liable to prosecution. But children no longer bear a corresponding *legal* obligation to provide goods and services for their parents, save when these are destitute, and siblings (brothers and sisters) have no such legal obligation to one another. In tribal society these obligations are strong and spread widely. A man's variegated relationships with others run through his chattels as well as his land; and the measure of how far he feels the correct sentiments in those relationships is the way he deals with his property and his produce. Anyone who feels he or she has been stinted will conclude that the other does not feel the right sentiments of love, demanded of their relationship. This is why in tribal life persons watch, apparently greedily, what their kinsmen do with their goods; and why bitter disputes can arise over amounts which appear negligible to us—such as being overlooked in the distribution of a small pot of beer. It is not the beer that counts: the invitation to drink is a symbol of recognition of kinship. The African has to eke out his distribution of his products with great skill, lest he offend some kinsman or woman. We ourselves feel hurt in similar situations: but however our kin and friends may offend us, it is not essential for our survival that they should feel the right sentiments and recognize their obligations to us. Our living depends on a wide series of impersonal relationships in the economic and political systems.

Another crucial fact arises from this situation. Ownership cannot be absolute, for the critical thing about property is the role that it plays in a nexus of specific relationships. Hence in Africa there is no clear definition of ownership: when an African court makes a decision on a dispute over property it states that X stands in a masterful position in relation to that specific object, privilege, or person, as against some other person who is counter-claiming—i.e. the decision is made as between persons related in specific ways.

Property law in tribal society defines not so much rights of persons over things, as obligations owed between persons in respect of things. Indeed, since there is relatively little in the way of goods, the critical property rights which a man or woman enjoys are demands on other persons in virtue of control over land and chattels—not as with ourselves, any set of persons, but persons related in specific long-standing ways with one. Correspondingly, if new relationships are being established, this is done through transfers of property, which create and define these relationships, as I have illustrated with marriage-cattle. Men similarly make payments when they enter into allegiance to a superior. Indeed gifts are given at all changes of relationships, as we give them; but in tribal society these gifts are believed to recognize and validate the new relationship of giver and recipient. Goods take on a high symbolic value.

Once we look at the situation of property from this point of view, we understand why a man pays cattle or other goods for a bride. He is not purchasing a woman to be a concubine or a slave: a wife's rights are very different from those of such a person. He is validating the transfer of certain rights over the bride from her kin to himself, and establishing 'friendship'—in-law relationship—with his wife's kin. The marriage-gifts also signify that he accepts the obligations of his status as husband, and that his own kin, who contributed to the payment, accept obligations to their new daughter- or sister-in-law and the rest of her family. We are misled if we think of a wife in this situation as a chattel of her father to dispose of as he pleases, to become a chattel to her husband. Father or husband may speak of himself as 'owner' of the woman: but this is shorthand for saying they have rights over her against each other, and accept duties towards her. The stress in this situation is on obligation to others.

This emphasis on obligation spreads to other branches of the law, as to the law of contract, which in tribal society tends to insist that all contracts are 'of the utmost good faith'. Seller, and not buyer, must look to the quality of goods exchanged under an implied warranty and the concept of latent defect is applied more widely and for a longer period than in modern, but not medieval Europe. If a Lozi sells a cow to another and it dies some months later, he must replace it. Among some Plains Indians the 'seller' of a horse bore some responsibility if it was stolen a day or two after its purchase, or was lamed in the first race it ran for its new owner. Firth has stated succinctly that 'the principle of *caveat emptor* would not function well in a [tribal] society'. Transfer of some property is necessary to establish a valid contract.[1]

I believe that this analysis, with its emphasis on status and obligation, bears out Maine's century-old generalization, that 'the movement of progressive societies has hitherto been a movement from *Status* to *Contract*'.

[1] See Chapters VI and VIII in my *The Ideas in Barotse Jurisprudence* (1965).

BIBLIOGRAPHY

Biebuyck, D. (ed.)
   (1963) *African Agrarian Systems.* London: Oxford University Press for the International African Institute.

Gluckman, M.
   (1965) *The Ideas in Barotse Jurisprudence.* New Haven and London: Yale University Press.

Résumé

DROIT DE PROPRIÉTÉ ET POSITION SOCIALE EN DROIT AFRICAIN

Cette communication considère les relations entre les droits de propriété et la position sociale. L'auteur soutient qu'il est faux de postuler une antithèse entre les droits communistes et les droits individualistes à la terre. Dans la pratique, les parcelles de terre et les biens et effets peuvent être soumis à des droits qui changent et que détiennent des personnes différentes. En Afrique, ces droits sur une parcelle de terre peuvent varier en fonction de l'usage qui en est fait et en fonction des périodes.

Le droit foncier des Lozi de Zambie est examinée en détail. Le roi Lozi peut jouir de droits considérables sur la terre mais ces droits se balancent d'obligations, surtout de l'obligation qu'il a de donner de la terre à tous ses sujets. Il accomplit ce devoir par l'entremise d'une hiérarchie de fonctionnaires subalternes. L'auteur soutient que la discussion de ces droits en langues européennes avec l'emploi de mots tels que possession, propriété et usufruit, déforme les droits effectifs que détiennent les différentes personnes. Il propose un groupe spécial de mots. On peut considérer le roi comme le 'propriétaire en tant que dépositaire pour son peuple'. Le roi donne aux subalternes du premier degré, un 'degré primaire d'administration' sur une parcelle de terre et ils donnent à leurs subalternes un 'degré secondaire d'administration' sur leur propre bien; et ceux-ci à leur tour, peuvent allouer un 'degré tertiaire d'administration', avant que nous parvenions à un usage effectif de la terre. On peut appeler ces parcelles de terre qu'on utilise, des 'degrés de production'. L'auteur croit que la supériorité de cette terminologie réside dans le fait qu'elle souligne le rapport intime entre le droit foncier et la hiérarchie de la société. L'auteur montre que plusieurs personnes apparentées peuvent aussi jouir de droits différents sur des biens mobiliers, par exemple le bétail. En vertu de la règle du 'vol privilégié', dans quelques tribus, un parent quelconque du propriétaire supposé d'une chose a le droit de se l'approprier. Le mot utilisé pour 'propriétaire' n'entraîne aucun droit exclusif; il indique seulement qu'un individu a un titre plus fort qu'un autre dans une dispute particulière.

Ces droits divers en matière de propriété désignent aussi les relations entre personnes. De là vient que la propriété obtient une valeur symbolique et que la générosité démontrée par le don de biens à autrui devient l'étalon, des sentiments corrects qu'on possède et de l'accomplissement de ses obligations. On transfère également des éléments de propriété afin d'établir de nouveaux rapports avec quelqu'un, par exemple, à l'occasion d'un mariage. Cette insistance sur la propriété et sur l'obligation apparaît dans le droit des contrats dans lequel un bien quelconque doit passer d'une personne à l'autre pour établir un contrat valable. Une fois le contrat établi, il entraîne la garantie que les biens sont en bon état.

XIII. The Breakdown of Traditional Land Tenure in Northern Nigeria

C. M. McDOWELL

I INTRODUCTION

This paper will examine the future of traditional land tenure in Northern Nigeria in the light of the various alien influences which have affected it since the Fulani conquest in 1804 and attempt an analysis of the role which traditional land tenure can play in a rapidly developing society. In general ownership of land depends on membership of a group and the relationship between the members and the group authority. The group may be a tribe, a lineage, a village, or a family in both the extended or nuclear sense. The authority may be a chief, village head, or council of elders. Whichever form the tenure takes, the amount of land acquired by an individual will depend on his status within the group, his relationship to the group authority, and his immediate needs. The authority may be religious, social, or political and will often be a mixture of all three.

Another factor which can influence the type of tenure found is the settlement pattern and the state of development in any given society. The Hausa and Yoruba, for example, are gregarious peoples whose settlement pattern consists of large towns interconnected with smaller towns and villages, the whole forming part of a complete and well-developed system of government based on a hierarchical aristocracy. Their type of tenure, therefore, will consist of attempts to establish security of tenure over particular areas of land in a society where status depends on a close relationship with a powerful authority. On the other hand, the Tiv live in a more egalitarian society based formerly on a semi-nomadic existence in which their rights to a piece of land in a new area depend entirely on their status within the lineage and their immediate farming requirements. They transfer their interpersonal rights to whatever piece of land they happen to occupy.

The dealings permitted in respect of land will depend on the state of development in its relation to environment. Where land is scarce, for example in an urban area, complex dealings such as sale, pledge, lease, loan, etc., may arise. Where, however, land is plentiful and the economy at a subsistence level the need to evolve such transactions will not be pressing. It is relevant, perhaps, to mention the religious aspect of land in traditional tenure as this may be a factor which militates against complete alienation.

The other principal means of acquiring land under traditional tenure is inheritance and this also relates to the transfer of authority from one generation to the next. Most societies in Northern Nigeria are patrilineal and authority transfers to the eldest son or other eldest male relative with actual benefits accruing either to the other sons or male relatives. Generally, the position of women is inferior as they are provided for by their husbands.

Land tenure in Northern Nigeria has great similarities with tenure patterns elsewhere in Nigeria and in Africa, but the pattern has been affected greatly by two major influences, namely, Islamic law and British rule. Both influences have had and are having direct and indirect consequences on the traditional pattern and are separated here merely for the purposes of systematic survey.

II ISLAMIC LAW

Islam was introduced into the Northern part of Northern Nigeria during the fourteenth century A.D., but it never became more than the religion of the upper classes. In fact, its hold was tenuous and over the centuries it was practised side by side with many pagan customs. It was this impurity which led to the holy war (*jihad*) waged by the Fulani against the Hausa Emirates and eventually the Fulani ruled most of present Northern Nigeria as an Empire based on the twin capitals of Sokoto and Gwandu.

The Fulani adopted a system of government based at any rate partly on traditional Islamic principles. In the sphere of land administration they considered Sokoto and Gwandu to be *mulk*, i.e. privately owned land in respect of which *ushr* (tithe) was payable, while the remainder of the country by virtue of the conquest fell into the category of public lands in the sense that ownership is vested in Allah through the Muslim community. In respect of such lands *kharaj* (tribute) was payable.[1] According to Anderson[2] *kharaj* lands fall into two categories: (*a*) where the land has been conquered by force of arms it becomes the property of the state but the former owners remain in possession and pay *kharaj* by way of rent; and (*b*) where the lands have been acquired by treaty (*sulh*) the original owners retain their rights and pay *kharaj* by way of tribute. In respect of such lands the ruler cannot grant full rights of ownership: 'Such lands are *wakf* or public lands and only the use of them can be granted.'[3] However, in the first flush of conquest the above rule was probably ignored. In Zaria, for example, there is evidence that extensive grants were made to the principal Fulani conquerors.[4]

Another aspect of land administration was the introduction of the fief system. After the conquest the various Emirates were placed in the fief of various imperial officials and this process was also adopted within the Emirates themselves. The system was used to ensure not only a steady stream of revenue from the various taxes imposed but also that administrative control could be tightly exercised.

It is not to be thought that the conquest led to the introduction in every respect of the rules of Islamic law relating to land tenure. It would seem that its application was in direct correlation to the strength of the religion in any given area, which meant that in urban areas it would be strongest and in rural areas weakest. To this day there are pagan Hausas, the Maguzawa, living in Muslim Emirates who remain relatively unaffected by either the religion or the law. Where the law is applied it is that of the Maliki School, although varying doctrines expounded in the authoritative texts find favour in different localities.

It is, however, probably true to say that the indirect influences of Islamic law have done more to affect the traditional

---

[1] Anderson, 1954, p. 185.　　　　[2] Cf. Meek, 1957, p. 116.
[3] Abdulahi, *Ta'limu Radthi*, quoted in Lugard, 1918, p. 360.
[4] Smith, 1955, p. 105.

concepts of land tenure and of society as a whole than the direct influences. For example, Meek discovered that the impact of Fulani rule had altered Jukun society from a matriarchy to a patriarchy.[1] The primary influence of this nature was what may be called the concept of the individual. Islamic law concerns itself with individual rights[2] as opposed to the group orientation of traditional African law. An indication of the two approaches can be seen in their attitude to the problem of partition of inherited property. Under Islamic law any co-heir has a unilateral right to demand partition, whereas, even under a sophisticated and modernized system of customary law such as that pertaining in Western Nigeria, partition is only permitted where all the members of the family have consented.[3]

This concept of the individual has undoubtedly played a major role in the breakdown of group tenure into individual tenure. The writers of memoranda for the Northern Nigeria Lands Committee in 1908 all found evidence that the group concept was being eroded by individual claims,[4] as did Cole and Rowling on Zaria and Kano Provinces respectively in 1948, although the latter were prepared to view the breakdown as a consequence of settled conditions rather than to admit that Islamic law was an influence. The same process was discovered by Luning[5] in Katsina Province in 1961 in an area where both traditional land tenure and Maliki law exist side by side. He found that the original group tenure had definitely broken down into individual tenure and shows how this is evidenced by a great increase in the number of transactions related to land.

One argument which can be raised against the full application of Islamic law is the fact that the pure *Shari'a* may be modified either by the ruler in accordance with political needs or by local customary law. There has been a constant conflict in Islamic law between judges whose interests lie in enforcing strict *Shari'a* and the state which is faced with the necessity of ruling. The same conflict exists in Northern Nigeria where *Alkalai* are loath to admit the existence of customary law and

---

[1] Meek, 1931, pp. 61–62.   [2] Schacht, 1964, pp. 208–9.
[3] Cf. *Balogun v. Balogun*, 9 W.A.C.A. 78.
[4] See generally *Minutes and Evidence before Northern Nigeria Lands Committee*.
[5] 1961, pp. 77–85.

insist that in the areas of their jurisdiction Islamic law is the law of the inhabitants in any case. The two systems are in many areas in an uneasy relationship. Nadel examined this relationship in terms of two systems of law, one belonging to the conquerors, the other to the conquered peoples, and showed that in general the latter defers to the former. He illustrated this by saying that it is in the interests of offenders and ligitants to dissociate themselves from their traditional system and adopt the alien system where their deviate behaviour in the former might be unexceptionable in the latter.[1] The reverse of this would also be true. Palmer gave examples of large-scale migrations taking place on the appointment of a new district head or *Alkali* who was known to enforce strict Islamic law without reference to local customs.[2]

One of the primary causes of the confusion between Islamic law and customary law at the present time is the fact that no attempt was ever made by the British Administration to differentiate between them. Both were considered to be 'native law and custom' and whether one or the other applied would depend on the particular structure of any given society to be deduced when the need arose. No systematic survey has even been carried out to discover just how far or in what areas Islamic law applies or to discover exactly in what respect it has been modified by local customary law. Much of the confusion in land matters in this respect can be traced to two primary aims of the original colonial government. The first was the necessity to preserve the existing system of Fulani rule while eliminating from it various unacceptable practices.[3] This meant that the dignity of the Fulani aristocrats had to be maintained while their traditional sources of income, that is, the fief-system, slavery and harsh taxation were abolished. This has meant a destruction of an integral part of the whole tradition and may explain the continual pressure to have the Islamic ideas of land ownership recognized as this is the only way in which ancestral claims can be maintained.

The second aim is best expressed in the words of Lord Lugard: 'Generally speaking, it should be the aim of the Administration to recognise and promote individual property

[1] Nadel, 1942, po. 165–74.   [2] *Minutes and Evidence*, etc., supra, p. 36.
[3] Lugard, 1906, Memo. 18.

in land.'[1] Lugard also insisted that it was the duty of the Government to protect the individual by preventing any tendency towards proprietary rights.[2] It is clear that this policy motivated the colonial government in its attempt to limit the acceptance of Islamic law in its full sense. Its attitude seemed to be that Islamic law must always bow to custom, especially in the area of land tenure. The confusion and conflict thus created is best summed up in the words of Anderson:

> It is in the matter of land tenure that native law and custom has won its most decisive victory over the general ascendancy of the Shari'a in the Muslim Emirates of Northern Nigeria. Yet even here the victory is not complete, and the situation remains somewhat fluid.[3]

Within recent years and especially since Independence this view has lost its validity.[4] In 1956 a Moslem Court of Appeal[5] was established as an appellate court for those cases 'to the determination of which it is lawful and appropriate that the principles of Moslem law shall be applied to the exclusion of any other system of law or of native law and custom'.[6] This in practice meant that the court would apply the strict *Shari'a* to those cases which might be from areas where the local law was a mixture of both Islamic and customary law although the *Moslem Court of Appeal Law* provided that in case of variation the view to be followed was the local one.[7] In 1960 the above court was replaced by the Shari'a Court of Appeal[8] following recommendations by the Panel of Jurists. It appears from cases decided by this court that the tendency to apply strict *Shari'a* in land matters has continued.[9] Due to this tendency, which undoubtedly springs from latent nationalism, traditional land tenure may in time disappear from the Muslim Emirates of Northern Nigeria.

[1] Lugard, Memo. 8, para. 32.
[2] Ibid., Memo. 10, para. 21.
[3] Anderson, op. cit., p. 184.
[4] Anderson himself has changed his mind; cf. Anderson, 1963, pp. 170–3.
[5] *Moslem Court Appeal Law*, N.R. No. 10 of 1956.
[6] Ibid., S. 3 (3).
[7] I.e. the doctrine of *amal* (practice).
[8] *Shari'a Court of Appeal Law*, N.R. No. 16 of 1960 now *cap.* 122 Laws of Northern Nigeria.
[9] Cf. cases in N.N. Case Note Series 1961–2.

III BRITISH RULE

British rule in Northern Nigeria started with the establishment of a Protectorate in 1900 which was one in name only until Lugard instigated the conquest of the Fulani from 1902 to 1903.[1] British rule existed until Independence in 1960.

It is unnecessary here to catalogue the extensive changes which this brought to the traditional African Society. But it is necessary to examine briefly the impact which British rule created in the field of land law, for the methods adopted were 'the root basis on which the policy of the country has been moulded'.[2] The first attempts were made by Lugard who saw the need for an overall land policy which would remove oppression from the peasantry while allowing the most rapid economic development. Under an agreement made between the Crown and the Royal Niger Company the government of the Protectorate had acquired, as it thought, absolute title to the lands of the Company. In addition Lugard claimed control of all lands formerly held by the Fulani, on the basis that the rights they had acquired by conquest had passed in turn to their conquerors. In his view the lands acquired from the Company were Crown lands and the absolute property of the Crown, while the remainder of the lands of the Protectorate fell into the category of Public lands over which the Government exercised general administrative control, private rights of ownership continuing unabated.

It was clear within a short time both that the original conceptions relating to the rights of the Fulani were incorrect and the land acquired from the Royal Niger Company was in fact not theirs to give. So in 1908 information was collected relating to land tenure and a committee was appointed 'to consider the evidence collected . . . and any other evidence available as to the existing system of land tenure in Northern Nigeria, and to report on the system which it is advisable to adopt'. The policy advocated by the Committee was that all the land in Northern Nigeria should be under the control of the Government and should be administered for the common

[1] Cf. generally *Colonial Annual Reports, Northern Nigeria, 1900–11*.
[2] Lugard, 1919, p. 37.

benefit of the natives.[1] This policy was adopted and enacted as the *Land and Native Rights Proclamation,* 1910, which was replaced with alterations and additions by the *Land and Native Rights Ordinance,* 1916. The Ordinance declared that all the lands of the Protectorate, whether occupied or not, were, with some exceptions, 'native lands' and were subject to the control of the Governor. The greatest interest recognized by the Ordinance was a right of occupancy which took two forms: a statutory right, which could be granted to either a native or a non-native, and a customary right of occupancy which was the title of a native community. The Governor had to pay due regard to native law and custom in administering the law.

This Ordinance was criticized on the grounds that it was an expropriation of native lands but in fact it protected native interests from exploitation while making provision for alien elements now present in increasing numbers. It also helped to preserve customary law for, while alienation to non-natives was prohibited without consent, alienation between natives was permitted and was subject to their native law and custom. Against this it may be said that the cardinal feature of centralized control may also have been a cardinal vice. Granted the Ordinance did not disturb the indigenous system under which an individual may only have had a right of occupancy anyway, but it did shift the emphasis from local control and local benefit to national control and national benefit. If the natives of Northern Nigeria had been allowed to develop freely as were their counterparts in southern Nigeria many of them would have been in a position to capitalize their land rights in a developing economy thereby increasing social and economic development locally. As it was the local interests were subordiated to the national ones, the justification being, rightly, in the early days, that exploitation would take place after the manner in other parts of Africa. In Southern Nigeria, however, exploitation was prevented by the *Native Lands Acquisition Ordinance* which enabled the Governor to control alienation to non-natives. It is not clear why one policy was followed in the North and another in the South, for, as Lugard remarks, writing on tenure in Southern Nigeria:

---

[1] See generally *Report of Northern Nigeria Lands Committee.*

It seems preferable that the natural evolution of land tenure should not be arbitrarily interfered with, either on the one hand by introducing foreign principles and theories not understood by the people, or on the other hand by arresting progress in evolution, by stereotyping by legislation primitive systems which are in a transitional state.[1]

It is also true that during the period of British rule the process of breakdown from group to individual rights continued unabated even though legally the right was no longer a right of full ownership but a right of occupancy. The reasons for this are many. On the one hand there was the impact of western ideas which expressed themselves in the peaceful state and economic expansion of the Region and in the concomitant transition from a subsistence to a money economy. On the other hand there was the development of townships and other settlement areas in which rights were granted to individuals. Added to this was the development of native authorities and an increase in their control over land matters. In addition a factor which may be relevant here is once again the process of individualization. Under British rule the individual became increasingly important in every respect. This whole process of individualization coupled with the similar ideas in Islamic law has been transferred to the process of holding land. No longer need a person feel so bound to his family by the ties of mutual protection and mutual assistance. These ideas have undoubtedly been speeded by the continual development of mass media and means of communication which has taken place in the last twenty years.

It may be said, therefore, that, while the introduction of a nationalized land policy prevented individual enterprise or the evolution of freehold tenures as has happened in Southern Nigeria (and with it the considerable volume of litigation and uncertainty of title), it has not prevented the individualization of tenure but has in fact helped it indirectly.

IV THE PRESENT POSITION

In 1962 the independent Parliament of Northern Nigeria enacted the *Land Tenure Law*. This Law, which has the same effect as, and is in terminology similar to, the *Land and Native*

[1] Lugard, 1918, memo. 10, para. 31.

Rights Ordinance, is an unqualified adoption by the government of Northern Nigeria of the principles relating to land tenure promulgated under British rule. However, the reasons for its adoption are not necessarily similar. The need to prevent exploitation is still considered necessary, but now it is not exploitation by Europeans that is feared but exploitation by other Nigerians. The tight control made possible by the Law may still be justified in terms of the national good, as the Government is virtually the only agency in the Region with sufficient funds to initiate large-scale development, but the demand for private, freely alienable rights is bound to increase as the economic well-being of the citizens increases, for the factors already alluded to are developing that much more rapidly now. This is particularly true of the urban areas where land is held on relatively short-term rights of occupancy. In such areas where individual enterprise is developing rapidly one brake on development is the difficulty of securing loans by mortgage. Because the right of occupancy may only be of short duration it will be difficult to borrow large sums of money on it. In addition, as alienation to non-natives without the consent of the Minister is unlawful, banks are loath to accept a right of occupancy as a security.

A further hardship is the great demand for rights in urban areas due to the enormous expansion of population. A non-native will accept a right for a very short period with onerous building covenants and a vague prospect of renewal. An example of this is the case of *Ejinkeonye* v. *Attorney-General*[1] in which the plaintiff was granted a right of occupancy for five years and covenanted to effect improvements to the value of £2,550. At the end of his term the right was not renewed and the improvements thereby vest in the Minister and may be granted again. This is perhaps an extreme case and it is true to say that in general the provisions of the Law do work for the benefit of the natives of Northern Nigeria.

The most important part of the Law within the scope of this paper is that relating to local government land administration. The position is governed by three sets of Regulations which replace earlier ones. The *Land Tenure (Native Authority-Control of Settlements) Regulations*, 1962, relate to the powers of

[1] Unreported, suit no. Z/19/1964, High Court, Northern Nigeria.

T

the native authority to create settlement areas for various purposes. The regulations are a kind of town-planning device at a low level. If, for example, a native authority wishes to create a new residential area, it lays out the ground in plots which are then allocated to individuals for a fixed term at a rent, so many to natives and so many to non-natives. The same principles apply to existing settlement areas in relation to the allocation of plots under the *Land Tenure (Native Authority-Right of Occupancy) Regulations*, 1962, and the *Land Tenure (Local Authority-Right of Occupancy) Regulations*, 1962.

The exercise of the powers under these Regulations will undoubtedly increase the process of individualization, particularly in areas where there are expanding settlements. In this way the number of people holding land under an individual right of occupancy will steadily increase and the law relating to such a right will not be customary law. As it is also possible for a native authority to create settlement areas in respect of agricultural holdings, fuel and forest areas, communal grazing areas, and reservoirs and catchment areas, it is theoretically possible for the whole of the land under its jurisdiction to become subject to statutory rights of occupancy. Whether this in fact happens will depend on the political and economic development of the Region, but signs of such expansion are already visible.

V CONCLUSION

How much relevance, then, has the system of traditional land tenure not only in the modern society of Northern Nigeria but also in relation to the increasing force of Islamic law and the pressures towards individualization? The experience in Southern Nigeria has shown that the traditional form of tenure can evolve and develop to meet new situations while still retaining its former validity. Most of the land in the South is held under customary law, but it is clear from decided cases that transactions are now permitted which were formerly not allowed. A whole body of rules has been created to deal with such problems as sale and partition of family property and the rights of members to that property. It is also possible for such property to leave the fold of customary law and become subject to English-type law.

On the other hand, in Northern Nigeria the interest capable of being held is certain, namely, a right of occupancy. What this interest actually is has never been judicially decided. It certainly bears many of the characteristics of a lease, particularly a building lease in the case of a statutory right, and has been described as such by several judges. On the other hand it bears many characteristics which are peculiarly its own, and is best described as an interest defined only in terms of the legislation and policy which gave it birth to the exclusion of alien legal concepts.[1]

While the emphasis of the present legislation is on central control and statutory individual rights, the role of traditional tenure, whether as modified by modern needs or not, is still very important particularly in the southern part of the Region. The present law protects such interests and there is no reason why they should not develop into individual rights. What will happen when the demand for individual ownership as opposed to individual rights of occupation occurs is for the future to determine.

BIBLIOGRAPHY

Anderson, J. N. D.
    (1954) *Islamic Law in Africa*. London: H.M.S.O.
    (1963) ed., *Changing Law in Developing Countries*. London: Allen & Unwin Ltd.
Bohannan, P. J.
    (1954) *Tiv Farm and Settlement*. London: H.M.S.O.
Cole, C. W.
    (1949) *Report on Land Tenure in Zaria Province; Report on Land Tenure in Niger Province*. Kaduna: Government Printer.
Hailey, Lord
    (1951) *Native Administration in British African Territories, Part III*. London: H.M.S.O.
Lugard, Lord
    (1906) *Instructions to Political and other Officers*. London: Waterlow and Sons.
    (1918) *Political Memoranda*. London: Waterlow and Sons.
    (1919) *Report on the Amalgamation of Northern and Southern Nigeria, Cmd. 468*. London: H.M.S.O.
Luning, H. A.
    (1961) *An Agro-Economic Survey of Katsina Province*. Kaduna: Government Printer.
McDowell, C. M.
    (1965) *An Introduction to the Problems of Ownership of Land in Northern Nigeria*. 1 Nig. L.J. 202, Lagos, A.U.P.

[1] Cf. Lord Morton, *Premchand Nathu v. Land Officer*, [1963] 2 W.L.R. 99 at 106.

Meek, C. K.
(1931) *A Sudanese Kingdom.* London: Kegan Paul.
(1957) *Land Tenure and Land Administration in Nigeria and the Cameroons.* London: H.M.S.O.

Nadel, S. F.
(1942) *A Black Byzantium.* London: Oxford University Press for the International African Institute.

Rowling, C. W.
(1949) *Report on Land Tenure in Kano Province; Report on Land Tenure in Plateau Province.* Kaduna: Government Printer.

Schacht, J.
(1964) *An Introduction to Islamic Law.* London: Oxford University Press.

Smith, M. G.
(1955) *The Economy of Hausa Communities of Zaria.* London: H.M.S.O.

Trimingham, J. S.
(1962) *A History of Islam in West Africa.* London: Oxford University Press.

United Kingdom
(1910) *Report of Northern Nigeria Lands Committee, Cd. 5102.* London: H.M.S.O.
(1910) *Minutes and Evidence before Northern Nigeria Lands Committee, Cd. 5103.* London: H.M.S.O.
(1900–11) *Colonial Annual Reports, Northern Nigeria.* London: H.M.S.O.

Résumé

LA RUPTURE DU SYSTÈME TRADITIONNEL DE DROIT FONCIER DANS LA NIGÉRIE DU NORD

L'objet de la présente communication est l'étude des espèces de droits fonciers qu'ont les individus dans la Nigérie du Nord, droits affectés par plusieurs influences.

Les droits coutumiers originaux, en ce qui concerne le droit foncier des indigènes, ont été souvent modifiés, en particulier par la conquête des Fulani musulmans, qui non seulement imposèrent un système de tribut, mais aussi introduisirent la loi de l'Islam.

Plus tard, la conquête britannique amena des décisions politiques et judiciaires qui ont modifié le droit foncier. Mais, des changements plus importants ont été provoqués par le développement économique.

On soutiendra qu'à l'origine, il n'y avait pas de concept précis de propriété foncière individuelle, mais qu'aujourd'hui ce concept est en train d'apparaître.

Dans la Nigérie du Nord, on n'a jamais défini juridiquement l'intérêt de l'individu sur la terre, bien que quelques juges l'aient considéré comme un bail. Néanmoins, cet intérêt a plusieurs caractéristiques qui lui sont propres.

XIV. Status, Responsibility, and Liability: A Comparative Study of Two Types of Society in Uganda
P. J. NKAMBO MUGERWA

The question has been asked whether there is individual responsibility in African customary law or whether any such responsibility as there is, is that of some group. The purpose of this brief discussion is to attempt to show that 'group responsibility' so called in truth arises only if the social group to which the individual belongs decides, for a variety of reasons, to adopt the offence or liability created by the individual's action as falling on the group as a whole. The reason why the group may so decide may be because the individual did the act in question while engaged on a mission which was considered to be of importance to the group as a whole. Or it may simply be due to an intense feeling of kinship binding the social group which makes every group member feel morally obliged to come to the aid of the offender or offenders. Whatever the reasons for group intervention, the effect is the same: such intervention prevents or inhibits the enforcement of what are otherwise legitimate demands against the offending member. The frustrated outsider is in turn forced to call upon similar forces in his own group to come to his aid.

When the group to which the offending individual belongs is a very large one, e.g. a nation of some two hundred million people, group interference on behalf of the individual acquires great respectability and is defended under such terms as 'protection of nationals' or 'persons engaged in national security work'. We are then lost in a maze of extradition laws and diplomatic intervention, questions of concurrent jurisdiction (in the home and foreign state) in respect of the same offence are raised, reparations by the state to which the individual belongs are demanded; and all appears well ordered and very civilized.

Most observers to date appear to view with far less enthusiasm the phenomenon where increasingly smaller groups of human beings, of a few thousands, or even hundreds, behave as if they were big nations. This differentation (on the part of the observers) is caused in the main by the absence of well-recognized means of settling such issues among simpler societies. Because the settlement procedure is uncertain, absent or ignored, these societies resort to physical violence with the result that they are in a constant state of war with their neighbours and even between the sub-groups within the same main group. Vendettas or blood-feuds are symptoms of past or constant failure on the part of a group of societies or sub-groups within a main group to observe the rule of individual responsibility.

The concept of individual responsibility seems to be universal among human beings and it flourishes most in those societies where the group's supreme authority does not need to appeal to kinship ties or clothe the act with the aura of group importance. In such circumstances the rule is that the issues be submitted to some settlement procedure and if the member be found guilty and/or liable he should make reparations to the injured party, sometimes with loss of property or freedom or even life. The background to this view of redressive sanctions is that in general—political and religious offences apart—African customary law made no or little distinction between civil and criminal responsibility. The object of the system was to ensure that any reparation or punishment that might be awarded should go to satisfy the victim or his relatives. The idea that the group should take fines or inflict punishment without these conferring any benefit on the injured party appears to be completely alien to African customary law.[1]

Before embarking upon a detailed comparative analysis of examples from Uganda, we must observe that frequently a society accepts completely the rule of individual responsibility as regards injuries between members of that group but applies an entirely different set of standards when it comes to injuries between group members and outsiders. Not infrequently,

[1] Driberg, 1934.

however, the group applies the same yardstick to injuries between group members and outsiders and shows great reluctance to fight outsiders for the sake of protecting one individual whose acts would have been punishable had they occurred internally. It is suggested here that the more centralized the rule which a society enjoys and the stronger and more just the supreme authority happens to be, the more likely that such a society will accept individual responsibility readily, not only as between members but also as between a member and an outsider. A strong, centrally organized society leads to the observance of agreed or imposed rules of conduct among its neighbours by the knowledge the latter undoubtedly have that if unjustified punishment or injury is meted out to a member belonging to the former severe retribution is likely to follow.

By way of illustration we shall cite the Iteso and the Karamojong on the one hand, and the Baganda on the other. The former group of peoples have clearly well-developed ideas relating to the individual responsibility as between themselves, but too often the tribe as a whole or groupings within the tribe intervene to protect the erring individual from the just demands of the outsider to the tribe or the sub-tribe. In the result what almost always starts off as the responsibility of one individual ends up by becoming the responsibility of the entire clan or tribe, with the result that the tribe or clan is constantly involved in punitive or defensive warfare.

In his book, *The Iteso*, Lawrance quotes several High Court judgments on various offences. First, with respect to adultery with married women:

If adultery was admitted by the lover, settlement was reached between the two families. Compensation ranged from three goats to three head of cattle. Refusal by the lover to admit adultery led to a clan feud often resulting in death (p. 218).

As regards fornication with unmarried women.

Should the girl die in childbirth, the man who made her pregnant is liable to pay blood-money of five head of cattle immediately.

This claim for blood-money may be enforced against the relatives of the man who made the girl pregnant if he himself is too poor to pay, or if he dies or absconds before payment (p. 227).

Concerning homicide:

Formerly cases of homicide were settled by taking the life of the killer or of a member of his extended family or clan; or by the gift of a girl by the relatives of the killer to the clan of the deceased; or by payment of cattle equivalent to prevailing bride-price rates to enable the deceased's clan to replace the life lost by taking a girl in marriage from another clan. This last method of settlement still prevails.

Blood-money is payable by the killer to the heir of the person killed in all cases of homicide in which the killer is not executed. If the killer is executed no blood-money is payable (p. 257).

An interesting side light is this note by the author:

Note: This rule was held to refer only to legal executions, but by High Court Revision 44 of 1952 must be taken to include any atonement by death.[1]

The following quotation is from High Court 44/52: D.C.23/52: D.N.C. 114/51: *Y. Okitoi v. P. Aisu:*

Aisu's father, Otaget, ran amok and killed a child aged five years and wounded several other persons. He was set upon by an angry crowd and done to death. Certain persons were prosecuted for his murder but in the preliminary inquiry in the District Court the magistrate did not commit them for trial and they were discharged. In this case Okitoi sued Aisu, as heir of Otaget, for customary blood-money. The District Native Court (a full bench of seventeen including all county chiefs) ruled that although Otaget had been killed it was not by legal execution and that Aisu must pay customary blood-money of five head of cattle to Okitoi, father of the murdered child. He in turn could claim blood-money from the killers of Otaget if they could be traced. With modifications this finding was upheld by the D.C. [District Commissioner] but reversed on petition to the High Court, which ruled that no blood-money was payable since Otaget had atoned for his crime with his life.

It is immaterial whether the killing amounted to murder or manslaughter or whether it was accidental; provided it was caused by the direct agency of the person sued for blood-money, he is liable to pay blood-money.

If the person liable to pay blood-money under section 3 above is unable to pay by reason of poverty or any other reason or if he

[1] All the above quotations on the Iteso are from Lawrance, 1957.

absconds or if he dies without paying, the debt must be paid by his nearest relative within the extended family (*ekek*).

Blood-money debts are not cancelled by the death of the judgement creditor and can be claimed by his heirs without time limitation (pp. 257–8).

Roscoe wrote of the Baganda in 1911 concerning adultery:

Though death was usually the punishment inflicted for adultery, an offender's life would sometimes be spared, and he be fined two women, if he were able to pay them; the culprit was, however, maimed; he lost a limb, or had an eye gouged out, and showed by his maimed condition that he had been guilty of a crime. A slave taken in adultery with one of his master's wives was invariably put to death. Women were compelled by torture to name their seducers; if the accused man denied the charge, the woman was asked to describe some personal peculiarity of his, or some mark on his body which could be identified; then if the man was found to have the peculiarity, he was either fined or put to death (p. 261).

If one peasant wronged another peasant by committing adultery with his wife, the offender was fined ten women, ten cows, ten goats and ten loads of barkcloths; part of this fine he would pay, and the rest he would leave unpaid for (possibly) several years, until he could bring some charge against the man in whose debt he stood; then when the case was tried, he would excuse the defendant from paying the fine, on condition that he forgave him his own debt. If a young man wronged an unmarried girl and she became pregnant, he had to take her to his father's house to live, until she had given birth to the child; afterwards he was required to pay her father the full dowry if he wished to marry her. If he declined to marry her, he was fined; and if he refused to pay the fine, the girl and her child were taken away from him by the members of her clan; if he paid the fine, but declined to marry the girl, she returned to her home after nursing and weaning the child, and the latter was brought up by one of the man's relatives (pp. 262–3).

As for theft:

If a woman was caught stealing food from another woman's garden, she was fined, and her husband, or her master, had to pay the fine. If a man was caught stealing food, he was killed on the spot; the food which he had stolen was tied round his neck, and his body was thrown into the road. House-breakers were killed on the spot, if caught; and the relatives would disown the offender, and would refuse to bury his body (p. 264).

With respect to homicide and murder:

If a man accidentally killed another, the case was tried, and the man was fined. For example, it might happen that a man would be cutting reeds or grass near to a road, and another man who was passing by and who heard the noise, would imagine that it was some wild animal, and would spear the workman, so that he died; or again, it might happen that in a quarrel over beer, one man would strike another so severely that after a few day's illness he would die. Such cases were settled by a fine, and were not punishable by death. It had to be proved that there was no malice attaching to them. The offender was detained until the case was tried, and the fine settled by the clans concerned; the fine for homicide was generally twenty cows, twenty goats, twenty bark-cloths, and twenty women. The clan to which the offender belonged sent him to beg from his friends and from all the members of his clan, till he could raise enough to pay about a quarter of the fine. During the time that the homicide was collecting the money to pay the fine, all the members of the deceased man's clan held aloof from him; but as soon as he paid a portion of it, they assembled together, and invited him to a meal, after which he was free to move about among them as before. The remainder of the fine was not paid for years, and perhaps never paid; it was held over until some member of the other clan committed an offence, and then one debt was made to clear off the other. During the meal at which the clans were reconciled, a pot of beer was brought in, and the head of the murdered man's clan would pour out a cup saying, 'There is no one here who has killed another'; he then gave each person present a cup of beer to drink. Murderers, as well as thieves, were discovered by the medicine-man through the ordeal. Suspected persons, if accused before a chief, would be brought before a council, and would be compelled there to submit to the poison ordeal, if they wished to prove their innocence; if they died under the ordeal, it would be concluded that they had been guilty, and that consequently the drug had taken effect; if, on the other hand, they suffered no ill-effect, it would be concluded that they were innocent, and the person who accused them would have to pay a fine for false accusation. Those who did not die from the effects of the drug, but who, owing to illness caused by the ordeal, were held to be guilty, were fined and in most cases put to death (pp. 266-7).

A small explanation is necessary to justify the choice of these two authors. Roscoe is acknowledged by most scholars as perhaps the best European scholar on the Baganda, writing at the time. Lawrance is about the only author who has attempted to describe Iteso institutions including their laws in any authoritative manner. An added advantage of using Lawrance is that he attempts to deal with the Iteso from the beginning of what is modern Uganda (i.e. about 1900) and takes the story to the present day. The Baganda are sufficiently brought up to date by Haydon in his *Law and Justice in Buganda* (1960):

> Generally responsibility for the wrong or tort was and is laid on the individual who did the act which caused the damage. The only clear exception to this rule is an accidental spearing of a fellow hunter when hunting [no responsibility on the killer]. There is also a quasi-exception in the case of cattle fighting and one killing the other; the owner of the animal killed takes the killer and the owner of the killer the carcase.
>
> As has already been observed, not only was there an individual responsibility in tort but also the family and ultimately the clan were liable for wrongs done by a member of their group. The final sanction against an habitual wrongdoer was, of course, to expel him from the clan. Nowadays only the individual responsibility, at any rate, in the courts of law, is enforceable except in certain specified cases which tend to follow the English law of the vicarious liability (p. 259).

It is clear from the above quotations that in both societies responsibility was principally individual but that groups exhibited a tendency to come to the aid of their kinsmen. The difference, however, is that while among the Iteso it was always possible for one clan to resort to force either to enforce a member's rights or resist an outsider's, this has not been possible in Buganda for several hundred years. The reason for this is, I think, the presence of strong centralized authority in which all persons enjoyed the king's protection more or less equally. In such circumstances, no inter-clan feuds would be tolerated let alone punitive expeditions against tribes outside the kingdom's boundaries. In the result a Buganda clan had to content itself with 'collections' towards a member's fine, etc., or with balancing one claim due from a clan member against another claim by a member against an outsider. Given these conditions we can see how the situation as described by Haydon had been reached in modern times.

In Teso, on the other hand, and until quite recent times, it has always been possible for one clan to use physical violence against another either in the enforcement or defence of clan rights. As the administration over the entire tribal territory became centralized in the latter days of the Protectorate, internal fighting ceased more or less, but this fact did not materially affect the attitude of the Iteso towards their predatory neighbours the Karamojong who continued to plunder their cattle chiefly because if the Iteso were willing to stop the raids the Karamojong were not. It is these twin factors—late centralization of authority in Teso and the presence of predatory neighbours—which explain the continued existence of traces of individual responsibility still being converted into clan responsibility. The case of *Okitoi* v. *Aisu* (quoted from Lawrance above) illustrates this continuity with the past.

The cost of clan attitudes being continued into the twentieth century has been amply demonstrated in Nazi Germany, and to a lesser extent in 1947 India and in present-day Cyprus. Similar tragedies have occurred between the Iteso and the Karamojong in the early 1960s when clans from one tribe in pursuit of their rights (real or imaginary) set out to avenge alleged wrongs committed against them. Intervention of the Central Government troops saved the attacked, but many among the attackers lost their lives. In answer to this tragic situation, the Independent Government of Uganda has gone to the root of the problem by utilizing the widespread acceptance by the clan of the responsibility of their individual members. It is this which explains the two most outstanding post-Independence pieces of legislation with regard to the administration of justice in Karamoja. These are:

(i) The Administration of Justice (Karamoja) Act, 1964, and

(ii) The Administration (Karamoja) Act, 1963, as amended by The Administration (Karamoja) (Amendment) Act, 1964.

Under the first Act, the jury system is introduced in Karamoja, while under the latter Act section 29 (4) empowers the Minister to make regulations for the maintenance of public order including measures for the payment of compensation for loss of life or property caused by cattle raids. By virtue of these provisions the Minister responsible for the administration of the Act has promulgated:

(a) Karamoja (Maintenance of Public Order) Regulations, 1964, (Statutory Instrument No. 265 of 1964), and
(b) The Restitution of Cattle and Payment of Blood-Money (Procedure) Regulations, 1965 (Statutory Instrument No. 101 of 1965).

The aim of the provisions of the first Act is to associate clan elders with the administration of justice. It is thought that these are the people who in the past have been in the habit of harbouring known criminals simply because these happened to be members of their clans. It is hoped that by the use of panels comprising jurors from different clans and by insisting on the rule of unanimity it will be possible to obtain more just convictions since the jurors who know what happened (the deaths almost always occurring in the course of raids either inside or outside Karamoja) will be faced with the task of having to convict an offender even if he happens to be a member of their clan or else risk being exposed, and thus attract the wrath of the members of the clan which was wronged in case of an unjust acquittal.

It is not expected that there will be much chance of jurors from the innocent or injured clan letting off offenders from opposing clans (and all clans in Karamoja seem to live in a state of constant opposition to one another). It is also hoped that the jurors from the wronged clan will stand for the interests of their clan members and, incidentally, those of justice.

With respect to the provisions of the latter Act, the responsibility for preventing cattle raids is placed squarely on the shoulders of the elders of the clan. Regulations 3, 5, and 6 empower a magistrate of the first class, if informed of an impending or likely raid or theft of cattle, to bind over the elders of the clans which are alleged to be involved and require them to execute bonds on behalf of the members of such communities that such communities shall keep the peace and be of good behaviour. Should the elders refuse to execute such bonds without good cause, the magistrate may forthwith order the seizure from the community concerned of cattle to the value of the amount of the bond. It is clear that it is in the interests of the clan elder to ensure that no raid or theft takes place. When a raid ending in bloodshed, etc., does in fact occur, the consequences for an elder who has been bound over are quite grave, for regulation 7 of the Regulations provides that when that happens and a magistrate is satisfied as to the truth of the information available to him, he may order the seizure from that elder's community of cattle to the value of the amount of the bond. The cattle seized are used for the compensation of the clan or clans that have been robbed or whose members have been killed in the course of the raid. If a raid involving bloodshed, etc., has not been preceded by the elders of the clans being bound over, then The Restitution of Cattle and Payment of Blood-Money (Procedure) Regulations, 1965, apply. Regulation 3 of these imposes an obligation upon, *inter alia*, the clan elder to report any raid or cattle theft. Then a committee set up by the Karamoja Administration and on which the clan elders involved would normally sit, proceeds to consider the claims and to give its award. Regulations 6 and 9 provide for this, while regulations 10 provides that the committee shall serve on the chief of the community adjudged responsible for the raid, notice of the claim. Regulations 13 makes provision for the manner of collecting the fine (in cash or cattle) from the members of the offending clan. Heavy penalties attend a clan elder or brother who neglects to comply with the award of the committee.

By setting a thief to catch a thief it is expected that convictions will be of real culprits and that sooner or later clans will tire of having to pay up for the misdeeds of a few of their number. In addition, with the gradual establishment of a strong centralized authority over the entire area occupied by the Karamonjong and the introduction and acceptance of more peaceful pursuits (as opposed to cattle raiding), it is hoped to stabilize Karamoja and thus give the Iteso a quieter existence than they have known to date.

We can now attempt to answer the question which we set ourselves, namely whether there is individual responsibility in African customary law or whether any such responsibility as there is is that of some group. It will be evident from the foregoing that the answer to that question is that in African customary law in general responsibility is individual, but that this general rule is modified whenever a human society is to be loosely organized or has fragmented into small units, or when a supreme political authority is lacking. In any event, and whatever the position may be elsewhere, in Uganda responsibility is primarily individual, although the less centralized and powerful the political authority, the more likely that the clan will step in to fill the gap. The process of fragmentation or decentralization can sometimes stretch to ridiculous limits, e.g. between family and family rather than clan. But within the unit which has been rendered uniform and viable politically (be it family or clan or tribe or kingdom) responsibility remains individual. It is the case that the break-up of large empires leads to constant warfare between smaller groups of human beings, on the other hand the establishment of strong centralized groups of people tends to ensure that the unit in which individual responsibility is the rule is as large as possible. Large, very well-organized political units have an interest in minimizing internal squabbles and therefore tend to promote a system of law in which the application of rules of self-help is at a minimum. It is my firm belief that as we in Uganda achieve a system of law in which the individual's rights are always taken care of by the courts, so will the need for groups of people within Uganda to resort to self-help methods decline.

BIBLIOGRAPHY

Driberg, J. H.
   (1934) 'The African Conception of Law'. *The Journal of Comparative Law Legislation and International Law*, xv, pp. 230–46.
Haydon, E. S.
   (1960) *Law and Justice in Buganda*. London: Butterworth.
Lawrance, J.
   (1957) *The Iteso*. London: Oxford University Press.
Roscoe, J.
   (1911) *The Baganda: Their Customs and Beliefs*. London: Macmillan.

Résumé

STATUT ET RESPONSABILITÉ—UNE ÉTUDE COMPARATIVE DE DEUX TYPES DE SOCIÉTÉ EN UGANDA

L'étude cherche à répondre à la question: la responsabilité individuelle existe-t-elle en droit coutumier africain ou une telle responsabilité est-elle limitée au groupe? Dans son introduction, l'auteur note que la responsabilité de groupe existe, mais seulement quand (à cause d'une diversité de raisons telle que la parenté ou l'acceptation par le groupe de l'importance pour lui d'incidents spécifiques) on l'accepte délibérément en contraste avec le principe habituellement admis de la responsabilité de l'individu. La responsabilité du groupe résulte de l'annulation des sanctions légitimes contre le coupable, et du recours de la partie coupable à des forces identiques. Alors que de telles réactions de la part de groupes très importants les rendent responsables, le cas n'est pas le même pour les groupes moins importants : familles, clans, tribus. Dans l'exemple précédent, un mécanisme international pour le règlement des litiges existe; cependant, il fonctionne imparfaitement. Dans les derniers exemples, aucune procédure certaine de règlement n'existe et, en conséquence, des solutions tendent à être obtenues par la force.

Toutefois, à ces réserves près, le concept de la responsabilité individuelle parait être universel: l'auteur examine la position à l'intérieur du contexte africain. Le droit coutumier africain ne fait, hormis dans quelques cas, aucune distinction entre la responsabilité civile et criminelle. L'objet du droit coutumier est d'assurer que tout châtiment ou réparation bénéficiera à la victime et le concept de l'action punitive ne résultant en aucun profit direct pour la partie lésée est complètement étranger. L'auteur suggère que la responsabilité individuelle entre membres d'un groupe et entre le groupe et les organisations extérieures, est gouvernée par le degré et l'efficacité de la centralisation de l'autorité. Plus l'autorité est effective, plus il est probable que la société acceptera la responsabilité individuelle, que se soit entre membres ou entre des membres et un individu extérieur au groupe.

Pour expliquer cette thèse, l'auteur prend pour exemple deux groupes tribaux de l'Uganda: les Teso-Karamojong, société composée de clans; et les Baganda, groupe très centralisé et capable d'adhérer à une structure hiérarchisée d'autorité bien définie. Référence est faite aux écrits de Roscoe sur les Baganda et ceux de Lawrance sur les Teso, pour montrer l'attitude de ces deux sociétés, envers l'homicide, la fornication et l'adultère en mettant l'accent sur la responsabilité individuelle et le système de réparations. Des cas cités, on déduit que dans les deux sociétés, la responsabilité est principalement individuelle, bien que, dans toutes deux, il y ait une tendance à aider la parenté.

L'auteur examine ensuite les remèdes adoptés par le gouvernement de l'Uganda depuis l'indépendance pour combattre des attitudes traditionnelles du clan parmi les Téso-Karamojong depuis le 12e siècle. L'objet, en bref, a été d'utiliser l'acceptation générale par le clan de la responsabilité pour ses membres individuels et d'associer les plus âgés du clan à l'administration de la justice. Deux lois importantes et récentes affectant l'administration de la justice dans le Karamoja sont examinées et référence est faite à l'introduction du système de jury (par quoi on espère que la responsabilité du jury remédiera aux rapports claniques), au placement de la responsabilité pour incursion de bétail sur les aînés (en leur demandant de s'engager au sujet de la bonne conduite de leurs communautés toutes les fois qu'une incursion est attendue) et en prévoyant la capture de bétail si les engagements ne sont pas exécutés ou si l'incursion n'a pas lieu. On espère que la communauté sera fatiguée de payer les méfaits des individus et que la responsabilité de groupe et les actions qu'elle facilite s'éteindront par leur propre usage.

En Uganda, conclut l'auteur, la responsabilité est, en principe, individuelle, bien que l'autorité politique soit moins centralisée et moins puissante; les sanctions du dernier groupe seront plus employées. 'Je crois fermement que, comme nous possédons en Uganda un système de droit dans lequel les droits de l'individu sont toujours pris en charge par les tribunaux, les groupes sociaux auront moins besoin de recourir à la justice administrée par eux en leur sein.'

XV. Injury and Liability in African Customary Law in Zambia

A. L. EPSTEIN

There has been little systematic discussion of the nature of liability for wrongs in African customary law though this is crucial for an understanding of any legal system and its underlying principles. Anthropologists have skirted this problem with descriptions of specific offences.[1] Colonial administrators, acting as magistrates, have seen the importance of the issues, but have sometimes generalized too hastily on insufficient evidence. Elias, a distinguished African lawyer trained in English law, has in his *The Nature of African Customary Law* (1956) criticized misconceptions that African law takes little account of the mental element and is marked by 'absolute liability', and insisted that on the contrary 'motive, accident, intention, etc., largely enter into every considered judgment'. But when he concludes that because English law looks at these elements in some instances and not in others, and that the position is more or less the same in African law, and links this with an earlier discussion of whether there is a law of contract or tort in African law, or 'just an undifferentiated and confused mass of obligations without any underlying assumptions in both of legal principles', I believe that the initial taking over of English categories evades problems for investigation and confuses analytical issues.

Loss or damage may be variously sustained (e.g. through physical violence, through unintended consequences of another's act; through failure to fulfil prescribed or voluntarily undertaken obligations; etc.). But not all loss or damage is recognized as an 'injury' founding suit in a particular society; and the basis of liability for ostensibly similar injuries may vary

[1] A notable exception is the recent study by Gluckman of *The Ideas in Barotse Jurisprudence* (1965), published after I had completed the draft of this paper.

between societies. On the face of it, the action which a Bemba father has against the man who seduces and 'eats the *cisungu*'[1] of his unmarried daughter has some similarity to the action for seduction in English law. But there are also important differences: the requirement of English law that in order to succeed the father has to show 'loss of services' would mystify the Bemba.

To establish categories of wrongs and to elucidate principles of liability we have to examine all forms of injury, and the extent to which liability (which should not be confused with responsibility) is affected not only by culpability but also by such factors as the circumstances in which an offending act occurred, the status and relationship of the parties, and so forth. This can only be done by sifting extensive and varied case-materials, and I shall outline how this may be done with data I collected in the African Urban Courts of Northern Rhodesia (Zambia) in 1950. There are no doubt important differences between these urban courts and those in tribal areas;[2] but urban court members had no training save experience in the tribal courts. Therefore in administering justice in the towns they operated with, and were guided by, the legal conceptions of their respective tribal laws.

Though I cite cases, I do not do so as if they were precedents in the sense of authoritative statements of customary law binding on the judges. There is not a complete consistency between cases, which vary with the circumstances; and there are good and bad judges, as well as good and bad decisions. But hearings and rulings are not haphazard: they are guided by expectations of both judges and litigants. Consistency is to be sought in the underlying structure of legal ideas and other assumptions of the judges, though they rarely formulate these explicitly.

The most obvious and elementary instance of injury is the direct application of physical violence by one person to the body of another. Let us examine first an example of this type

[1] A Bemba girl on reaching puberty traditionally went through a series of ceremonies known as *cisungu*. The first man to have sexual intercourse with her after she has reached this stage is said to 'eat the *cisungu*'. This should be the man to whom she has been properly married. For anyone else to do so is a serious offence.

[2] See Epstein, 1953, *passim*.

heard by the African urban court at Ndola. The matter involved a husband and wife, both Bemba, and had been referred to the court by the municipal location authorities. The gist of the wife's complaint was that she had been assaulted by her husband, once on a public path when returning from a beer drink, and a second time when he had seized her violently and bitten off a piece of her ear and swallowed it. The husband's reply to these charges took the form of a statement made in the usual way. The trouble was, he said, that his wife had an excessive love of fornication. In Livingstone she had committed adultery twice, and in Ndola twice again. Once when he had gone on a visit to Livingstone he had left her at the Farms (a short distance out of Ndola), but she had decided to move back to the location. On his return he found his wife naked in the path, fighting with a man. They exchanged words and then, being drunk, they all started fighting. On the second occasion they were again drunk, and he had bitten her ear because she refused to listen to what he said: she behaved like a goat, and couldn't resist adultery when he was away for a short time. The statement of the parties concluded, they were questioned at length by the court. Part of the examination ran as follows:

Per curiam (to complainant): On the occasion when you were fighting and he 'broke your ear' were you drunk?
Comp: No, not in the slightest.
Per cur: And the other time, where were you coming from?
Comp: We were coming from the Farms.
Per cur: And you were all drunk?
Comp: Yes, we were all completely drunk.
Per cur: Was there any man to whom you had given beer?
Comp: No, none at all.
Per cur: How long have you been together with your husband?
Comp: It is seven years.
Per cur (to defendant): Where were you married?
Def: Here on the line of rail.
Per cur: And how many times has your wife committed adultery?
Def: On four occasions [i.e. with four different men].
Per cur: Is your wife then a cross-cousin?
Def: No, there is no relationship.
Per cur: How is it then that you did not divorce her and marry another?
Def: I hoped perhaps that one day she would give up her ways.

Per cur: Well, since it appears that you like your wife, what have you to say about this case?
Def: She herself knows the answer to that.
Per cur: Right. Now when you want to 'instruct' your wife, is it your custom to bite her ears?
Def: Well, I bite her ears because I get so angry.
Per cur: And you say that you want your wife?
Def: Yes, that is so and no lie.
Per cur: When you committed the assault were you drunk?
Def: Yes, we were all very drunk indeed.
Per cur: Well, what is the reason for all this?
Def: It's that she went and slept with other men when she ran away from her brother's house at the Farms.
Per cur: How many times have you assaulted her?
Def: Twice.
Per cur: Did you do wrong in 'breaking' her ear?
Def: Yes, as for that I was completely in the wrong indeed.

The defendant had earlier agreed that there were no witnesses who could speak on his behalf. His wife, however, was accompanied by her brother, who was invited to make a statement before the court. He confirmed the husband's testimony, saying that his sister seemed to think only of drinking and running after other men. He had nothing to say about his brother-in-law at all. The fact that his sister had had her ear bitten off was her own affair entirely since she always refused to listen to what he told her. At last the court passed judgment:

As to all this, you, Frazer, we find that you have a case for [are guilty of] 'breaking' your wife's ear and swallowing it. Therefore the court finds that you should pay £5. You will take £3 and give it to your wife, the remainder will be paid to the court. Furthermore, we feel that you ought to divorce her otherwise you will kill her one day with your beatings. As for you, girl, we see that you have no child. This is because you love only fornication. So that the fact that you had your ear bitten off is your own fault (*mulandu*) entirely. You must cease this habit of committing adultery as though you were a dog which knows nothing of respect (*mucinshi*).

The facts in issue in this case were never really in dispute. The husband admitted the main charges against him, and he agreed in the end that what he had done was wrong. Yet the court devoted a good deal of time to the hearing, and it is clear from the whole line of questioning, as well as from the judgment, that it considered the husband had suffered considerable aggravation. In a sense the woman got what she deserved. But if this is so, why should she have been made an award of a fairly substantial sum of money? In many matrimonial disputes the court will often award a small sum—10s. or a chicken—to the aggrieved party. Such awards are best regarded not as compensation, but as an earnest of goodwill opening the way to full reconciliation. In the present case, however, far from seeking to reconcile the parties, the court actually advised a divorce. The award to the woman has to be seen therefore as compensation for damages received. Does it follow, then, that assaulting one's wife is an offence for which the husband is always liable irrespective of the blame that may attach to the wife's prior conduct? Clearly not, for a husband's beating of his wife is recognized as an appropriate way of asserting his authority in the household, and I have recorded cases where an outsider who has attempted to intervene in a marital squabble has himself been found at fault. If, on the other hand, liability derives from the gravity of the damage sustained, why did the court not simply treat the matter as a penal offence and just impose a fine? I want to suggest that the court members here were not being inconsistent in their thinking, but that their finding flowed from certain assumptions about the nature of the human person which derive from tribal culture and philosophy.

A clue to the nature of these assumptions is contained in the court's reprimand to the woman that she should cease behaving like a dog that knows nothing of *mucinshi* (respect). The phrasing, of course, is designed to emphasize the repugnance of her behaviour in the eyes of the court, but the contradistinction of humans and animals recurs so frequently in judgment as to suggest that something more fundamental is involved than mere rhetoric. Thus in another case at Mufulira we find the court admonishing a man who sought a divorce because his wife complained of his frequent adulteries: 'You, fellow, you are a lunatic, you have no sense. It is time you came to learn that a man of sense ought not to roam about as though he were a wild animal of the bush.' That is to say, one is entitled to expect

Injury and Liability in African Customary Law in Zambia 297

of one's fellow-men that their behaviour will conform to certain standards: man enjoys the gift of intelligence (*amano*), and knows therefore that in his behaviour he must display proper manners and respect (*mucinshi*); in so far as one does not measure up to these expectations one's humanity (*ubuntu*) is diminished. But there is also a further attribute of the person which is involved here. This is conveyed in the Bemba word, -*tuntulu*. -*Tuntulu* is an adjective meaning whole, complete, in good health, etc., but it also has overtones of wider import. Thus one may ask 'Is the animal dead (*Bushe nama naifwa*)?', and receive the answer, 'No, it is still alive (*iyo, ituntulu*).' This association of wholeness with life was brought home to me on one occasion when I was discussing with Bemba hereditary councillors the connection in Bemba thought between the east and life on the one hand, and the west and death on the other. One of the councillors (*Bakabilo*) present had especially important ritual duties to perform on the death of the Paramount Chief, and whenever he came to visit the capital he was required to stay in a section to the west of the village. He was being playfully chided by the other *Bakabilo* who always stay to the east, one of whom finally remarked: 'You are a prince of the dead, but we are of the living (*ifwe tuli batuntulu*).' The life-principle is a sacred value which finds its highest embodiment in the whole human person, which ought not therefore to be diminished, save in special circumstances. It is this basic postulate, I believe, which accounts for the overriding concern that the courts display in regard to physical violence to the person, and leads to the principle that one is liable in damages for any act which has as a direct consequence the diminishing of another's person, even though the act itself may have been prompted by that other's prior wrong.

In order to substantiate what might seem to be a somewhat fanciful line of analysis, and before seeking to develop the argument further, let me cite another and perhaps stronger case. This concerned a man who assaulted another for attempting to rape his daughter. He was ordered to pay £5 compensation for knocking out two of the other's teeth. He appealed to the African Court of Appeal on the grounds that the compensation awarded was excessive. I record below a few extracts from this hearing.

Per curiam (to appellant): Did you not beat John?
Appellant: I did.
Per cur: And is beating another person a good thing?
App: No, it is very bad indeed.
Per cur: Listen. If this seemed to you a case of rape why did you not report the matter at the [Police] Charge Office? We do not want to have people beaten here in Ndola. We want people to stay in peace here, and not be engaged in fighting. This person John was made by God but you want to destroy him. . . . What do you want the court to do for you?
App: I have appealed because the money was too much. In my opinion for the two teeth that he lost I should have been made to pay only £2. If three had come out I should have paid £3.
Per cur: Can you beat a person because you know just how much you will have to pay him?
App: No, that is not it.
Per cur: One thing you should remember is that John did not commit rape on your daughter. Did you find that he had done so?
App: No, but when I asked my daughter she told me that John had attempted to rape her.
Per cur: You should know that rape is a 'civil' case; murder is a 'criminal' case, and so is assault.[1] Suppose that you had killed John, which would be the more serious case—that or 'rape'?
App: Murder would be the bigger one.
Per cur: Suppose you remove the frame from a bicycle do you think you can ride it?
App: No.
Per cur: Well, it is the same here with John's teeth. Since you knocked out two of his teeth he is unable to chew meat and other hard foods. You have spoilt the 'wealth' which was given to him by God. If a pot breaks, can it be mended?

The court then proceeded to point out how seriously such offences were regarded in former times. Some court members even thought the compensation awarded was inadequate, but they finally agreed that they ought not to interfere with the finding of the court of first instance, and the appeal was dismissed.

It will be observed that in this case, as in the previous one, the defendant did not seek to dispute liability for the injuries he had

---

[1] Here the court was referring to the classification of English law which appears in the court warrant and sets out its constitution and legal powers. That the distinction is not always understood or followed in practice is seen in the reference to rape as a civil case. See also below, p. 300.

caused; his objection was merely to the amount he was required to pay as compensation. Again there is the concern with actual physical damage, a concern seen here in two ways. First, there is the stress placed by the court on the fact that the girl had not been raped, although the evidence seemed fairly clear that this would have occurred if the father had not intervened. Second, the gravity of the offence is reiterated as though it were tantamount to homicide. But what also seems important is that in both cases the offending acts, like the act of homicide itself, lead to consequences which are irreversible.[1] Under tribal conditions, at least, a person who has lost his ear or his teeth can never be made whole again. In the second case, indeed, wholeness as an attribute of the person was given quite explicit expression: like life itself it is a gift of God. The clear lesson of both cases, then, is that he who resorts to violence, even in defence of his legitimate interests, does so at his peril, since the consequence of his act may well be the maiming, or most heinous of all, the complete physical destruction of another person.

The tribes with which we are concerned are of the type characterized as 'states':[2] there was usually some degree of central administration, and the exercise of power and authority was controlled institutionally, often through an elaborate system of political offices. In such systems the application of physical violence becomes a monopoly of the state: not only does the state deny to the individual the right to take the law into his own hands, but it also arrogates to itself the right to inflict physical punishment for certain classes of offence. It is clear, therefore, why men who resort to violence should do so at their peril. But this still leaves unanswered certain questions posed by the case-material I have cited. Why, for example, was compensation awarded in both cases where the imposition of a fine or some other penalty would seem sufficient for the court to make its point? Africans in Zambia, however, do not see the matter in quite this way. For them the award of compensation for damages suffered to the person is one of the most basic and distinctive principles of their customary law. Indeed,

[1] I am grateful to Dr. R. Frankenberg for drawing this point to my attention and for other comments on the original draft.
[2] Fortes and Evans-Pritchard (eds.), 1940, Introduction.

among the most educated and Westernized Africans to whom I talked, the fact that compensation was so rarely awarded in a Magistrate's court was one of the major differences between the African and the European legal systems; it was this aspect of the latter which most puzzled them and aroused their criticism. In other words, the aims of an African court are seen as being as much redressive as penal. The judges should be as much concerned with the nature of the damage sustained as with wrongful acts as such, and this I suggest has its roots in assumptions about the human person as a whole being. I suggest further that this view of the problem also helps to account for a number of other features of legal doctrine and practice among the Bemba and certain other tribes of the region. Thus where a man has sustained physical injuries there is a reluctance to hear his case until the wounds have fully healed: once a case has been settled it cannot be reopened if the injury turns out to be more serious than was at first suspected; and here again the question of reversibility is relevant. Secondly, it may help to explain the widely differing responses of Africans and Europeans towards certain kinds of offence. A good instance of this is rape which, as mentioned earlier, was referred to by an African court as a 'civil' case. Such cases were indeed a source of much misunderstanding between urban court members and White magistrates. For the latter the essence of the offence is the forceful seizure of a woman and having intercourse with her without consent, and it commands a severe penalty. By contrast, African judges tend to treat such matters relatively lightly; the offence is classified as *bucende*, adultery or illicit fornication, and it is the infringement of the husband's marital rights rather than the affront to the woman herself which is the basis of the action.[1] The assumption here is that women in general are complaisant in sexual matters: if the offence occurs within earshot of a place of habitation and she does not cry out or make report immediately afterwards it is presumed that she consented to the act which carries no threat to her integrity as a person. On the other hand, if the offence took place in the bush it was viewed quite differently. The

---

[1] The rape of a nubile girl (*uwa cisungu*) would be regarded in quite a differen light. 'Eating the *cisungu*' is, of course, yet another type of act whose consequences are irreversible.

woman was no longer a person in a position to give or withhold her consent freely, since she had no protection against the threats of a man who, it was said, might kill her if she refused him. Such an offence was indeed a thing of mystical ill omen (*mupamba*) which defiled the country (*kushikule calo*); if it were not reported but was subsequently discovered, both parties were severely punished.

This reference to mystical notions also serves as a reminder that in traditional African thought the gravest threat to life and limb was not always provided by physical violence alone. There was—and is—a whole range of acts which Africans would immediately recognize as serious offences, actionable in customary law, but which the modern European would ordinarily react to with scepticism or dismiss as trifling or eccentric. In many of these cases the cause of action rests in a particular tribal belief which postulates a direct (though as we see it unverifiable) causal nexus between an act and its consequences, as for example in the notion that a woman who serves her husband with food while she is in an impure state may cause him to develop a serious bronchial ailment. In yet others the injury arises not from the physical damage as such that flows from the trespass but because the act itself appears as so unnatural that it at once indicates witchcraft. I want to suggest that the inference of witchcraft in these cases, which is the basis of legal liability, becomes less puzzling if seen in relation to those assumptions about the human person to which I have referred. Take the following example: among ourselves a man who preferred to have sexual intercourse with his wife while she was asleep might simply be regarded as having curious tastes in such matters. I was told that European District Officers to whom such complaints by African women were occasionally referred would dismiss them as a matter for the individual parties concerned. But to the African court members who have to judge such cases the practice has quite a different connotation. It is an abhorrent and unwholesome act which no 'reasonable man' would contemplate because it is tantamount to using a woman as a corpse. By his act the husband violates the integrity of his wife as a person: he has deprived her of part of her life-substance which he can then put to use magically in order to grow wealthy and powerful. The whole thing smacks of witchcraft and is believed to carry a serious threat to the woman's life.

In his work on *The Judicial Process among the Barotse* (1955), Gluckman has shown how the concept of the 'reasonable and customary man' lies at the heart of their jurisprudence, and I myself have analysed the juridical thinking of urban court members in broadly similar terms.[1] If my present argument is valid that the concept of injury is bound up with assumptions about the nature of the human person, then I think we can see why 'the reasonable man' should assume such importance in African legal thought since, as I pointed out earlier, reason is seen as one of the defining characteristics of the human being. On the other hand, as an analytical concept 'the reasonable man' presents some difficulties, and Lord Devlin is not alone in seeking a word that would free us from some of its ambiguities.[2] In one of its aspects the stress is on rationality, the ability to see, for example, that certain consequences are likely to flow from a certain course of action. Yet the character of 'the reasonable man' in African law does not derive from the faculty of ratiocination alone, any more than does that of his English counterpart. He is a creature of custom and morality as much as of reason; in African thought he is above all a 'whole' man. Hence a man who has intercourse with his wife while she is asleep, or commits an act of sodomy with a boy, forfeits his claim to be a full human being. His behaviour is by definition 'unreasonable' because it confounds and confuses the basic dichotomies of African thought, here for example, of life and death, of male and female. His offence is much more serious than that of a physical assault: it is in the Biblical sense an abomination[3] and carries the most heinous threat of all to the integrity of the person—death by witchcraft.

This essay indicates that the notion of injury in some Zambian tribes is rooted in a concern to protect the integrity of the person. The cross-examinations cited inquire into motive, but in no case did drunkenness, provocation, or legitimate grievance affect liability. The irrelevance of motive emerges

[1] Epstein, 1954. [2] Devlin, 1965, p. viii.
[3] Dr. Frankenberg reminds me that the data presented throughout this paper suggest many parallels with ancient Jewish law. The topic is one that might repay further examination,

even more clearly in those cases which turn on the presence of witchcraft. In short, the data suggest that the courts concentrated on the acts and their consequences rather than on the motives from which they sprang. Nevertheless, it would be unwise on this basis to proceed to erect a general theory of 'absolute' liability in tribal law. The judicial process, I have said, is dominated by the presence of 'the reasonable man', and in the cases quoted the consequences which flowed from the defendants' acts were all of a kind that could reasonably have been foreseen and anticipated, even if they were unintended. In working towards a general theory of liability it would be necessary to carry the analysis further than I have been able to do here by examining cases where damage sustained was an unforeseen consequence or the result of negligence, the failure to take due care.

BIBLIOGRAPHY

Devlin, P.
  (1965) *The Enforcement of Morals*. London: Oxford University Press.
Elias, T. O.
  (1956) *The Nature of African Customary Law*. Manchester: Manchester University Press.
Epstein, A. L.
  (1953) *The Administration of Justice and the Urban African*, Colonial Research Series No. 7. London: H.M.S.O.
  (1954) *Juridical Techniques and the Judicial Process*, Rhodes–Livingstone Paper No. 23. Manchester: Manchester University Press.
Fortes, M. and Evans-Pritchard, E. E. (eds.)
  (1940) *African Political Systems*. London and New York: Oxford University Press for the International African Institute.
Gluckman, M.
  (1955) *The Judicial Process among the Barotse of Northern Rhodesia*. Manchester: Manchester University Press for the Rhodes–Livingstone Institute.
  (1965) *The Ideas in Barotse Jurisprudence*. New Haven and London: Yale University Press.

Résumé

DU PRÉJUDICE ET DE LA RESPONSABILITÉ DANS LE DROIT COUTUMIER AFRICAIN EN ZAMBIE

Les conceptions en matière de préjudice et de responsabilité dans les droits africains n'ont pas reçu l'examen et la discussion systématique qu'ils méritent. Le problème est complexe et pose nombre de questions dont il est important qu'elles soient analytiquement distinctes. La première question concerne les formes de perte ou de dommage qui confèrent une cause d'action et constituent donc des 'préjudices'. Le travail est ici d'établir les principes mêmes de la responsabilité. Un deuxième groupe de questions étudie jusqu'où la responsabilité peut être affectée par d'autres facteurs et pose la question entière de la responsabilité.

La présente étude cherche à explorer quelques uns des points relatifs aux préjudices subis par les personnes dans le droit coutumier de quelques tribus de Zambie. Deux cas sont examinés en détail. Ceux-ci suggèrent que, quoique les tribunaux examinent le mobile, le principe de base est que celui qui cause des dommages physiques irréparables à un autre, même quand ils sont provoqués ou quand ils résultent de la défense de ses intérêts légitimes, agit ainsi à ses risques et périls. On suggère que ce principe est fondé sur certaines conceptions au sujet de l''intégrité' et de la 'modération' comme attributs fondamentaux de la personne humaine. Des considérations semblables aident à expliquer les réactions différentes des Africains et des Européens devant certaines catégories d'infractions (par exemple l'enlèvement) et pourquoi certaines atteintes aux personnes sont regardées très sérieusement par les Africains et considérées comme des manifestations de sorcellerie. Cependant, les données présentées se rapportent seulement aux actes, dont les conséquences, même si elles sont involontaires, ont pu être raisonnablement anticipées. Ce qui a besoin d'être étudié davantage, ce sont les cas où le dommage subi était une conséquence imprévue, ou le résultat d'une négligence. Un problème intéressant posé dans l'étude et méritant un examen ultérieur est le rapport entre la définition du devoir, l'opération des croyances en la sorcellerie et l'apparition d'un concept juridique d'accident qui exclue la responsabilité.

XVI. The Customary Law of Wrongs and Injuries in Malawi

J. O. IBIK

In no branch of customary law is there so much uniformity of the general principles involved as in the laws of civil wrongs and injuries. However, there are a few variations of principle and detail between the uxorilocal and virilocal peoples, compared as two separate entities. Thus whereas among the uxorilocal and matrilineal Chewa people of the Kasungu district the husband will not be vicariously responsible for the delicts of his wife, among the virilocal and patrilineal Tumbuka of the neighbouring district of Mzimba the converse situation applies with possible exceptions, e.g. murder. Even among similar groups of uxorilocal or virilocal peoples, variations of principles and details can be detected. Thus, although a Chewa father in the Sabinia area may not be held responsible in damages for delicts committed by his child, a different attitude seems to have evolved among the Chewa residing in the Lilongwe urban area. They consider that a father should be liable for all minor delicts of his child. It is not the object of this paper to establish that similarities exist in the customary laws applying to the various African communities of Malawi. The main purpose of emphasizing the apparent similarity is rather to provide a justification for dealing generally with the contemporary customary laws of civil wrongs applied in Malawi today. Notable differences, where they occur, will be mentioned to make clear that complete uniformity does not exist.

I CLASSIFICATION OF WRONGS

Before embarking upon a discussion of the general principles of liability for wrongs, let us firstly consider briefly the question whether a distinction is, in fact, drawn between crimes, delicts or torts *strictu senso*, and breaches of agreement. Well-known jurists have corrected the false notion, which held sway throughout southern Africa for a considerable time, that African law draws no distinction between crimes and civil wrongs. While endeavouring to keep out of a general Africa-wide discussion on this point, I am emboldened by my findings in the field[1] to state, categorically, that a valid distinction can, and appears to, be drawn between the customary notions of crimes and other wrongs. To illustrate with one example, by the customary law of the Tumbuka people of Rumpi district, a person can pull down and destroy his house with or without good reason. Such an act is not actionable *per se* as a civil or other wrong. He can also, if he is so minded, burn the debris. Again this act of burning is not actionable *per se*; but should he damage another's property as a result of the fire spreading, he will be as much liable in compensation as if he had caused the damage with his own hands. If, however, he sets the house on fire without first dismantling it, he becomes *ipso facto* liable to the chief or village headman of the area where that house was erected, regardless of whether any actual damage has been caused or not. Among the Nyanja-speaking people, the offence thus committed is called *kuyuyura mwene muzi*—literally, 'breach of the village-owner's code'.

This head of liability bears a striking similarity to the 'Western' notion of crime in that:

> (i) the only person who can enforce the law against the culprit is the chief or village headman, i.e. a person empowered by his official status as a guardian of the law;
>
> (ii) the culprit's liability to the imposition of a fine or the penalty of expulsion from the village attaches independently of any actual or even threatened damage caused by his wrongful act.[2] Thus it makes no difference that the house burnt was located in a remote solitary part of the village; and
>
> (iii) the person entitled to exact penalty can, in his discretion, pardon the culprit, especially if there are extenuating circumstances.

[1] Research conducted between 1963 and 1964 in Malawi.
[2] As stated, any actual damage suffered by another person as a result of the culprit's wrongful act is a separate cause of action.

What is the chief or village headman entitled or bound to do with the fine extracted from the culprit? Does the vernacular expression for this fine differ from the vernacular word for ordinary compensation? To take the second question first, the answer is, regrettably, in the negative. The creeping doubt raised by this admission will, understandably, be strengthened by a further admission, in answer to the first question, that the fine collected may legally be pocketed by the collector. The objection may well be taken that the act cannot possibly be classified as a 'crime' at all. This, with respect, is not a valid objection. The true classification of the wrong in question can hardly be denied simply on linguistic considerations.[1] A spade, by whatsoever name called, will remain a spade. Equally groundless for rejecting this classification is the *ex post facto* consideration that the alleged fine is not treated as public property. The explanation for this is presumably the absence of central control in the traditional system of government. One other point, which the antagonists are especially fond of raising, involves the question, for example, whether murder is punishable by hanging or similar severe punishment. Will ordinary compensation atone for the evil act of murder? (In dealing with this question it must be noted that murder, if classifiable as a crime in customary law, is in the same category as most other customary crimes in so far as redress solely by compensation is concerned.) The answer to this question is, again, in the affirmative. Enough has been said to show that a distinction exists between a crime and other wrongs. We may note in conclusion that customary criminal offences have been virtually abolished, and no court established for Malawi can impose any criminal sanction for the breach of any such offence unless incorporated by an enacted law.[2]

Is there a distinction between a tort and a breach of agreement? Generally a tort or delict in the strict sense is actionable, whereas the breach of an agreement *simpliciter* is not actionable. A typical example of a breach of agreement not giving rise to compensation or action is failure or refusal by a vendor to deliver goods to the purchaser. This is so even though the agreed

---

[1] As will be seen later, one vernacular word often has more than one meaning.
[2] An example of this restriction is contained in the *proviso* to section 12 of the Local Courts Ordinance of 1962, as amended.

purchase money has been paid in advance. It will make no difference to the disappointed purchaser's position that the seller has resold the contract goods at an enhanced value and pocketed the profit. All that is due to the purchaser is the return, in full, of the money that he has prepaid. Again, a farm labourer who sits by and allows the whole farming season to expire without cultivating the crops and without notifying his employer of his unwillingness to honour the agreement is not suable by the aggrieved employer. The sole liability in these circumstances is dismissal without notice, and repayment of any wages and perquisites he may have wrongfully received from his employer. There are, however, instances where a breach of agreement is actionable—though not for the recovery of general damages. Thus among the Tumbuka people of Rumpi district, if a farm labourer has been unjustly dismissed after working on the farm, he will be entitled to recover proportionately more wages from the employer than might have been paid *pro rata*. In relation to the loan of farmland, although an ordinary breach of an agreement to lend is irredressible like the refusal of a purchaser to pay the purchase money and accept the goods, there is a special circumstance which ought to be considered. Thus among the Chewa people of Lilongwe district, where the borrower of land has actually commenced planting his crops, a purported breach of the agreement by the lender asking the borrower to vacate the land forthwith is ineffectual. Looking at this situation from the borrower's point of view, it is apparent that should he complain to the elders about the lender's monstrous act, they will order the latter to desist from re-entering until the former had reaped his crops. This is the closest example of an order for specific performance clearly distinguishing a delict from a breach of agreement. This line of distinction seems rather tenuous and will not therefore be further pursued. The criterion for the distinction between delicts and breaches of agreement is, as we have already observed, the non-actionability of the latter. This distinction is sometimes blurred. Thus a pledgee who fails to return the pledge is strictly liable to make good the loss of the pledge regardless of the cause for his failure. The distinction is, none the less, a valid one because an owner of a kraal through whose negligence the cattle consigned under a herding agreement have

The Customary Law of Wrongs and Injuries in Malawi 309

died or depreciated in value is not suable by the aggrieved consignor. Whereas anyone causing damage to another's cattle or goods, whether through negligence or intentionally, will be liable in compensation to the aggrieved person.

So far our discussion discloses a threefold classification of wrongs into crimes, delicts, and breach of contract. At least one common basis for these three categories of wrongs is the likelihood of an award of pecuniary compensation. This sole factor distinguishes these wrongs from other wrongs which are either not redressible pecuniary-wise or only redressed by expiatory sanctions. Wrongs not redressible at all are exemplified by a wicked omission where no positive duty to act exists.[1] Thus a person who fails to warn an unsuspecting victim of a concealed danger, e.g. a pit caused by flood, will not be held liable to compensate the unfortunate person for injuries suffered by him when he fell into the pit and broke his arm. Wrongs attracting expiatory remedies are mostly concerned with the breach of the sexual moral code by a spouse. Thus among the Chewa of Dedza district sexual intercourse with a wife during advanced pregnancy, or soon after childbirth, or even during menstruation, is a matrimonial offence requiring the use of special medicine (*mankhwala*) for ritual purification. These two types of wrongs can be added to the three categories, enumerated above, as the fourth and fifth categories. For completeness, one could add as a sixth category, wrongs consisting of breach of the rules of secret societies such as the Chewa *Nyau* or ordinary association such as the age group (typified by the *Ingulilo* among the Ngonde, Nyakyusa, etc., of the Karonga district). As these three additional categories of wrongs are rather special in that they are mostly concerned either with morality *simpliciter* or exclusive clubs and associations, they will only be noted here and not considered in the pages that follow.

II THE GENERAL PRINCIPLES OF LIABILITY

Having shown that breaches of agreement are, in general, non-actionable, and that crimes and delicts have a great deal in common, we now propose to devote the remaining pages

---

[1] Thus a house-owner who fails to maintain or pull down his dilapidated building will be liable to his neighbour whose property is damaged by the house collapsing naturally because he is under a duty to repair or pull down the house.

of this paper mainly to a review of the principles of liability in crimes and delicts. Reference to a delict or civil wrong in these pages shall include a crime unless the contrary is indicated. This is because the general principles applying to both categories of wrongs are practically the same.

A person can be liable in delict either because of his:

(i) actual perpetration of the wrong complained of; or
(ii) close relationship with the perpetrator of the civil wrong.

Actual Perpetration

Any human being, regardless of age, sex, marital state, mental and physical condition, social or political status, is capable of committing a civil wrong. The relationship (consanguineal or affinal) between the wronged person and the wrongdoer is immaterial. Thus a father can commit a wrong against his child and vice versa. Husbands and wives can be guilty of committing wrongs against each other. A village headman who commits adultery with the wife of a villager is as much a wrongdoer as if he had been a 'nobody'. One is liable as the perpetrator not only for wrongful acts done by oneself but also for injuries caused by one's property, especially livestock. The classification of liability in respect of cattle trespass under this head can be rationalized as the act of the cattle-owner consisting in his *omission* or failure to keep the cattle under effective control. Liability for injuries caused by property other than cattle, dogs, goats, etc., is typified by the house-owner's liability for the damage caused by the collapse of the building. A notable exception to this rule is occupier's liability for safe premises. Thus the occupier of a house cannot be held answerable for any injury or damage suffered by 'a visitor' as a result of dangers (whether apparent or latent) arising from the poor state of repair of the house. It is irrelevant whether the occupier has warned the visitor of the dangers to enable him to take good care of himself.

Aiding and Abetting

A person who aids and abets the actual perpetrator of a civil wrong will not be himself liable as a co-perpetrator:

(a) A person who supplies matches to another person to enable him to set fire to the building of a third party is not liable in compensation as a party to the civil wrong of burning down another's house.

(b) Two adults, A and B, decide to kill C's chicken. A supplies B with a knife. B catches the chicken and eventually kills it. They both abandon the chicken and run away. B, alone, is liable in compensation to C. A's conduct may be reprehensible and quarrelsome.

(c) A, an adult, hands two eggs, which belong to B, to C, an eight-months-old child of D. C drops and breaks the eggs. D is, none the less, answerable in compensation. A's conduct is reprehensible as anti-social and quarrelsome.

Close Relationship with the Perpetrator

Liability under this head has been variously described as *respondent superior*, vicarious, or 'group responsibility'. To those well acquainted with the English legal terminology, where consensus that vicarious liability is but one aspect, albeit a major one, of *respondent superior*, one may cautiously use these two expressions interchangeably to describe this head of liability in customary law. A special word of caution must now be given. From available evidence, it is not strictly correct to refer to this head of liability in customary law as vicarious, bearing in mind the English legal connotations of vicarious liability. Thus a father[1] will not escape liability for his son's delicts by showing that he had not been negligent or had exercised reasonable care to prevent the wrongdoer from committing the alleged wrong. Among the Ngonde of Karonga district a father will be answerable for the wrong committed by his son in the course of employment of another. Except in extreme cases of complicity, it is doubtful if an employer, *qua* employer, will be liable for injury suffered by a third party as a result of negligence by an employee in the performance of his duties as such. The notion of group responsibility is much harder to justify although one can see semblance of that notion in this head of customary liability. Thus it is recognized as a definite moral obligation on the well-to-do relatives of the wrongdoer to contribute towards the

[1] Among the uxorilocal people, a father is not necessarily held responsible for the wrongs of his child.

payment of compensation. This is clearly not a legal responsibility; for one thing, the wrongdoer himself is not entitled to exact contribution from the relatives. Secondly, although the head of an extended family can impound the property of the wrongdoer to raise the necessary fund for paying the compensation, he cannot exercise a similar right with regard to the property of other members of the family unless specifically empowered by an *ad hoc* agreement of the family elders.

What degree of relationship can give rise to vicarious liability in the sense described? Among the virilocal patrilineal peoples, the following persons are recognized as those essentially liable vicariously: the father, and the head of the extended family. In the case of an illegitimate child, the person vicariously liable is its maternal grandfather unless it has been affiliated to its natural father by redemption.[1] The 'vicarious relationship' between father and child will normally devolve upon the successor to the deceased father's name and position as the head of the simple family. Similarly, the successor to the name and position of the deceased head of an extended family will automatically assume a similar sort of relationship, vis-à-vis the members of the extended family. Similar rules apply among the uxorilocal matrilineal peoples except that:

(i) the position of responsibility is assumed by the senior maternal uncle of the culprit; and

(ii) the special care of an illegitimate child does not arise since all children of a union (born in or out of wedlock) are regarded as 'belonging' to their mother's matrilineal group under avuncular *potestas*.[2]

[*Editorial note.*—A section dealing with disputes in the same family has been deleted.]

III GENERAL DEFENCES

Before illustrating these general principles of liability with specific examples, a word must be said about general defences. These are not exhaustive, but are defences that can apply to

[1] Act of legitimation includes subsequent marriage of its natural parents. Among the patrilineal Ngonde of Karonga district, a child can be redeemed by the payment of *Ikiposolo* (compensation usually consisting of two head of cattle).

[2] This group is called *Mbumba* in Chinyanja (a local vernacular).

practically all specific delicts. For completeness, we ought also to mention factors which are not considered good defences. Valid or good defences may be classified into two groups, namely:

(i) absolute unconditional forgiveness;
(ii) complainant's consent (*volenti non fit injuria*).

Unconditional Forgiveness

This consists of the injured party's accepting the apology of the wrongdoer, and voluntarily communicating to him an intention never to take steps to recover compensation in regard to the particular civil wrong suffered by him. No formal procedure is required. Usually the wrongdoer is accompanied by one or more of his elderly blood relatives[1] when he offers an apology to the injured person. It is not of the essence of unconditional forgiveness as a valid defence that it must be *ex gratia*. Thus it may be given in consideration of the wrongdoer's offering a token apology, or assuming a special obligation towards the wronged person. It is, however, the essence of this defence that the forgiveness must be 'present' and 'unconditional'. Where a conditional forgiveness has been procured, the wrongdoer cannot rely on it as a good defence unless the condition on which the forgiveness was granted is performed or satisfied. Lastly, the communication of an intention never to seek compensation need not be express. It can be inferred from the surrounding circumstances.

Complainant's Consent ('Volenti')

A person who, in good faith, voluntarily consents to the infliction of a particular harm by the defendant cannot subsequently recover compensation in respect of that injury. *Bona fide* consent must be carefully distinguished from 'connivance' or acquiescence, intended as a trap to facilitate: (i) the commission of a civil wrong, and (ii) proof that such wrong has been committed by the defendant. Thus where a husband assists his wife to lure the defendant into having immoral sexual intercourse with her, he will not be precluded from recover-

---

[1] E.g. father or maternal uncle. A friend can also be accepted as a witness instead of a blood relative.

ing compensation against the defendant by reason of the fact that he connived with his wife. It is of the essence of this defence that the complainant's consent is: (i) made in good faith; (ii) communicated to the defendant; and (iii) the cause of the act complained of.

The communication of the consent need not be express; it suffices if it can be inferred from the surrounding circumstances.

Both of these defences can arise from the act of the complainant's father in the case of: (i) a very young person (e.g. a dependent child under twelve years of age); and (ii) a mental defective incapable of managing his own affairs.

Undue Delay

Undue delay in seeking a remedy is not considered a good defence, although it can impair credibility unless there are extenuating circumstances or a satisfactory explanation.[1] The general principle of proceedings requires that the injured person should seek the appropriate remedy as soon as he becomes aware of: (i) the commission of the wrong alleged; and (ii) the true identity of the wrongdoer.

Delay in bringing an action will jeopardize a complainant's right of recovery should the wrongdoer die in the meantime. Thus among the Yao of Fort Johnston district no action for cattle trespass can be instituted after the wrongdoer's death, although when such action has been commenced prior to that time, the complainant can successfully pursue it afterwards.

Regarding the effect of death on the right of action, it must be noted that a valid distinction is drawn between actions for liquidated and unliquidated damages. Thus where the complainant has been awarded a sum of money as compensation, his delay in collecting the judgment debt prior to the death of the wrongdoer will not deprive him of his right to enforce the 'judgment' against the culprit's successor. Similarly, where a creditor has failed to recover a sum from the debtor and has not commenced proceedings before the death of the debtor, he

---

[1] If the delay is protracted and unjustified, it can be used as a relevant circumstance for the inference that the complainant had compromised his right or was *volens*.

will, none the less, be entitled to sue and recover the debt against the culprit's successor. In both examples, it is apparent that delay, however long, can afford no defence whatsoever. These cases are to be contrasted with others, e.g. action for defamation or personal physical injuries where delay, even if unprotracted, will be fatal if the defendant should die in the meantime.[1]

Factors such as: (1) the involuntariness of the wrongful act complained of; (2) accident; (3) act of God; (4) remoteness or non-foreseeability of damage suffered; (5) insanity; (6) drunkenness; (7) juvenile delinquency; (8) official or consanguineal relationship; and (9) superior racial or political status, do not found a good defence generally, although they may be taken into account in assessing the *quantum* or kind of damages or redress to award. Thus a village headman who has committed adultery with a villager's wife can be ordered by the chief to pay compensation to the aggrieved husband.[2]

Finally it must be emphasized that no complainant can successfully bring an action for compensation unless he can establish a satisfactory connection between the injuries suffered and the act complained of. Normally the elders insist that such a connection must be direct.

Lack of space prevents me from dealing with specific civil wrongs.

Résumé

LES DROITS COUTUMIERS DU MALAWI CONCERNANT LES DOMMAGES ET PRÉJUDICES

Classification des infractions

Les infractions peuvent être classées en trois catégories principales à savoir: celles résultant de (1) délits; (2) actes dommageables; (3) ruptures de contrat.

---

[1] Among the Lomwe of Mlanje district, delay followed by the death of the defendant will be equally fatal to an action for defamation brought but not concluded prior to the occurrence of the death. This principle is by no means peculiar to the Lomwe people.

[2] A Chief committing a similar offence may be difficult to bring to justice on account of social and political considerations. In the past (as well as today) such misdemeanour was usually the cause or justification for witchcraft and similar 'supernatural' recourse.

Les délits et actes dommageables peuvent être, d'une part, facilement différenciés d'une rupture de contrat parce qu'une rupture de contrat présuppose l'existence d'un contrat, et peut, par conséquent, engager seulement les personnes intéressées par cet acord. D'autre part délits et actes dommageables peuvent se produire, qu'un accord existe ou non, entre les parties. De plus il n'y a pas de limite au nombre de personnes qui peuvent être entraînées dans un seul délit ou acte dommageable. Une autre raison moins élémentaire de distinguer entre ces deux larges groupes d'infractions est que la rupture de contrat n'est généralement pas réparable par un dédommagement ou une autre décision, tandis que les délits et actes dommageables sont souvent causes d'actions pécuniaires. Une distinction moins claire existe entre délits et actes dommageables puisque la plupart des infractions qui peuvent être considérées et punies en tant que l'un peuvent aussi l'être en tant que l'autre. La mince distinction disparait complètement dans les cas où les procédures séparées n'existent pas pour les deux types d'infractions. Il y a en effet extrêmement peu de cas où elles sont traitées séparément. Peu nombreux sont aussi les actes dommageables qui peuvent être seulement punis en tant que délits. Ainsi changer l'utilisation d'un terrain, sans la permission du chef ou de l'autorité du village, est un bon exemple d'infraction traitée seulement en tant que délit.

Principes généraux de responsabilité

Aucune personne ne pourra être responsable pour un délit ou un acte dommageable à moins que le demandeur ne puisse démontrer que :

(i) le défendeur a commis un acte positif ;
(ii) un préjudice a été subi par le plaignant ;
(iii) un préjudice a été causé immédiatement (ou médiatement) par l'acte en cause.

Le défendeur sera aussi responsable si le demandeur peut montrer que l'acte causant le dommage a été commis, soit par quelqu'un dont le défendeur est responsable, soit par un animal, ou un bien appartenant au défendeur.

Une personne sera responsable pour son acte injuste bien qu'elle n'ait pas eu l'intention de le commettre ou qu'elle n'ait pas prévu le dommage réel subi par le demandeur, pourvu qu'il y ait un rapport de cause à effet entre son acte et le dommage en question.

Il est clair, selon ce qui précède, qu'un acte plutôt qu'un simple oubli est le fondement habituel d'une infraction. Il y a, cependant, des cas où un acte dommageable peut être fondé sur une omission ou inaction voulue, par exemple dans le cas d'une négligence volontaire de subvenir aux besoins de sa femme et de ses enfants. Ces cas présupposent toutefois l'existence d'un devoir positif.

Défenses

Il existe bon nombre de défenses (celles-ci coexistent avec n'importe quelles défenses spéciales qui peuvent être applicables, c'est-à-dire (1) le pardon et (2) le consentement). Ainsi, une personne qui a été pardonnée sans condition pour son méfait par la personne lésée, n'est plus en péril d'être poursuivie pour la même infraction. Si elle est poursuivie, elle peut plaider le pardon comme cause d'excuse.

XVII. Contract in Tswana Law
I. SCHAPERA

I INTRODUCTION

This account is based on data gathered during field studies of several Tswana 'tribes' (chiefdoms) in Bechuanaland Protectorate, notably Kgatla, Kwena, Ngwaketse, Ngwato, and Tawana. Those studies were made, intermittently, in the years 1929–43. My main source of information, apart from personal observation and the statements of Tswana themselves, is a collection of 1,932 records of cases tried by tribal courts, mainly during 1935–40.[1] Of those cases, 310 (16 per cent) related directly to breach or alleged breach of contract. (This figure excludes cases about rights and duties associated with status, e.g. those created by marriage and kinship, membership of tribe or local group, clientship, and serfdom.) I confine the discussion to rules reflected, and occasionally stated, in the case material; if others are not mentioned the reason is, simply, that they did not come before the courts during the period covered by the records.

The main kinds of contract about which there was litigation were for employment of service (42 per cent), sale or barter of goods (19 per cent), and loan of goods (17 per cent); other fairly common disputes were due to breach of promise to marry (6 per cent), and breach of trust by men who had agreed to buy, sell, or transmit goods for someone else (also 6 per cent); and the remainder included a few each about donation, hire of property, and partnership. The services mostly involved were, in descending order of frequency, herding and other care of

[1] The Protectorate Administration in 1935 made the keeping of written case records obligatory everywhere; previously only the Ngwaketse had done so systematically, for 1910–16 and 1928–34. As opportunity offered, I made an abstract (and occasionally a complete copy) of every case recorded by the chiefs' courts and a few others. There is a preliminary analysis of that material in Schapera, 1943b. For an earlier description of Tswana contracts, based mainly on Kgatla and Ngwato sources, cf. Schapera, 1938 (new edition, 1955), Chapter XIV.

livestock, manual labour (e.g. digging wells, building huts, and ploughing), and 'doctoring' by professional magicians (*dingaka*); and the goods mostly involved were livestock (roughly 60 per cent of the total), money, utensils, clothing, and (in only ten instances) land.

The generic Tswana term for 'contract' is *tumalano*, 'mutual agreement' (from *dumela*, 'to agree, consent'). This covers a variety of transactions more specifically distinguished, for example *adima*, lend, borrow; *ananya*, exchange, barter; *fa*, donate (*mpho*, donation); *reka*, buy; *rekisa*, sell (lit., 'cause to buy'); *thapa*, engage, employ (nowadays almost universally replaced by the loan-word *hira*, from Afrikaans *huur*, which applies also to the hire of goods, e.g. wagons); and *tsaya molato*, incur ('take') a debt, e.g. by borrowing something and promising to repay it in kind. There are also certain specialized terms, such as *mafisa*, livestock herded under agistment; *letsema*, work-party at which the helpers are fed, and usually also paid, for a day's work; *tsaya letsema*, take advance payment for help at a (future) work-party; and *tsaya mogwang*, take corn and promise to repay as much after the harvest. A debtor is *yoomolato*, 'the one in debt or at fault' (the same term is used for a 'guilty' person in any other context), cf. English 'liable', and a creditor is *mong wamolato*, 'owner of the debt'.

II FORMATION

In its simplest form, a contract in Tswana law is a promise which the courts will enforce. All contracts impose obligations upon one (or both) of the parties concerned, and reciprocally confer rights upon the other (or both). Both A's obligation, and B's right to its performance, are called by the same term, *tshwanelo*, most suitably translated as 'due' (cf. 'due by A', 'due to B'). The obligation is occasionally one-sided, as when A donates goods or services to B, who gives him nothing in return. In most contracts, however, both parties incur obligations and simultaneously acquire rights; for example, they agree to exchange goods (as in sale and purchase), or to exchange goods for services (as in employment of labour).

The vast majority of contracts are concluded by oral agreement.[1] Except in regard to betrothal, there is apparently no

---

[1] For the exceptions, see below, p. 327.

set form of 'offer' and 'acceptance'. People sometimes deny having made an agreement, but the issue does not depend upon whether or not they have satisfied certain formal requisites; in none of the cases recorded, or described to me, was there any question of the precise stage at which it could be said that an agreement had now been effected.

However, all but the most trivial contracts (such as simple purchases paid for at once) are usually made in the presence of witnesses (*basupi*, from *supa*, show, point out). This is not essential to validate contracts, for the courts have upheld some to which there were no witnesses at all. It is done, rather, as an obvious and useful precaution in case of future dispute; the records show, for example, that a claim may be rejected owing to lack of corroborative evidence.

Normally, the parties first reach their agreement privately. They then call relatives or friends to listen while they repeat in detail its nature and terms. Alternatively, either or each of them will soon afterwards mention it to members of his family, and if livestock are involved he will in any case inform the herdboys. If the parties consider the agreement important enough, they may also go to the local *kgotla* (council-place) and describe it to the chief or village headman and all other men present; this ensures that its terms will be widely known and remembered. (The same procedure is occasionally followed by a man who wants to make a will.)

A bare promise is sufficient to make an agreement legally binding. For example, courts have upheld promises not to become a polygamist (Ngwaketse, 74/1913),[1] or to claim compensation for damage done by cattle to standing crops; they have, similarly, enforced promises to pay compensation for such injuries as damage to crops or the seduction (followed by pregnancy) of an unmarried girl; and, to mention but one more instance, when a man hired to build a hut complained that he could not start work because his employer had not supplied the bricks promised, the latter was ordered to do so (Ngwaketse, 9/1930).

Contracts must as a rule be made directly between the parties

---

[1] i.e. Case No. 74 of 1913, chief's court, Ngwaketse. For a selection of the cases referred to here, and of others also illustrating the Tswana law of contract, see Schapera, 1965.

themselves; for example, courts dismissed claims for a plough allegedly promised, 'because A had not himself told B he would give him the plough' (Ngwaketse, 84/1913), and for compensation for stolen rafters, 'because A had not agreed with B himself that B should look after his rafters' (Ngwaketse, 27/1915). Normally, too, people can only sue or be sued by those with whom they have actually agreed. Sometimes, however, an agreement is made for the benefit of a third party (as when A sells B something on behalf of C, or A gives B something to transmit to C); in such cases C, although not a party to the original agreement, can himself sue B if it is not carried out. Similarly, parents can bind their children, for example by arranging whom they shall marry, or hiring out their services (say as herdboys).

Another instance of rights being enforceable by third parties is that a man may successfully claim payment of debts in kind or money due to his father or brother, whether dead or even alive; in the latter event he presumably acts on behalf of his kinsman (usually away working abroad), since there is nothing in any of the case records to suggest that the debt had been ceded to him. Correspondingly, people can be held liable for the debts not only of a dead kinsman but also of one who is still living. In this particular context, the following rules emerge from the records: (i) only the chief heir (normally the eldest son by the first wife) is liable for a dead man's debts; (ii) a person is not liable for a kinsman's debts unless the debtor himself cannot be sued, e.g. owing to absence abroad; and (iii) a defaulter's relatives cannot be made to pay debts of which they were previously ignorant (cf. Ngwaketse, 48/1913, 2/1930).

III CAPACITY TO CONTRACT

In principle, women and unmarried children cannot make valid contracts without the consent of their male guardian (husband, father, etc.), who then also represents them at court in case of dispute; informants described instances (there are none in the records) of a father successfully reclaiming livestock or other goods disposed of without permission by a son. In practice, women nowadays engage independently in many kinds of transaction, and can also conduct their own cases at court; examples of such transactions found in the records include the sale of beer, hire of transport or a 'doctor', loan of livestock, employment of a herdsman, and practice as a midwife.

On the other hand, even men occasionally need the consent of their near relatives before entering into agreements. This applies especially in regard to marriage: a betrothal, to be legally valid, requires the approval not only of the parents on both sides, but also of their siblings and other close kin (cf. Ngwaketse, 34/1934, in which the judge told a girl's father that he 'was wrong to join the children without the agreement of all their people, this is not marriage'). Informants said that in the old days a man also needed his kinsmen's approval before he could take cattle as *mafisa* (under agistment); and that, even nowadays, a man should not give away or lend arable land without his neighbours' consent, which they can refuse if the prospective beneficiary has a bad reputation, say for being quarrelsome. I was given a few instances of the latter among the Ngwato; none appear in the records.

There were only three instances, in all, suggesting that capacity to contract is limited in other ways too. In these, courts ruled that: (i) 'one woman does not give another woman cattle to herd' (Ngwaketse, 39/1930); (ii) a man had 'acted wrongly' in buying an ox from another who was 'sick' (Malete, 27/1941);[1] and (iii) 'because the parties are closely related [how, is not stated], there can be no question of contract' (Tawana, 1/1939–40). The last (where the complaint was that a man had refused to hand back an ox given him to herd) may be a local variation; in other tribes, agreements between such very close relatives as siblings have been held binding (e.g. Kgatla, 19/1938, Ngwaketse, 47/1940). In any event, as these cases show, capacity to contract is seldom an issue raised in court.

IV CONTRACTUAL OBLIGATIONS

In contracts for transfer of goods or employment of service (and they constituted nearly 80 per cent of all those about which

[1] In this case, the seller of the ox had disposed of an animal he was herding, and was sued by its owner; the nature of his 'sickness' does not appear in the record, where he is merely referred to by the term ordinarily used for any 'sick person' (*molwetse*). In another case a few days later (28/1941), when he was again defendant, no reference at all was made to his 'sickness'.

there was litigation), the parties must agree on the nature and amount of the payment due, including the sex and age of any animals involved in the transaction. They may also, but need not, agree on such other details as the time of payment or delivery of goods purchased, or when a loan should be repaid.

In addition to such specific conditions, contracts of these kinds normally entail what may be called 'standard' or 'customary' obligations. These do not have to be stipulated whenever an agreement is made, but are generally taken for granted, and the courts in case of dispute will always assume that they apply. The following are examples of those featuring most prominently in the case records:

(a) The parties must have valid title to what they give. The issue arises most commonly in regard to livestock, as when A sells (or pays) to B an animal he has stolen or otherwise misappropriated. The purchaser or recipient must then restore the animal to the true owner (who, if necessary, sues him for it), and can recover whatever he himself may have given for it; i.e. the contract is cancelled. The seller or giver is sometimes, though not always, also punished for theft; in only one case, out of many, was he further made to repay more than he had received, viz. double the original purchase price of 10s. (Tawana, 187/1939).

(b) Animals or other goods involved must be delivered in sound condition (and according to the specifications agreed upon). Failing this, they can be rejected; or, as in cases where a rifle was repaired badly, or a whisk for which magical powers ('of producing water and milk') was claimed did not meet the test, the price paid must be refunded; or, if an animal was known to be unfit when lent, and then died in the borrower's possession, a claim for compensation will be dismissed (cf. Ngwaketse, 3/1934).

(c) In either sale or purchase on credit, ownership passes once something has been given in return for a promise to deliver or pay. But risk does not pass simultaneously; for example, if an animal purchased dies before having been taken away, the seller must give another in its place.

(d) If a cow or other female animal is bought and left for the time being with the seller, the purchaser when taking

Y

delivery (by going to fetch the animal) is entitled also to its offspring. The same rule applies to female stock one man may be holding for another under any other condition, say as *mafisa* (under agistment).

(*e*) A man looking after another's livestock must inform him promptly of losses due to death, straying, theft, etc., and must give him the hides of those that have died. Failing this, he can be held liable for the loss. He is also liable for losses or injury due to his own negligence (e.g. if he does not search for stray animals).

(*f*) The holder of *mafisa* cattle is entitled to a heifer as payment, either after a year or so, or when the owner takes back the cattle. But it can be withheld, or refused altogether, if he has not looked after the animals properly. Similarly, a man hired for some special task (such as building a hut, digging a well, or 'doctoring') is not entitled to payment until he has satisfactorily completed that task.

(*g*) A gift of any kind, once made, is irrevocable (unless given to children or other dependants). The issue often arises when a man claims, or tries to retain, goods he has given a concubine who afterwards abandons him. The courts have similarly ruled that a man who gives someone else arable land is not entitled to use it again himself or to say afterwards that the recipient must plough it for him.

(*h*) A debt must be paid on demand (or at the time agreed upon), and is always due, no matter how long ago it was incurred. *Molato gaobole, gobola nama,* says the proverb, 'A wrong [or debt] does not rot, [only] meat rots.' But the creditor should not wait too long before making his claim. Correctly, he should first approach the debtor directly, several times if need be, and sue only as a last resort. On the other hand, he may also prejudice his claim (and be denied the right to natural increment of livestock, or even to any payment at all) if he needlessly postpones legal action, as in cases where he did not go to court until twenty years or more after the transaction in respect of which he claimed. The principle applied is that he must act while the matter is 'still fresh' (*esale metse*, lit. 'still wet')—if only because, as occasionally stated in a judgment, 'the spoor may be lost', i.e. the facts can no longer be ascertained.

V REMEDIES FOR BREACH

Many transactions are completed at once, or almost at once; for example, goods purchased may be paid for and taken away immediately, or people helping at a work-party may be rewarded the same day. Such transactions very seldom give rise to litigation, if at all; no instances occur in the case records. The disputes that do come to court are almost all about agreements not yet carried out, like those in which A is still under obligation of some kind to B.

Of the 310 cases in the records seen, 163 (53 per cent) were claims for payment due in respect of services rendered or goods taken (including money lent); 64 (21 per cent) were for restitution of goods deposited (e.g. *mafisa* cattle), donated or lent (e.g. betrothal gifts, fields, etc.), or entrusted for transmission, sale, etc.; 59 (19 per cent) were for compensation (e.g. for loss of animals herded, breach of promise to marry, or failure to render services promised); and the remaining 20 (6 per cent) were for actual performance (e.g. delivering goods specified, or doing work promised). In 216 cases (70 per cent) the claim was awarded in full, and in 17 others (5 per cent) it was awarded in part. The principles reflected in the judgments included the following:

(*a*) If payment of a debt is refused or withheld, the debtor is ordered to pay; and if there was no excuse for his delay (e.g. if he had been approached several times in vain), he may have to pay more than was in fact originally due. In the old days, it may be added here, a man whose debtor would not pay had another remedy than going to court: he could 'seize' (*thukhutha*) cattle or other property from the latter and hold it as security. This practice, though still found at times, is tending to be frowned upon by the tribal authorities, because of the many disputes to which it leads; among the Ngwaketse it was actually prohibited in 1898 by Chief Bathoen I, who decreed that any man 'seizing' another's goods would not only have to return them, but would also forfeit what was due to himself (a penalty that was enforced in, e.g., 16/1916).

(*b*) A defaulter may similarly be ordered to do work he has promised, or to finish a task he has abandoned or done badly; specific examples include digging a well, transporting goods, ploughing, and 'doctoring'. Occasionally this applies also to breach of promise to marry, the judge ordering that the marriage must take place. But if the defendant can show that performance was impossible he may be excused, as in cases where a herdsman could not search for stray stock because his employer had given him other work to do (Ngwaketse, 3/1928), or a man could not plough a field for someone else because it was waterlogged (Tawana, 233/1940).

(c) But if any payment has already been made, the court will usually order its refund, and thus cancel the contract. This applies also in cases of a girl's refusing to marry her fiancé: he is then entitled to recover the whole of his betrothal gifts.

(d) A person who has suffered actual loss through breach of contract may be awarded special damages. Thus, when A did not plough a field for B at the time agreed upon, the court awarded B part of A's own crops (Tawana, 21/1937); and a man who borrowed and did not return another's bull for several years was ordered to give him the five calves that bull had sired on his own cows, 'because the owner's cows had been without the services of their bull for a long time' (Kgatla, 22/1938). This applies also in cases where a girl is jilted by her fiancé, especially after she has borne him a child; in one such case (Kwena, 16/1936), the court specifically awarded her eight head of cattle as damages 'because he has spoiled her chances of getting married to someone else'.

(e) If a case for breach of contract is due primarily to the defendant's obstinacy or other misconduct (e.g. if he has appealed from a lower court when he was clearly in the wrong, or if he told lies), the court, in addition to any other award, may inflict special punishment upon him, e.g. fine him 'for letting the matter come to court unnecessarily' (Kgatla, Mathubudukwane district court, 3/1936). Such penalties were imposed in 22 of the 310 cases.

As many of the cases show, the court in giving judgment tends to stress obligations. Occasionally the emphasis is on rights instead: for example, 'pay what is claimed'; *otshwanelwa kegoboelwa kedikgomo tsetharo*, 'he is entitled to a refund of three cattle' (Malete, 21/1941); *abaneelwe ditshwanelo tsabona*, 'let them be given what is due to them' (Tlokwa, 35/1937). But the phrasing is more commonly the other way round: 'pay what you owe', 'pay as you promised', 'carry out your promise', 'pay according to your agreement', and, perhaps most often of all, *omolato*, 'you are at fault (or in the wrong)'. It will be seen, incidentally, that here it is sometimes explicitly stated that an agreement had been made, and should therefore be kept. I regard this, and the diversity of ways in which a single rule may be applied, as good evidence that Tswana do have the idea of 'contract' as such, and thus differ from the Barotse among whom, Gluckman says, 'each transaction is regarded as a specific complex of rights and obligations, and there is no general model of contract'.[1]

VI INNOVATIONS

Contact with Europeans has introduced several new features in Tswana contracts. Occasionally, for example, they are nowadays made in writing. As early as 1915 Ngwaketse courts were accepting promissory notes as confirmation of debt, and in 1937 relatively complex written agreements were being made among the Kgatla by small groups of men for sharing the cost and use of boreholes in grazing areas.[2] Money is very widely used in transactions, and effects of its adoption are seen, *inter alia*, in loans at a specified rate of interest, and the employment of herdsmen and other labourers for monthly cash wages. There was one Kgatla case (3/1935) in which money had been lent on condition that it was repaid in three annual instalments; and in two others (Ngwaketse, 45/1912; Tawana, 215/1939) the contract even contained what was in effect a 'penalty clause', stipulating that if money was not paid by a certain time the sum due would increase progressively the longer the delay. Other new kinds of transaction, likewise due to the adoption of European goods, include for example the hire of wagons and the employment of men for such work as ploughing, repairing rifles, building brick houses, and breaking in horses.

In addition, certain kinds of transaction have been forbidden by chiefs. The most widespread prohibitions are against the sale of livestock or grain to European traders without permis-

[1] Gluckman, 1965, p. 176.
[2] One such agreement is reproduced in full in Schapera, 1943, p. 253.

sion from the tribal authorities; almost everywhere, too, chiefs regulated in various ways the sale and purchase among the people themselves of 'Kafir beer' and other intoxicants. Examples of others, localized in distribution, include the following: Ngwato and Ngwaketse may not levy payment from passing travellers for watering cattle at their wells; the Ngwaketse were in 1914 forbidden to seek a 'doctor', if they needed one, except through the chief (this was replaced in 1929 by the rule that no 'doctor' might 'practise' without a permit from the chief); and Tlokwa may not donate or lend fields except to close relatives. It has 'always' been Tswana law, I may add here, that land may not be sold or rented; the only apparent exception is among the Kgatla, where a heifer is occasionally 'paid' for a field (though informants said the payment is really compensation for the original cost of clearing the land).

Violation of such prohibitions (the list is by no means exhaustive)[1] is usually punished by a fine. The offenders are also deprived of any benefit; whatever they received in payment is either confiscated by the chief, or must be returned to the purchasers. Informants said the chief will usually also confiscate goods (e.g. livestock or beer) illegally offered for sale but not yet sold, and gave some examples; none appear in the case records.

VIII SUMMARY

The following seem to be distinctive characteristics of the Tswana law of contract. (*a*) The basic principle that an agreement of any kind must be kept, unless performance is impossible. (*b*) A bare promise may be sufficient to make an agreement legally binding. (*c*) If a contract is made for the benefit of a third party, he himself can sue if it is not carried out. (*d*) The existence of generally recognized 'standard' obligations, which do not have to be specified whenever an agreement is made but which the courts will always assume to apply. (*e*) The award of special damages to persons who suffer actual loss through breach of contract, and the infliction of special penalties upon recalcitrant debtors and others who provoke needless litigation.

[1] Schapera, 1943a, pp. 36–38, 47–49.

BIBLIOGRAPHY

Gluckman, M.
    (1965) *The Ideas in Barotse Jurisprudence.* New Haven and London: Yale University Press.

Schapera, I.
    (1938, 1955) *Handbook of Tswana Law and Custom.* London: Oxford University Press for the International African Institute.
    (1943) *Native Land Tenure in the Bechuanaland Protectorate.* Lovedale, South Africa: The Lovedale Press.
    (1943a) *Tribal Legislation among the Tswana.* London School of Economics and Political Science Monographs, No. 9. London: Percy Lund, Humphries.
    (1934b) 'The Work of Tribal Courts in the Bechuanaland Protectorate', *African Studies*, ii, pp. 27–40.
    (1965) 'Contract in Tswana Case Law', *Journal of African Law*, ix, 3, pp. 142–53.

Résumé

CONTRAT DANS LE DROIT TSWANA

Le sujet présenté dans ce résumé a été étudié dans les décisions des cours de justice des Tswana dans le Protectorat du Bechuanaland, principalement pendant la période de 1935–40. Parmi ces cas, 310 avaient trait directement à des ruptures ou mettaient en cause des ruptures de contrat. Le discussion se borne aux règles énoncées occasionellement dans les registres; si d'autres règles ne sont pas mentionnées, c'est qu'elles ne sont pas apparues pendant cette période.

Formation. Un contrat dans le droit Tswana est fondamentalement un accord volontaire (*tumalano*) entre deux parties, imposant des obligations à l'une (ou aux deux) et réciproquement conférant des droits à l'autre (ou aux deux). Dans la plupart des contrats, les deux parties contractent des obligations et simultanément acquièrent des droits. Quelquefois, cependant, les obligations ne sont que d'un côté, par exemple: quand A donne des marchandises ou rend des services à B qui ne lui donne rien en retour.

Les traits spéciaux qui suivent peuvent être notés:

(*a*) la plupart des contrats sont conclus oralement. Des témoins ne sont pas essentiels pour engager les parties juridiquement, mais si aucun n'est produit, cela peut causer préjudice à l'accusation on à la défense.

(*b*) une simple promesse peut être suffisante pour rendre un accord juridiquement valable.

(c) un accord doit normalement être conclu directement entre les personnes intéressées. Mais, dans l'intérêt d'une troisième personne, cette personne elle-même, peut les poursuivre si l'accord n'a pas été conclu dans les règles. De la même façon, des personnes peuvent quelquefois poursuivre, ou être tenues responsables des dettes d'un parent, mort ou même vivant.

(d) en principe, les femmes et les enfants célibataires ne peuvent pas contracter sans le consentement de leur tuteur mâle; en pratique, les femmes, de nos jours, s'engagent seules dans toutes sortes de transactions et en cas de litige, peuvent plaider leur propre cause devant la cour.

Obligations-type. A part des détails changeants comme la nature des biens et le paiement dû pour des produits achetés ou pour des services rendus (qui doivent être spécialement approuvés par les personnes intéressées), la plupart des contrats incorporent certaines conditions-type ou coutumières. Celles-ci n'ont pas à être stipulées toutes les fois qu'un accord est conclu mais elles sont acceptées, et en cas de litige, les tribunaux assumeront toujours qu'elles s'appliquent. En voici les plus communes.

(a) les personnes doivent avoir un titre valable sur ce qu'elles donnent; animaux ou autres produits engagés doivent aussi être remis en bon état.

(b) dans la vente ou l'achat à crédit, la propriété est transférée aussitôt que quelque chose a été donné en échange d'une promesse de délivrer ou de payer. Mais le risque n'est pas transféré simultanément; par exemple, si un animal acheté meurt avant qu'il ait été emporté, le vendeur doit le remplacer.

(c) si A doit à B une femelle, ou si B s'occupe pour lui d'animaux femelles, B a aussi le droit à leurs petits.

(d) un homme s'occupant du bétail de quelqu'un doit l'informer rapidement des pertes dûes à la mort ou au vol etc. . . . S'il ne prévient pas, il peut être tenu pour responsable de la perte.

(e) un homme embauché pour un travail spécial n'a pas droit au paiement avant qu'il ait accompli ce travail d'une façon satisfaisante.

(f) une dette doit être payée à la demande, ou à la date fixée et est toujours dûe; le temps depuis lequel elle est contractée est sans importance. Mais si le créancier tarde trop longtemps pour demander à être réglé, il peut nuire à ses chances de recevoir son dû.

Recours pour infractions. Voilà les règles les plus employées:

(*a*) si le paiement d'une dette est refusé ou repoussé, le débiteur peut être poursuivi et il devra payer; s'il n'y avait pas de raison à son retard, il peut avoir à payer plus qu'il ne devait à l'origine.
(*b*) similairement, on peut ordonner à un défaillant d'accomplir un travail qu'il a promis, ou de finir une tâche qu'il a abandonnée ou mal faite. Mais on peut l'excuser s'il peut prouver que l'exécution est impossible.
(*c*) si quelque chose a déjà été payé sans avoir été livré, la Cour peut ordonner un remboursement; ceci résilie le contrat.
(*d*) une personne qui a souffert d'une perte actuelle à cause d'une rupture de contrat peut se voir attribuer des dommages et intérêts spéciaux.
(*e*) si un cas de rupture de contrat est dû principalement à l'obstination du défendeur ou à sa mauvaise conduite, la Cour peut lui infliger une sanction spéciale en plus de toute autre.

De temps en temps, les tribunaux exposent explicitement qu'un marché a été conclu et doit par conséquent être tenu. Ce cas et la diversité de ceux dans lesquels une simple règle peut être appliquée peuvent être considérées comme une preuve que les Tswana ont vraiment l'idée de 'contrat' et diffèrent ainsi des Barotse, parmi lesquels, dit Gluckman, 'chaque transaction est considérée comme une collection spécifique de droits et obligations, et il n'y a pas de modèle général de contrat'.

Innovations. Les contrats avec les Européens ont introduit de nouveaux traits dans les contrats Tswana. Quelquefois, de nos jours, ils sont fait par écrit. De plus, ils assument de temps en temps des formes telles que le prêt d'argent à un taux fixé d'intérêt, l'embauche de pâtres ou autres ouvriers payés mensuellement, et l'emploi de main d'oeuvre pour des travaux tels que le labour des champs, la réparation de carabines, la construction de maisons de briques ou le transport de marchandises par chariot. Les chefs ont aussi introduit des décrets interdisant certaines sortes de transactions telles que la vente du bétail ou de grain aux commerçants européens. Mais, dans l'ensemble, les Tswanas ont trouvé dans leur droit traditionnel des contrats suffisamment flexibles pour leur permettre d'affronter les nouvelles sortes de transactions dans lesquelles ils sont maintenant souvent engagés.

XVIII. Customary Contracts and Transactions in Kenya[1]

Y. P. GHAI

I INTRODUCTION

In Kenya cases in which both parties are Africans fall under the jurisdiction of African courts under Chapter II of the African Courts Act, 1952, continuing the situation under earlier statutory provisions. Hence contracts between Africans do not fall under the law of contracts of England, which is generally applicable. Hannigan has argued that the passing of the 1961 Contract Act, providing that English law of contract in general shall apply in Kenya, imposes this also in 'native courts, and excludes native custom on contractual matters'.[2] Hannigan's contention is by no means certainly valid. Whatever the constitutional position, in practice the customary law of contracts is still recognized and enforced in African courts.[3]

II CONTRACTS IN CUSTOMARY LAW

A study of the records of the African courts reveals two types of contractual transactions that come before them. One set of transactions are of traditional type, and solutions of disputes arising out of them are based on well-established principles of law and precedents. Other transactions are created by modern developments and present courts with novel problems. The courts seem to maintain that they can deal with these often in terms of traditional customary rules, and they also act on occasion in terms of what we can call 'natural justice'. These

---

[1] This paper is an initial essay on some features of contracts at customary law in Kenya. I was only able to look at a few tribes—Kikuyu, Meru, Embu, Luo, and Kipsigis. My main sources were the records of the African courts, and conversations with court panels and elders. This method of research was far from satisfactory.

[2] Hannigan, 1961, p. 5.

[3] [Editorial note.—This paragraph is a précis of a much longer introduction giving detailed references to the development of legislation on this point.]

cases are often a useful source of customary law concepts; this is particularly true in the field of damages, where the principles are clearer in the modern type of cases, since evaluations are made in monetary terms as opposed to stock or produce. Light is also thrown by these cases on the traditional concepts of negligence and risk, though the need remains to use such cases with extreme caution, for the courts are anxious to do justice, which is sometimes achieved at the expense of consistency, and also because law influences other than customary law play a part in the process of decision-making.[1]

There is no generalized concept of executory contract in customary law, which is to say that the mere exchange of promises by itself has no legal validity. This point is illustrated strikingly by a case from the Meru African court.[2] The case concerned the sale of a piece of land. B had agreed to buy the land from A, at 2,330s. All the negotiations had been carried out as was shown by the evidence given by the witnesses; the final agreement was reduced to writing, which was produced in court. After the agreement had been reached, A changed his mind and claimed his land back. The court upheld his claim, as, although B had occupied the land, he had so far paid nothing for the land and mere agreement was held not binding. The necessity of executed consideration on one side is crucial. It is crucial not only to make agreements binding, but also because it creates liability even though there is no agreement, somewhat on quasi-contractual principles. The same court which refused to enforce the land agreement mentioned above held that there was liability in the following situation.[3] X had paid a fine for his brother Y in the Resident Magistrates' court, as well as given some money to the African court for compensation ordered to be paid by his brother, although the brother was in jail at this time and had not requested X to make these payments. Nor was there any understanding that Y was to pay back these sums. When X sued Y to recover the money, Y could not plead in his defence the lack of agreement or understanding to pay back the money. X had made a payment for Y,

---

[1] One judge told me that whenever a case involving the modern type of partnership came up before him he reached for the laws of Kenya to look up the Partnership Act.
[2] No. V of 1964.
[3] No. V of 1960.

and therefore was entitled to the recovery of it. This is not to say that the conception of consent or agreement is not important. Such a conception is well known to the courts and has helped in the expansion of contractual categories, noticeably partnership. But because the conception and boundaries of contract are not clearly defined, the courts are willing to spell contracts out of non-contractual situations, in order to do justice. This situation is not dissimilar to the common law concept of unjust enrichment but whereas the common law accepts that the remedy in this kind of situation is not contractual, the African court in this case tended to treat it as arising out of contract. In the traditional form of contracts there is widespread knowledge of the rights, liabilities, and obligations involved. There is seldom any discussion between the parties as to the terms of the contract, and such discussion takes place only if it is intended to vary the customary terms. But there are also *ad hoc* individual contracts, including modern contracts like partnerships. The courts have much difficulty with the second type. Primarily because traditionally most contracts were standard in form, sufficient thought is not given to the detailed terms of these new type of contracts, nor indeed is there as yet enough experience of joint enterprises, commerce, etc., to anticipate future contingencies and make provision for these. The result is that the courts are obliged to write in certain missing terms. The courts do not indulge in the sophistry of the reasoning of the Moorcock case,[1] but are gradually creating what may be called modern standard form contracts, of which partnership is the outstanding example.

Traditional contracts largely concern land and stock, reflecting the rural, non-monetary economy of tribal societies. Among the Luo a common kind of contract is what is known as the '*singo*' pledge.[2] In this contract A gives B one heifer in exchange for a bull. B keeps the heifer, till it gives birth to a female calf. When a female calf is born, B returns the heifer and gives one more bull, but retains the calf. If the heifer dies before producing a female calf, then A must provide another cow. Luo regard one cow as equal in value to two bulls. This type of contract benefits both parties; A often enters into this

[1] (1889) 14 P.D. 64.
[2] See case No. 38 of 1965 at Winam court (Kisumu).

transaction because he needs a bull to kill for ceremonial reasons. An outright exchange is also possible among the Luo. This is known as '*wilo*', and one cow is exchanged for two bulls.

The Meru have a somewhat similar institution, called '*ngwato*'. In this, one party gives a cow to the other, and the latter pays for the first heifer of that cow with goats by instalments (five goats is the average, but the number can vary). When the heifer is in fact born, the cow is returned to the original owner. If the cow dies before producing a heifer, the owner must provide another cow, or return the goats.[1] If the cow produces a bull, the person who has the cow keeps the bull till such time as a heifer is born. When that happens, he returns the cow and the bull, but retains the heifer. The buyer of the calf must complete payment before the calf is born, as if it is born before he has paid, it belongs to the owner of the cow.[2] Such a contract is a traditional way of enabling people without cattle to have some; it also acts as a cohesive force in the community, creating and strengthening ties of friendship.[3]

Herding contracts are also quite frequent. If a person owns some cattle, he may not be able to look after them himself, either because he has something else to do or because he has no land on which to graze his cattle. It is usual in such circumstances to ask someone else to look after the cattle. No payment is made for this kind of service. In some tribes the keeper is allowed to take blood from the animals, according to his need, and normally keeps the milk. In other tribes payment of some kind is made—this takes the form of one of the offspring of the animals. Among the Kikuyu, if a person keeps one cow in another's corral, and the cow produces ten calves, one bull out of the ten calves belongs to the herder. Similarly, one goat out of ten belongs to the herder (*rithio*). Among the Embu also, payment must be made, and in a case where the herder brought an action to recover payment, the court said: 'According to Kimbere custom, if someone is giving his cows to the other to look after for him, always something is given to the other by

[1] No. II of 1965 (Meru African court).
[2] According to a Meru case, No. 43 of 1965, if the calf dies after birth, two sheep have to be given instead.
[3] 'Ngwate' is also the word used to refer to the relationship that arises between two families which are joined by marriage.

the person to look after the cows.'[1] However, there is evidence to show that payment for such services is becoming the rule among most tribes, and even the milk is given to the owner if he lives near by. As we shall see later, the risks are generally with the owner.[2]

There are also well-defined traditional land transactions, and the rules about sale of land and about tenancies are clear. Tenancies are basically gratuitous loans of land. Among the Embu, the user can be evicted at any time but if there is any permanent crop in the land, he must be given compensation. Among the Kikuyu similar practices obtain (a tenancy is called *Uhoi wa githaka*). Someone who is given building, cultivation, or grazing rights on another's land without any payment whatever is called a *muhoi*. He cannot give or sell this land to anyone. If the *muhoi* does any act which displeases the giver, *muheani*, he may be required to leave the land immediately. In the past no compensation was required to be paid to the evicted tenant, but now compensation is made obligatory, to encourage the progressive development of the land. There is a judgment of the Court of Review which claims that according to Luo law, a tenant cannot be evicted except for good cause, such as misbehaviour.[3] It is not clear how far this accurately represents the Luo law. Misbehaviour would include acts which are incompatible with the owner's title. In the Court of Review case it was alleged that the tenant had forfeited his rights by planting trees and thus claiming the land as his. The land can be given on conditions, and land given only for cultivation cannot be built on.[4]

The second type of contracts is mainly of two kinds—*ad hoc*, individual contracts which have probably always played a part in tribal society, and the newer kind of contract, a response to the commercial, monetary changes resulting from colonialism. Many of the traditional contracts have been carried over into the new age, serving the needs of a somewhat different kind. An outstanding example of this is debt. In the old type of contract, there are instances of bailment and agency. It was, and still is, common practice to put one's cattle in someone's

[1] No. 20 of 1965 (Embu court).
[2] For a cattle contract among the Kipsigis, '*kimangan*', see Peristiany, 1939, p. 150.
[3] (1955) III C.O.R.L.P. 1.   [4] (1959) VII C.O.R.L.P. 4.

corral if night falls when one is still some distance from one's home. Sometimes the cattle are left there for a few days. Or it can happen that someone is given money by another to buy cattle to take back to his corral till collected by the new owners. These are to be distinguished from contracts of herding. The cattle cannot be used without permission, otherwise there is a valid claim for damages.[1] In another case, timber was left with the defendant for safe custody, and it was agreed that if he got someone who wanted to buy it, he should bring that man to the plaintiff and they could agree on the price. The defendant, without consulting the plaintiff, sold the timber for 400s. The plaintiff alleged that the value of the timber was 490s., and because the defendant had broken the terms of the bailment, he was ordered to make up the balance.[2] There are several cases of agency as well, in which a person was asked to receive money on someone else's behalf, or to buy or sell for someone. It is interesting to note that in one sense the African contracts of agency display a mature rule of agency: the agent falls out once the transaction for which he was employed is complete. In one case A gave money to B to be given to X Company. B gave it to an official of the company, who probably absconded with it (this is not clear from the facts of the case). A brought an action against B for recovery of the money. His claim was dismissed, and the court held that he only had a claim against the company.[3] The explanation of this rule is not the same as in the common law. It is more likely that the agent drops out not because he has completed what he was supposed to do, but because he no longer has the money. The ability of customary law to reach the person in possession of the goods in question is quite striking; the notion of privity of contract is only very rudimentary, and occasionally makes difficult the classification of a case as tort or contract.

Debts constitute the most important contractual transactions to come before the courts, about 25 per cent of all the civil cases. The debts that are claimed in these cases are of various kinds—maize, cattle, money. They arise either out of customary dealings in cattle—exchange of presents and so forth—or the

[1] See case No. 163 of 1965 in the Winam court (Kisumu).
[2] 161 of 1965 Winam court (Kisumu).
[3] 48 of 1965 Winam court (Kisumu).

modern credit system. Another important group of contracts is partnerships. The courts exercise a lot of discretion here, as there is hardly any law to guide them. Commercial aspirations among the Africans are growing, and more and more of them are opening shops, replacing, to some extent, the Asian storekeepers. The shops are often partnerships. Disputes seem quite common, partly because these enterprises frequently do not succeed, due to lack of experience, and partly because the accounting system, etc., generally are non-existent. There is hardly any law to settle these disputes; the local African District Councils lay down some rules, but often there is total ignorance of these rules. The courts are trying to evolve rules to deal with these disputes. It now seems accepted that parties share in the profits in proportion to their capital contribution, and at the dissolution of the partnership, the assets are divided in a similar way. But the courts are not particularly suited for this task: there is little notion of binding precedents; and the cases are often most complicated and require skilled presentation.[1] There is urgent need for some kind of legislation or guidance on this matter, if the governmental policy of Africanizing the economy is to succeed.

III CONCEPTIONS

From this discussion of some contracts adjudicated on in the African courts, it is obvious that customary law comprehends notions of continuing relationships arising out of contractual transactions, and subsisting outside of family ties. The concept of consent is important, even though it is not adequate by itself, executed action of some kind being necessary for validity. There are few formalities necessary for the formation of a contract; in some cases consent of other parties besides the principals is required. For example, family land cannot be sold without the whole family's consent;[2] in some instances, the permission of the clan has to be obtained. Certain transactions required the performance of special ceremonies; marriage contracts are a good example, but in some tribes, sale of land as well. These are becoming increasingly less important, and customary contracts

---

[1] The courts are astute to infer partnerships even when there is no agreement. See case No. 23 of 1960 (Embu).
[2] (1959) C.O.R.L.P. 2; (1953) VI C.O.R.L.P. 2.

are in general marked by extreme informality. There are very few qualifications on the capacity to contract; among the Kikuyu and the Meru women cannot own stock or land, and this limits their capacity, but among the Luo the women are relatively free to dispose of their property as they see fit. Minors are also able to make contracts, though contracts made by minors often involve vicarious liability for the father, unless the minors have established their own household. Drunkards seem to be afforded little protection against their injudicious bargains; the explanations I was given for this rule were somewhat inconsistent: 'No drunk will ever make a contract' and 'all our contracts are made over a glass of beer anyway!'

Mistake is a vitiating factor. As will be pointed out later, customary law has great capacity for opening up transactions and its remedial rules have much flexibility. Therefore the incidence of mistake does not offer any great problem. If the parties have acted under a misapprehension, they are allowed to ask to be put back to their original position. If the bride-price is delivered to a wrong person, it can be recovered from him,[1] and in a case of mistaken identity, consensus was held to be inoperative.[2] Allegations of duress are rare; I found only one case when duress was pleaded. The court dismissed the plea rather summarily—'We do not easily believe that kind of defence'[3]—but presumably, in a genuine case of duress, no contract will be held to have arisen. Again, I could find no case when illegality was considered relevant, though there were at least two cases where arguments based on illegality would have been conclusive at common law.[4] Some judges said they would throw out cases involving illegal acts, others denied that customary law was familiar with illegality as a vitiating, contractual factor. The second view is probably near the truth. Customary law seems greatly concerned to establish what belongs to whom and to restore it to him; *in pari delicto potior est conditio defendentis* is somewhat incompatible with this aim. There are no developed ideas of warranties. Expressed warranties have force, but there are few implied warranties; the reason seems to be

[1] See case 102 of 1964 (Winam, Kisumu).
[2] See case 50 of 1965 (Meru).
[3] See case 110 of 1965 (Thika).
[4] 8 of 1959 (Embu), sale of beer without licence; 221 of 1964 (Kisumu), buying maize without permit.

that defects in cattle and produce are not easily detected or identified. The general feeling seems to be that one cow is as good as another. The rule is *caveat emptor*.

When discussing mistakes, misrepresentation, duress, illegality, fraud, it is important to remember the kind of relief the courts give. I shall come back to this point later; consequential damages are not awarded, and the court's judgment as a rule aims at putting the parties in the position they were in before the contract was formed.

As mere agreements do not conclude a contract, it becomes necessary to see when a contract is formed, and when the risk and title to property pass. A contract is formed when some object has been transferred or some act done. In sale, risk generally remains with the seller until delivery.[1] Increments accrue to the benefit of the buyer, but only if he has completed payment. Delivery does not necessarily pass the title; it does so only if the payment has been completed. Nor in such cases does risk pass till the last instalment has been paid, if the payment is by instalments. It would thus appear that risk passes from the seller to the buyer when both delivery and payment have been made. In contracts of bailments and herding, the owner bears the risks. The risk can pass to the keeper only if he delays in the return of the object or cattle, and this is specially so if the request for the return has been made and not complied with.[2] Apart from this, the risk does not pass. Negligence does not displace risk, unless delay is regarded as a form of negligence. If a cowherd is foolish enough to take another's animals in the forest so that they are devoured by a lion, the loss is the owner's. Similarly, if cattle escape from someone's corral the keeper is not responsible; nor if they are stolen. This retarded development of the concept of negligence as affecting risk must be due to a whole variety of natural hazards so prevalent in tribal society.

The bailee, however, can become responsible if he fails to adduce satisfactory evidence of the loss of the animals.[3] If the owner lives near by, then the meat and the skin must be returned to him; if he lives too far, then only the skin need be

---

[1] See case No. 96 of 1964 (Winam, Kisumu); case No. 41 of 1965 (Embu, Appeal case).
[2] Case No. 4 of 1961 (Embu).   [3] See 41 of 1965 (Meru, Appeal case).

sent. In any case he must be informed immediately of the loss or death, and given an opportunity to identify the dead animal as his, and not the bailee's. In case of loss, the bailee must assist him in the search. Failure to inform promptly, and to produce satisfactory evidence, can result in the bailee's liability to replace the animal.[1] These rules, while recognizing the natural hazards of life, minimize opportunities and incentives for deceit.

As was hinted earlier, customary law does not know any rigid ideas of the privity of contract. In an appellate case at Meru,[2] the plaintiff sold a cow to the defendant; the cow became pregnant before the sale was finalized, and according to Meru customary law, the calf which would be born would belong to the plaintiff. The defendant sold the cow to a third party before the cow had produced; the calf would be given to the defendant who would in turn give it to the plaintiff. The calf unfortunately died at birth, and after the defendant and the third party had gone to court, the defendant was awarded two sheep, which he offered to pay to the plaintiff. The plaintiff refused this and insisted on a calf, alleging that the transaction between the defendant and the third party could not affect his right. The court in a somewhat unclear judgment held that the transaction between the defendant and the third party was crucial to the question of liabilities in the first contract, saying that it was absurd to expect the defendant to pay more than he had received. In another case, A took B's cattle in settlement of a purported debt. The debt was in fact owed by C, B's half-brother. A was allowed to retain the cattle when he proved that B owed money to C.[3] The lack of concern with privity does enable the court to do justice between the parties, where the common law court might easily be thwarted by a technicality. On the other hand, its absence prevents a clear distinction of the contractual category from other legal categories; and might well inhibit its growth.

Perhaps the greatest weakness of the customary law of contracts is in its provision of remedies. Specific performance in the sense of ordering the carrying out of the agreement is unusual, though orders requiring the transfer of cattle or produce

---

[1] See 3 of 1960 (Embu).   [2] No. 45 of 1965.
[3] 16 of 1959 (Winam, Kisumu).

are common.[1] There is a certain lack of finality about transactions. People who come to court alleging a breach of contract by the other party merely claim to be put into the position they were in before they made the contract. Thus whether there was mistake, fraud, duress, or misrepresentation, the consequences are not much different. Nowadays when damages are being increasingly awarded in a monetary form, no consequential damages are given. Damages seem to be related as much to the benefit gained by the defendant as the loss suffered by the plaintiff. D entered into an agreement with P to hire P's sewing machine and to pay 25s. for it every month; no other terms were agreed upon. After the first month D terminated the contract and refused to pay for more than one month; he had the machine with him for nine months as P refused to accept it. D was ordered to pay the rental for only one month, but it is interesting to note that the court justified this result by remarking that if D had actually used the machine for a longer time, he would have had to pay for it.[2] Another case is even more striking on this point. A borrowed some money from B at interest to start a business. The business failed and was closed down after two months. The money was not returned for several months. The court held that interest for only two months was payable.[3]

In many of the modern type of contracts, like transport, loan, hire, consequential damages are not awarded. The instinct perhaps is right: I was frequently told in justification of this rule that it is difficult for the defendant to know the purposes for which the plaintiff wants the defendant's goods, or services, and so it was unfair to attach liability beyond knowable damages. Notions of ordinary, constructive, or imputed knowledge are not accepted, nor indeed actual knowledge if they lead to consequential damages.

Thus there is no great legal deterrent against committing breach of contract. Most contracts, other than the 'once and for all' transactions, are broken wherever any party feels like it.

---

[1] In the only genuine case of specific performance I found, the court was rather apologetic about granting it, saying that it had no option as one party had already consumed the goods of another and so could not be asked to return them. So he had to do what he had contracted to do—i.e. deliver his animals (136/64, Winam, Kisumu).

[2] No. 4 of 1959.   [3] No. VIII of 1964 (Meru).

It is unlikely that contracts would be abandoned so casually if customary law had the concept of consequential damages. If small-scale African efforts at commerce are to succeed, then it will be necessary to provide for consequential damages. Many African traders have had to give up their businesses because their customers did not pay for years and no interest was awarded; or their partners pulled out without notice and the courts allowed them to withdraw their capital.

Contracts also exhibit a lack of finality, in that sales of land are redeemable in some instances, and there is no limitation of action. If customary law is to promote the development of commerce, then changes will be needed in the rules about mistake, misrepresentation, warranties, damages, and remedies.[1] For though there is a conception of contract, there is no clear or sufficient differentiation between the concepts in contract, and partly as a result, the courts have not been able to solve satisfactorily the problems presented by novel contractual situations.

BIBLIOGRAPHY

Hannigan, A. St. J.
   (1961) 'The Imposition of Western Law Forms upon Primitive Societies', *Comparative Studies in Society and History*, iv (November).
Peristiany, J.
   (1939) *Social Institutions of the Kipsigis*. London: Routledge.

Résumé

LES TRANSACTIONS ET CONTRATS COUTUMIERS AU KENYA

Au cas où les deux parties sont africaines, le litige est porté devant les tribunaux africains et le droit coutumier est appliqué. Deux sortes de contrats se présentent devant de tels tribunaux: (1) les contrats traditionnels et coutumiers, (2) les contrats qui comportent des situations inconnues au droit coutumier traditionnel, mais pour la solution desquels des concepts coutumiers sont employés.

Les contrats traditionnels intéressent principalement les terrains et le bétail. Pour les contrats concernant le bétail, il

---

[1] [Editorial note.—These sentences summarize a longer exposition.]

s'agit d'une personne qui confie le soin de son bétail à une autre personne. Les animaux figurent aussi dans des échanges et la société traditionnelle connaissait l'évaluation d'un type d'animal par exemple, une vache, par rapport à un autre type d'animal, par exemple un mouton. Les transactions ayant pour objet des terrains sont principalement des locations. Jadis, il n'était pas toujours possible de vendre un terrain. De nos jours, il est même possible de trouver des contrats de mandat et de caution. Les tribunaux s'occupent aussi dans beaucoup de cas de contrats de type moderne résultant du système de crédit et de l'existence des sociétés. Les tribunaux ne savent pas toujours quelle attitude adopter. Les contrats traditionnels mentionnés dans le paragraphe précédent sont dans l'ensemble standards dans leur formes de telle sorte que même dans les types de contrats les plus récents, les personnes intéressées ne se préoccupent pas beaucoup des détails. Ainsi, à l'heure actuelle, il est difficile de dire qu'un droit coutumier précis naît de ces contrats.

Le droit coutumier n'accepte pas les contrats exécutoires, c'est-à-dire qu'on ne répond pas du simple échange de promesses. Le consentement cependant est un concept important, mais il doit être accompagné par quelque exécution afin que soit créée la responsabilité contractuelle. Peu de formalités sont requises pour former un contrat, sauf dans les contrats spécialisés comme le mariage et la vente de terrain. La plupart des gens ont la possibilité de contracter; dans quelques tribus, la possibilité des femmes est limitée par la règle disant qu'elles ne peuvent pas posséder de terrain ou de fonds; quelquefois, la permission du mari est une condition préalable. Les enfants peuvent contracter, mais, en cas de litige, les parents sont responsables.

La livraison de la marchandise est nécessaire pour conclure une affaire, et dans la vente, jusqu'au moment de la livraison, les risques sont généralement du côté du vendeur, de sorte que, si le bétail est perdu ou est tué, le vendeur subit la perte. Dans les contrats de 'pâture' et de caution, les risques sont du côté du propriétaire. La négligence de la personne en charge du troupeau est hors de propos, mais s'il a tardé à remettre les animaux, la responsabilité lui en incombe. Cependant, il doit produire une preuve satisfaisante de la perte de l'animal: produire la peau ou la tête suffit. S'il n'y a aucune trace, il doit aider le propriétaire à essayer d'en retrouver une.

La notion de relativité du contrat n'est pas développée; les tribunaux s'intéressent davantage à voir qui possède les biens en question et à les restituer à leur propriétaire légitime. Cela rend difficile une démarcation précise par rapport à d'autres transactions entraînant une responsabilité juridique. L'erreur, le dol, la violence ont de l'importance en ce sens que, si ceux-ci existent, la personne innocente peut réclamer que le contrat soit annullé; aucune conséquence pénale n'en résulte.

Index

Abdulahi: *Ta'limu Radthi*, 268 n.
abene, judgment fee, 117
abomination, 67–68, 302
Abrahams, R. G.: 'Neighbourhood Organization', 146, 149
abusus, 243–5, 248–9
accident, 68
acculturation, 223
Adangme (Ghana), 242, 244
adjudication, 31
administration
  estates of, 57–58, 256–7
  powers of, 58
  under probate, 51
  of property, 49–55, 259
Administration of Justice (Karamoja) Act (1964), 286
Administration of Justice Proclamation (1942), 163
Administration (Karamoja) Act (1963), 286
  Amendment (1964), 286
Afavie v. *Banyea*, 113
affiliation, 224–5, 228–9, 232–3
  action, 225
aformi (men whose wives are abducted), 213, 220–1
African Conference on Local Courts, Dar es Salaam (1963), 79, 123 ff.
African Court(s), 110
  of Appeal, 297
African District Councils, 339
African Reserves, 56
African Urban Courts of Northern Rhodesia (Zambia), 293
Afrigie v. *Dotwaah & anr.*, 110 n.
agency, 337–8
agistment, 71
  mafisa, 322, 324–5
agreement(s), 71–78
  breach of, 306–8
  conception of, 334–5
  judgment by, 144
  written, 327
Akan (Ghana), 38, 40–41, 44, 57, 74, 113–15, 190
  law, 183, 187–8, 192
  property rights, 182
Akim (Ghana), 179 n.
Akomea & ors. v. *Biei & ors.*, 111 n.
Ala (land deity), 182

alienation of land in Northern Nigeria, 273
Alkalai, 269–70
allodial title, 58 n.
Allott, Antony N., 6, 31, 38–47, 57–58, 113–14
  Akan Law of Property, 182 n., 190, 192
  essays by, 1–78, 179–92
  Essays on African Law, 114 n.–116 n., 118 & n., 119, 145, 146 & n., 149
  ed., *Judicial and Legal Systems of Africa*, 79
  Native Authority Estimates, Northern Nigeria, 134
  Northern Nigeria Local Government Handbook, 134
  ed., *Record of Proceedings of the Conference on the Future of Law in Africa*, 134
amal (practice), 271 n.
amano (intelligence), 34, 297
America, 10
  legal rules in, 9
American
  small-claims courts, 8, 30, 139, 143
American Law Institute, 13 n.
ancestor(s)
  and cessation of legal personality, 185–6
  cult, Malagasy, 169, 172, 174, 176–7
  social identification/solidarity with, 110, 184
ancestral
  claims in Northern Nigeria, 270
Anderson, J. N. D.: *Changing Law in Developing countries*, 271 & n., 277
  Islamic Law in Africa, 268 n., 271 & n., 277
Adriana (noble caste: Madagascar), 173
Andrianampoinimerina, 170–3
Anglo-Muhammadan Law, 133
Anglo-Saxon common law, 1, 23
Ankrah & ors. v. *Dabra & anr.*, 113–14, 116
appeal/appellate court(s), 24, 271
  of Gurage, 156
  tribunal de ville, 223, 232
arbitral proceedings, 118–19
arbitration(s), 26, 29–31, 111–19
Arbitration Ordinance, 119

348 Index

Archer, P.: *The Queen's Courts*, 142 n., 143, 149
archives, used in research, 105 & n.
arina, 34
ario, see primary marriage
aristocracy
  Fulani, 270
  hierarchical, 266
asafo companies, 116, 118
aseda, 114, 117
Asenso v. *Nkyindwo*, 111 n.
Ashanti (Ghana), 40, 149, 179 n., 185–6
  infants' rights in, 184
  slaves in, 184 n.
Asian storekeepers, 339
assessors, African, 14, 28, 30
Assim (Ghana), 179 n.
association, legal, 48
assumpsit, 77
ategburu (ritual aggregates), 211–12
Austrian courts, 143
award in arbitration, 115–19
  see also compensation
Awradja Gizat (district court), 164

Baganda (Buganda), 281, 283–4
Bagua(fo) (arbitrators), 115–17
bailment, 337, 341–2
Bakabilo (councillor), 297
Balogun v. *Balogun*, 269 n.
banishment, 161, 185
Banton, M.: 'Tribal Headmen in Freetown', 116 & n., 119
Bantu law, 196
bare
  agreement, 72–74
  promise, 73–74
Barnes, 53
Barotse, 44, 56, 68, 72, 75–77, 111, 138, 147, 164, 242–4, 247–8, 321
  judges' wide conception of evidence, 143 n.
  law, 19
  Lozi tribe, 61, 253–63
  see also Gluckman
barter, 71
Basotho, Basuto, 49, 53, 59, 197, 202, 205, 259
  law/customs, 203
Bathoen I, Chief, 325
Beattie, J. H. M.: 'Informal Judicial Activity in Bunyoro', 146, 149
Bechuanaland, 253
  Protectorate, 318–28
Bedford, S.: *The Forces of Justice*, 143 n., 149
Beecham–Taylor trial, 140–3
Belgian law, 6
  on illegitimacy, 224

Belgium, 241
Bemba (Northern Rhodesia), 67, 259, 293, 294, 297, 300
beneficial ownership, 58 n.
Bentsi-Enchill, K.: *Ghana Land Law*, 58 n., 79, 180 n., 192
Bereng Griffiths v. *'M'Antsebo Seeiso Griffith*, 199, 201
betrothal, 64, 319, 322
  conciliation of, 326
  of infants (Kadara), 213
  of infants (Madagascar), 173, 176
  teshi, 212
  see also breach of promise to marry
Bhaca court procedure, 142
Biebuyck, D.: ed., 'Introduction' to *African Agrarian Systems*, 18 n., 79, 264
black magic, 98
  see also magicians; medicine-men; sorcery; witchcraft
blasphemy, 68
blood-feuds, 6, 280
  in Gurage (*bado*), 156–7
  ritual arbiter of (*wäg*), 163
blood-money, 160, 165, 281–3, 287
bo nkuro (informal investigations), 115
Boadu v. *Fosu*, 190 n.
bohali, see bride-wealth
Bohannan, L., 45, 139
  'Dahomean Marriage', 61 & n., 79
Bohannan, P. J., 137 n.
  Justice and Judgment among the Tiv, 20 n., 79, 144 & n., 145–6, 149, 164 n., 166
  Tiv Farm and Settlement, 277
breaches
  of agreement/contract, 66, 306–8, 318–28
  of promise to marry, 318, 325–6
bride-price, 18 n., 60, 282, 340
bride-wealth, 18 n., 60, 165, 213, 218–19, 226–7, 232–4
  bohali, 198, 206
  debts, 147
British
  legal systems compared with African, 137
  Magistrates' courts, 30 (see also England)
  rule in Northern Nigeria, 272–4
  territories, 28
British Administration (Northern Nigeria), 270
British India, 32
British Privy Council, 257
British Provincial Administration, 210
British South Africa Company, 257, 260

Index

Brooke, N. F.: 'The Changing Character of Customary Courts', 119
bucende (adultery), 300
Buckland, W. W. and McNair, A. D.: *Roman Law and Common Law*, 39 n., 79
Budu II v. *Caesar & ors.*, 117
Buganda, 68
bukoleshi, 227
bureaucracy, 27
Busia, K. A.: *The Position of the Chief in the Modern Political System of Ashanti*, 110 n., 116 & n., 119

Cameroon, 101
capacity, definition of, 46
capitalism, 246
Capitant, H.: *Vocabulaire juridique*, 237 n., 249
Cardozo, 70, 139
caretaker of property, 51
Casely, Hayford: *Gold Coast Native Institutions*, 119
cattle
  'beget children', 61
  as blood-money, 160, 165
  compensation for, 309
  contracts, 337 & n.
  debts, 338
  defects in, 341
  grazing in Bechuanaland, 253
  held as security, 325
  as *mafisa* (under agistment), 322, 324-5
  marriage-, 261-3
  -owning tribes, 260-1
  raids, 286-7
  trading, 71, 342
  trespass, 73, 310, 314, 320
  see also herding
caveat emptor, 76, 263, 341
caveat vendor, 75
Central Africa, French-speaking, 52
ceremonies in marriage contracts, 339
Chaha tribe (Gurage), 154-5
'champion-at-law' (*maro*), 162
chattels, rights in, 259-63
Cheshire, G. C.: *The Modern Law of Real Property*, 58, 79
Chewa people, 305, 308-9
chiefs, 32 and *passim*
  under independent democracy, 27
Chief's Tribunal, 116
child(-ren), 45
  bound by parents, 321
  definition of, in customary law, 197-8
  illegitimate, 6-7, 198, 206, 312
  legitimation of, *see* legitimation
'child-wealth', 18 n.

cisunga, 293 & n., 300 n.
civil code/law, countries with tradition of, 32, 39
Civil Service, Nigerian, 129
clan(s) of Madagascar (*foko*), 173
clan courts, 156
code, definition of, 33
Code Napoléon, 224
Codes of Madagascar: of Ranavalona Ière (1828), 171-2
  of 101 Articles (1868), 174-5
  of 305 Articles (1881), 175
codification of law, 14 n., 31-33
cognatic
  kin, 160
  systems, 54
Coker, Justice, 73
Cole, C. W.: *Report on Land Tenure in Zaria Province*, 269, 277
Coleridge, Lord Justice, 42
Colloque du Droit Malgache, 102
Colloquium on African Law (London 1964), 197
colonial régime(s), 25, 27
  changes resulting from, 337
Colson, E.: *Marriage and the Family among the Plateau Tonga*, 50 n., 79
Columbia, U.S.A., 143
Commission on the Laws and Customs of the Basotho (1873), 202-3, 207
common law, 16, 338, 340
  countries of Africa, 32
  systems, Anglo-American, 138
common-sense justice, 30, 141
communication, development of means of, 274
'communistic' tribal societies, 252
comparative law, European-based, 180
compensation, 69, 145, 306-15
  for cattle raids, 286-8
  claims in Tswana law, 325
  in Gurageland (*yäsäda*), 156-7, 159-61
  Ikiposolo (Malawi), 312 n.
  for injury, 296, 299-300
  in Kenya, 337
  promises upheld, 320
  for reversionary rights, 257 & n.
compurgation, 36
conciliation, 31
  as function of inferior courts, 143
concubinage, 61, 64, 229
  suits, 233, 324
Conference on the Future of the Law in Africa, London (1960), 123 ff.
Conferences on Local Courts and Customary Law (1963), 26-27
Congo
  dualistic system in, 223
  individual land property in, 236, 238

Index

Congolese
  law, 224, 229, 233
  Constitution (June 1967), 227
conjugal rights, 60
Conseil de Cité, 227-8
  Social Commission of, *see* Social Commission
consent, concept of, 339
consolidation of law, 25
contract(s), 32, 71-78
  formation of, 74-75
  herding, 336, 338
  in Kenya, 333-44
  law, 10, 263
  law in Tswana, 318-28
  marriage, 8, 19
  status/commercial, 19
Contract Act, Kenya (1961), 333
corporate groups, 67
  African, 187
corporations, 39-45, 183
  aggregate/sole, 40, 43-44
  doctrine of, 39 & n.
  legal, 48
Corpus Juris, 39 n.
Côte d'Ivoire, 52
courts
  of appeal, *see* appeal
  Gurage, 153-66
  integration of, *see* integration
  magistrates', 8, 30, 110, 127-8, 132, 139 ff.
  primary, 29
  small claims, 8, 30, 139, 143
  superior, 139, 143
  traditional, 110-19
  tribal, 318
  see also tribunal
Court of Review (Kenya), 337
coutume évoluée de Kinshasa, 223
crime(s), 66-67
  and civil wrongs, distinction between, 305-6
Criminal Code, Ethiopia (1930), 163
criminal law, 32
curator ad litem, 198
Customary Courts, 110
  of the first instance (*tribunaux de centre*), 223, 230
Cyprus, 286

Dahomey, 29, 61, 101
damages, 76-77, 314, 326, 334, 343-4
  for breach of contract, 328
  consequential, 341, 343-4
  see also compensation
Danquah, J. B.: *Akan Laws and Customs*, 115, 117 & n., 119
Dar es Salaam, 26

Conference, *see* African Conference on Local Courts
debts, liability for, 321
  in Kenya, 337 ff.
decree, judgment by, 144
Dekkers, R.: *Précis de droit civile belge*, 237, 249
delicts, 66, 305 ff.
delictual liability, 73
  wrongdoing, 67
democracy, independent, 27
Deschamps, H., 5 n., 12, 29, 31 n., 32, 34, 56
  essay by, 169-77
Devlin, P.: *The Enforcement of Morals*, 302 n., 303
devolution of property
  oblique, 52
  traditional, 49
  vertical, 52
District Governor (Malkanya), 163
divination, 35
divorce, 62-65, 142
  documents relevant to, 106
  excluded among Kadara, 210-11, 214
  in Kinshasa, 232
  laws, 29, 32
  in Madagascar, 100
  rate, 54
Djaka & ors. v. *Amemadokpor*, 113 n.
'doctors', *see* magicians
dot, 18 n., 60, 106
dowry, 18 n., 198, 206
Driberg, J. H.: 'The African Conception of Law', 280 n., 289
droit parallèle, 29, 31
droit de paternité, *see* paternity
droit secret, 22, 29, 31
droit du seigneur, 57
'dry the blood', 157
Duhamel, J. and Smith, J. D.: *Some Pillars of English Law*, 139 n., 150
duress, plea of, 340

economy
  Africanization of, 339
  rural, non-monetary, 335
Edo, Northern, 59
education, purpose of, 34
Ejinkeonye v. *Attorney-General*, 275
elders, 32
election *vs.* succession, 27
Elias, T. Olawale: *The Nature of African Customary Law*, 67, 79, 143 n., 146, 150, 237-9, 249, 292, 303
élite, new African, 27
Embu (Kenya), 333 n., 336, 337 & n., 339 n.-342 n.
eminent domain, *see propriété éminent*

Index

Emirates, 268
  Muslim, 268, 271
  see also Hausa
Emmet, I.: *A North Wales Village*, 146, 150
England
  law of contracts of, 333
  lay justices in, 27
  sanctions in judicial procession, 148
  see also British
English law, 77
  classification of wrongs in, 66–67
  on corporations, 39–43
  on divorce, 65
  on land, 58
  and litigation, 146
Epstein, A. L., 22, 24, 30, 34–35, 67–70, 73, 137 & n., 139
  The Administration of Justice and the Urban African, 293 n., 303
  essays by, 1–78, 292–303
  Juridical Techniques and the Judicial Process, 68, 72 n., 144 & n., 150, 302 n., 303
  'Some Aspects of the Conflict of Law and Urban Courts in Northern Rhodesia', 150
esoteric: customary law, 98, 104
  technical knowledge, 139
estate(s)
  of administration, 57, 256–7
  definition of, 21, 49
  primary/secondary/tertiary, 256–7
  of production, 57, 257
  succession to, 48–59
estoppel, 117
Ethiopia, 30, 32–33, 153
  see also Gurage
Ethiopian Civil Code (1960), 32
Ethiopian Penal Code (1957), 164
European inheritance systems, 52
Evans-Pritchard, E. 44 n.
  see also Fortes, M.
evidence, 32, 36
  circumstantial, 36, 70
  in Gurage courts, 158
  hearsay, 24, 36, 111, 159
  primary, 24, 36
  selection of, 24
  in traditional courts, 110–19
exoteric customary law, 98
extended family, 43, 266
  ekek, 283

'face-to-face' societies, 148
familia, 47
family
  allowances, 232 n., 233
  consent to sale of land, 339
  extended, 43, 266, 283

groups, structure and legal functioning of, 181
moots, 30
nuclear, 29, 266
ties, weakening of, 118
family law, 27, 31, 126
  and customary courts/law, 124, 128, 130–1
  Sesotho, 13
Fante (Ghana), 74, 179 n.
  fishing communities, 192
  land tenure, 190
farming, large-scale development of, 15
  see also cattle
Feifer, G., *Justice in Moscow*, 143 n., 150
Fetha Negast ('laws of the King'), 163
feudal systems, 256
fiduciary, 206
fie asen (family or domestic settlement), 116
fief system in Northern Nigeria, 268, 270
Firth, R., 260, 263
foko (clans of Madagascar), 173
fokon'olona (village assembly), 100, 107, 173, 176
Forde, C. D., 42
  ed. *African Worlds*, 38 n., 79
forgiveness, unconditional, 313
Fortes, M., 47 n.
  'Kinship and Marriage among the Ashanti', 40, 79
  Kinship and the Social Order, 79
  and Evans-Pritchard, E. E.: eds., *African Political Systems*, 299 n., 303
francophonic African states, 31, 101
Frankenberg, R., 299 n., 302 n.
Franklin, E., *see* Stafford, W. G.
Fréchou, J.: 'Le régime foncier dans la région des Timbi', 242 n., 243 n., 249
Freetown, 116
French: civil code, 3, 16
  law, 19
  territories, 28
fructus, 248
Fulani
  conquered by British (1902–3), 272
  conquest of Northern Nigeria (1804), 266–8, 272
  rule in Jukun, 269
  rule in Northern Nigeria, 270

Ga state (Ghana), 111
Ganda, 61
garde, droit de, 228–9, 232 & n.
Gardiner, Lord, 128
generations, conflict between, 27
genetricial rights, 45, 60
  services, 60
German courts, 143 n.

Index

Germanic laws, 18
Ghai, Y. P., 28, 72–73, 75–76, 77
  essay by, 333–44
Ghana, 14, 24, 26, 28–29, 32, 39, 43, 62, 64, 71, 73, 118, 179 n., 180–92
  English-based legal system in, 189
  Supreme Court of, 24–25
Ghana Courts Act (1960), 110 n.
Ghana Courts Decree (1966), 28
ghost-marriage/husband, 54, 63, 180, 183, 186
Giles, F. T.: *The Magistrates' Courts*, 139 n., 142 n., 143, 149 n., 150
Gluckman, Max, 56–58, 72–73, 75–77, 137, 139, 143, 146
  essay by, 1–78, 252–63
  The Ideas in Barotse Jurisprudence, 43–44, 47, 72 n., 79, 150, 242 n., 243 n., 247, 250, 252 n., 263 n., 264, 292 n., 303, 327 & n., 329
  The Judicial Process among the Barotse of Northern Rhodesia, 18 n., 19, 24 n., 38, 68, 79, 111 n., 119, 138 & n., 143 n., 144, 147, 150, 164 n., 165 n., 166, 302–3
  'Kinship and Marriage among the Lozi of Northern Rhodesia', 63 n., 79
  Politics, Law and Ritual in Tribal Society, 143 n., 150
  'The Reasonable Man in Barotse Law', 111 n., 120
grazing lands, community, 11
  see also cattle
Griffith, C. J. Branford, 111
group
  liability, 279
  orientation of African law, 269
  personality, 183, 187
  tenure, 269
guardian, powers of, in property, 52
guardianship
  action (*droit de tutelle*), 225
  in Kinshasa, 224, 226
  Sesotho, 196–207
guilt
  determination of, 35–36
  in Gurage judicial system, 153–66
  presumption of, 23–24
Gulliver, P. H.: *Social Control in an African Society*, 137 n., 150
Gurage (Ethiopia), 30, 36
  courts, 24
  judicial system, 153–66
  justice, 34
Gurvitch, G.: *The Sociology of Law*, 221
Gwandu, 267

Hailey, Lord: *Native Administration in British African Territories*, 277

Hammond-Tooke, W. D.: *Bhaca Society*, 142, 150
Hannigan, A. St. J.: 'The Imposition of Western Law Forms upon Primitive Societies', 333 & n., 344
Hart, H. L. A.: 'Punishment and the Elimination of Responsibility', 66, 80
Hausa, 71, 220, 266
  courts, Muslim, 211
  Emirates, 267
  -land, 127
  pagan, 268
  slaves in, 184
Haydon, E. S.: *Law and Justice in Buganda*, 285, 289
Hebrew law, 67
heir under Sesotho customary law, 196–207
heluka, 34
herding contracts, 336, 338, 341
hierarchy of segments of kinship groups, 57–58
High Courts, 125
  of Gurage, 155–66
  of Lozi (*kuta*), 165
Hohfeld, W. N.: 'Fundamental Legal Conceptions as Applied in Judicial Reasoning', 21 n., 80
Holleman, J. F.: 'An Anthropological Approach to Bantu Law', 144 & n., 145, 150
homicide, 161, 282, 284, 299
'house(s)'
  burning of, 66, 306
  definition of, 203
  of Gurage, 154 n.
house-property complex, 53–54, 63
Howell, P. P.: *A Manual of Nuer Law*, 180 n., 186 n., 192
hunting tribes, 252–3
husband, 'primary', 7
  see also ghost-marriage; marriage

Ibik, J. O., 66–69, 73, 76
  essay by, 305–15
Ibo, 44, 64, 147, 242, 244
  law, 180–3
  property rights, 182
idda (Islamic rule of remarriage), 7, 65, 210–21
Ijaw, 59
illegitimacy, 6–7, 198, 206, 312
  in French and English law, 223
  see also legitimation
illiteracy, 119
inadvertence, 68
incorporation, 179
  and customary law, 187
  see also corporation

Index

India, 286
Indian Empire, 133
Indian village communities, 190
individual
  concept of the, 269, 274
  responsibility, concept of, 280 ff.
  rights of occupation, 277
individualization
  in Nigeria, 269, 274, 276
Indonesian law, 16
industry, large-scale development of, 15
infants, rights of, 184-5
  see also children
inferior criminal courts of America, 143
inheritance, 47-55
  and land tenure, 267
  laws, 29
  systems, double unilineal, 53
  see also succession
initiation, purpose of, 34
injuries, 66-71
  law of, in Malawi, 305-15
  liability for, see liability
innocence in Gurage judicial system, 153-66
insanity, 315
integration
  of courts system, 25, 28-29
  of law(s), 14, 28
intestacy, 45
Isifu v. Donkor, 117 & n.
Islamic law, 5 & n., 7, 30, 126, 130, 133
  and inheritance, 52
  and land tenure, 267-71, 274, 276
  see also Muslim
Iteso (Uganda), 281-2, 285-6, 288
Ivory Coast, 32

Jewish law, ancient, 302 n.
jihad (holy war) of Fulani, 267
Jowitt, W. A. J.: *Dictionary of English Law*, 237 n., 250
judges
  danä (Gurage), 155
  new types of, 12
  professional, 25-26
  in role of counsel, 23
  selection of, 15
  traditional jurists as, 12, 23, 26
judgeships
  hereditary, 165
Judicial Commissioner's Court, 203
judicial: law, 15
  structure in Ghana, 115
  types, 97-108
Judicial Service Commission, 126-7
judiciary
  separate from executive, 139
  status of, in England, 139
Jukun, 269

jural: corporation, 56
  postulates, 70
  unit, 47 n., 52, 54
juristic: legal person, 181
  personality, 183
jury system, 286
jus dicere, 6
juvenile delinquency, 228, 315

Kadara, 59, 60
  Northern, 210-21
Kafir beer, 328
Kagoro, 210
Kajuru District Council, 217
Kajuru Town, 211
Kano Province, 269
Karamojong, 6, 281, 286, 288
Karamoja, 286-8
Katsina Province, 269
Keay, E. A. and Richardson, S. S.:
  Native and Customary Courts of Nigeria, 135
  Statement by Government of Northern Nigeria, 135
kenela, 44 n.
Kenny, C. S., 66
  Outlines of Criminal Law, 80
Kenya, 11, 32, 75-76, 144
  contracts and transactions in, 333-44
Kgatla, 318, 322, 326-8
kgotla (council-place), 320
kharaj (tribute), 268
Khatala, M. B. v. Khatala, F. B., 200, 203
Kiambu District (Kenya), 144
Kikuyu, 61, 333 n., 336, 337, 340
Kimbere, 336
'king is also a beggar', 254
Kinshasa (*formerly* Leopoldville), 6, 26, 60-61, 223-34
kinship groups/network, 38
  cognatic system of, 29, 53
  extended, 29
  in Gurageland, 30, 164
  and land ownership, 252
  law of Kinshasa, 225
  in legal disputes, 181
  nesting (incapsulate), 51
  omnilineal, 53 & n.
  unilineal, 53
  and succession, 48-59
Kipsigis (Kenya), 11, 61, 333 n., 337 n.
Kisumu, 338 n., 340 n., 341 n., 342 n., 343 n.
Kohler, 70
kola-nut trading, 71
kraal, 308
Kuba, 244
  law, 20 n.
Kufana, 211, 216-17, 220
kufunda (legal theft), 259-60

Kuper, H. and L.: eds., 'Introduction' to *African Law*, 20 n., 80, 154 n., 166
Kwasi v. Labri, 113–14
Kwena, 318, 326

labour, employment of, 318–19
labour-service, 60
Lambert, H. E., 144
land
  disputes over, 319
  law, 27, 31
  —, and customary courts, 128
  ownership, 20
  —, characteristics of African, 191
  —, of Gurage, 160 & n.
  —, inheritance of, 48–59
  —, law of, 124
  property, individual, 236–49
  rights in, 55–59
  tenure, 252–9
  —, in Northern Nigeria, 266–77
Land and Native Rights Ordinance, Northern Nigeria (1916), 273–5
Land and Native Rights Proclamation (1910), 273
Land Tenure Law, Northern Nigeria (1962), 274–5
Land Tenure (Local Authority—Right of Occupancy) Regulations, Northern Nigeria (1962), 276
Land Tenure (Native Authority—Control of Settlements) Regulations, Northern Nigeria (1962), 275
Land Tenure (Native Authority—Right of Occupancy) Regulation, Northern Nigeria (1926), 276
language(s), African, 16–17
  legal, 16–21
  terms for succession/inheritance, 49 n.
Lansdowne, J., 199
Law in Africa, 71
Laws of Lerotholi, 13, 197, 200–2, 203–4, 207
Law Reform Committee (Ghana), 29
law schools, 26
Lawrance, J.: *The Iteso*, 281–2, 285–6, 289
lawyers
  as judges, *see* judges
  training of, in customary law, 26
lefielo (servant-wife), 198–9
legal personality, 38–48, 179–92
legal unit, 47–48
legitimation
  action, 225, 312 n.
  of children in Kinshasa, 223–34
  see also illegitimacy
Lekaota, R. v. Lekaota, A. R., 200, 202–3
Lele, 59

Leopoldville (*now* Kinshasa), 6, 26, 60–61, 223–34
Lerotholi Code, *see Laws of Lerotholi*
Lesotho, 61, 196, 200
levirate(-ic marriage), 44 & n., 53, 60, 63
  in Madagascar, 173, 176
Lewis, I. M.: ed., *Islam in Tropical Africa*, 80
liability
  for injuries, 66–71
  —, in Malawi, 305–15
  —, in Zambia, 292–303
  in Uganda, individual/group, 279–89
limited liability company, 43
literacy, 64
Lloyd, D.: *The Idea of Law*, 139 n., 150
Lloyd, P. C.: *Yoruba Land Law*, 42, 80, 182 n., 188 n., 192
Local Courts Ordinance, Malawi (1962), 307 n.
local government land administration (Northern Nigeria), 275
locus poenitentiae, 114
Logoli, 242, 244–5
Lomwe (Mlanje), 315 n.
London Conference, *see* Conference on the Future of the Law in Africa
Lozi (Barotse) tribe, 61, 253–63
Luba, 227
Lugard, Lord, 272
  Instructions to Political and Other Officers, 270 n., 271 & n., 277
  Political Memoranda, 268 n., 273–4 & n., 277
  Report on the Amalgamation of Northern and Southern Nigeria, 272 n., 277
Luning, H. A.: *An Agro-Economic Survey of Katsina Province*, 269 & n., 277
Luo (Kenya), 182, 333 n., 335–6, 340

McDowell, C. M., 12, 26–28, 30
  essay by, 266–77
  An Introduction to the Problems of Ownership of Land in Northern Nigeria, 277
McNair, A. D., *see* Buckland
Madagascar, 29, 32, 56, 99, 101–3, 107, 169–77
mafisa, *see* agistment
magicians/'doctors' (*dingaka*), 319, 328
  see also black magic; medicine-men; sorcery; witchcraft
magistrates
  colonial administrators as, 292
  in colonial period, 28
  courses for, 27–28
  courts, 8, 30, 110, 127–8, 132, 139, 140 ff.
  professional, 28
  —, need for, 126–7

Index

Maguzawa, 268
Maine, H. S., 47, 73, 190
  Ancient Law, 80, 263
Malagasy law, 34
Malawi, 27, 32, 49, 68–69
  law of wrongs/injuries in, 305–15
  Tonga of, 62, 147
Malengreau, G.: 'Le régime foncier dans une société indigène', 239, 242, 243 n., 250
Malete, 322, 326
Maliki law, 125, 211, 268–9
Maluti Mountains, 197
Marien, M.: *The Ethiopian Empire Federation and Laws*, 164 n., 166
market-place, justice in, 143
marriage
  -cattle, 261–3
  civil/religious, 63
  contracts, and ceremonies, 339
  —, in Madagascar, 99–100
  establishment of, 63–64
  father's right to dispose of daughter in, 29
  forced, 31
  forms of, 59–63
  ghost-, *see* ghost-marriage
  law(s), 29, 31, 32
  leviratic, *see* levirate
  payment, 18 & n., 59–63
  primary, 59, 65
  — (*ario*), 212
  registration of, 64
  'secondary', 7, 59–60, 210–21
  Sesotho, 196–207
  systems, 14
  see also divorce; monogamy; polygamy
Masarwa, 46
Maseela v. *Maseela*, 199
maternity, *droit de*, 225
matriarchy, 269
matrilineal tribes/peoples/systems, 28–29, 41, 61, 187, 225
  Kongo, 226 n., 227
  systems of inheritance under, 49, 52–54, 63
  Yombe, 227
  see also uxorilocal
matrimonial offence(s), 309
  see also marriage
Mauretania, 29
medicine-men, 284
  see also black magic; magicians; sorcery; witchcraft
Meek, C. K.: *Land Tenure and Land Administration in Nigeria*, 268 n., 278
  Law and Authority in a Nigerian Tribe, 147, 150, 182 n., 192
  A Sudanese Kingdom, 269 & n., 278

Menilek II, Emperor, 163
Mensah v. *Takyiampong*, 113 & n.
Merina Kingdom (Madagascar), 169–73, 177
Meru (Kenya), 333 n., 336, 340 & n., 341 n., 342
  African Court, 334
methods of investigating customary law, 104–8
migration
  effects of, on Gurage judicial system, 165
  on Northern Nigeria, 270
mining, large-scale development of, 15
minors and contract, 340
Minutes and Evidence before Northern Nigeria Lands Committee, *see* Northern Nigeria Lands Committee
missionaries, 5
  influence of, in Madagascar, 171, 175–6
  Paris Evangelical, 197
Mitchell, J. C.: 'Marriage Stability and Social Structure', 63 n., 80
mobility, influence of, in Madagascar, 174
Mohaleroe, Tsepo, 196
monogamy, 64, 200, 205
  see also marriage
monopole du droit d'exploitation, 57
Moorcock case (1889), 335 & n.
Moore, Sally F.: 'Introduction' to Part IV of *The Anthropology of Law*, 18 n., 80
  'Public and Private Law', 67 n., 80
moots, 29–30, 146
  see also arbitrations
Morton, Lord, 277 n.
Moscow courts, 143
Moshoeshoe, George Tlali, 202
Moslem Court Appeal Law, 271 & n.
Mosotho, 198
movables, *see* property
mucinshi (respect), 34, 295–7
Mufulira, 296
Mugerwa, P. J. Nkambo, 6, 41 n., 67, 68–69
  essay by, 279–89
multiplex relations, 22 & n., 138, 147–9
mupamba (ill omen), 301
Muslim
  Hausa courts, 211
  personal law, 125, 131
  traders, 71
  see also Islamic law
Mutchi v. *Annan & ors.*, 112
Myers, F. H.: 'The Small Claims Court in the District of Columbia', 143 & n., 146, 150

356   Index

Nadel, S. F.: *A Black Byzantium*, 270, 278
Natal, 64
Natal Native Code, 1896, 16, 60
Nathu, P. v. Land Officer, 277 n.
nation-building, 28–29
National Council of Basutoland, 197
National Oath (Ghana), 115
nationalism in Northern Nigeria, 271
nationalized land policy in Nigeria, 274
Native Administration Ordinance (1927), 111, 115
Native Authority (Nigeria), 130–1
Native Authority Estimates, Northern Nigeria, 131 n.
Native Courts, 110, 113, 117
Native Courts Inspectorate, 28
Native Courts Law (Nigeria), 130
Native Jurisdiction Ordinance (1883), 111–12
Native Lands Acquisition Ordinance (Southern Nigeria), 273
native tribunals, *see* tribunals
'natural justice', 333
Nazi Germany, 286
Ndebele king, 257
Ndola, 294, 298
negligence, 68, 341
   concept of, 334
'negotiations for settlement', 31, 113, 116, 117–18
ngoetsi (shadow wife), 200
Ngonde, 311, 312 n.
ngwate, 336 & n.
Ngwaketse, 318 & n., 320 & n., 321–3, 325–8
Ngwato, 318, 322, 328
Nigeria, 26, 71, 73, 128–34
   Eastern, 129
   Northern, 28, 30, 125–6, 129
   —, land tenure in, 266–77
   Southern, 273–4, 276
   Western, 128–9, 269
   see also Northern Nigeria Lands Committee
Nkrobo, 117
Northern Nigeria Lands Committee (1908), 269
   Minutes and Evidence, 269 n., 270 n., 278
   Report, 272 n., 273, 278
Ntsin v. Ekutey & ors., 111 n.,
nuclear family, *see* family
nuda pacta, 72
Nuer law, 180, 183, 186
Nyanja-speaking people, 306

oaths
   ritual, in Gurage, 158–9, 161, 165
   use of, 24, 35, 137

Obi, S. N. C., 44
   The Ibo Law of Property, 180 n., 182 n., 193, 239 n., 242 n., 243 n., 250
obligations, standard/customary, 323
occult, 68
   evil, women as source of, 54
   and reason, 34–37
official customary law, 98–100
Okitoi, Y. v. Aisu, P., 282, 286
Ollennu, N. A., 8 n., 22–25, 26, 28–29, 31, 35, 62, 74–75
   essay by, 110–19
oman, 188–9
omnilineal
   inheritance, 54
   systems, 63
onipa (person), 188
ordeals,
   poison, 284
   use of, 24, 35, 98, 103, 137
Ordinance (Northern Nigeria), *see* Land and Native Rights Ordinance
Ordinance (1927), *see* Native Administration Ordinance
Osborne: *Concise Law Dictionary*, 72 n.
ownership, definitions of, 55

pagan law, 30
   tribes, 210 (*see also* Kadara)
Pakistan Government and Law Commission, 133
palliations, 36
Palmer, R., 270
parallel law, 98, 101–2
Paris Evangelical Missionaries, 197
parliament, 33
partition of inherited property, 269
partnership, 192, 334–5, 339
Partnership Act (Kenya), 334 n.
pasturage, 253
   see also cattle; grazing
paterfamilias, 205
paternity
   disputes, 215, 218–19
   rights of/*droit de*, 7, 60–61, 224–9, 232–3
patriarchy, 269
patrilineages (*ute*), 211–12, 214
patrilineal tribes/peoples/systems, 28–29, 41, 60, 63, 225
   adelphic, 53–54
   in Kadara, 213 ff.
   in Kinshasa, 227, 229
   in Madagascar, 172
   in Malawi, 312 & n.
   Ngombe, 226 n.
   in Northern Nigeria, 267
   systems of inheritance under, 52–54
   see also virilocal
patrilocal marriage, 212

Pauwels, J. M., 3, 6, 7, 26, 31 n., 32, 60–61
  'Le droit coutumier et la constitution du Congo', 223 n., 234
  essay by, 223–34
peasantry
  in Northern Nigeria, 272
  rights of, 184
peculium, 183
penal law, 31
penalties for breach of contract, 327–8
'people of law' (*yäzänga säb*), 162
Perham, M.: *The Government of Ethiopia*, 163 n., 166
Peristiany, J.: *Social Institutions of the Kipsigis*, 337 n., 344
perpetué rights, 56
persona, 38, 39 n., 45–48, 181
personal law, 28
personality
  corporate, 39 & n.
  legal, 38–48, 179–92
  total social, 38
Petit, M., 230
  'A propos d'un jugement', 230 n., 234
  'La reconnaissance d'enfant adultérin et l'ordre public', 230 n., 234
Peul (Fouta Djalon), 242, 244
Phillips, A.: *Report on Native Tribunals*, 144 n., 150
  A Survey of African Marriage and Family Life, 231 n., 234
Plains Indians, 263
Ploscowe, M.: 'The Inferior Criminal Courts in Action', 143 & n., 150
Pogucki, R.: *Report on Land Tenure in Adangme Province*, 239 n., 242 n., 243 n., 250
Poirier, J., 8, 12, 22, 29, 31, 50 n., 52–53, 57, 73
  essay by, 97–108
polygamy, 59, 320
  in Kinshasa, 229
  in Madagascar, 173, 176–7
  in relation to divorce rate, 106
  of Sesotho, 205, 207
  women's rights in, 200
polygyny, 54, 231–3
polysegmentary societies, 69
pooling of property, *see* property
Pospisil, L.: 'Kapauku Papuan Laws of Inheritance', 52, 80
potestas, avuncular, 312
Pound, 139
privity of contract, 338, 342
Privy Council, 113 n., 114
procedure, flexibility/informality of, 23, 137–49
produce, sharing of, 252

production, 259
  land as unit of, 257
programmatic legislation, 32
promises, exchange of, 334
promissory notes, 327
proof in traditional courts, 110–19
  see also evidence
property, 41
  durable/fungible, 52
  injuries caused by, 310
  movable/immovable, 52, 59
  pooling of, 53–54
  rights, 182, 252–63 (*see also propriété*)
  succession to, *see* succession
  see also house
propriété, 236–49
  éminente, 56–57, 104
  rights, 56, 242–3
proprietory occupancy, 58
Public Service Commission for the appointment of Magistrates, 132

Qadi, 126, 133–4

Radama I, 170
Radama II, 174
Radcliffe-Brown, A. R., 38
  ed., *African Systems of Kinship and Marriage*, 18 n., 80
  'Patrilineal and Matrilineal Succession', 58, 80
Ramangasoavina, M., 102
Ramolefe, A. M. R., 5 n., 13–15, 41 n., 44 n., 49, 50 n., 53, 59, 61, 64
  essay by, 196–207
Ranavalona Ière, 170–2, 174
Ranavalona II, 174–7
rape in Bemba law, 67, 300–1
rationality, 302
Rattray, R. S., 44
  Ashanti, 185 n., 193
  Ashanti Law and Constitution, 149, 150, 184 n., 186, 193
realist schools of lawyers, 4
reason
  definition of, 34
  and occult, 34–37
'reasonable man', 19, 34–35, 301–3
reconciliation, 117, 137–49
  as goal of court proceedings, 22, 24
  in Gurage, 156
  pagan modes of, 30
  pre-trial, 146–8
  'promotion of', 31
  see also negotiations for settlement
reconnaissance, 224–5, 228
Record of Proceedings: African Conference on Local Courts (1963), 112 n., 120
redemption of illegitimate child, 312 & n.

Index

registration of title to land, 32
relevance, conception of, 138
religion
  among Gurage, 154
  Islamic, see Islam
  and secret law, 103
  see also missionaries
religious
  aspect of land tenure, 267
  beliefs, role of, 22
  crimes among Gurage, 157
  offences, 68
remarriage of Kadara, 219–21
Report of Native Tribunal, Gold Coast (1943), 120
Report of Northern Nigeria Lands Committee, see Northern Nigeria Lands Committee
repugnancy clause, 230
respect, 34
respondent superior, 311
responsibility
  civil, 280
  criminal, 280
  individual or group/clan, 279–89, 311–12
  for injuries, 66–71
  vicarious, 311–12
restatement of law, 13 & n.
Restitution of Cattle and Payment of Blood-Money (Procedure) Regulations (1965), 287–8
reversionary rights, 257 & n., 259
Revue Juridique du Congo, 232 n.
Rhodesia, 144
  Northern, 60–61
Richards, A. I., 47
  'Mother-right among the Central Bantu', 47 n., 80
  'Social Mechanisms for the Transfer of Political Rights', 47 n., 80
Richardson, S. S., 26
  essay by, 123–34
  see also Keay, E. A.
rights
  of land, 55–59
  perpétué, 56
  propriété, 56
Ripert, G. and Boulanger, J.: eds., *Traité élémentaire de droit civil du Planiol*, 237 n., 250
risk(s), 341
  concept of, 334
ritual
  aggregates (*ategburu*), 211
  consequences of supernatural punishment, 157
  groups, 220
  illnesses, 159
  intercourse, 60

oath, see oaths
  of pouring libation, 185
  practices, role of, 22, 147
  purification, 309
Robert, André-P.: *Évolution des coutumes de l'Ouest africain et la législation française*, 236, 238, 239, 250
Roberts, T. L.: *Judicial Organisation and Institutions*, 80
Roman law, 16, 258
Roman–Dutch law, 1, 16, 39, 207
Roscoe, J.: *The Baganda: Their Customs and Beliefs*, 283–4, 289
Rowling, C. W.: *Report on Land Tenure in Kano Province*, 269 n., 278
Royal Niger Company, 272
'rumours wreck a nation', 111
Ruxton, F. H.: *Maliki Law*, 211 n., 221
Rwanda, 138

säbat bet Gurage, 154 n., 155
sacrifice,
  to appease ancestors, 169
  funeral (Madagascar), 173
  peace-making, 163
'sailor and his wife' case, 140–3
Samanfo (spirit ancestors), 186
sanctions, 148
  expiratory, 309
  redressive, 280, 309
  religious, of Madagascar, 169, 172
  ritual, 163
  social, 163–4
Sarbah, J. M., 191
  Fanti Customary Law, 120
  Fanti Law Report, 120
  Fanti National Constitution, 120, 190 n., 193
Schacht, J.: *An Introduction to Islamic Law*, 269 n., 278
Schapera, I., 5 n., 21, 64, 73 & n., 76–77, 243 n., 253
  'Contract in Tswana Case Law', 73 n., 74, 81, 320 n., 329
  essay by, 318–28
  A Handbook of Tswana Law and Custom, 18 n., 72, 80, 182 n., 239 n., 242 n., 250, 318 n., 329
  'Matrilocal Marriage in Southern Rhodesia', 61 & n., 80
  Native Land Tenure in the Bechuanaland Protectorate, 327 n., 329
  'The Ngwato of the Bechuanaland Protectorate', 116 & n., 120
  Tribal Legislation among the Tswana, 328 n., 329
  'The Work of Tribal Courts in the Bechuanaland Protectorate', 318 n., 329

Index

secret law, 102-4
  societies, 309
segmentary state (Gurage), 154
Sesotho, 44 n.
  family law, 13
  marriage, 196-207
settlement
  family/domestic (*fie asen*), 116
  negotiations for, 31, 113, 116-17
  procedure and individual responsibility, 280
settlement patterns/areas and land tenure, 266, 274, 276
sexual moral code, 309
Shack, William A., 12, 22, 24, 30, 34
  essay by, 153-66
  The Gurage, 154 n., 166
  'On Gurage Judicial Structure', 155 n., 166
  'Urban Tribalism', 165 n., 166
shadow-wife (*ngoetsi*), 200
Shari'a Court of Appeal, 125, 131, 133-4, 269, 271
  Law, 271 n.
Sheddick, V.: *Land Tenure in Basutoland*, 57 n., 81
Shona, 61, 144-5
simplex relations, 22 n., 138, 147, 149
single-interest relationships, 138
singo pledge, 335
Sky-god, 34, 154, 156-7
slander (*qånema*), 159
slaves, rights of, 46, 184
slavery
  and legal personality, 183
  in Madagascar, 171-2, 176
  in Northern Nigeria, 270
Small Claims Courts, 8, 30, 139, 143
'small-scale' societies, 148-9
  see also multiplex relations
Smith, J. D., *see* Duhamel
Smith, M. G., 7, 41 n., 59-60, 65
  The Economy of Hausa Communities of Zaria, 268 n., 278
  essay by, 210-21
  'Secondary Marriage in Northern Nigeria', 210 n., 221
  Secondary Marriage and Social Change, 210 n., 221
  The Social Structure of the Northern Kadara, 210 n., 215 n., 221
  'The Sociological Framework of Law', 41 n., 81
Social Commission (*Conseil de Cité*), 227-8
social life
  law in relation to, 137
  role of courts in, 146
social workers, 31
Sohier, Antoine: *Traité élémentaire de Droit coutumier du Congo belge*, 236, 238-9, 250
Sokoto, 267
Sonius, H. W. J.: *Introduction to Aspects of Customary Land Law in Africa*, 20 n., 81
sorcery, 36-37, 98, 103
  see also black magic; magicians; medicine-men; witchcraft
sororate, 54, 59-60, 63
Sotho, 44 n.
South African native law, 196
South-East Asia, system of land-holding in, 259
souveraineté, rights of, over land, 56
Stafford, W. G. and Franklin, E.: *Principles of Native Law and the Natal Code*, 203, 207
status, 47
  definition of, 46
  and land-holding, 58
  and property rights, 252-63
  rights and duties, 318
  in Uganda, 279-89
  of wives, 54
Stephen, H. J.: *Commentaries on the Laws of England*, 237 n., 250
stipendiary magistrates, 128
'stool' (chieftainship), 39, 43, 110, 180, 186-92
  Adonten, 187
  Mampong, 187
strangers, rights of, 46, 184
substantive law, 137
succession, 48-55, 204
  circular, *see* inheritance
  discretionary, 49
  vs. election, 27
  in Madagascar, 174
  positional, 47
  (Roman) universal, 44, 46-47
succession, laws of, 14, 20, 32
Sudan, 134
sulh (treaty), 268
Sunday Times, 128 n.
Superior courts, 139, 143, 149
supernatural, 35
  entities and legal system, 180
  punishment, 157, 159
  sanctions of Gurage, 158
Supreme Court of Ghana, 117
Swaziland, 32
Swiss courts, 143

taboo (*fady*), 169
Tanganyika, 28-29
Tanzania, 27-28
tape recordings used in study of customary law, 108
Tawana, 318, 322-3, 326-7

taxation in Northern Nigeria, 270
Tennent, J. R. M.: 'Administration of Criminal Law in some Kenya African Courts', 120
Teso, 285-6
  see also Iteso
testators, 49
Thika, 340 n.
thunder god (Božä), 154, 157
Tikopia (Oceania), 260
Tiv: courts, 144-5, 164
  society, 266
Tlokwa, 327-8
Tonga of Malawi, 62, 147
tort, 18, 66-67, 305 ff., 338
  customary law of, in Ghana, 14
  individual responsibility in, 285
townships, development of, in Nigeria, 274
trading, 71
transactions, 71-78
  customary, in Kenya, 333-44
  see also agreements; contracts
transactors, 48
  legal, 48, 71
treaty (*sulh*), 268
tribal affiliations, 27
tribal: courts, 318
  law/legal systems, 30, 138, 156
tribes
  matrilineal, see matrilineal
  patrilineal, see patrilineal
tribunal(s),
  de centre (customary court), 223, 230
  de District, 230
  native/indigenous, 111, 115-19, 153
  de territoire, 230
  village, 115
  de ville (appeal court), 223, 232 (*see also* appeal courts)
  see also courts
tribute (*kharaj*), 268
Trimingham, J. S.: *A History of Islam in West Africa*, 278
trustee, 21
Tswana, 21, 46, 56, 64, 72-73, 76-78, 242-4
  law, 184
  law, contract in, 318-28
  property laws, 182
Tumbuka, 305-6, 308
-*tuntulu*, 297

ubuntu (humanity), 34, 297
Uganda, 279-89
Uganda Government, 6
uncle(s), paternal, in Sesotho law, 205-6
unification of law(s), 14 n., 25, 28-29

unit(s), right- and duty-bearing, 38-39, 46
University(-ies)
  Law Schools, 134
  of Natal, 196
  Nigerian, 133
unjust enrichment, concept of, 335
urbanization and Gurage judicial system, 165
usufruct, 55, 245 n., 258
usufructuary, 206-7
ute (patrilineages), 211-12
uxorilocal peoples, 305, 311-12
  see also matrilineal

Vanderlinden, J., 55-56, 58 n.
  essay by, 236-49
  'Principes de droit foncier zande', 239 n., 242 n., 243 n., 250
Vansina, J.
  'Le régime foncier dans la société kuba', 239, 242 n., 243 n., 250
  'A Traditional Legal System', 20 n., 81
van Velsen, J., 2, 7, 22 & n., 24-25, 27, 30, 35-36, 62
  essay by, 137-49
  The Politics of Kinship, 147 n., 150
Venda, 182, 188
vendettas, 280
  see also blood-feuds
village(s), 189
  assembly (*fokon'olona*), 100, 107
  community, 190-2
  courts, 126
  — of Gurage (*yäqaya danä*), 155, 158 & n.
  headman (*goro*), 158
  — (*odekuro*), 190
  law (*sera*), 158
  of Lozi, 253 ff.
  moots, 30
virilocal marriage, 212
  peoples, 305, 312
  see also patrilineal
vocabulary, legal, 16-21
volenti non fit injuria, 68, 313-14

Wagner, G.: *The Bantu of North Kavirondo*, 242 n., 250
Wakils, 134
Ward, W. E. F.: *A History of Ghana*, 120
van Warmelo, N. J.: *Venda Law*, 182 n., 193
warranties, 340
West Africa, 71
West African Court of Appeal, 113 & n.
western
  ideas, impact of, in Nigeria, 274
  jurisprudence, 20 n.

Index

legal theory, 40
modern law, 7–8
White, C. M. N.: 'The Changing Scope of Urban Native Courts', 120
widows, 212
  status of, 200–7
widow-inheritance, 53, 60
  alelalako, 212
widower-inheritance, 60
wife, *see* shadow wife
will(s), right to make, 49
Willan, Sir Harold, 199
Wilson, Gordon: *Luo Customary Law and Marriage Laws and Customs*, 182 n., 193
Wilson, Mark, C. J., 112–13, 113, 116
witchcraft, 103–4, 301–3, 315 n.
  accusations, 31, 36
  death by, 302
  in Madagascar, 171
  women accused of, 54
  see also black magic; magicians; medicine-men; sorcery
witnesses to contracts, 320
wizards, 155–6
women
  have no capacity to contract, 321
  marrying women, 54 (*see also* sororate)
  position of, in Northern Nigeria, 267
  powers/liabilities of, 7, 340
  restricted rights of, 45
  as source of occult evil, 54
  status of, 199–200
  see also marriage; widows
work-associations, 190
wrongs, customary law of, in Malawi, 305–15

yägŏka (high court, Gurage), 154–5, 157, 163
yämsaya danä (council of judges), 162 & n.
Yao (Fort Johnston), 314
yäsäwä danä (body of informal judges), 155
Yoruba, 188, 266
  customary law, 133
  lineages, 42
  property rights, 182

Zambezi River, 253
Zambia, 27, 32, 292–303
Zande, 244–5, 248
Zaria Province, 210, 268–9
  Northern, 211
Zulu, 61, 259
Zulu law, 19